Information Security and IT Risk Management

Manish Agrawal, Ph.D.
Associate Professor
Information Systems and Decision Sciences
University of South Florida

Alex Campoe, CISSP
Director, Information Security
University of South Florida

Eric Pierce
Associate Director, Information Security
University of South Florida

Vice President and Executive Publisher	Don Fowley
Executive Editor	Beth Lang Golub
Editorial Assistant	Jayne Ziemba
Photo Editor	Ericka Millbrand
Associate Production Manager	Joyce Poh
Cover Designer	Kenji Ngieng

This book was set by MPS Limited.

Founded in 1807, John Wiley & Sons, Inc. has been a valued source of knowledge and understanding for more than 200 years, helping people around the world meet their needs and fulfill their aspirations. Our company is built on a foundation of principles that include responsibility to the communities we serve and where we live and work. In 2008, we launched a Corporate Citizenship Initiative, a global effort to address the environmental, social, economic, and ethical challenges we face in our business. Among the issues we are addressing are carbon impact, paper specifications and procurement, ethical conduct within our business and among our vendors, and community and charitable support. For more information, please visit our website: www.wiley.com/go/citizenship.

ISBN 978-1-118-33589-5 (paperback)

10 9 8 7 6 5 4 3 2

Table of Contents

List of Figures

Preface

Unlike the problem facing the Superb Fairy-Wren (front cover), most information security problems we humans face are not matters of life and death (for more on the Wren's problem, please see the critical thinking question in chapter 9). However, they are vexing, expensive and frequent enough to make information security a contemporary profession and the topic of information security a worthwhile subject to study.

This book is designed to serve as the textbook for a one-semester course devoted to information security. It is focused on helping students acquired the skills sought in the professional workforce.

We start by introducing the professional environment of information security. After the student is convinced of the merits of the subject, the book introduces the basic model of information security consisting of assets, vulnerabilities, threats and controls. The rest of the course is devoted to characterizing assets, vulnerabilities and threats and responding to them using security controls. The book ends by integrating all these topics within the general umbrella of organizational risk management. At the end of the course, students should have an awareness of how information security concerns have evolved in our society and how they can use contemporary frameworks to respond to these concerns in a professional environment.

The book comes with a full set of end-of-chapter exercises. There are five kinds of exercises at the end of every chapter:

1. Traditional end-of-chapter questions are designed to improve student understanding and recall of common topics in information security.

2. An example case at the end of each chapter allows students to apply the knowledge in the chapter to business contexts.

3. There is a threaded design case running through all the chapters in the book. In this case, students play the role of the Chief Information Security officer of a typical state university and are confronted with situations related to the topics discussed in the chapter. They are required to analyze and evaluate the situation in light of the knowledge in the chapter to create a solution that addresses the present problem.

4. A critical thinking exercise introduces students to analogous situations and relate the ideas from the chapter to these situations. The problem confronting the Superb Fairy-Wren falls in this category.

5. Finally, each chapter has a detailed hands-on activity using a customized distribution of the CentOS Linux OS to be installed as a virtual machine using VirtualBox. We take great pride in this aspect of the book. We have carefully selected exercises that will help students become familiar not only with rudimentary information security tasks, but also with Linux systems administration. Eric in particular, has spent countless hours testing,

curating and maintaining the distribution. You may download the distribution from the textbook's companion website.

While the book is self-sufficient without the hands-on activity, this content is in direct response to employer demands and we do hope you will give your students the advantage of this aspect of the text. Chapters 2 and 3 introduce the basic setup and usage of the virtual machine. The instructions are detailed enough for students to be able to complete the exercises on their own.

When using the book, class time may be used in various ways. A traditional lecture format will work very well. Instructors interested in using class-time for more interactive activities will find that the end-of-chapter activities are a very useful way to use class time.

The author team integrates the different perspectives necessary to teach information security to an aspiring professional. Manish Agrawal is an MIS faculty member who designed this course and has taught it to MIS and Accounting students at the University of South Florida for over 5 years now. Alex Campoe is the Director of Information Security at the University of South Florida where he is at the frontline of the university's information security activities including incident response, policy development and compliance. Eric Pierce is responsible for identity management at the university. Many of the topics covered in the book are informed by their knowledge of the most important day-to-day activities that fall under the information security umbrella.

The Superb Fairy-Wren, though not strictly facing an information security problem, happens to use a solution that adopts many of the information security controls discussed in the text. The context also includes all the components of our basic information security model – assets in the form of the life of offspring, vulnerabilities in the form of delayed hatching, threats in the form of parasitic birds and controls including passwords. We think it succinctly describes the text.

We are eager to hear any comments you may have about the book – suggestions for improvement, errors and omissions, bugs in the virtual machine, and any other issues you may encounter. We will do our best to respond directly to you with corrections, and also address them as errata to be published on the textbook companion site. We obviously would also like to hear complementary things if the book helped improve your understanding of the subject, improved your teaching, helped you land a job, or helped you on the job. Those comments can give us indications on how to strengthen future editions of the book. Comments may be sent to the first author at magrawal@usf.edu.

Introduction

## CHAPTER 1

Overview

This chapter motivates the topic of information security and lays out the structure for the rest of the text. At the outset, we describe why information security is a useful area of study with the hope of getting you excited in the topic. We then provide a brief history of the subject, highlighting important developments that have led to the current state of the industry. Finally, we outline the procedures adopted by the industry to maintain information security. These procedures will be examined in detail in the rest of the book. At the end of this chapter, you should know:

- Why information security is an important topic for everyone today
- The important developments that led to the current state of the information security industry
- Key terms used in information security
- Broad outlines of the procedures used in the industry to maintain information security

Professional utility of information security knowledge

If you are reading this book as part of a college course, it is probably offered by a professional school – business, information, or engineering for example. These schools are expected to graduate students who can hit the ground running when they join the work force. Naturally, we expect that the question foremost on the minds of students in these college is – where are the jobs? What is the professional relevance of this subject? What is the demand for professionals in this subject? What drives organizations to hire graduates with skills in this subject? When hired, what are graduates in this subject typically expected to do? What competencies will help graduates meet or exceed these expectations of employers? Before you decide to spend any more time with this book or the subject of information security, we would like to take this topic head-on and address these issues.

Demand estimates

The standard source for employment estimates is the Bureau of Labor Statistics[1] (BLS), a government agency that gathers employment statistics from extensive surveys of employers. BLS has created a taxonomy called the "standard occupational classification (SOC)" for all the major occupational categories. Information security analysts are given the SOC identifier 15-1122 (Figure 1.1). They fall under the major group of "Computer and mathematical occupations (15-0000)." Statistics for information security analysts is aggregated along with those for

---

[1]http://www.bls.gov/

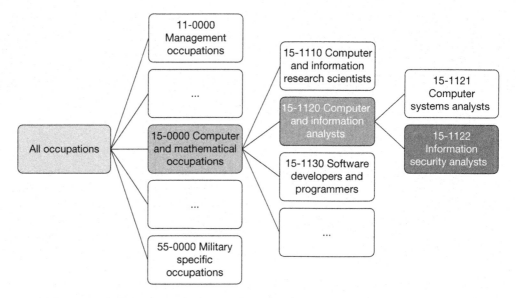

FIGURE 1.1   Classification of information security analysts

web developers and computer network architects and may be obtained from the BLS website.[2] The total employment for this group in May 2010 was estimated to be 243,330, with a mean annual wage of $79,370.

Other sources for obtaining estimates of the demand for information security professionals are the professional certificate action organizations involved in the industry. One of the leading organizations is (ISC).[2] Based on a survey of over 10,000 information security professionals around the globe, this organization estimated that there were approximately 2.28 million information security professionals worldwide in 2010, of who over 900,000 were in the Americas. This number was also estimated to be growing at over 13%.[3] The average annual compensation was estimated at over $78,000. The wide difference in estimated employment between the two surveys could be attributed to a difference in the characteristics of the organizations sampled by the two surveys. It may however be noted that both surveys are quite consistent in their estimates of average annual compensation.

Demand drivers

A number of factors are driving the demand for information security professionals. Primary among these is the increasing criticality of information to individuals and organizations and the resulting increase in the amounts of information gathered by organizations and stored in computer systems for easy retrieval. Possession of a username and password combination could be more useful to a thief today than possession of a $100 bill. A successful attack at a bank or other commercial establishment could yield hundreds of thousands of vetted username and password combinations. The most motivated attackers are therefore increasingly targeting information stores rather than physical stores.

[2]http://www.bls.gov/oes/current/oes151179.htm

[3]https://www.isc2.org/uploadedFiles/Landing_Pages/NO_form/2011GISWS.pdf

Even as information is becoming more valuable, unwittingly, users are also making it easier for attackers to obtain this valuable information. For example, most users use a small set of usernames and passwords wherever usernames and passwords are required. They also often prefer that their devices remember these usernames and passwords to save typing effort at websites. Now consider what happens if an attacker is able to lay their hands on a laptop, tablet, or other mobile device belonging to a user in possession of sensitive information. The attacker could easily get access to hundreds of thousands of records with minimal effort. With millions of knowledge workers leaving their workplaces with billions of mobile devices every day, organizations are compelled to act proactively to ensure that they do not appear on the front pages of newspapers and TV channels for losing customer information or other sensitive data.

The value of information described above is just one of the demand drivers for information security professionals. Other factors include dealing with application vulnerabilities, the constant stream of viruses and worms reaching organizations, regulations, customer expectations of privacy, and disgruntled employees.

The demand drivers for information security professionals have also been changing very rapidly. For example, until as recently as 2008, mobile devices such as smart phones and tablets were not common in companies. Having a company-issued phone was a matter of pride for executives. Then by 2010, most employees preferred to use their personal smart phones and tablets to do company work rather than the company-issued phones that did not have web browsers and other desirable features. Information security professionals had to scramble to deal with the far-reaching implications of this change. Whereas earlier they could issue phones such as Blackberries and impose the desired security policies on these devices, the security policies on personal devices were controlled by the users, not by the companies they worked for. As a result, information security professionals reported in 2010 that dealing with mobile device security was one of their top concerns. These concerns, and hence the demand for information security professionals, are only likely to increase in the near future, securing the professional prospects for information security professionals.

Professional activities

What do information security professionals do? The BLS website describes the role of information security analysts as:

> Plan, implement, upgrade, or monitor security measures for the protection of computer networks and information. May ensure appropriate security controls are in place that will safeguard digital files and vital electronic infrastructure. May respond to computer security breaches and viruses.

> Illustrative examples: Computer Security Specialist, Network Security Analyst, Internet Security Specialist

This is a fairly technical set of activities. However, a lot of the work done by information security professionals is non-technical in nature. Figure 1.2 shows the distribution of the top four most time-consuming activities reported by respondents to the (ISC)² survey.[4] It is seen that regulatory issues, policy development, and managerial issues constitute the bulk of information security work.

---

[4]https://www.isc2.org/uploadedFiles/Landing_Pages/NO_form/2011GISWS.pdf

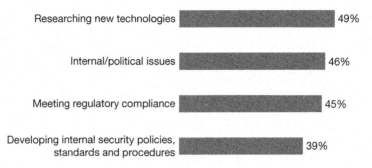

FIGURE 1.2 Time-consuming activities for information security professionals

Desired competencies

The primary responsibilities of information security professionals are to anticipate information-related problems and to minimize their impact. Responses to the ISC[2] survey highlighted the eight areas with the greatest need for training, as shown in Figure 1.3. These are very good indicators of the competencies expected of information security professionals. It can be seen that successful information security professionals are expected to have expertise in systems analysis and design to identify possible vulnerabilities entering homegrown applications, system administration skills to examine systems and identify traces left behind by hackers (forensics), and risk management. In addition, the business continuity and disaster recovery expectations require that information security professionals also have a very good understanding of the business as well as the IT infrastructure to be able to identify the most mission-critical applications in the organization so that these can be quickly brought up online in the event of a natural or man-made disaster.

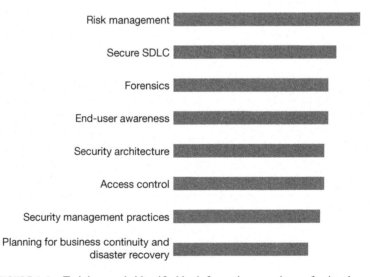

FIGURE 1.3 Training needs identified by information security professionals

The intent of this section was to satisfy you that information security is a viable profession. Hopefully, it has also conveyed that information security is a very exciting profession. Further, since information security lapses attract a lot of public scrutiny, the activities of information security professionals are of great interest to top management of organizations, probably more so than those of many other parts of an organization's IT infrastructure. In fact, according to the ISC^2 survey, the information security group reports to executive management, i.e., the CEO, CIO, or equivalent, in almost 25% of the organizations.

Brief history

From this point on, we assume that you are interested in learning about information security from a professional perspective. That is, you are interested in learning about the subject for use in your career. Almost everything we do today regarding information security is the result of famous lapses that have occurred over the years and the responses by industry to these experiences. Many of these incidents are now part of the professional folklore. It is useful for you to know about these incidents in order to better appreciate regulatory requirements, the concerns of managers as well as to build your vocabulary in the profession. The list below is not intended to be comprehensive;[5] it only captures the major incidents that led to regulatory or industry actions or serve as a barometer for information security concerns at the time.

1981 – Development of the core Internet technologies (TCP and IP): The core technologies of the Internet were finalized in 1981. There was no mention of security in these technologies, indicating that at that time the *technology world* was not concerned about information security. Since TCP and IP were available for free, they became the preferred networking technology for UNIX systems, widely used at universities and various intensive organizations such as hospitals and banks.

1982–1983 – Gang of 414's: Computer intrusions began soon after TCP and IP were integrated into industrial equipment. The most highly publicized incident of this time was the gang of 414's, a group of six teenagers from Milwaukee, who got their name from the telephone area code for Milwaukee. These teenagers found it exciting to get into systems that were supposed to be out of their reach. Using home computers, phone lines, and default passwords, this group was able to break into approximately 60 high-profile computer systems, including those at the Los Alamos Laboratories and the Memorial Sloan-Kettering Cancer Center in New York. The incident received wide coverage, including a Newsweek cover story titled "Beware: Hackers at play." This is believed to be first use of the term "hacker" in the mainstream media in the context of computer security. While the teenagers themselves did no harm, it was easy for the industry to see that the simple techniques used by the kids could easily be replicated by others. As a result, the US Congress held hearings on computer security. After more such incidents, Congress passed the Computer Fraud and Abuse Act of 1986, which made it a crime to break into federal or commercial computer systems.

1988 – Morris worm: Robert Morris, then a graduate student at Cornell, and now a Professor of Computer Science and Artificial Intelligence at MIT, released a 99-line self-replicating program on November 2, 1988, to measure the size of the then nascent Internet. As a result of a design feature of the program, it brought down many systems it infected, and

---

[5] A more comprehensive source is Wikipedia: http://en.wikipedia.org/wiki/Timeline_of_computer_security_hacker_history

achieved several landmarks in the process. It is considered the first Internet worm. In percentage terms, it is estimated to have brought down the largest fraction of the Internet ever (10%). It also resulted in the first conviction under the 1986 Computer Fraud and Abuse Act. Robert Morris was sentenced to probation, community service and a fine. The Morris worm prompted the US Government to establish the CERT/CC (CERT coordination center)[6] at Carnegie Mellon University as a single point to coordinate industry–government response to Internet emergencies. Prof. Morris was also a co-founder of Viaweb, an e-commerce firm bought by Yahoo!, and renamed it as Yahoo! Store.

> As an interesting anecdote, Robert Morris' father, Bob Morris, designed the password encryption system for the UNIX operating system that is used even today. Even more interestingly, at the time of this incident, the senior Bob Morris was the chief scientist for the National Computer Security Center (NCSC) of the National Security Agency (NSA),[7,8] the federal agency responsible for designing secure computers.

1995–1998 – Windows 95/98: Microsoft released Windows 95 on August 24, 1995. The operating system had a graphical interface and was designed to run on relatively inexpensive computers). The release was supported with a heavy marketing push, and within a very short time, it became the most successful operating system ever produced, and drove most other operating systems out of the market. Windows 95 was designed primarily as a stand-alone single-user desktop operating system and therefore had almost no security precautions. Most users ran Windows 95 without passwords and most applications ran on Windows 95 with administrative privileges for convenience. However, Windows 95 supported TCP/IP, thereby bringing TCP/IP into mainstream businesses. This combination of a security-agnostic networking technology (TCP/IP) combined with an equally security-agnostic business desktop created a fertile environment for information security compromises to flourish. In talks, security experts sometimes refer to this environment as the source of the information security profession.[9] Even the introduction of Windows 98 on June 25, 1998, made no change to the basic security design of Windows desktops.

1996 – Health Insurance Portability and Accountability Act (HIPAA): This Act which primarily focused on protecting health insurance for US workers when they change or lose jobs also had important information security implications. Many government leaders believed at the time that electronic health records (EHR) were an important instrument to lower rising healthcare costs in America. The Act therefore also pushed for electronic health records. Since information security was getting recognized as an important concern, the law had provisions to make organizations responsible for maintaining the confidentiality of patient records in the healthcare industry. At the current time, the healthcare industry has until 2014 to move over

---

[6] While CERT typically stands for Computer Emergency Response Team, CMU has registered the name as a service mark with the US Patents and Trademark Office

[7] http://cm.bell-labs.com/cm/cs/who/dmr/crypt.html

[8] For another very interesting account of Bob Morris, read the amazingly humorous book by Cliff Stoll, "The Cuckoo's Egg," ISBN 0671726889

[9] For example, Dan Geer (chief information security officer for In-Q-Tel, the venture capital arm of CIA) referred to this in his talk at the ISSA meeting in Tampa, December 2011.

completely to EHR. This is a major driver of demand for information security at the time of writing this edition (2012–2013).

2000 – ILOVEYOU virus: On May 5, 2000, this virus was released by a student in the Philippines (Figure 1.4). The virus deleted images on infected computers and automatically sent itself as an email attachment to the Outlook contacts list of infected computers. The virus infected millions of computers worldwide, and caused billions of dollars in damage. The creators of the virus, Reomel Ramores and Onel de Guzman, were traced within hours of the release of the virus. However, investigators realized very quickly that Philippines had no law against writing computer viruses, and had to drop all charges against the students.[10] This incident led to the realization that information security was a global phenomenon and led to a push from developed countries for developing countries to revamp their information security laws. However, even today there are significant differences between countries regarding information security laws. For example, while writing a virus can lead to fines of up to $250,000 and 10 years of imprisonment in the United States, the punishment in the Philippines can range from 100,000 Pesos (about $2,500) and up to an amount commensurate to the damage and up to 3 years in prison.[11]

2002 – Sarbanes–Oxley Act: During 2000–2002, America witnessed many unpleasant incidents of corporate fraud involving such legendary companies as Enron, Tyco, and WorldCom. For example, Enron claimed revenues of over $100 billion in 2000 and declared bankruptcy the next year. MCI-WorldCom revealed in 2002 that it had overstated its earnings by over $72 billion in the past five quarters. These frauds were enabled by fraudulent manipulation of accounting systems, believed to be at the behest of firm leadership. However during trials, the CEOs consistently tried to escape blame by pleading ignorance of accounting procedures, and blind trust in their highly paid and well-educated lieutenants. Since the retirements of most Americans are invested in large publicly traded firms, their downfall affects most American families. Compelled to act and ensure correctness in financial reporting, Congress enacted the Sarbanes–Oxley Act in 2002. The Act focused on making the key executives personally

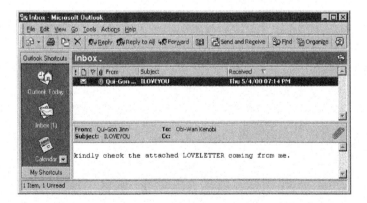

FIGURE 1.4   ILOVEYOU virus

[10] Arnold, W. "TECHNOLOGY: Philippines to drop charges on e-mail virus," New York Times, August 22, 2000.

[11] http://www.chanrobles.com/ecommerceimplementingrules.htm (accessed 02/28/2012)

accountable for the correctness of financial reports filed by publicly traded companies. The Act had three major provisions. Section 302 of the Act requires the CEO and CFO of firms to sign a declaration of personal knowledge of all the information in annual filings. Section 906 of the Act imposes criminal penalties including imprisonment of up to 20 years for incorrect certification. Section 404 of the Act has had a major impact on the information security profession because it requires that the certification in Section 302 be based on formal internal controls. This has led to significant investments in internal controls over financial reporting in publicly traded firms.

2005–2007 – Retailer attacks: In December 2006, T.J.Maxx reported that its computer systems, which processed credit card payments, had been breached (Figure 1.5). On investigation, it was found that the breach had started a year and a half ago in July 2005 and over 45 million credit card and debit card numbers had been stolen. It turned out that the leader of the group involved in the breach was Albert Gonzalez, an informer for the US Secret Service and in fact Albert was cooperating with the Secret Service in connection with another case at the time of these attacks. Investigations also revealed that the group had also hacked into the systems at other retailers such as BJ's Wholesale Club, DSW, Office Max, Boston Market, Barnes & Noble, and Sports Authority. The modus operandi of the group was to drive along US Route 1 in Miami and seek out an insecure store with wireless networks to enter the corporate networks. Later the group improved its methodology and used SQL injection attacks to enter the networks at Hannaford Brothers and Heartland Payment Systems, a credit card payments processing company. Over 125 million credit card numbers were estimated to have been stolen from Heartland, and the company estimated damages at over $12 million. In March 2010, Albert Gonzalez was sentenced to 20 years in prison. He also forfeited over $1.65 million that he had earned from selling fake credit cards based on the stolen information. These incidents highlighted that even large firms had glaring information security weaknesses, which could lead to serious embarrassment and losses. The SQL injection attacks in particular created an awareness of the need to pay attention to information security during software development, and introduced the term "secure SDLC" to the IT lexicon.

2008 – Denial of service attacks in Georgia: Coinciding with the military war between Georgia and Russia in 2008, Georgia was the victim of massive distributed denial of service

© Michael Neelon(misc)/Alamy

FIGURE 1.5 T.J.Maxx

attacks. The attacks defaced the websites of many media and government organizations, limiting their ability to communicate their viewpoints about the war to their citizens (Figure 1.6). The circumstances of the incident led many people to believe that the cyber-attacks[12] were caused by Russia as part of a war strategy. If so, these were the first known incidents of cyber-war being used as an instrument of warfare.

June 2009 – Establishment of the US Cyber Command: In April 2009, the Wall Street Journal reported that intruders had broken into the computer networks of defense contractors developing the Joint Strike Fighter, also called the F-35 Lightning II.[13] The $300 billion project was the Defense Department's costliest weapons program ever, and used 7.5 million lines of computer code. Intruders had stolen terabytes of data related to the aircraft's design and electronics. It was believed that the theft would help enemies plan their defenses against the fighter. The contractors involved in the project include Lockheed Martin, Northrop Grumman, and BAE Systems. Also in April, the Wall Street Journal reported that the US electricity grid had been penetrated by spies from China, Russia, and other countries. The spies also inserted computer software in the grid, which could be used to cause damage by remote control.[14]

Soon thereafter, on June 23, 2009, the US Cyber Command was created to defend US military computer networks against attacks from adversaries and also to respond in cyberspace as necessary). At the time of creation of the new command, there were concerns that the initiative might impose undue restrictions on the civilian Internet under the pretext of defense.

2010 – Operation Aurora and Google-China: On January 12, 2010, a blog post by Google's Chief Legal Officer reported that the company had detected an attempt to steal its intellectual property originating from China (Figure 1.7). The attacks were also aimed at accessing emails of Chinese human-rights activists. The US Government soon escalated the incident with Congress announcing its intention to investigate the allegations and the Secretary of State labeling the Chinese censorship of the Internet to an information-age Berlin Wall. Further investigations traced the attacks to two educational institutions in China – Shanghai Jiaotong University and the Lanxiang Vocational School. Jiaotong is home to one of China's elite computer science programs, and Lanxiang is involved in training computer scientists for the Chinese military.[15]

FIGURE 1.6 Defaced Georgian foreign ministry website

---

[12]Cyber is a prefix that refers to anything related to computers or networking

[13]Gorman, S., Cole, A. and Draezen, Y. "Computer spies breach fighter-jet project," Wall Street Journal, April 21, 2009.

[14]Gorman, S. "Electricity grid in US penetrated by spies," Wall Street Journal, April 8, 2009.

© Lou-Foto/Alamy

FIGURE 1.7 Google-China offices

China has however denied formal government involvement and called the attacks simply an attempt by students to refine their computer skills.

April 17, 2011 – Sony PlayStation Network (PSN): Sony announced that an external intrusion had compromised its PlayStation Network and Qriocity service), and that hackers had obtained personal information on the 70 million subscribers of the network. The company could not rule out the possibility that credit card numbers may also have been stolen. In response, the company took the network offline while it tried to ensure that all traces of the offending software had been removed from the network. During the time, millions of kids all over the world who had planned their summer breaks around catching up with online gaming on PSN had to find alternate ways to pass their time. For this reason, while the intrusion affected a relatively innocuous network, the impact on families around the world was huge and almost every family with kids followed the daily developments around the attacks.

This brief chronology highlights how information security attacks have evolved from technical proofs-of-concept to commercially driven attacks to steal credit card information. Of late even governments are being suspected of pursuing their agendas through cybercrime. In Europe, a remote Romanian town, Râmnicu Vâlcea, has emerged as the focal point in global cyber money laundering. In the middle of nowhere, this town has car dealerships selling Mercedes-Benz and other expensive cars.[16] Social response has evolved as well, from judges merely warning intruders and laws making specific exceptions for juveniles in spite of their known involvement in cyber-attacks (414's) to governments establishing entire military commands to deal with cyber security.

---

[15]Markoff, J. and Barboza, D. "2 China schools said to be tied to online attacks," New York Times, February 18, 2010, http://www.nytimes.com/2010/02/19/technology/19china.html (accessed January 8, 2012).

[16]Bhattacharjee, Y. "How a remote town in Romania has become cybercrime central," Wired Magazine, January 31, 2011, http://www.wired.com/magazine/2011/01/ff_hackerville_romania/all/1 (accessed January 8, 2012).

Definition of information security

That is the background which has defined organizations' concerns about information security. If you were observant, you may have noted that the incidents had different impacts on information security. In the case of the 414's, the primary concern was loss of privacy. In the Enron case, it was accuracy of information, and in the case of Georgia, it was the ability of citizens to access relevant information. Information security can mean different things to different people.

> *Information security is now defined as protecting information and information systems from unauthorized access, use, disclosure, disruption, modification, or destruction in order to provide integrity, confidentiality and availability.*

While the above definition is based on the code of law of the United States (section 3542, Chapter 35, title 44),[17] the definition is remarkably consistent across the industry. For example, RFC 2196[18,19] on information security states that the basic goals of security are availability, confidentiality, and integrity.

The CIA triad

The law writes the dimensions of information security in the sequence – integrity, confidentiality, and availability. However, these three dimensions are better remembered in a slightly different sequence as the CIA triad, where C stands for confidentiality, I for integrity, and A for availability. To maintain symmetry with this popular phrase, we will henceforth discuss the information security dimensions in the sequence of this triad – confidentiality, integrity, and availability.

Confidentiality

According to section 3542 of the US code, *Confidentiality means preserving authorized restrictions on access and disclosure, including means for protecting personal privacy and proprietary information.*

The law recognizes the right of individuals to privacy, and such right extends to information which, if made public, could cause harm or embarrassment to the person. Confidentiality is the responsibility of custodians of information to provide that privacy to the individuals whose information they have in their possession. All the examples of credit card theft discussed in this chapter relate to the failure of organizations to maintain confidentiality of the information in their possession.

If you ask most people to define information security, they typically will respond with some variant of "information security means not losing credit card information." Most people associate information security with confidentiality.

---

[17]The US code is available online from many sources, though the publishers frequently change the URLs to their sites. It is best to simply Google for "US code 3542" to find a site. As of January 8, 2012, the top result was the Cornell University Law School at http://www.law.cornell.edu/uscode/usc_sec_44_00003542----000-.html

[18]RFCs or requests for comments are the documents published by the Internet Engineering Task Force, the group that defines Internet standards including TCP and IP.

[19]Fraser, B. RFC 2196 site security handbook, September 1997, http://www.ietf.org/rfc/rfc2196.txt

Integrity

Integrity means guarding against improper information modification or destruction, and includes ensuring information non-repudiation and authenticity.

When you pull information from an information system, for example, your grades from the university, or the monthly statement from your bank account, you trust that the information provided is reliable and actionable. For example, when the bank reports the balance in your checking account, you do not think it necessary to tally the totals of credits, debits, and interest income yourself to verify the amount. Rather, you trust that the bank has made the right calculations. Imagine how complex life would be if the information you received from IT systems could not be trusted to be accurate. Integrity is the aspect of information security that prevents that from happening.

In the examples above, the inability of IT systems to prevent senior executives at Enron and WorldCom from manipulating company records to serve their personal interests were examples of failure of integrity.

Availability

Availability means ensuring timely and reliable access to and use of information.

When you log into your course site online, you expect it to be online. That in essence is availability. The relevance of availability to information security is self-explanatory. An information system that is unavailable is an information system that is not useful. In the example above, the response of the Sony PSN was an example of failure of availability. Most viruses also have the same impact – they typically delete important files, causing a loss of availability. Even if the files can ultimately be recovered from backup systems or other sources, the time lost in recovering those files represents time not spent doing useful work, i.e., lack of availability.

The right to privacy

Of the three dimensions of information security, confidentiality is probably the most difficult to define precisely. This is because the social expectations of privacy are very dynamic. What one person considers private, photographs for example, another may consider public. What was once considered private may now be considered public. While organizations may fiercely protect the privacy of their employees, the same employees may willingly share much of the same information voluntarily on social networks and other websites.

In fact, the right to privacy is fairly recent in US law. The first modern reference came in an 1890 article in the Harvard Law Review, where Louis Brandeis (who later became a Supreme Court Justice) and his law partner Samuel Warren wrote:[20]

Recent inventions and business methods call attention to the next step which must be taken for the protection of the person, and for securing to the individual what Judge Cooley calls the right "to be let alone."

---

[20]Brandeis, L.D. and Warren, S.S. "The right to privacy," Harvard Law Review, December 15, 1890, 4(5): http://groups.csail. mit.edu/mac/classes/6.805/articles/privacy/Privacy_brand_warr2.html (accessed 1/12/2012)

Instantaneous photographs and newspaper enterprise have invaded the sacred precincts of private and domestic life; and numerous mechanical devices threaten to make good the prediction that "what is whispered in the closet shall be proclaimed from the house-tops." For years there has been a feeling that the law must afford some remedy for the unauthorized circulation of portraits of private persons; . . . The press is overstepping in every direction the obvious bounds of propriety and of decency. Gossip is no longer the resource of the idle and of the vicious, but has become a trade, which is pursued with industry as well as effrontery . . . modern enterprise and invention have, through invasions upon his privacy, subjected him to mental pain and distress, far greater than could be inflicted by mere bodily injury.

The article was an outburst by Samuel Warren in response to media coverage of high society events of the time, including events in the Warren family which following the social conventions of the time, greatly embarrassed the Warren family.[21] Readers may find an eerie similarity between these thoughts from the 19th century and the privacy debates of the 21st century surrounding Facebook and other social media websites.[22]

In recent years, as organizational concerns over information security have intensified, many experts have proposed expanding the definition to include aspects of information security such as non-deniability (if a company charges a service ordered by phone to your credit card and you deny ordering for the service, how do you prove that you did indeed place the order?). However, for the purposes of this text, we will focus on the traditional definition of information security of integrity, confidentiality, and availability.

Personal guide to maintaining information security

If you are studying information security, perhaps it is a good idea to develop a 2-minute elevator speech on information security that answers the question, "how can I best maintain my information security." You may get this question from friends and family members who are concerned about their own information security. Every professional will give you a different answer, based on their own experiences. Here is ours.

If you wish to maintain your information security, you will get the best returns for your efforts from the following:

Antivirus: Make sure that you are using antivirus software and that its subscription is current. Many people can get the software and subscription for free as part of their ISP subscription or from their employers or school.

Automating software updates: Wherever possible, configure your operating system and application software to apply updates automatically.

Passwords: If possible, use a different password at each site that requires a password. If this is difficult, at the very least, use two passwords – one for the "fun" sites such as newsletters, email etc and

---

[21] Gordon Crovitz, L. "The right to privacy from Brandeis to Flickr," Wall Street Journal, 7/25/11.

[22] Facebook has a very well-written "Guide to Facebook security," at https://www.facebook.com/notes/facebook-security/ownyourspace-a-guide-to-facebook-security/10150261846610766

another for financial organizations such as banks and brokerages. Never share the financial password anywhere or with anyone.[23] For an easy way to add security, pad your chosen password with characters, e.g., *pass – word* is not very difficult to remember, but it is vastly more secure than *password*.

SUMMARY

This chapter provided an overview of information security. We started by looking at why companies have found it necessary to invest in information security and what activities information security professionals spend their time on. There was a quick review of the important information security incidents in the last quarter century. We saw how based on these experiences, the industry has defined information security as the CIA triad – confidentiality, integrity, and availability.

In the rest of this book, we will focus on developing skills to implement information security. We start with essential system administration and scripting so that students can experiment with technology throughout the semester. We do this because in our opinion, system administration and scripting skills are extremely important differentiators in the workplace, particularly for entry-level positions. We then move on to more conceptual issues in Part 2. To implement information security, we present the framework composed of assets, vulnerabilities, threats, and controls and show how assets are determined, threats are identified, and incidents are handled. Finally, in Part 3, we examine the managerial and regulatory context.

EXAMPLE CASE – WIKILEAKS, CABLEGATE, AND FREE REIGN OVER CLASSIFIED NETWORKS

In February 2010, the then relatively unknown WikiLeaks began releasing classified memos from the archives of the US State Department. In summer 2010, Wikileaks reached an agreement with leading newspapers around the world, including the New York Times in the United States and Der Spiegel in Germany, to publish selected cables from the archives in redacted form, i.e., after removing identifying information. The first of these were published in November 2010. By September 2011, the security on the files at Wikileaks had been compromised and all memos were visible online in full text form to anyone. About half the leaked memos were classified as "unconfidential," 45% were "confidential," and the remaining were marked "secret." None of the leaked memos was classified as "top secret." The incident had acquired the moniker "Cablegate."

Wikileaks is a non-profit organization launched in 2007. The leading force behind Wikileaks is Julian Assange, an exceptionally competent computer programmer from Australia, who has a strong zeal for reform using the freedom of the press. Accordingly, the mission of Wikileaks is to help whistleblowers reach journalists anonymously by providing a secure and anonymous electronic drop box. It is motivated by the principles of freedom of speech and media publishing. It is proud of its record of defending its journalists and anonymous sources against legal and political attacks aimed at obtaining the identities of these sources.

The memos leaked by Wikileaks were the result of decades of information collection effort by US diplomatic offices from around the world. The earliest memo dates back to 1966 and the leak was a source of considerable embarrassment to the US State Department. The leaked memos summarized analysis by world leaders and US diplomats. Reflecting geopolitical realities, often these analyses were at odds with the leaders' public positions. The leaders shared their analyses based primarily upon complete trust in the ability of the US State Department to maintain the confidentiality of the information and their identities. With no

---

[23]This recommendation comes from the fact that many compromises occur when websites store passwords without encryption. If the website is compromised, the hacker will get access to your password and will definitely use it at all bank and brokerage sites. For an interesting, but lengthy account, read the article by James Fallows, "Hacked!," The Atlantic, November 2011, http://www.theatlantic.com/magazine/archive/2011/11/hacked/8673/ (accessed 01/13/12)

known information leaks in the past, US diplomats around the world had a high degree of credibility in the diplomatic community. This gave them unparalleled access to sensitive and privileged information.

In fact, once the memos were leaked, leading newspapers in many countries published excerpts from memos that related to their country to satisfy their readers' curiosity about what the United States knew about their country.

The source – Pfc Bradley Manning

Private First Class (Pfc) Bradley Manning is a US army soldier, 23 years of age at the time of Cablegate. He enlisted in the Army in 2007 and trained as an Intelligence analyst. Around this time, through friends, he also came in touch with the programmer-enthusiast community at Brandeis University near Boston. In 2008, when he was deployed to Iraq, his job gave him access to two information networks – SIPRNet and the Joint Worldwide Intelligence Communication System (JWICS). More than 3 million US Government personnel and soldiers have access to these networks. The wide access to these networks was the result of the 9/11 attacks where it was believed that gaps in information-sharing within the government was responsible at least in part for the failure of the US Government to prevent the attacks.

Through these networks, Pfc Manning obtained access to the leaked memos. Sometime in 2009–2010, he decided to pass these confidential memos on to Wikileaks. In May 2010 Adrian Lamo, a former hacker and information source about the hacker community was profiled in Wired magazine. Probably as a result of the article, Pfc Manning contacted Lamo and chatted with him on AOL Instant Messenger (IM). During the chat, Manning revealed that he had leaked the memos and suggested his motivations for doing so. Lamo decided to report this to the authorities, which led to Pfc Manning's arrest and the revelation of the identity of the Wikileaks source. Wired magazine published the transcripts of the chats between Pfc Manning and Adrian Lamo.[24] One of the most memorable lines in the transcript is *(12:15:11 PM): hypothetical question: if you had free reign over classified networks for long periods of time . . . say, 8–9 months . . . and you saw incredible things, awful things . . . things that belonged in the public domain, and not on some server stored in a dark room in Washington DC . . . what would you do?*

Pfc Manning was charged before a military court on February 23, 2012, with offenses including aiding the enemy. Though aiding the enemy is a capital offense (i.e., can lead to the death penalty), prosecutors did not seek the death penalty in this case.

REFERENCES

http://en.wikipedia.org/wiki/United_States_diplomatic_cables_leak

http://en.wikipedia.org/wiki/Bradley_Manning

http://www.bbc.co.uk/news/world-11047811

http://www.wired.com/threatlevel/2011/07/manning-lamo-logs/

http://www.cablegatesearch.net/

CHAPTER REVIEW QUESTIONS

1. What are some of the strengths of information security as a career choice?

2. What are some of the ways in which stolen information can be used for profit?

3. What are some of the most common ways in which the carelessness of end users can lead to a loss of sensitive information?

4. What are some of the common professional responsibilities of information security professionals?

5. Provide a brief description of the activities on which information security professionals spend most of their time.

6. Briefly describe the most important skills that information security professionals are expected to possess to succeed in their job.

7. How did the development of inexpensive computer networking technology (TCP/IP) affect information security?

8. Briefly describe the activities of the gang of 414's.

9. Briefly describe the impact of the gang of 414's on information security.

10. Briefly describe the Morris worm. What are some of the factors that make it a landmark in the evolution of information security?

[24]http://www.wired.com/threatlevel/2011/07/manning-lamo-logs/

11. What was the impact of Windows 95/98 on information security?

12. How does HIPAA (the Health Insurance Portability and Accountability Act) affect the profession of information security?

13. What are the provisions in the Sarbanes–Oxley act that are related to information security?

14. What were some of the immediate factors that led to the creation of the US Cyber Command?

15. Provide a brief description of the US Cyber Command and its activities.

16. What was operation Aurora?

17. Briefly describe the outage that affected the Sony PlayStation Network in 2011.

18. What is information security?

19. What is confidentiality?

20. What is integrity?

21. What is availability?

22. Provide an example of a violation of confidentiality.

23. Provide an example of a violation of integrity.

24. Provide an example of a violation of availability.

25. Which in your opinion is the most important of the three components of information security? Why?

EXAMPLE CASE QUESTIONS

1. Of the three dimensions of information security, which was/were affected by Cablegate?

2. What do you think motivated Pfc Bradley Manning to release the memos to Wikileaks, and then discuss his actions with Adrian Lamo, well aware of the risks of these actions?

3. Based on publicly available information, what were some of the measures taken by the US Government to secure the memos?

4. To what extent were these measures effective?

5. If you were responsible for the information security of these memos, what would you have done to prevent an incident such as Cablegate from happening?

6. Why do you think the recommended actions above were not taken by the experts responsible for the information security of these memos?

HANDS-ON ACTIVITY – SOFTWARE INSPECTOR, STEGANOGRAPHY

The hands-on activities in every chapter are designed to help you become familiar with the common tools used by information security professionals. These activities also help you apply the material covered in the chapter within the context of real systems.

Secunia Online Software Inspector

As the first hands-on activity, you will use a simple, free resource to identify the most important security problems in the computers you use for daily work. This process is called an audit, and PC audit tools are available from many software companies and ISPs. While this exercise uses the tool provided by one such firm – Secunia, you are free to use similar tools from a provider of your choice.

The Secunia Online Software Inspector is available from the firm's website.[25] The product's webpage appears as in Figure 1.8.

Using the software is straightforward. Clicking on the "Start Scanner" button on the page starts the scan with default options and the scan takes a few minutes to complete. When it is done, the report appears at the bottom of the page. A sample report is shown in Figure 1.9.

---

[25] URLs are very volatile. As of 02/12/12, the URL was http://secunia.com/vulnerability_scanning/online/. The most reliable method of course is to use a search engine to find "Secunia Online Software Inspector."

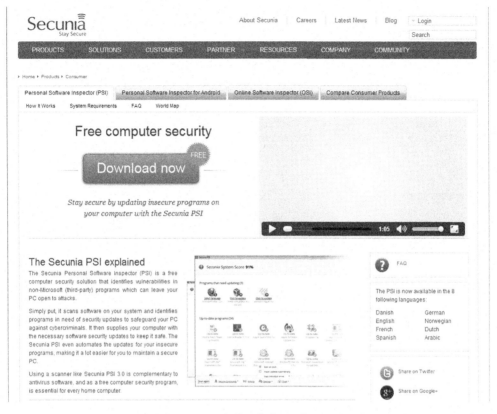

FIGURE 1.8   Online Software Inspector

The report shows that the scanned computer had many software applications that needed to be updated to their latest versions. We have seen in this chapter how older versions of software typically have known vulnerabilities that can be exploited by viruses and hackers. It is a good idea to periodically run an audit tool such as this and update or remove outdated software.

PC audit questions

1. Run a PC audit tool such as Secunia's Online Software Inspector on one of your home computers. Submit a screenshot such as the one shown in Figure 1.9.

2. What are some actions you are considering after viewing the results of your PC audit?

Steganography[26]

This exercise gives you the opportunity to take a look at the "dark side" of information security. You will act as a revolutionary trying to secretly send a message to a friend. You are trying to fix the time and place of a meeting with a group of friends. You believe that all your emails are being scanned.

While there a numerous ways of doing this, in this exercise you will use a particularly easy and interesting method – you will hide the text with the relevant information inside an image (say your university's logo) and send it to your friends. If your friends know where to look for, they can easily get the information.

The goal of the exercise is to demonstrate how easy it is to create information security challenges and therefore

---

[26] Source: http://lifehacker.com/230915/geek-to-live--hide-data-in-files-with-easy-steganography-tools

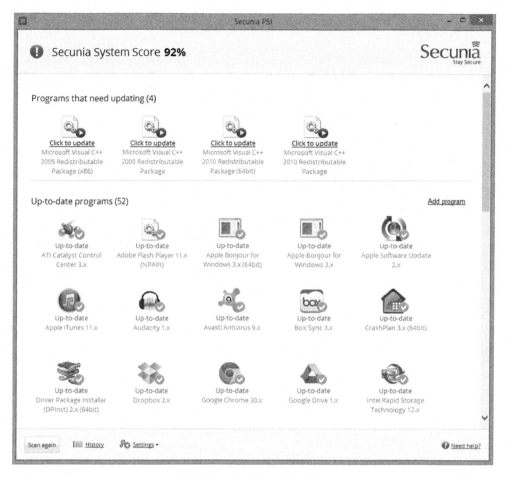

FIGURE 1.9   PC audit report

how challenging it can be to eliminate information security problems.

To do the exercise, you will need the following:

1. An image file. While almost any image will do, it is most convenient to take a small .jpg or .gif file. Usually your school's logo will work fine. Save the file on your computer. In this exercise, we will assume that all files are saved in the Downloads folder. It is a particularly convenient location on Windows and Mac computers. For this example, the file is called logo.gif (if gif image) or logo.jpg (if jpg image).

2. A text file containing the date, place, and time of the meeting. Save the file in the same folder as the image

above (an easy way to create this file is to open Notepad, type in the contents and save the file in the Downloads folder). For this example, the file is called msg.txt.

When you complete the above, your Downloads folder will look as in Figure 1.10.

We are now ready to hide the text file inside the image files. You will need to open the Command prompt for this. In Windows, this is accessed from All programs → Accessories → Command Prompt. On Mac, this is accessed from Applications → Utilities → Terminal. To reach the Downloads folder, type in the command:

```
Cd Documents\Downloads
```

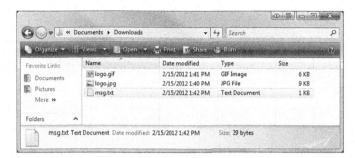

FIGURE 1.10   Contents of Downloads folder for Steganography exercise

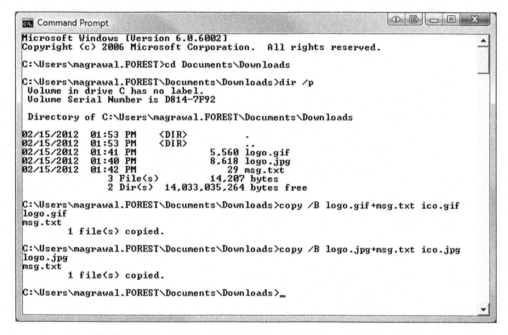

FIGURE 1.11   Commands to hide text files at the end of image files

On Windows, the following command will append file2 at the end of file1 and save the results as file3:

```
Copy /B file1+file2 file3
```

To use this command to hide our text file in the image file, we can use the following commands:

```
Copy /B logo.jpg+msg.txt ico.jpg (for the
jpg image)
Copy /B logo.gif+msg.txt ico.gif (for the
gif image)
```

The sequence of commands is shown in Figure 1.11.

After you run these commands, the contents of your Downloads folder appear as shown in Figure 1.15 (to preview the images, you can select Views → Large icons).

You may notice that the manipulated images (ico.gif and ico.jpg) are indistinguishable from the original images (logo.gif and logo.jpg respectively). A person without knowledge of your activities would not find anything amiss in the manipulated images. You can verify that these images can be opened in browsers and other applications and be used anywhere images can be used.

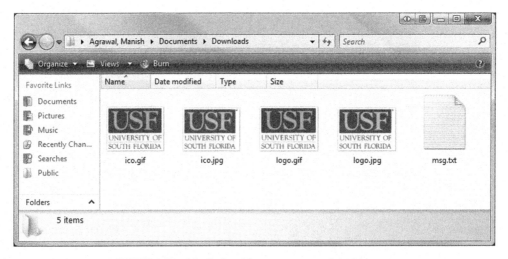

FIGURE 1.12 Manipulated images among original images

FIGURE 1.13 Opening image files in Notepad

But how can your friends recover the information hiding in the images?

Turns out, it is quite easy; they just need to use the right application – Notepad in this case. Start Notepad, select File → Open and navigate to the Downloads folder. Change the file type to All files (*.*) as in Figure 1.13 and select either the ico.gif or ico.jpg file. Ignore the unreadable text and scroll to the end of the file. You will see something like what you see in Figure 1.14. You see that it is possible to create interesting information security challenges using simple, every day IT tools available to everybody. You may also appreciate why these possibilities create nightmares for information security professionals.

What you did in this exercise is called Steganography – *hiding information in a way such that no one suspects the existence of the message.*

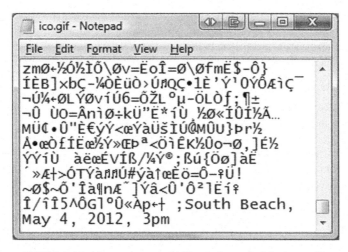

FIGURE 1.14   Secret message hidden at the end of the image file

Table 1.1   Major information security incidents and their impacts

Incident	CIA area(s) affected	Potential preventive measures
414's		
Morris worm		
ILOVEYOU virus		
T.J.Maxx		
Websites of the government of Georgia		
Joint Strike Fighter		
Google-China		
Sony PlayStation Network		

Steganography questions

1. Create one steganographic image following the directions in this section.

2. Submit printouts of the original image, the modified image, and a screenshot of the text embedded in the image as in Figure 1.14.

CRITICAL THINKING EXERCISE: IDENTIFYING CIA AREA(S) AFFECTED BY SAMPLE REAL-LIFE HACKING INCIDENTS

This chapter introduced some of the most damaging (and hence well-known) information security incidents. These are listed in Table 1.1 for your convenience. For each incident, identify the information security area (confidentiality, integrity, or availability) that was most affected. While we have not yet discussed measures organizations take to defend themselves against these kinds of incidents, make an initial attempt to identify some actions organizations can take to ensure that these incidents do not happen to them.

DESIGN CASE

To give students the opportunity to walk through the process of developing the information security architecture for an organization, we will use a threaded design case that runs throughout the book. In each chapter, you will use the concepts covered in the chapter to build the information security architecture for the organization. To help in the exercise, the chapters in the book are arranged in approximately the sequence in which the issues relevant to information security are addressed in practice. Therefore, your activities in earlier chapters will help you build up your solution in later chapters.

The organization we consider in the case is a typical state university. We call it the Sunshine State University. Modern universities such as the Sunshine State University share most characteristics of medium-to-large businesses. They serve upwards of 20,000 demanding users, have thousands of employees, have budgets in excess of a billion dollars, and comply with various regulations. To meet the needs of all these constituencies, universities have all the business processes and IT systems found in a typical corporation such as HR, payroll, finance, and travel in addition to typical services such as email and calendar. Also, many research centers at universities act as custodians of sensitive personal data associated with research projects, creating information security needs comparable to the needs of most large businesses. In fact, it is not surprising to find state universities being some of the largest deployments of leading information technologies.

From the perspective of students and faculty, one of the greatest advantages of using the university as the context for the threaded design case is that it is very familiar to everyone. If necessary, faculty can customize the context to suit any special needs of their institution. In most cases, students will have encountered some of the issues discussed in the case, which greatly facilitates learning.

The organization

Sunshine State University is a State University. Like many state universities, about 30% of its funding comes from state taxes; another 30% comes from student tuition, and 30% from student financial aid (Figure 1.15). The remaining 10% comes from an assortment of sources including research grants, alumni contributions, and revenue-generating academic programs such as executive education. The university is trying to move towards a more elite profile by reducing its dependence on state taxes and tuition to about 20% each. The difference would be made up by increasing revenues from other sources to about 30% of the total budget from the current 10%. The current enrolment at Sunshine State

University is about 20,000 students. To serve these students, the university has about 700 faculty members (leading to a student–faculty ratio of about 29). There are also about 1,500 administrative support personnel performing functions such as academic counseling, scholarships, IT, finance, payroll, office managers, and so on.

To improve the student educational experience, Sunshine State University has begun to increase its focus on research opportunities for graduate and undergraduate students. At the current time, this emphasis is led by the colleges of Engineering and Medicine. Recently hired faculty members in both these colleges have strong records of attracting research funding from sources such as the National Science Foundation and the National Institutes of Health. While these projects create great opportunities for students to earn scholarships while working on research projects, university administrators have been advised by their colleagues that the university should upgrade its systems for handling the data created by these projects. Universities have been taken to court for violating the privacy of research subjects and students.[27]

Organization structure

An extract from the organization structure of the university is shown in Figure 1.16. The discussion in the book will be limited to these units of the university. Provost is responsible for all Academic Affairs on the campus. The Chief Operating Officer is responsible for all business and finance activities on campus. The General Counsel manages legal affairs and compliance.

Students in the College of Medicine do their residency in the local Downtown Hospital. The hospital itself is part of a larger conglomerate and has its own IT support personnel. A major research project initiated by college faculty has enrolled 4,000 newborn children to study the medical impacts of interactions between environmental factors and genetic structures. The study will follow these children for up to 15 years. The college maintains its own IT services that primarily consist of providing email services and shared document storage.

The College of Fine Arts is known for its School of Art, graduating several well-known graphic artists. While the location of the university is not home to a major movie studio, some of its recent graduates have leveraged the video capabilities of DSLR cameras to gain success as movie directors in the indie movie circuit.[28]

---

[27] See http://blog.alertsec.com/2012/01/univ-of-hawaii-settles-data-breach-lawsuit/ for an example

[28] "Indie" refers to independent movies. Indie films are typically produced and marketed on a shoestring budget without the assistance of major film studios. Many leading movie directors first attracted attention on the indie movie circuit.

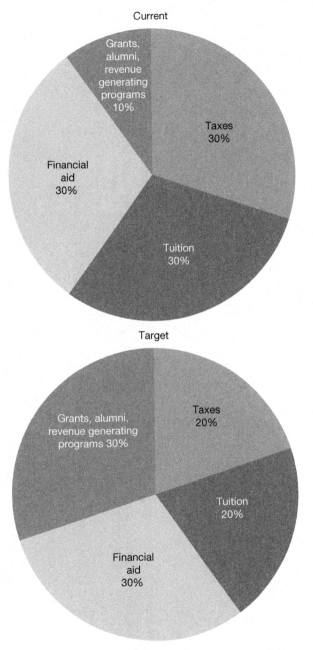

FIGURE 1.15   Sunshine State University funding sources

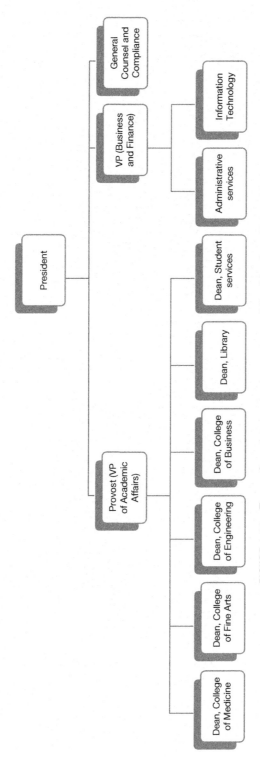

FIGURE 1.16 Extract from the organization structure of Sunshine State University

The School of Engineering is beginning to gain traction with funding agencies, attracting some seed funding from the US Department of Defense for developing sensors and associated applications for battlefield deployment.

In addition to its regular teaching and research activities, the College of Business supports local minority businesses in the community by providing a business incubator, where small disadvantaged business (SDBs) can utilize IT resources and mentoring from local faculty on writing business proposals, marketing, distribution, etc.[29]

The Library is small but very active. In addition to the traditional library services, the library offers undergraduate and graduate degrees in library sciences. The library is actively looking for partnerships with vendors and publishers in order to migrate to an e-textbook model. They are also leading an effort to combine collections with other state and local government libraries and improve their interlibrary loan systems.

Student Services supports students by attending to their non-course-related needs such as student loans, housing, code of ethics, student government, and other student organizations.

The business and finance services on campus are largely centralized. The administrative services component handles purchasing, physical plant, grounds maintenance, and University Police. They also deal with payroll, hiring procedures, and benefits. Information Technology deals with all enterprise-wide IT efforts, including the Enterprise Business Systems. The Student Information System, HR systems, and payroll and financial systems are operated centrally by IT.

Some ancillary IT services are operated as a mix of centralized services and local support. These services include desktop support and management, file share management, print management, account provisioning, and server management. To save costs, the management of some of these services is led by non-tenured faculty members whose primary responsibility is to teach classes. Generally speaking, technical staff is over-worked, under paid, but is well-trained and qualified. They do their best to meet student expectations on a limited budget. The information security department is part of IT.

Security design case questions

Answer the following questions with regard to Sunshine State University:

1. What are some of the ways in which weaknesses in information security can potentially cause embarrassment or financial losses to the university?

2. List three items of information stored in the university's information systems for which the university is expected to maintain confidentiality. What are some of the ways in which the confidentiality of each of these items may be compromised?

3. List three items of information stored in the university's information systems for which the university is expected to maintain integrity? What are some of the ways in which the integrity of these items may be compromised?

4. List three items of information stored in the university's information systems for which the university is expected to maintain availability? What are some of the ways in which the availability of these items may be compromised?

---

[29] From Wikipedia: A small disadvantaged business (SDB) is a small business that is at least 51% owned by one or more individuals who are both socially and economically disadvantaged. SDB status makes a company eligible for bidding and contracting benefit programs involved with federal procurement.

## CHAPTER 2

System Administration (Part 1)

Overview

As we stated in Chapter 1, the goal of information security is to protect information and information systems by ensuring *confidentiality*, *integrity*, and *availability* of information. You have seen some examples of how security can be breached and the consequences of such a breach. Evidently, businesses would like to defend themselves and their customers. So, how can they do that? The rest of this book is devoted to answering just this question. This chapter introduces you to system administration, one of the core components of an organization's response to information security concerns. At the end of this chapter, you should know:

- What is system administration
- Why system administration is important to information security
- What are the general system administration facilities provided by enterprise software systems

Introduction

The overall information security response by an organization has many components including standard procedures, user training, and managerial accountability. All of these will be addressed in the appropriate sequence in this text. However, the first line of defense is the effort undertaken by system administrators to secure critical information systems. *The system administrator is the person who is responsible for the day-to-day operation of a technology system.*[1] Given the importance of information security for day-to-day technology operations, system administrators often also perform the role of system security officer. *The system security officer is the person who is responsible for writing, enforcing, and reviewing security-operating procedures.* System administrators are some of the most important IT personnel in an organization.

This chapter introduces you to system administration and describes why it is vitally important to information security. We then introduce you to some of the standard system administration facilities provided by common enterprise software using the major operating systems currently in use as examples. The hands-on activity in this chapter gives you the opportunity to download, install, and configure your own copy of a customized version of the Linux operating system. This operating system has been customized by the authors of this book and includes tested versions of the most common information security utilities used by system administrators. These utilities will be used in the hands-on activities in later chapters. The operating system also includes a mini-simulation of Sunshine State University, which you may find useful in the threaded design case on Sunshine State University used in the book.

---

[1] ATIS Telecom glossary: http://www.atis.org/glossary/default.aspx

Why introduce system administration so early in the text? And why emphasize hands-on system administration?

Effective system administration requires a good amount of discipline and technical skill. It takes time to develop these skills. It is tempting to relegate system administration to an appendix or to direct students to online resources to develop these skills. However, we believe that system administration is also a foundational skill for an aspiring information security professional. We therefore introduce the topic early in the text. We will use the hands-on activities after every chapter to help you refine your system administration and technical skills. Many students find this to be the most valuable component of this course. Most employers also value these skills for entry-level positions.

What is system administration?

System administration is a set of functions that provides support services, ensures reliable operations, promotes efficient use of the system, and ensures that prescribed service-quality objectives are met. System administration includes the installation, configuration, and maintenance of network equipment (switches, routers, DHCP, DNS servers, etc.) and computer systems (database systems, email systems, ERP systems, etc.). Depending on the size and complexity of the systems involved, the time required to provide these services could range from just a small portion of one IT person's time per week to an entire dedicated team of administrators, programmers. and support personnel. If you have ever installed new software or replaced faulty hardware in your PC, you have done the job of a system administrator, albeit on a small scale. At the other extreme, companies like Google employ thousands of system administrators and other personnel to support hundreds of thousands of computers.[2] Every minute that a critical business system is off-line could mean thousands, even millions, of dollars of lost revenue. Therefore, skilled system administrators are highly sought-after in the industry.

Related trends – Cloud Computing

In response to the complexities of system administration, two major technology trends have emerged in recent years. Both of these trends fall under the category of cloud computing. *Cloud computing is the delivery of software and other computer resources as a service, rather than a product and provided over the Internet.*[3] The first trend is Software as a Service (SaaS). *Software as a Service is a software delivery mechanism in which an application and all of the associated resources are provided to organizations by the SaaS vendor, typically through a web browser.* The SaaS provider provides all hardware and software and takes on the responsibility for all aspects of system administration. Pricing is typically as a subscription, with a per-user cost paid on a monthly or annual

---

[2] http://www.datacenterknowledge.com/archives/2011/08/01/report-google-uses-about-900000-servers/

[3] http://en.wikipedia.org/wiki/Cloud_computing

basis. Some SaaS applications are provided free of charge and provide revenue through displaying advertisements. If you have used any of the web-based applications such as Google Docs or used an online storage service such as DropBox, you have used a SaaS application.

The second major trend is Infrastructure as a Service (IaaS). *Infrastructure as a Service is a business model in which an organization uses hardware equipment such as processors, storage, and routers from the IaaS provider.* IaaS is also considered a form of cloud computing. Unlike SaaS, the IaaS provider provides only the hardware and takes responsibility for just the hardware installation and maintenance. All operating system and application administration must be performed by the organization's system administrators. Pricing is typically on a subscription basis and is based on usage (e.g., per GB of storage, per million CPU cycles). Amazon[4] and Rackspace[5] are some of the better known IaaS providers.

In recent years, system administrators have begun to deploy a technology called virtual machines to increase the efficiency of utilization of their computer hardware. *A virtual machine is a software container into which an operating system and applications can be installed.* Virtual machines function exactly like their physical counterparts but without the possibility of hardware failure. Virtual machines can be started and stopped on demand, so during times of business' peak load, such as the holiday season for an online merchant, new virtual machines can be started to run as web servers. Once the holidays are over and load returns to normal, the extra virtual servers can be removed. As an example of the utility of virtual machines, in the hands-on activity at the end of this chapter, you will create your own virtual machine and use the virtual machine for most hands-on activities in the rest of this book. When an organization hires an IaaS provider, they are buying access to a virtual machine.

Combining IaaS and virtual machines, instead of buying and maintaining enough physical servers to handle peak load, organizations can pay only for the exact number of servers they need, when they need them.

System administration and information security

At this point, you may be asking yourself "what does system administration have to do with information security?" In fact, system administration is the first line of defense for all the three dimensions of information security – confidentiality, integrity, and availability. Consider *availability*. If critical information, such as your grades, is not available because the server that it is stored on has failed and there is no way to recover it, you would be directly impacted by a system administration failure. It was the responsibility of the system administrator to anticipate this issue and use appropriate methods to prevent the hardware failure from affecting end users. For most system administrators, the majority of their time is spent planning for, repairing, and recovering from hardware failures. As another example, consider *confidentiality*. What if critical information, such as your transcript, was stolen from your university systems and put up on the web for anyone to see? This too would be a system administration failure. It was the

---

[4]http://aws.amazon.com/

[5]http://www.rackspace.com/cloud/

responsibility of the concerned system administrator to anticipate this issue and use the appropriate file permissions to ensure that unauthorized people could not read or copy your transcript.

As you see, virtually everything that system administrators do is related to information security and most technical aspects of information security are addressed by system administrators. The next section describes some of the common tasks performed by system administrators and the section after that describes some of the common tools provided by enterprise software systems to help system administrators perform these tasks.

Common system administration tasks[6]

Every stage of using a technology involves system administration tasks. These tasks include installation and configuration of the system so it can be used, access control and user management so users can find what they need without inadvertently causing damage to the system, ongoing monitoring of the system to ensure all components are operating as expected, applying updates when monitoring reveals performance or security-related issues

Installation and configuration

Installation is the act of writing the necessary data in the appropriate locations on a computer's hard drive for running a software program. The first task when setting up a new computer is installing the operating system. If you have ever installed a version of Microsoft Windows or a Linux distribution, you are familiar with the process; you start the computer up with an installation disk, answer a few configuration questions, select which hard drive to install on, select which programs to install, then wait while the files are transferred. The steps are very similar no matter which OS you are installing. While the installation and configuration of software on one computer is quite straightforward, the challenge for system administrators is to streamline this process across hundreds or thousands of computers in the organization. In the next section, we provide an overview of some utilities commonly used for these tasks.

Configuration is the act of selecting one among many possible combinations of features of a system. Configuration has several information security implications. Complex configurations can create vulnerabilities due to the interactions among components and the inability of system administrators to fully comprehend the implications of these interactions. Many desirable software components are not maintained, creating information security hazards. For these reasons, whereas the general rule of thumb among consumers regarding configuration may be

> Peter Bos, an engineer at MIT, is credited with using his privileges as a system administrator to send the world's first spam message in 1971. The message was addressed to about a thousand fellow engineers, including at the Pentagon. The intent of that first spam message was to:
>
> A   Sell used computers
> B   Oppose the Vietnam war
> C   Find a job
> D   Recruit students to his lab
>
> (Answer on page 31)

---

[6]Source for the spam snippet:

   1. Morozov, E. "The common enemy," WSJ Book Review, May 9, 2013.

   2. Brunton, F. "Spam: a shadow history of the Internet (infrastructures)," MIT Press, ISBN 026201887X.

"when in doubt, install or update," among professional system administrators it is "when in doubt, do not install."

Access control and user management

Access control is the act of limiting access to information system resources only to authorized users, programs, processes, or other systems. Access controls establish what users can do on a system. Typically, this refers to which files or directories a user can read, modify, or delete, but in some operating systems, access to network ports and other OS-level structures can also be limited. Access controls can also be applied at the application level, limiting which rows and/ or columns a user can see in a database or which screens are available in a business application.

A key component of access control is user management. *User management refers to defining the rights of organizational members to information in the organization.* Creating and removing user accounts are probably the first thing that people think of when they hear the term user management. However, user management also includes updating records appropriately when users change roles. To manage large numbers of users, it is common to organize users with similar privileges into groups. For instance, all faculty members in the Computer Science department can be made members of the `Compsci-Faculty` group. This group could then be used for granting access to certain resources on the department's website or as mailing list for email discussions.

The relationship between access control, user management, and the first two component portions of the CIA triad – *confidentiality* and *integrity* – is straightforward. A system administrator establishes access controls on pieces of information to ensure that only the authorized users are allowed to view (confidentiality) or modify (integrity) them. This process can be simple, but as the size of the organization and amount of data grows, the complexity and chance for error increases dramatically. We will look at these issues in depth in Chapter 7.

Monitoring and testing

Once installed, configured, and running, a system needs to be continuously monitored to ensure desired performance and security. *Monitoring is the act of listening and/or recording the activities of a system to maintain performance and security.* The system administration tasks in this category come in two varieties: reactive monitoring and proactive testing. *Reactive monitoring is the act of detecting and analyzing failures after they have occurred.* For example, administrators can use automated monitoring tools such as Nagios[7] to get an overall view of the "health" of their network and instant notifications when problems occur. Similarly, log management tools collect and analyze the system logs from all of the servers across a network and correlate events between servers. Monitoring tools such as these assist system administrators in detecting unusual patterns or events, which may indicate a security compromise and, once a compromise is detected, how many systems are potentially affected.

Proactive testing is the act of testing a system for specific issues before they occur. One common practice is to use vulnerability scanners to access systems and look for potential vulnerabilities. These vulnerabilities can then be prioritized and resolved. Usually carried out by a professional security firm, penetration testing takes this one step further, actively exploiting vulnerabilities found and assessing the level of access that is gained.

---

[7]http://www.nagios.org/

Software updates

Ongoing use and monitoring of software usually reveal vulnerabilities or feature requirements. Software updates are used to fix these issues. *A software update is the act of replacing defective software components with components in which the identified defects have been removed.* Software updates can be broken into two categories: operating system updates and application updates. *Operating system updates are software updates that fix issues with the low-level components of the system software and are developed and released by the operating system vendor directly.* All modern operating systems include software for automatically checking for and installing required updates without system administrator intervention. Application updates fix problems in individual applications. These typically involve much more work on the system administrator's part because applications are often customized with plugins from other vendors and sometimes even by in-house developers. Many of these customizations are not well documented or well tested. It is not easy to predict the impact of an application update on these customizations. Therefore, manual updates are often necessary to deploy application updates.

> Peter Bos
> Answer: (B). The text of the message was: "There is no way to peace. Peace is the way."

Keeping systems updated is extremely challenging in organizations because of the unpredictable behaviors of installed applications on updated systems. For this reason, system administrators typically install the update on a development server and test all applications on the development system before deploying the update to production systems.

Facebook, email discovery, system administration, and the law

Mark Zuckerberg started thefacebook.com on February 4, 2004, while still a student at Harvard. Over time, this site grew to become the well-known company – Facebook. About 9 months before launching the Facebook, while still a Harvard student, Mark had signed a contract with Paul Ceglia, an upstate New York serial entrepreneur to create a website called StreetFax. In 2010, Paul Ceglia filed a lawsuit in Buffalo New York, claiming that the StreetFax contract was in fact the contract for Facebook. According to the terms of the contract, Paul was entitled to a 50% stake in Facebook. At the time of the lawsuit, it was estimated that this stake could be worth as much as $50 billion. In support of his claim, Paul produced a copy of his contract with Mark.

Ok. So what does this have to do with information security in general and system administration in particular? Before you read further, pause to think for a moment what Facebook might be able to do to demonstrate that Paul's claim is false (Figure 2.1).

In its motion to dismiss the claim, Facebook produced the results of its search of Harvard's email server. Facebook's motion for dismissal states, ". . . [we reviewed] all of Zuckerberg's emails contained in the email account he used while a student at Harvard. That account contains emails from the 2003 to 2004 time period. The emails Ceglia quotes in his Amended Complaint do not exist in the account. They are complete fabrications. . . . [we ran searches] on all emails in the account using search terms containing the words and phrases taken from the purported emails excerpted in Ceglia's Amended Complaint. . . . the purported emails were not in Zuckerberg's email account. . . . not a single one exists on the Harvard server. What does exist in the Harvard account are numerous emails between Zuckerberg, Ceglia, and StreetFax employees concerning Ceglia's failure to pay Zuckerberg for his StreetFax work – and Ceglia's repeated pleas for forgiveness and his promises to scrape together the

FIGURE 2.1 Paul Ceglia

money he owed Zuckerberg. The real emails in Zuckerberg's account show that Zuckerberg never discussed Facebook or any social networking website with Ceglia or his colleagues, and that Ceglia's story of a purported "partnership" with Zuckerberg to launch Facebook is a complete fiction.

The article in Wired Magazine is quite detailed and worth a read for those interested in the matter.

References

1. Paul D. Ceglia vs. Mark Elliott Zuckerberg, "Memorandum of law in support of defendant's motion to dismiss," March 26, 2012.
2. Raice, S. "A Facebook founder fight," *Wall Street Journal*, March 27, 2012, B7.
3. Kravets, D. "How forensics claims Facebook ownership contract is 'forged'," *Wired Magazine*, March 27, 2012, http://www.wired.com/threatlevel/2012/03/facebook-ownership-forensics/ (accessed 07/23/2013).

Single points of failure

The above are the standard system administration activities related to software that have information security implications. There is also one important system administration activity related to hardware with information security implications. *A part of a system whose failure will stop the entire system from working is a single point of failure.*[8] Single points of failure have availability implications. For example, a common single point of failure in desktop computers is the power

> What is the oldest email in any of your email accounts?
> What is the subject matter of that email?

---

[8]http://en.wikipedia.org/wiki/Single_point_of_failure

supply. If the power supply fails, the computer cannot function until a replacement is installed. The standard solution to deal with single points of failure is redundancy. *Redundancy is surplus capability, which is maintained to improve the reliability of a system.* For example, to minimize downtime, you could have a spare power supply ready to install right away. Extra parts like this are known as **cold spares** and are useful for minimizing downtime, but there is still some amount of time that the system would be unavailable. Most large computer servers utilize **hot spares**. *Hot spares are redundant components that are actually housed inside the server and can replace the failed component with no downtime.* Redundant components even allow system administrators to handle external failures as well. For instance, battery backups allow system administrators to deal with power failures (Figure 2.2).

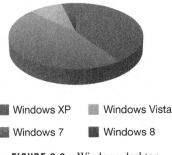

■ Windows XP   ▨ Windows Vista
■ Windows 7   ■ Windows 8

FIGURE 2.2   Windows desktop usage – April 2013

System administration utilities

Given the important role of system administration in an organization and the very high value of a system administrator's time, specialized system administration utilities have evolved over time for enterprise-grade hardware and software. In this section, we provide an overview of the common utilities available for the administration of common operating systems – Windows and Linux/UNIX. Similar system administration utilities are available for other enterprise systems as well – e.g., databases, routers, and hardware.

We first take a look at the general features of the two operating systems and then look at some popular system administration utilities for these two systems.

Microsoft Windows

With 92% of the desktop computer market as of April 2013,[9] if you use a computer, it is most likely running Microsoft Windows. Since the mid-1990s when Windows 95 and Windows NT were released,[10] Microsoft has released versions of Windows in two lines: desktop and server. The desktop line includes the familiar version numbers (Windows 95, 98, ME, XP, Vista, 7, 8) and includes support for the wide range of computer hardware and peripherals used on home computers. You have most likely used one or more of these versions. The server line (NT, 2000, 2003, 2008, 2008 R2, 2012) in contrast supports a much smaller set of hardware and peripherals and is focused on business desktops and the server market. The most important differentiator, however, is that the server line includes a number of services for access control and user management that are not available for the desktop line. The most important of these services are the *Active Directory Domain Services.*

Active Directory is a collection of technologies that provide centralized user management and access control across all computers that are "members" of the domain. Once domain memberships are defined, *Group Policies* can be applied to domain users and computers to control user access to features on specific computers in the organization. Microsoft defines *group policy as an infrastructure that allows you to implement specific configurations for users and*

---

[9] http://netmarketshare.com

[10] http://windows.microsoft.com/en-US/windows/history

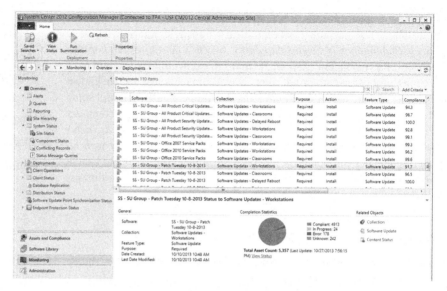

FIGURE 2.3 System Center Operation Manager

computers.[11] Group Policies are often used to restrict certain actions that may pose potential security risks, e.g., to disable the downloading of executable files or to deny access to certain programs. *The server that implements the active directory rules within a domain is called the Domain Controller for the domain.* The Domain Controller maintains information on user accounts, authenticates users on the domain based on this information, and authorizes these users to access resources on the domain based on the group policy. Each domain requires at least one Domain Controller, but more can be added for redundancy.

System administration utility – System Center

Microsoft provides several tools for securely installing and configuring Windows under the name **System Center.**[12] The System Center Configuration Manager (SCCM) allows system administrators to manage the Windows installation process on hundreds of servers and desktops from one console, including the services and software to be installed. In addition to operating system installation, SCCM also automates the update process, both for Windows and other software packages that have been installed. The tools provided by System Center give a system administrator the ability to deploy new software or changes in a repeatable manner that can be easily automated and, more importantly for information security, audited.

System Center also includes a monitoring system called System Center Operations Manager (Figure 2.3), which can alert system administrators to hardware failures or other issues affecting the availability of data. Recognizing the developments of IaaS and virtual machines, SCCM can create or remove virtual servers to maintain the level of availability set by the system administrator.

---

[11] http://technet.microsoft.com/en-us/library/cc779838(v=ws.10).aspx

[12] http://www.microsoft.com/en-us/server-cloud/system-center

Windows SysInternals

For personal use, you may like to use a set of utilities provided by Microsoft called System Internals, better known in the industry as SysInternals. They are available from Microsoft's website.[13] These tools were first created by Mark Russinovich in 1996, and the company he founded, Winternals Software, was later acquired by Microsoft. SysInternals provides excellent visibility into the ongoing activities such as file and registry changes on a running computer. Many screenshots in this book use information from Sysinternals.

Unix/Linux

The Unix operating system was first developed under the name UNICS in 1969 by a group at AT&T's Bell Labs led by Ken Thompson and Dennis Ritchie.

Trivia

We can credit an early video game, *Space Travel*, for the development of UNIX – Thompson had originally written the game for an operating system (Multics) and hardware that the group no longer had access to. During the process of rewriting the game for new hardware, he wrote the basis of what would become Unix.[14]

In 1975, AT&T licensed Unix to several educational and research institutions. Because the source code was provided with Unix, many of these institutions modified and extended Unix to meet their needs. The University of California, Berkley, released the **Berkley Software Distribution (BSD) Unix** in 1978, which introduced many enhancements that are still present in modern Unix systems.[15] Dozens of Unix "flavors" have been released – each based on either the BSD or AT&T code-bases, but adding their own particular enhancements. The final AT&T version of Unix, System V, was released in 1988, but versions of Unix based on their code (referred to as **SysV-based Unix**) are still in development today.[16] A family tree showing the most popular releases is shown in Figure 2.4.

Linux

In 1991, Linus Torvalds, a Computer Science graduate student at the University of Helsinki, released the first version of a new *Unix-like* operating system: **Linux**. Linux is referred to as Unix-like because it does not contain any source code from earlier Unix operating systems,

---

[13] At the time of writing (April 2012, the URL was http://technet.microsoft.com/en-us/sysinternals/bb545021

[14] http://www.livinginternet.com/i/iw_unix_dev.htm

[15] http://en.wikipedia.org/wiki/Berkeley_Software_Distribution

[16] http://www.levenez.com/unix/

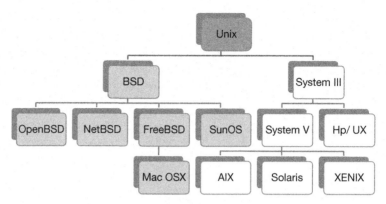

FIGURE 2.4 Unix family tree

but it provides an environment that includes virtually all of the tools and features provided by a BSD or SysV-based Unix. Linux was released as Open Source Software. *Open source software is a software in which anyone is able to modify the source code and distribute his or her changes to the world.* The motivation behind developing an independent code base and adopting the unique licensing model was to allow developers an opportunity to distribute their own innovations to the world, without being obstructed by the restrictions imposed by commercial operating systems. This free exchange of ideas in software was greatly enhanced by the rise in Internet-connectivity beginning in the mid-1990s. Instead of just one or two students at a university or a few dozen developers at a commercial software vendor, Linux soon had thousands of developers from around the world working to improve it.[17] In the two decades since it was first released, Linux has been modified to run on everything from supercomputers to cell phones. With many GPS devices, home wireless routers, Android devices, and the Amazon Kindle using Linux for their operating system, chances are you have used a device running the Linux operating system. Also, as of November 2012, all of the world's 10 fastest supercomputers use Linux as the operating system.[18]

An interesting result of the open nature and flexibility of Linux is the number of different Linux versions that have been created. Everyone is free to create their own Linux "distribution," and there are literally hundreds in active development.[19] Unlike Microsoft Windows and the commercial Unix operating systems, there is not an "official" version of the Linux operating system, but there are several major distributions. By far, the most common Linux distribution in a business setting is *Red Hat Enterprise Linux* (RHEL). RHEL is a commercial Linux distribution, but Red Hat also freely provides the source code for the entire operating system. The developers of the CentOS project[20] have compiled this source code and built a free Linux operating system that is nearly identical to RHEL. All of the hands-on activities in this text, beginning with the one at the end of this chapter, will utilize a customized version of CentOS.

---

[17] http://www.ragibhasan.com/linux

[18] http://www.top500.org/lists/2012/11

[19] http://distrowatch.com/search.php?ostype=Linux&category=All

[20] http://www.centos.org

System administration utilities

Automated operating system installation and configuration tools have many names in the Unix and Linux world (Jumpstart on Oracle Solaris, Kickstart on RHEL, and Network Installation Manager on IBM AIX to name just a few), but they all work in a very similar fashion. The system administrator creates a file that contains instructions on how to configure network devices, hard drives and any other common hardware, and a list of software packages that should be installed. Finally, it includes any post-install programs that need to be run to finish the configuration process.

Several applications provide cross-platform support for configuring software after operating system installation.[21] The most popular of these packages is Puppet,[22] which is used heavily by major Internet companies such as Google and Twitter. A system administrator creates a "puppet manifest" which lists the software to be installed and the desired configuration, the manifest can then be sent to one or more remote servers, and the software is installed, regardless of the underlying operating system.

SUMMARY

This chapter sets the groundwork for the technical component of this course. System administrators perform most of the technical activities related to information security. This chapter therefore defined system administration and introduced the role played by system administrators in organizations. It also introduced the common information security tasks performed by system administrators. Finally, it provided an overview of the common utilities used to simplify these tasks in large organizations.

The hands-on activity in this chapter will lay the stage for the hands-on activities you will perform in all the remaining chapters of this book.

EXAMPLE CASE – T.J. MAXX

Corporate interest in information security was dramatically raised in 2007 following the revelations of embarrassing information security breaches at several well-known companies. Hackers had complete access to credit-card databases at many of the leading retailers in the country including T.J. Maxx, Barnes and Noble, and Office Max (Figure 2.5).

Hackers know that it is safe to be outside the target country to avoid prosecution. It was therefore initially believed that the attacks were caused by hackers outside the country. However, investigations revealed that the attacks were mostly from domestic sources and led to the prosecution of 11 men in 5 countries, including the United States. Most interestingly, the ringleader turned out to have been an informer for the US Secret Service.

Outcome

On August 5, 2008, the US government charged 11 individuals with wire fraud, damage to computer systems, conspiracy, criminal forfeiture, and other related charges for stealing credit-card information from prominent retailers such as T.J. Maxx, BJ's Wholesale Club, Office Max, and Barnes and Noble.

In August 2009, many members of the same gang were again charged with compromising Heartland Payment Systems, a credit-card processing company, and stealing approximately 130 million credit-card numbers. With approximately 100 million families in the United States, this translates to almost 1 credit card stolen from every American family. 5 members of the gang were indicted on July 25, 2013.[23,24]

---

[21] http://en.wikipedia.org/wiki/Comparison_of_open_source_configuration_management_software

[22] http://projects.puppetlabs.com/projects/puppet

[23] http://www.justice.gov/opa/pr/2013/July/13-crm-842.html (accessed 10/11/13)

[24] http://www.justice.gov/iso/opa/resources/5182013725111217608630.pdf

© HO/Reuters/Corbis

FIGURE 2.5 Albert Gonzalez, at the time of his indictment in August 2009

Background

The gang involved in all these incidents had been in operation since 2003. Between 2003 and 2007, the gang used simple methods to exploit weaknesses in wireless security at retail stores. At T.J. Maxx, they had found that many stores did not use any security measures in their store wireless networks. As a result, obtaining employee user names and passwords was as simple as waiting outside the stores in the morning with laptops and listening to the network traffic as employees and managers logged into their accounts.

Worse, these user accounts had access to the corporate IT systems at T.J. Maxx, including those that stored credit-card information. Using this information, the hackers had a free run of the company's credit-card information. For almost a year, the gang members extracted the data, stored it on the company's own servers, and retrieved it at their own convenience. Their goal was to use this information to sell fake credit cards at pennies on the dollar.

This was the method used by the gang in the attacks that formed the basis of the 2008 indictment. Beginning in August 2007, the gang refined its skill set and began to use SQL injection attacks to place malware on web applications and gain access to corporate databases. The gang used this method in the attacks for which it was indicted in 2009.

The ring leader and his activities

Albert Gonzalez, the ringleader of the gang, was a resident of Miami, Florida. Beginning around 2003, he is believed to have driven around Miami, using his laptop computer to locate insecure wireless access points at retail stores. Stores typically use these networks to transfer credit-card information from cash registers to store servers. When an open network was located, the gang would use a custom-written "sniffer" program to collect credit-card account numbers (one of the most popular sniffers is Wireshark, an easy to use program that is available for free use[25]). Fake cards using these numbers were then sold in the gray market. The biggest victim was T.J. Maxx, which lost information on over 40 million credit cards.

Later, when the gang graduated to SQL injection attacks, it would visit stores to identify the transaction processing systems these companies used. The gang used this information to determine suitable attack strategies to target the specific systems used by these companies. The gang also studied the companies' websites to identify their web applications and to develop appropriate attack strategies for these websites.

The ringleader, Albert Gonzalez, earned over $1 million in profits by selling this card information. Apparently, at one time, his counting machine broke and he had to manually count $340,000 in $20 bills. In August 2009, Albert Gonzalez agreed to plead guilty to charges in the T.J. Maxx case, which had been filed in 2008.

Gonzalez became an informant for the Secret Service in 2003 after being arrested for various crimes. As an informant for the Secret Service, in October 2004, he helped the Secret Service indict 28 members of a website Shadowcrew.com. Shadowcrew stole credit-card information and sold it for profit. While in operation, Shadowcrew members stole tens of thousands of credit-card numbers. After the Shadowcrew operation was completed, however, Albert began his own exploits.

Impact

The direct damage from the attacks in terms of fraudulent charges on customer credit cards was limited. In March 2007, one gang in Florida was caught using cards stolen from T.J. Maxx (TJX) to buy approximately $8 million in goods at various Wal-Marts and Sam's Club stores in Florida. However, the collateral damage from the incident has been colossal. TJX Companies, Inc. (TJX) (T.J. Maxx Stores is one of the companies owned by the group, Marshalls is another)

---

[25]http://www.wireshark.org

settled with Visa for $40 million in November 2007 and with MasterCard in April 2008 for $24 million.

The impact was nationwide. Tens of millions of customers had to be reissued credit cards. Customers who had set up automated payments on the stolen cards received collection notices from service providers when charges did not go through because the cards had been canceled and new ones had been issued in their place.

Surprisingly, sales at T.J. Maxx do not seem to have been significantly affected by the intrusion (Figure 2.6). Fraudulent expenses were refunded to customers by the credit-card companies through the automatic protection programs offered by credit cards. Customers do not seem to mind their cards information stolen so long as they are not held liable for fraudulent transactions.

Significance

The T.J. Maxx case is significant for the study of information security and its relationship with other professions because

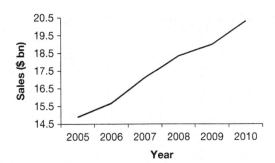

FIGURE 2.6   T J Maxx sales (2005–2010)

the case has been extensively documented in the press. In addition, details are also available from the indictments made in the case. These readings provide a rich account of the actors involved in information security, their motivations, and the legal processes that follow major information security incidents.

REFERENCES

Pereira, J. "How credit-card data went out wireless door," *Wall Street Journal*, May 4, 2007.

Pereira, J., Levitz, J. and Singer-Vine, J. "U.S. indicts 11 in global credit-card scheme," *Wall Street Journal*, August 6, 2008: A1.

United States of America vs. Albert Gonzalez, Criminal indictment in US District Court, Massachusetts, August 5, 2008 (the T.J. Maxxcase).

United States of America vs. Albert Gonzalez, Criminal indictment in US District Court, New Jersey, August 17, 2009 (the Heartland case).

Zetter, K. "TJX Hacker was awash in cash; his penniless coder faces prison," *Wired*, June 18, 2009.

Gorman, S. "Arrest in Epic Cyber Swindle," *Wall Street Journal*, August 18, 2009.

Gorman, S. "Hacker sentenced to 20 years in massive data theft," *Wall Street Journal*, 2010: A1.

"Albert Gonzalez," Wikipedia, http://en.wikipedia.org/wiki/Albert_Gonzalez.

T.J. Maxx, 10-K reports, 2006–2010.

T.J. Maxx, 8-K filing, January 18, 2007; April 2, 2008; November 30, 2007.

CHAPTER REVIEW QUESTIONS

1. What is system administration?

2. Why is system administration important?

3. Who is a system administrator?

4. What are some of the important day-to-day activities performed by system administrators?

5. Define Infrastructure as a Service (IaaS).

6. What are some of the benefits of using an IaaS provider?

7. What is a virtual server?

8. What are some benefits of virtualization?

9. What is the role of a system administrator in maintaining information security in an organization?

10. What is software configuration?

11. How does software configuration impact information security?

12. Define access control. How can weak access controls impact information security?

13. Define user management. How does user management impact information security?

14. What is monitoring? How does it help information security?

15. What is reactive monitoring? What are some common reactive monitoring methods?

16. What is proactive testing? What are some common proactive testing methods?

17. What is a system update? What are the challenges in keeping systems updated? Why is it important for information security?

18. What is a single point of failure? How do system administrators typically deal with single points of failure?

19. What is the difference between cold spares and hot spares?

20. What is Active Directory? What role does it play in maintaining information security on Windows computers?

21. What are group policies? How do group policies assist system administrators in maintaining information security?

22. What is a domain controller?

23. Provide a brief description (two to three sentences maximum) of the information security features of the latest version of Microsoft's System Center or comparable product.

24. What is Linux? Why is it popular? What are some of the most popular distributions of Linux?

25. Provide a brief overview (two to three sentences maximum) of the capabilities of Puppet, the IT automation software used by many system administrators.

EXAMPLE CASE QUESTIONS

1. Based on the information provided above, list as many example of violation of confidentiality, integrity, and availability identified in the case.

2. Based on the case, identify the failures in execution of the common system administration tasks at T.J. Maxx at the time of the case.

3. If you were responsible for system administration at T.J. Maxx, what are the things you would have done to prevent the occurrence of the incidents reported in the case?

HANDS-ON ACTIVITY – LINUX SYSTEM INSTALLATION

Disclaimer

The activities you are about to perform can harm your computer if not done correctly. While every effort has been made to prevent mishaps, please note that it is ultimately your responsibility to protect the data on your computer and your computer itself.

In order to get practical hands-on experience on essential information security and system administration skills, the book includes a series of hands-on activities, which use the Linux operating system. You will create the required environment as the hands-on activities in this chapter. When you complete the activity, you will have your own working copy of CentOS Linux (http://centos.org) that we have configured for use with this course. In our experience, at the end of the course, students find these hands-on activities to be the most useful component of this course, and in fact, one of the most interesting activities in their college studies. The specific configuration used here has been chosen because it allows you to create the required infrastructure on almost any computer you may own. We have taken considerable effort to make this resource available for you because these are skills that are highly sought after by employers and which differentiate you from competitors in the marketplace. We hope you find these activities as exciting as we are excited about creating them (Figure 2.7).

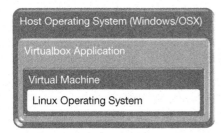

FIGURE 2.7   Virtual machine structure

The activity for this chapter is completed in two steps. In the first step, you will install VirtualBox, a virtualization environment. In the second step, you will use VirtualBox to create a virtual machine containing a preconfigured Linux operating system.

Step 1 – Installing VirtualBox

Before you begin, note the minimum system requirements:

* Windows XP, Windows 7, Windows Server 2003, or Windows Server 2008

* Macintosh OSX 10.5 or greater

* 2 GB of RAM

* 10 GB free hard drive space

VirtualBox is an open source computer application that can be installed on any computer running an Intel or AMD processor to create virtual machines on the computer. Guest operating systems can be installed on these virtual machines so that a Windows computer with adequate storage and processing power can run multiple operating systems. Follow these steps to install VirtualBox on your personal computer. At the time of this writing, the product is being updated very rapidly, so your version numbers may differ from those shown here. It should be safe to follow the configuration management rule for consumers, "when in doubt, install the latest version." For more details on VirtualBox, check the VirtualBox manual,[26] particularly Chapter 1 of the manual.

1. Visit the VirtualBox download page (Figure 2.8) to obtain the installer. This URL changes often; it is best to search for "Download VirtualBox" to locate this link. The page looks as below. Download the appropriate installer for your system. The instructions below are for Windows. The procedure for other systems will be similar.

2. Double-click the downloaded file to start the installation. Click "Next" on the welcome screen (Figure 2.9) to begin the installation.

3. You are now asked to select the location where you would like to install VirtualBox. The default location is

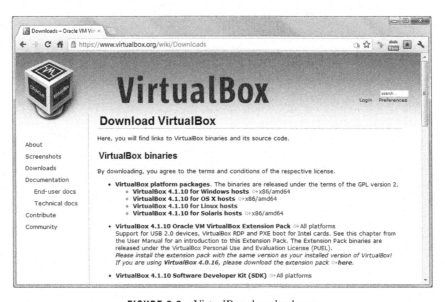

FIGURE 2.8   VirtualBox download page

---

[26] https://www.virtualbox.org/manual/

your Program Files folder. Click "next" if the default install location is OK (Figure 2.10).

4. The installation now proceeds like any normal application. You may receive an alert from the UAC (user acceptance control). Allow the installation and proceed through the screens by clicking "Next."

5. You may receive a warning that your network connections will be restarted. If you have any network traffic (file downloads, music streaming, etc), you may want to wait until those transfers are complete before proceeding.

6. If you are asked whether you would like to install USB support, it is recommended that you elect to do so.

FIGURE 2.9 VirtualBox installer welcome screen

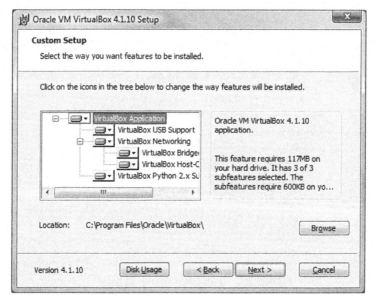

FIGURE 2.10 Default install Location

7. Click "Finish" to complete the installation. When installation is complete, you will see the confirmation (Figure 2.11). If you enable the checkbox to start VirtualBox, you will see the VirtualBox manager (Figure 2.12). It is currently empty. You will populate it with your own customized Linux operating system in the next step of this exercise.

Step 2 – Install the OS

As you may have read in the VirtualBox documentation, you can install almost any modern desktop operating system as a guest OS. For this book, we have customized a distribution of Linux. Using Linux in allows us to circumvent commercial licensing limitations. Fortunately, most security concepts are generalizable across operating systems and most of the general concepts you will learn here also apply to Windows. Follow the instructions below to install the customized Linux distribution in a new virtual machine on your computer:

1. Download the CentOS Linux virtual image from the companion website for the text. The .ova file extension stands for "Open Virtual Appliance," an industry

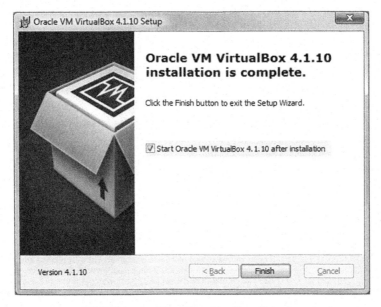

FIGURE 2.11   VirtualBox install confirmation

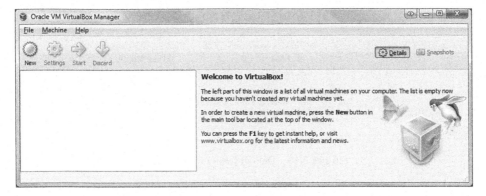

FIGURE 2.12   VirtualBox manager

standard for operating systems packaged for installation into a virtual machine.[27] The format was created by VMWare, a leading firm in the virtualization industry. Note that this is a VERY large (over 2.5 GB) file and can take several hours to download, even over broadband.

2. Double-click on the CentOS_6.ova file, the "Appliance Import Wizard" will start. The default values should be fine, and you can start the process of creating your virtual machine by clicking "import," as shown in Figure 2.13. The import may take 10–20 minutes depending upon the speed of the computer and the location of the installation.

3. When the installation is complete, the VirtualBox manager shows the new VM in the list of VMs (Figure 2.14). You can now start VirtualBox at any time, select the VM and click on "start" to start up the VM. When the VM is running, you can click on "stop" to terminate the VM.

4. At this point, you are probably eager to see what all this leads to. After the virtual machine has been imported, click on "Start." The Linux operating system will start. Common issues and their solutions are listed below. After any such issues are resolved, you will see the CentOS Linux login screen.

Known issues

1. You may get a warning suggesting that you download and install the expansion pack since your computer had USB 2.0 enabled. You may ignore this message, or if you feel comfortable, you may download and install the extension pack available on the VirtualBox website.

2. You may get warning messages regarding mouse movements, window size, etc. These may be ignored.

3. If you get an error message that says that indicates a problem with the CPU, please select the VM, select "Settings" in the VM manager, then System →Processor and select the "enable PAE checkbox (Figures 2.15 and 2.16)."

4. If you are unable to connect to the network, go to settings → network and attach the network adapter 1 to the NAT as shown in Figure 2.17. You may also be able to just scroll down on the front page and select "Network."

Starting the virtual machine

1. When the virtual machine boots up, you will see the login screen as shown in Figure 2.18.

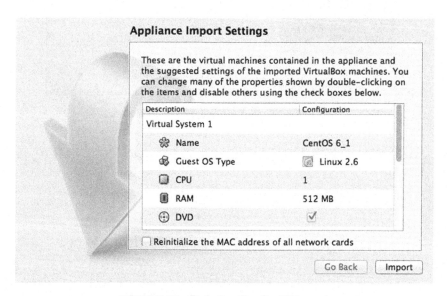

FIGURE 2.13 Default setting for OS import

---

[27]For more details, see http://www.fileinfo.com/extension/ova

FIGURE 2.14   Virtual machine in Virtual machine manager

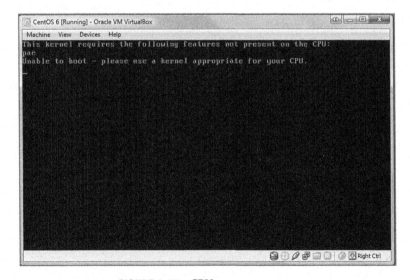

FIGURE 2.15   CPU error

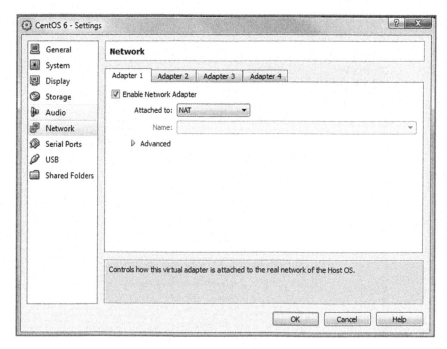

FIGURE 2.16 Enabling PAE

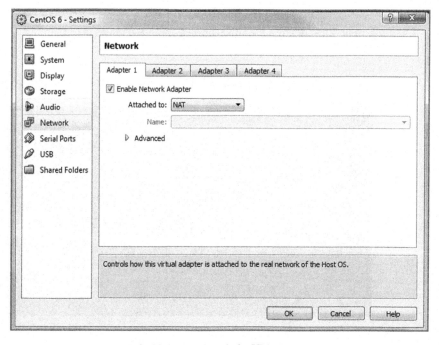

FIGURE 2.17 Attach the VM to NAT

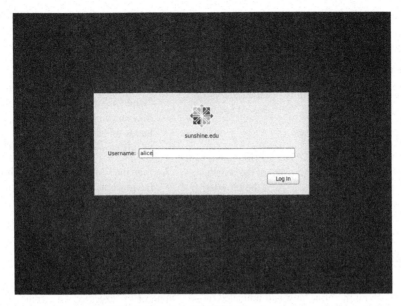

FIGURE 2.18 CentOS VM login screen

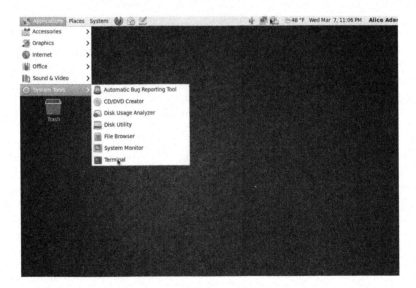

FIGURE 2.19 CentOS Linux desktop

2. At the Login prompt enter the username *alice* and use the password *aisforapple*. This will bring up the CentOS desktop as shown in Figure 2.19.

1. To stop the virtual machine, select Machine → Close (*Virtual Box* → *Quit on OS X*) from the running CentOS VM window.

2. To start the machine again, use Start → Programs → Oracle VM VirtualBox → Oracle VM VirtualBox (*Applications* → *Virtual Box in OS X*).

3. In the next chapter, you will learn some basic UNIX/ Linux system administration, including folder navigation, using the vi editor, and creating user accounts.

Hands-on activity questions

1. Provide a brief description of VirtualBox and its uses.

2. Provide a brief description of the OVA file format.

To demonstrate that you have successfully installed the VM, submit the following:

3. A screenshot of the CentOS desktop.

4. Start the browser using Applications → Internet → Firefox web browser. Submit a screenshot of the browser window showing the default home page of the browser.

5. Start the system monitor using Applications → System tools → System monitor. Submit a screenshot of the System monitor.

6. Start the terminal by selecting Applications → System Tools → Terminal. At the prompt, type in the command "whoami." Submit a screenshot of the terminal window showing the command and its output. (Most of the hands-on activities in the book will make extensive use of this terminal window.)

7. Stop the VM by selecting Machine → Close → Poweroff the machine.

CRITICAL THINKING EXERCISE – GOOGLE EXECUTIVES SENTENCED TO PRISON OVER VIDEO

In September 2006, four classmates bullied a boy suffering from autism at their school in Turin, Italy, and uploaded the clip to Google video (the predecessor to YouTube). The video became popular and was viewed over 5,500 times over the next 2 months and even reached the top of the list of "most entertaining" videos at Google's Italian site.

When Google was notified about it by Italian Police, Google removed the video. However, the boy's father and Vivi Down, an organization representing people with Down's syndrome, sued four Google executives for defamation and illegal personal data handling. Google claims it was swift in removing the video upon being alerted.

On February 24, 2010, the Court of Milan acquitted all executives of the defamation charge, but held three executives guilty of illegal personal data handling and being slow to remove the video upon being informed about it by the police. They were senior vice president and chief legal officer David Drummond, former Google Italy board member George De Los Reyes, and global privacy counsel Peter Fleischer. Personal liability was assigned because corporate officers are held legally liable for a company's actions in Italian law. None of the executives was present in Italy for the hearing and since the sentence was suspended pending appeal, none were under immediate threat of imprisonment.

Google's stand, articulated by its communications manager, was that "They didn't upload it, they didn't film it, they didn't review it and yet they have been found guilty." In his 111-page judgment, the judge Oscar Magi wrote "the Internet [is] not an unlimited prairie where everything is permitted and nothing can be prohibited. . . . Instead, there were laws regulating behavior and if those laws were not respected, 'penal consequences' could ensue." According to Italian law, not stopping a fact is equivalent to causing it. The data protection law requires prior authorization before handling personal data and the posted video was personal data. Therefore, Google was responsible for ensuring that the user who posted the video had the consent of everyone involved in the video.

On December 21, 2012, an Italian appeals court overturned the conviction and acquitted the executives.

REFERENCES

Manuela D'Alessandro, "Google executives convicted for Italy autism video," 02/24/2010, http://www.reuters.com/article/2010/02/24/us-italy-google-conviction-idUSTRE61N2G520100224 (accessed 07/16/2013).

Hooper, J. "Google executives convicted in Italy over abuse video," *The Guardian*, 02/24/2010, http://www.guardian.co.uk/technology/2010/feb/24/google-video-italy-privacy-convictions (accessed 07/16/2013)

Povoledo, E. "Italian judge cites profit as justifying a Google conviction," *New York Times*, April 12, 2010.

EDRi-gram, "First decision in the Italian criminal case against Google executives," 02/24/2010, http://www.edri.org/edri-gram/number8.4/decision-italy-vs-google-executives (accessed 07/16/2013).

Pfanner, E. "Italian appeals court acquits 3 Google executives in privacy case," *New York Times*, December 21, 2012.

CRITICAL THINKING QUESTIONS

1. What is your opinion about the incident?

2. Should system administrators and companies be responsible for the content posted by users of a website?

3. Say you are the system administrator of a website and you receive a request from a user to delete a picture

uploaded by a friend at a party that includes the user. Would you consider the request reasonable?

4. How would you respond to such a request?

DESIGN CASE

For this design case, we will use the Sunshine State University used on the first chapter. Like many other IT-related services at the University, email support is divided into two major systems:

1. Information technology, which reports to the VP of Business and Finance, supports email for all administrative personnel. For historical reasons, the Provost Office pays IT for support of faculty email as well.

2. Student email is supported by the technical staff reporting to the Dean of Students.

The current Student Email system runs on a single server purchased 6 years ago. The server has two internal drives. The internal drives contain the operating system and applications and an external JBOD holds all the data. The server has a single power supply and a single network port. The server runs Linux and the open source SMTP program Sendmail for email delivery.

A recent hardware issue brought the Student Email Servers crashing. The first time this happened, there was an outage of 13 hours. Unfortunately, the root cause of the initial outage was not determined and problem happened again

but this time things were a bit more serious: a critical storage failure caused all of the emails to be lost. The System Administrator in charge of the server could not handle the pressure and resigned. You were the Student Assistant to the Sys Admin. The Dean of Students is in a bit of a bind and offers you a job with great pay, benefits, and tuition waiver program to help you finish your degree.[28]

Two weeks later the server is back online and all email has been recovered from tape. The failure happened at 1:00 p.m. on a Wednesday. The last backup ran at 2:00 a.m. on Tuesday. Email delivered between those times was irrevocably lost.

The student population is up in arms and the Provost gets involved. Together with the Dean of Students, you are asked to recommend a choice for email service among the following options, along with your reasons for the same:

• Maintain email services locally

• Replace the entire email infrastructure with a SaaS email solution

• GoogleApps for Education (http://www.google.com/apps/intl/en/edu).

SECURITY DESIGN CASE QUESTIONS

1. What is a JBOD anyway?

2. As you research your options for Sunshine State University, you are advised to start with a common procedure – looking at what your closest peers are doing. Businesses call this benchmarking. In your context, this means what peer universities are doing in terms of email systems.

   a. List three universities or colleges in your area that you would consider the closest peers to Sunshine State. (Keep this list handy. You will find yourself

returning to this list often to research what these schools are doing to address the challenges you face in this and later chapters.)

   b. Which of these options has each of the institutions selected for email service? Why did they select this choice? (You may find information regarding this on their websites. You can also call their technical support help line).

   c. If your own institution is not on the list in (a), what is your own institution doing for email service? Why?

---

[28]While there is some dramatization, the scenario is based on an actual incident.

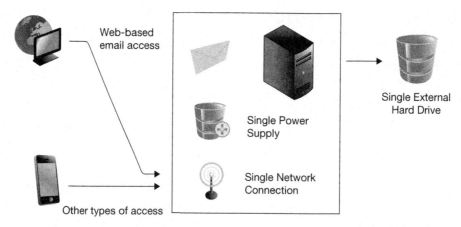

FIGURE 2.20 Sunshine State University email infrastructure

3. What problems can you anticipate from Sunshine State's current system as shown in Figure 2.20? What are the single points of failure? What would have to happen for the local system to be able to safely handle email service if any of these single points of failure were to fail?

4. What features (if any) do the cloud service models (IaaS and SaaS) offer that could not be currently provided locally?

5. During your research you find that one of the common queries fielded by technical support is restoration of accidentally deleted email. What facilities (if any) does each alternative provide in the restoration of accidentally deleted emails?

6. Another important feature request from the student body is email access from a wide variety of devices, especially non-web clients such as smart phones and traditional email clients such as Thunderbird and Eudora. What support does each of the choices provide for email access from these devices. What advantages or disadvantages does each system have for such access?

System Administration (Part 2)

Overview

In the previous chapter, we introduced system administration and described the role that system administrators play in information security. This chapter continues the discussion of system administration by introducing a core set of technical operations used by system administrators. These operations are demonstrated using the Linux virtual machine created in the previous chapter. At the end of this chapter, you should know:

- The core components of a modern operating system
- How to use the command-line interface (CLI)
- Basic operations to navigate the filesystem
- File permissions for users and groups
- User account management
- Software management

Operating system structure

Computer operating systems are software that manage computer hardware and provide common services to user applications. Modern operating systems are made up of many separate programs (or processes) that all work together to produce the desired results. *At the core, the kernel is the software which provides controls for hardware devices, manages memory, executes code on the computer's CPU, and hides the details of the underlying physical hardware from user applications.* This allows application developers to ignore the details of the underlying hardware when developing applications, greatly simplifying application development.

The shell is a text-based program that allows the user to interact directly with the kernel. Common operations performed using the shell include starting and stopping programs, controlling the execution of programs, and starting or stopping the computer. The shell hides the complexity of the kernel from the user so that the user can enter commands in plain English and rely on the shell to translate these commands into the binary code necessary for the kernel to execute them.

While graphical operating systems such as Windows keep the shell hidden, Unix-based operating systems like Linux or Mac OSX automatically start a shell on start-up. This shell runs behind the scenes, starting and stopping programs in response to GUI operations. The shell is also accessible directly as a terminal. This terminal is the preferred environment used by administrators for most system administration tasks. Unless otherwise specified, all system administration tasks in this book will be performed using the terminal window in a Linux operating system.

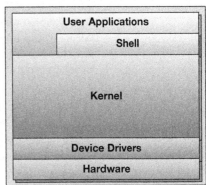

FIGURE 3.1 Operating system structure

Table 3.1 Common shell programs

Name	Developer	1st Release	Details
Bourne Shell (sh)	Stephen Bourne	1977	The de facto standard on Unix. Every major Unix-based OS includes at least one Bourne-compatible shell[1]
C Shell (csh)	Bill Joy	1978	Syntax is based on the C programming language. Popular for interactive use, but not recommended for use as a general scripting language.[2]
Korn Shell (ksh)	David Korn	1983	POSIX 1003.2 compliant, Bourne-compatible and added many features needed for shell scripting.[3]
Bourne-again Shell (Bash)	Brian Fox	1989	Developed as an open-source replacement for Bourne Shell. Bash is very popular for both interactive use and scripting as it combines many of the features from C shell with those from Korn shell and adds many of its own enhancements. Bash is the default shell on Mac OSX and most Linux distributions.[4]

Like all software, shells have evolved over time. Table 3.1 provides an overview of the common shells available. Most administrators prefer the Bash shell, the shell used in this book.

Running a Shell on Windows

There are several options for running a shell on Microsoft Windows. Microsoft's basic command shell (COMMAND.COM or cmd.exe depending on the Windows version) has not changed much since the mid-1990s. It provides the ability to execute commands and supports a few basic tools for manipulating the filesystem. Later versions added the ability to connect to the local network for file transfers and remote administration, but overall the abilities of the shell are limited.

Microsoft now includes an alternative shell and scripting language called *Windows Powershell*.[5] Powershell was designed primarily for scripting and is relatively unique in shells in that it is an object-oriented language that can interact directly with .NET objects and classes. It has quickly become the main scripting language on Windows, and several major applications, such as Microsoft Exchange 2010, rely on it heavily.[6]

For enthusiasts, in addition to the shells provided by Microsoft, open-source developers have re-created much of the UNIX environment on Windows – including the popular Unix shells. The Cygwin project was developed in the 1990s to allow programs compiled on a Unix system to run on Windows. It has evolved into a collection of software that provides a complete Unix-like environment, including command shells and graphical programs. Bash is the default shell in Cygwin, but virtually all of the popular shells used in Linux distributions are now available through the Cygwin installer.

---

[1] http://en.wikipedia.org/wiki/Unix_shell

[2] http://www.faqs.org/faqs/unix-faq/shell/csh-whynot/

[3] Rosenblatt, B. *Learning the Korn Shell*. (O'Reilly), 1993.

[4] http://www.gnu.org/software/bash/manual/bashref.html#What-is-Bash_003f

[5] http://technet.microsoft.com/en-us/library/bb978526.aspx

[6] http://social.technet.microsoft.com/wiki/contents/articles/exchange-2010-powershell-scripting-resources.aspx

The command-line interface

Before proceeding to system administration tasks, this section introduces the command-line interface and the rudiments of using the interface (Figure 3.2).

The Bash prompt

To start a terminal window in the version of CentOS Linux provided with this text, open the "System Tools" panel under the "Applications" menu as shown in Figure 3.2. When you open the terminal window, you are presented with a **prompt** from the Bash shell. The Bash prompt is the entry point for all commands that you type, but it can also provide information about the account and server you are using and the environment Bash is running in. Here is a typical Bash prompt:

```
[alice@sunshine usr]$
```

Files and directories

Files and directories in all operating systems are organized in a hierarchical structure. In UNIX, each "layer" of the hierarchy is separated by a slash (/). The top of the hierarchy is referred to as the *filesystem root* and is represented as a single slash. Each directory can contain files or sub-directories, or a combination of both (Figure 3.3).

The location of a file or directory in the hierarchy is referred to as its **path**. There are two ways to express the path of a file, as given in Table 3.2.

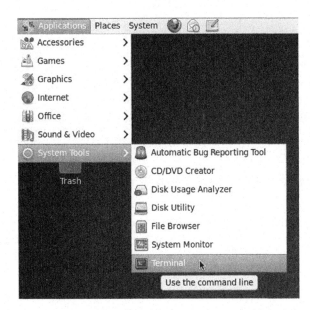

FIGURE 3.2   Reaching the command prompt window

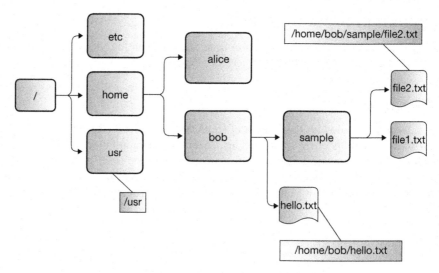

FIGURE 3.3 Unix file hierarchy

Table 3.2 Specifying fie paths

Type	Examples	Description
Absolute	/home/bob/hello.txt/etc	Absolute paths are the exact location of the file that is being referenced. They include **each directory above the current one up to the filesystem root**.
Relative	sample/file2.txt hello.txt	Relative paths give the location of the file **in relation to the current directory**.

Case Sensitivity

Almost all UNIX filesystems are case sensitive, so hello.txt and HELLO.TXT are two distinct files. An exception to this rule is the default filesystem used in Mac OSX (HFS+), which is case insensitive. On Mac OSX, hello.txt and HELLO.TXT would be interpreted as the same filename. For this reason, when copying files from a case-sensitive filesystem to case-insensitive one, it is necessary to check for possible filename conflicts.

Moving around the filesystem – pwd, cd

The first thing you need to know is where you are and the pwd command provides that to you. pwd **stands for "print working directory"** and returns the absolute path of the directory you are currently in. When you login to a UNIX system or open a terminal window, you will normally be placed in your home directory. *Your home directory is your personal space on the UNIX system, analogous to the Documents folder in Windows.*

```
[alice@sunshine ~]$ pwd
/home/alice
```

Now, to move to another directory, we can use cd. *cd, the change directory command, allows us to switch to another directory. The target folder name is specified as the argument to the command.*

```
[alice@sunshine ~]$ cd /usr
[alice@sunshine usr]$ pwd
/usr
```

Thus, the command "cd /usr" takes us to the /usr folder. In this instance, we used the absolute path of the directory. We can also use relative paths.

```
[alice@sunshine usr]$ cd bin
[alice@sunshine bin]$ pwd
/usr/bin
```

What about moving "up" the tree? In other words, what if we want to move from /usr/bin to /usr? We can use the absolute path as above, but there is also an alternative. The **parent directory**, *the directory directly about the current one in the hierarchy*, is represented by two periods (..)

```
[alice@sunshine bin]$ pwd
/usr/bin
[alice@sunshine bin]$ cd ..
[alice@sunshine usr]$ pwd
/usr
```

Similarly, the current directory is represented by a single period (.) This isn't very useful when changing directories since "cd . " would instruct the shell to *change directories to the current directory* (i.e., *don't do anything*), but it will be very useful with some of the other commands we will learn.

Listing files and directories

To list the contents of the current directory, use ls .

```
[alice@sunshine usr]$ cd /home/alice
[alice@sunshine ~]$ ls
Desktop  Documents  Downloads  hello.txt  Music  Pictures  Public
Templates  Videos
```

Depending on the version and particular configuration of the operating system you are using, the results may be in multiple colors to represent the different types of files or directories shown. (In this instance, items in blue are directories and those in black are files.) Because these colors can vary from version to version of each operating system, it is best not to rely on them. There is an alternative setting, or **switch**, that can be passed to ls that prints results in a more standardized format: -F .

```
[alice@sunshine ~]$ ls -F
Desktop/  Documents/  Downloads/  hello.txt  Music/  Pictures/
Public/  Templates/  Videos/
```

ls -F appends a slash (/) to each directory. You can now easily differentiate between files and directories. However, the ls command does not list hidden files in this directory by default. All files and/or directories whose names begin with a period (.) are considered hidden files. *Hidden files are files whose existence is hidden from users by default.* To list all files, including the hidden ones, you must use the -a switch:

```
[alice@sunshine ~]$ ls -aF
./                .bash_logout   Desktop/    hello.txt   Public/
../               .bash_profile  Documents/  Music/      Templates/
.bash_history   .bashrc        Downloads/  Pictures/   Videos/
```

As you can see, several hidden files (bash_history, .bash_logout, etc.), are now visible. Also two hidden directory entries, /(current directory) and ./(parent directory) are now visible. Since all directories in the Unix filesystem have both a current directory and parent directory entry, *there will always be at least two hidden directory entries in each directory.*

When auditing a system, watch out for hidden directories. A common trick that attackers use after compromising a system is to camouflage their directory of tools by naming it . . . (three periods). It's an effective way of hiding in plain sight – it can be very easy to miss unless you are watching for it.

```
[alice@sunshine compromised]$ ls -aF
./    .../        Documents/   hello.txt   Pictures/   Templates/
../   Desktop/    Downloads/   Music/      Public/     Videos/
```

Shell expansions

Expansions are special characters or strings that the shell will use to build the list of files or directories a command will be run on. There are several different types of expansions recognized in the Bash shell.

Tilde expansion

The Bash shell interprets the tilde character (~) as the user's **home directory**.

```
[alice@sunshine Expansion]$ cd ~
[alice@sunshine ~]$ pwd
/home/alice
```

If you follow the tilde with a username, Bash expands it to the location of that user's home directory. You will not be able to cd into their home directory unless that user has granted you permission to do so, but this is an example of this type of expansion in use:

```
[alice@sunshine Expansion]$ cd ~bob
[alice@sunshine ~]$ pwd
/home/bob
```

File name expansion (wildcards)

To simplify command entry, the Bash shell offers some wildcards, as listed in Table 3.3. The `,` `[..]`, and `*` characters are the available **wildcards**. Bash expands words containing these characters by replacing the word with a list of files or directories that match the filter created by the wildcard.

```
[alice@sunshine ~]$ cd /opt/book/system-admin/shell_expansion
[alice@sunshine shell_expansion]$ ls
goodbye.doc  heap.txt  helicopter.txt  hello.doc  hello.txt  help.txt
[alice@sunshine shell_expansion]$ ls *.doc
goodbye.doc  hello.doc
[alice@sunshine shell_expansion]$ ls he?p.txt
heap.txt  help.txt
```

File management

Now that you know how to move around the filesystem, let's learn how to modify files and folders.

Creating and deleting directories

`mkdir` and `rmdir` are used to create and remove directories.

```
[alice@sunshine ~]$ cd /opt/book/system-admin/work
[alice@sunshine work]$ mkdir new_directory
[alice@sunshine work]$ ls -aF
./  ../  new_directory/
[alice@sunshine work]$ rmdir new_directory/
[alice@sunshine work]$ ls -aF
./  ../
```

> `rmdir` will only work on empty directories. An error will be given if you attempt to run `rmdir` on a directory containing files and/or directories

Table 3.3 Bash wildcards

Wildcard	Filter	Example
?	Matches **zero or one** character with all characters	**re?d** matches **red**, **reed**, and **read** but *not* **reads**
[..]	Contains a list or range of letters/numbers that should be matched	**re[a,e]d** matches **reed** and **read** but not **red**
*	Matches **zero or more** characters with all characters	**re*** matches **red**, **reed**, **read,** and **reads**

Copying and moving files

Use the `cp` command to copy files and `mv` to move them from one directory to another. *To change the name of a file, simply "move" it from the old filename to the new one. The syntax is <cmd> <source> <target>.*

```
[alice@sunshine work]$ cp ../shell_expansion/hello.txt hello_world.txt
[alice@sunshine work]$ ls -aF
./  ../  hello_world.txt
[alice@sunshine work]$ mv hello_world.txt HELLOWORLD.TXT
[alice@sunshine work]$ ls -aF
./  ../  HELLOWORLD.TXT
```

Adding the `-r` *(recursive)* switch allows `cp` to work with directories as well as files (`mv` always works recursively). *Recursion is the act of defining a function in terms of itself.*

```
[alice@sunshine work]$ cd ~
[alice@sunshine ~]$ ls -F
Desktop/  Documents/  Music/  Pictures/  Public/  Videos/
[alice@sunshine ~]$ cp -r Documents/ Documents-copy
[alice@sunshine ~]$ ls -F
Desktop/  Documents/  Documents-copy/  Music/  Pictures/  Public/
Videos/
[alice@sunshine ~]$ mv Documents-copy Documents-moved
[alice@sunshine ~]$ ls -F
Desktop/  Documents/  Documents-moved/  Music/  Pictures/  Public/  Videos/
[alice@sunshine ~]$ ls -aF Documents
./  ../  notes.txt  readme  sample_file.mp3
[alice@sunshine alice]$ ls -aF Documents-moved/
./  ../  notes.txt  readme  sample_file.mp3
```

As you can see, the directory `Documents/` and all of its contents were first copied to `Documents-copy/` and then moved to the new name `Documents-moved/`; the directory name was changed but the contents were unaffected.

Deleting files

To delete a file, use the **rm** command.

```
[alice@sunshine ~]$ cd Documents-moved/
[alice@sunshine Documents-moved]$ ls -aF
./  ../  notes.txt  readme  sample_file.mp3
[alice@sunshine Documents-moved]$ rm notes.txt
[alice@sunshine Documents-moved]$ ls -aF
./  ../  readme  sample_file.mp3
```

> **To help prevent accidental data loss, use the `-i` switch for `cp`, `mv`, and `rm`.** You will be prompted for confirmation before deleting a file or copying/moving a file that would overwrite an existing file.

```
[alice@sunshine Documents-moved]$ rm -i readme
rm: remove regular file 'readme'? n
[alice@sunshine Documents-moved]$ cp -i sample_file.mp3 readme
cp: overwrite 'readme'? n
[alice@sunshine Documents-moved]$ ls -aF
./   ../   readme   sample_file.mp3
```

Recursive delete

As with `cp`, the recursive switch (`-r`) can be used with `rm` to delete directories, however, using the recursive switch with `rm` is potentially much more dangerous. `rm -r` works by first deleting each and every file in the directory, then deleting the directory itself. The potential for disaster here should be obvious. **Always check and recheck the path that you enter when using** `rm -r`

```
[alice@sunshine ~]$ ls -F
Desktop/   Documents/   Documents-moved/   Music/   Pictures/   Public/
Videos/
[alice@sunshine ~]$ rm -r Documents-moved/
[alice@sunshine ~]$ ls -F
Desktop/   Documents/   Music/   Pictures/   Public/   Videos/
```

Viewing files

So now you can make your way through the filesystem, move things around, and change their owners, but how do you see what is in a file? The vast majority of files on a Linux server are text files, so they can be viewed using a few simple commands.

less

`less` allows you to view text files one screen at a time.

```
[alice@sunshine ~]$ less /usr/share/doc/openssl-1.0.0/FAQ
```

Table 3.4 gives the keys you can use to navigate and search the file. The search term will be highlighted and the file will scroll down until the first occurrence of the term will be at the very top of your terminal.

head and tail

If you only need to see a few lines from the beginning or end of a file, use `head` and `tail`. The `-n` switch controls the number of lines the program displays – the default is 10 lines.

```
[alice@sunshine ~]$ head /etc/passwd
root:x:0:0:root:/root:/bin/bash
bin:x:1:1:bin:/bin:/sbin/nologin
daemon:x:2:2:daemon:/sbin:/sbin/nologin
adm:x:3:4:adm:/var/adm:/sbin/nologin
lp:x:4:7:lp:/var/spool/lpd:/sbin/nologin
```

Table 3.4 Commonly used vi keyboard shortcuts (also used in less)

Command	Description
Down arrow	Scroll forward one line
Up arrow	Scroll backward one line
SPACE BAR	Scroll forward one full screen
b	Scroll backward one full screen
g	Scroll the start of the file
G	Scroll to the end of the file
/pattern	Search from the current location toward the end of the file for the pattern
?pattern	Search the current location toward the beginning of the file for the pattern
n	Scroll the file to the next occurrence of a match
N	Scroll to the previous occurrence of a match
q	Quit

Note: Some of these shortcuts have carried over to Gmail. For example, typing/while reading mail puts the cursor in the search box.[7]

```
sync:x:5:0:sync:/sbin:/bin/sync
shutdown:x:6:0:shutdown:/sbin:/sbin/shutdown
halt:x:7:0:halt:/sbin:/sbin/halt
mail:x:8:12:mail:/var/spool/mail:/sbin/nologin
uucp:x:10:14:uucp:/var/spool/uucp:/sbin/nologin
[alice@sunshine ~]$ tail -n5 /etc/group
sales_grp:x:504:
engineering_grp:x:505:
marketing_grp:x:506:
eric:x:507:
accounting_grp:x:508:
```

Searching for files

A typical Linux server contains thousands of files and looking through them for one, specific file can seems like searching for a needle in a haystack. However, a very powerful file search tool, find, is there to help. In its most basic form, find takes two arguments: the directory that the search should start from and the name of the file to search for. Here is an example of searching for the Apache (webserver) configuration file:

```
[alice@sunshine ~]$ find /etc -name httpd.conf
/etc/httpd/conf/httpd.conf
```

As you may have noticed, find uses a slightly different syntax than the other commands we have worked with so far. In all the other commands you have seen, the command switch has followed the command name. However with find, the -name switch comes *after* the first argument (/). The find manual refers to the -name httpd.conf part of the command as an

---

[7]http://support.google.com/mail/bin/answer.py?hl = en&answer = 6594

expression. There are many operators that can be used in an expression such as -user (finds files owned by a particular account) or -empty (finds empty files). Multiple expressions can also be combined to narrow search results:

```
[alice@sunshine ~]$ find /opt -user alice -empty
/opt/book/system-admin/my_file.txt
```

Access control and user management

Permissions

Linux and most other Unix-based operating systems control access to files through two mechanisms: **file permissions** and **Access Control Lists** (ACL). File permissions are the traditional method of controlling access to files and has been in use since the early days of Unix. They are fully supported by all shell commands and work consistently across the different operating systems. ACLs are a more recent addition and provide much finer-grained control of not only who can access a file, but also what can be done with it. Unfortunately, there is little standardization yet among the multiple ACL implementations on different OSes and limited tool support. ACLs are therefore usually passed over in favor of file permissions. We will look at both mechanisms, focusing primarily on file permissions, but demonstrating where the extra control provided by ACLs is useful.

ls (again)

To view the current file permissions, use the -l switch for ls. This switch returns the directory listing in the 'long' format, broken up into 7 columns. Table 3.5 describes the information provided in each column:

```
[alice@sunshine ~]$ cd /home/shared
[alice@sunshine shared]$ ls -laF
total 56
drwxr-xr-x.  5 root root      4096 Jan 29  2012 ./
drwxr-xr-x. 12 root root     36864 Feb 15 19:57 ../
drwxr-xr-x.  6 root root      4096 Jan 29  2012 academic_affairs/
drwxr-xr-x.  5 root root      4096 Jan 29  2012 business_finance/
drwxr-xr-x.  2 root legal_grp 4096 Jan 29  2012 legal/
```

Table 3.5   Column descriptions in long file listing

Column position	Description	Example
1	File/directory permissions	drwxr-xr-x
2	Number of Filesystem "hard" links	2
3	File/directory user ownership	Root
4	File/directory group ownership	engineering_grp
5	File/directory size (in bytes)	4096
6	Modification Timestamp	Jan 28 19:06
7	File/directory name	engineering/

Symbolic notation

Let's take a closer look at the file/directory permissions in column 1. `ls -l` reports file permission in **symbolic notation**:[8] See table 3.7 for examples.

The first character indicates the type of file:

d Directory

-Regular file

b Block/special file

c Character/special file

l Symbolic link

p Named pipe

s Socket

The next nine characters are broken up into three groups of three characters:

1. What the owner can do

2. What the members of the group that owns the file can do

3. What all users (*the world*) can do

Each group is broken into three columns:

r – Read

w – Write

x – eXecute

In addition to execute, the third column can also represent special attributes that can be applied to a file:

s – **setuid/setgid** – Instead of using the permissions of the user executing the file, this file will "run as" the owner (**setuid**) or group (**setgid**) specified here.

T – **sticky bit** – When a directory has this attribute set, any user with write access can create files in the directory, but *only the owner can move or delete them.*

Octal notation

In addition to symbolic notation, some commands use **octal notation** to represent file permissions. Octal notation consists of 3 octal (base-8) numbers, each represents one component of the permission: user, group, and world. The values are calculated by adding the 3 octal bits together (see Table 3.6):

---

[8]http://en.wikipedia.org/wiki/Filesystem_permissions#Symbolic_notation

Table 3.6 Octal notation

Octal	Symbolic	Description
0	- - -	No permissions
1	- -x	Execute
2	-w-	Write
3	-wx	Write/Execute
4	r- -	Read
5	r-x	Read/Execute
6	rw-	Read/Write
7	rwx	Read/Write/Execute

Table 3.7 File permissions examples

Symbolic notation	Octal notation	Explanation
d rwx r-x r-x	755	Directory with read/write/execute permissions to the owner and read/execute permissions to the group and the world.
- rw- r-- ---	640	Regular file with read/write permissions to the owner and read permissions to the group and no permissions to the world.

1. The read bit adds 4 to the total (binary: 100)

2. The write bit adds 2 (binary: 010)

3. The execute bit adds 1 (binary: 001)

Changing Permissions

The chmod command is used to change the permissions on a file or directory. chmod uses octal notation when entering permissions. In the next example, we will change the permissions of the /home/shared/legal directory to give read/write/execute permissions to the owner of the directory, read/write/execute permissions to everyone in the legal_grp group and read/execute permissions to everyone else.

> Many of the following commands must be run with **super-user privileges.** The super-user account usually has the username of **root** and is the most powerful administrative user on a Unix-based system. The super-user has the ability to view, modify, and delete any file on the system. Obviously, access to the super-user account must be guarded very closely. We will discuss ways to share some of these privileges with other user accounts later, but for now, we will be switching user accounts with the su command and using the super-user account.

```
[alice@sunshine shared]$ su -
Password: thisisasecret
[root@sunshine ~]#
```

Notice that the command prompt has changed – it shows your current username (root) and the dollar sign ($) has been replaced with a hash (#). The hash sign is used as root's command prompt in many operating systems and shells – whenever you see it, be extremely careful with the commands you type. A simple mistake can be disastrous when using the super-user account.

```
[root@sunshine ~]#[cd /home/shared
[root@sunshine shared]#[ls -laF
total 56
drwxr-xr-x.  5 root root      4096 Jan 29  2012 ./
drwxr-xr-x. 12 root root     36864 Feb 15 19:57 ../
drwxr-xr-x.  6 root root      4096 Jan 29  2012 academic_affairs/
drwxr-xr-x.  5 root root      4096 Jan 29  2012 business_finance/
drwxr-xr-x.  2 root legal_grp 4096 Jan 29  2012 legal/
-rw-r--r--  1 root root       3969 May 29 10:20 README
[root@sunshine shared]#[chmod 775 legal
[root@sunshine shared]#[ls -laF
total 56
drwxr-xr-x.  5 root root      4096 Jan 29  2012 ./
drwxr-xr-x. 12 root root     36864 Feb 15 19:57 ../
drwxr-xr-x.  6 root root      4096 Jan 29  2012 academic_affairs/
drwxr-xr-x.  5 root root      4096 Jan 29  2012 business_finance/
drwxrwxr-x.  2 root legal_grp 4096 Jan 29  2012 legal/
-rw-r--r--  1 root root       3969 May 29 10:20 README
```

The permissions on the legal directory have been changed from drwxr-xr-x to drwxr-wxr-x In simple terms, the group write permission has been added, so any member of the legal_grp group can now read and write files in this directory.

Access control lists

The standard UNIX file permissions are very powerful, but their main weak point is that each file can only be owned by one user and group at a time. If you have multiple people that need to have differing levels of access to a file, UNIX file permissions are not enough. You must take advantage of the filesystem Access Control Lists (ACLs) provided by most modern UNIX operating systems. Here is an example: say you have a file that you want to give two users read and write access to and you also want to give read-only access to a separate group of users, all other users should have no access. With standard file permissions, this isn't possible but it is relatively easy using the **setfacl** command.

```
[root@sunshine ~]# cd /opt/book/system-admin/access_control
[root@sunshine access_control]# ls -laF
total 52
drwxr-xr-x  5 root root      4096 Jan 29  2012 ./
drwxr-xr-x 12 root root     36864 Feb 15 19:57 ../
-rw-r--r--  1 root root     43836 May 29 10:06 document.txt
[root@sunshine access_control]# chmod 600 document.txt
[root@sunshine access_control]# ls -laF document.txt
-rw-------  1 root root     43836 May 29 10:06 document.txt
[root@sunshine access_control]# setfacl -m u:alice:rw document.txt
[root@sunshine access_control]# setfacl -m u:bob:rw document.txt
[root@sunshine access_control]# setfacl -m g:legal_grp:r document.txt
[root@sunshine access_control]# setfacl -m o-: document.txt
```

The setfacl -m command takes two arguments, the first is the ACL to apply and the second is the file that the ACL should be applied to. The ACL entry is broken up into three fields separated by colons.

The first field indicates what type of entry this ACL is:

u User – modifies file access for a single user

g Group – modifies file access for a group of users

o Others – modifies file access for all users that have not been granted access through a user or group ACL

The second field indicates whom this ACL applies to. In the case of user and group ACLs, this will be the name of the user or group, respectively. In the case of an ACL applied to "others," this field is left empty.

Finally, the third field is the list of permissions that should be granted by this ACL. Like the chmod command, setfacl uses symbolic notation for expressing read (r), write (w), and execute (x) access.

The **getfacl** command lists the ACLs that have been set on a file.

```
[root@sunshine access_control]# getfacl document.txt
# file: document.txt
# owner: root
# group: root
user::rw-
user:alice:rw-
user:bob:rw-
group::---
group:legal_grp:r--
mask::rw-
other::---
```

You can also see if ACLs have been applied to a file using **ls -l**

```
[root@sunshine access_control]# ls -laF document.txt
-rw-------+  1 root root        43836 May 29 10:06 document.txt
```

The plus symbol in the final column of the permissions indicates the presence of ACLs.

File ownership

Let's take another look at the output from ls -l

```
[root@sunshine ~]# cd /home/shared
[root@sunshine shared]# ls -laF
total 56
drwxr-xr-x.  5 root root        4096 Jan 29  2012 ./
drwxr-xr-x. 12 root root       36864 Feb 15 19:57 ../
drwxr-xr-x.  6 root root        4096 Jan 29  2012 academic_affairs/
drwxr-xr-x.  5 root root        4096 Jan 29  2012 business_finance/
drwxr-xr-x.  2 root legal_grp   4096 Jan 29  2012 legal/
-rw-r--r--   1 root root        3969 May 29 10:20 README
```

Column 3 reports the **file owner**, the user that either created the file or had ownership transferred to him/her by the previous owner or an administrator. Similarly, the fourth column lists the **group** that file belongs to. This normally defaults to the creator's group when a file is created; however, we will learn how to affect what default group is used later in the chapter.

Changing ownership

To change the owner and group of a file, you will use the chown and chgrp commands, respectively. In this example, we will change the ownership of /home/share/README to the user dave and group library_grp

```
[root@sunshine shared]# cd /home/shared
[root@sunshine shared]# chown dave README
[root@sunshine shared]# chgrp library_grp README
[root@sunshine shared]# ls -laF
total 56
drwxr-xr-x.  5 root root       4096 Jan 29  2012 ./
drwxr-xr-x. 12 root root      36864 Feb 15 19:57 ../
drwxr-xr-x.  6 root root       4096 Jan 29  2012 academic_affairs/
drwxr-xr-x.  5 root root       4096 Jan 29  2012 business_finance/
drwxr-xr-x.  2 root legal_grp  4096 Jan 29  2012 legal/
-rw-r--r--   1 dave library_grp 3969 May 29 10:20 README
```

Editing files

Now that you can see the contents of file, you need to know how to create and edit files yourself. There are literally hundreds of programs available for editing files,[9] from the simplest command-line text editors to graphical programs that can rival Microsoft Word in features. However, over the course of your career, you will be using many different types and versions of Unix-based operating systems and your favorite editor may not be available on all of them. There is only one editor that is included with all Unix-based systems: vi

The six editor?

The first thing you must know about vi is how to pronounce it. Don't try to pronounce it like the word 'vie' and never read it as a roman numeral six (VI), just say each letter separately (vee-eye). One more thing – Unix users typically use vi as a verb ("vi this file") instead of a noun ("open this file in vi").

vi was written by Bill Joy in 1976 and has been an integral part of Unix operating systems since it was released with BSD Unix in 1979. It's gone through many changes and rewrites since then and has been ported (rewritten to work on another hardware or operating system) to every major operating system released since then. Because it exists on so many systems, vi is the de facto standard for text editing. Although features have been added to the various versions of vi, there are a standard set of functions that all versions employ.

This text will stay within those standard functions, but all examples will be drawn from the main version of vi used on Linux, vim (vi improved).

---

[9]http://freecode.com/search?q = text+editor&submit = Search

vi basics

Many people are intimidated when they open vi for the first time. There are no menus or help of any kind and there is generally very little information displayed. To help first time users of vi, a short tutorial program (vimtutor) was developed. It takes you through all of the basic vi functions and introduces you to some of features that make vi an indispensible tool even 35 years after its initial development. It is highly recommended that you complete the vimtutor exercise for your own personal benefit.[10]

```
[alice@sunshine ~]$ vimtutor
```

This command will bring up vimtutor, as shown in Figure 3.4.

vi and Gmail

Many users are not aware of the many keyboard shortcuts available in Gmail.[11] On closer inspection, some of these keyboard shortcuts seem to have been inspired by the corresponding vi shortcuts. Examples include / to search, k to move to newer conversation, and j to move to older conversation.

Software installation and updates

In the Linux world, applications are often called packages. Some of the most important day-to-day functions of a system administrator are to install new software and keep the software packages on

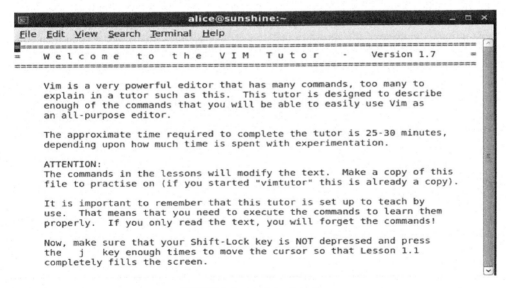

FIGURE 3.4   vimtutor interface

---

[10] See vi keyboard shortcuts at http://www.viemu.com/a_vi_vim_graphical_cheat_sheet_tutorial.html

[11] http://support.google.com/mail/bin/answer.py?hl = en&answer = 6594

all servers upgraded. The can be a challenge because of the sheer number of packages that make up a typical server operating system. Even a relatively basic Linux installation, such as the one used for the exercises in this book, includes well over a thousand separate packages.

Package formats

If you have never worked with UNIX-based operating systems, you may not be familiar with **software packages**. In Microsoft Windows and Mac OSX, operating system updates are commonly distributed as large bundles, which update many pieces of the operating system at one time. Similarly, application updates on those platforms are distributed as one installer file that replaces multiple files contained in the old version of the application.

Linux and most of the other UNIX-based operating systems distribute operating system and application updates as software packages. Instead of packaging all of the files needed by an application into a single file, applications are split into smaller components that could be reused by other applications. These components are then turned into software packages. Each package includes a list of dependencies – packages that must be installed before this package can be installed correctly. These dependency lists can get extensive, even for applications that seem fairly simple. As an example, enter this command to see the list of dependencies for the Firefox browser. You will see that firefox depends on many other packages:

```
[alice@sunshine ~]$ repoquery --requires firefox
```

The YUM package manager

CentOS Linux includes the yum package manager to assist the system administrator in the tasks of installing new packages, tracking dependencies, and updating packages. Yum works by building a database of the currently installed RPM packages on the system and then comparing them to online *package repositories*, HTTP or FTP sites that contain all of the packages that have been released. To ensure that repositories are always available and packages can be downloaded quickly, the files are replicated between hundreds of servers around the world.[12] Each of these "mirrors" of the main repository contains all of the files of the original and can be used for all installation or update procedures. Before downloading any files, yum automatically tests the download speed for the mirrors that are available and selects the one that is the fastest.

yum install and yum remove

yum install downloads the requested package(s) and any package dependencies from a package repository. As an example, let's install the gnome-games package, which includes a few games such as Solitaire and Sudoku.

```
[root@sunshine ~]# yum install gnome-games
Loaded plugins: fastestmirror, refresh-packagekit, security
Loading mirror speeds from cached hostfile
```

---

[12] http://www.centos.org/modules/tinycontent/index.php?id = 30

```
 * base: mirrors.gigenet.com
 * extras: mirrors.gigenet.com
 * updates: centos.mirror.choopa.net
Setting up Install Process
Resolving Dependencies
--> Running transaction check
---> Package gnome-games.i686 1:2.28.2-2.el6 will be installed
[Output shortened to conserve space]
Dependencies Resolved
================================================================
==================================
 Package           Arch            Version
Repository        Size
================================================================
==================================
Installing:
 gnome-games       i686            1:2.28.2-2.el6              base
3.3 M
Installing for dependencies:
 clutter           i686            1.0.6-3.el6                base
320 k
 ggz-base-libs     i686            0.99.5-5.1.el6             base
189 k
 guile             i686            5:1.8.7-5.el6              base
1.4 M
Transaction Summary
================================================================
==================================
Install      4 Package(s)
Total download size: 5.1 M
Installed size: 18 M
Is this ok [y/N]: y
Downloading Packages:
(1/4): clutter-1.0.6-3.el6.i686.rpm
| 320 kB      00:00
(2/4): ggz-base-libs-0.99.5-5.1.el6.i686.rpm
| 189 kB      00:00
(3/4): gnome-games-2.28.2-2.el6.i686.rpm
| 3.3 MB      00:03
(4/4): guile-1.8.7-5.el6.i686.rpm
| 1.4 MB      00:01
----------------------------------------------------------------
----------------------
Total                                               744 kB/s
| 5.1 MB      00:07
[Output shortened to conserve space]
Installed:
  gnome-games.i686 1:2.28.2-2.el6
Dependency Installed:
```

```
    clutter.i686  0:1.0.6-3.el6      ggz-base-libs.i686  0:0.99.5-5.1.el6
guile.i686 5:1.8.7-5.el6
Complete!
[root@sunshine ~]# gnome-sudoku
```

The three default package repositories (base, extras, and updates) are listed along for the mirror that was chosen as the fastest for that repository. yum then downloaded the list of dependencies for gnome-games and compares that list to the packages that are already installed on this system. Then a list of all the packages that will be installed is presented to the system administrator. If the system administrator wishes to continue, the packages are installed and the application is ready to be used.

If a package is no longer needed, the yum remove command will delete the package and any packages that depend on it. Obviously, great care must be taken while using the yum remove command to ensure that packages that are necessary to the function of the server are not affected.

```
[root@sunshine ~]# yum remove gnome-games
Loaded plugins: fastestmirror, refresh-packagekit, security
Setting up Remove Process
Resolving Dependencies
--> Running transaction check
---> Package gnome-games.i686 1:2.28.2-2.el6 will be erased
--> Finished Dependency Resolution
Dependencies Resolved
================================================================
===================================
 Package               Arch            Version
Repository        Size
================================================================
===================================
Removing:
 gnome-games              i686            1:2.28.2-2.el6      @base
14 M

Transaction Summary
================================================================
===================================
Remove       1 Package(s)

Installed size: 14 M
Is this ok [y/N]: y
Downloading Packages:
Running rpm_check_debug
Running Transaction Test
Transaction Test Succeeded
Running Transaction
  Erasing    : 1:gnome-games-2.28.2-2.el6.i686
1/1
Removed:
  gnome-games.i686 1:2.28.2-2.el6
Complete!
```

yum list and yum search

We've seen that the yum install command allows you to install new packages, but how do you know what packages are available? The yum list command will display all of the packages that are available and yum search allows you to search for packages whose title and/or description contain your search terms.

```
[root@sunshine ~]# yum list
Loaded plugins: fastestmirror, refresh-packagekit, security
Loading mirror speeds from cached hostfile
 * base: mirrors.gigenet.com
 * extras: mirrors.gigenet.com
 * updates: centos.mirror.choopa.net
Installed Packages
ConsoleKit.i686                 0.4.1-3.el6                  @anaconda-
CentOS-201112130233.i386/6.2
ConsoleKit-libs.i686            0.4.1-3.el6                  @anaconda-
CentOS-201112130233.i386/6.2
ConsoleKit-x11.i686             0.4.1-3.el6                  @anaconda-
CentOS-201112130233.i386/6.2
[Output shortened to conserve space]
zlib-static.i686                            1.2.3-27.el6
base
zsh.i686                                    4.3.10-4.1.el6
base
zsh-html.i686                               4.3.10-4.1.el6
base

[root@sunshine ~]# yum search games
Loaded plugins: fastestmirror, refresh-packagekit, security
Loading mirror speeds from cached hostfile
 * base: mirrors.gigenet.com
 * extras: mirrors.gigenet.com
 * updates: centos.mirror.choopa.net
===N/S Matched: games
=========================================================
gnome-games.i686 : Games for the GNOME desktop
gnome-games-extra.i686 : More games for the GNOME desktop
gnome-games-help.noarch : Help files for gnome-games
kdegames.i686 : KDE Games
kdegames-libs.i686 : Runtime libraries for kdegames
kdegames-devel.i686 : Header files for compiling KDE 4 game applications
```

yum update

The yum update command provides a simple way to scan all of the packages installed on a system, compare their versions to the latest available and report on the ones that need to be updated.

```
[root@sunshine ~]# yum update
Loaded plugins: fastestmirror, refresh-packagekit, security
Determining fastest mirrors
```

```
    * base: mirrors.gigenet.com
    * extras: mirrors.gigenet.com
    * updates: centos.mirror.choopa.net
base                                                              |  3.7 kB
00:00
extras                                                            |  3.5 kB
00:00
updates                                                          |  3.5 kB
00:00
updates/primary_db                                               |  2.8 MB
00:03
Setting up Update Process
Resolving Dependencies
--> Running transaction check
---> Package firefox.i686 0:10.0.3-1.el6.centos will be updated
[Output shortened to conserve space]
Transaction Summary
================================================================
==========================
Install        1 Package(s)
Upgrade       23 Package(s)
Remove         1 Package(s)
Total download size: 92 M
Is this ok [y/N]: y
Downloading Packages:
(1/24): firefox-10.0.4-1.el6.centos.i686.rpm                     |  20 MB
00:24
(2/24): kernel-2.6.32-220.13.1.el6.i686.rpm                      |  22 MB
00:30
(3/24): kernel-firmware-2.6.32-220.13.1.el6.noarch.              |  6.2 MB
00:07
(4/24): kpartx-0.4.9-46.el6_2.2.i686.rpm                         |  45 kB
00:00
(5/24): libpng-1.2.49-1.el6_2.i686.rpm                           | 184 kB
00:00
[Output shortened to conserve space]
Complete!
```

As you'll notice, the output is very similar to yum install. One interesting thing to note is that yum update can install and remove packages in addition to upgrading them. As software packages are developed and updated, they may change the packages that they depend on or the packages may change names, requiring the old package to be removed and be replaced by the new one.

Account management

Depending on the environment that the system administrator is working in, account management may take up a large part of his/her time or almost no time at all. Some of the factors that impact the amount of user management that must be done are the total number of user accounts and the percentage of users that are added or removed on a regular basis. With organizations such as universities and large corporations, the number and complexity of account management tasks is much too great to process manually. In these situations, an Identity Management solution is used to build account management rules that can be applied automatically to all current and potential users. We will cover Identity Management in depth in a later chapter, but for now we will look at the procedures for manual account management.

User manager

The easiest way to manage user accounts and group memberships in CentOS is to use the User Manager, a graphical tool included with a typical CentOS installation. You can start it by selecting "User and Groups" from the Administration menu (Figure 3.5).

The interface is very similar to the user administration pages included with Windows and Mac OSX (Figure 3.6). To add a new user, just click the "Add User" button and fill out the new user form. By default, the tool will generate a home directory for the user in the /home filesystem and issue the next available user and group id numbers. However, you can override this behavior and input custom values if needed. You can also delete a user by selecting the "Delete" button.

Finally, you can edit an existing account by selecting the account from the list and clicking on the "Properties" button. In the account editor, you can change any of the values set when the account was created. In addition, you can also modify some access control settings for the account, such as:

- Account Expiration – After this date, the account will not be allowed to authenticate. A system administrator must unlock the account for the user to regain access.

- Lock Local Password – If this setting is enabled, the user will not be able to authenticate with the password in /etc/passwd. However, external authentication (LDAP, Kerberos, NIS, etc.) is still allowed.

- Password Expiration – Settings for the minimum and maximum amount of time that can pass between changing passwords. Once the maximum amount of time has elapsed, a system administrator must unlock the account for the user to regain access.

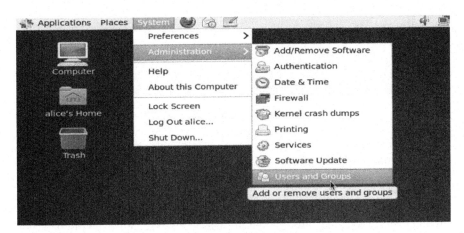

FIGURE 3.5   Reaching users and groups manager

FIGURE 3.6 Adding users

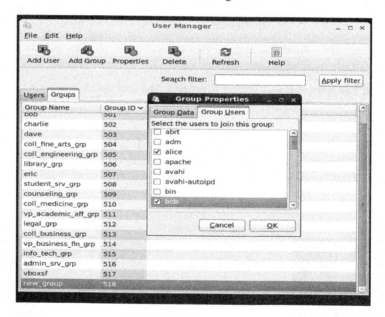

FIGURE 3.7 Group manager

- Force password change on next login – Action is self-explanatory. This setting is used frequently for new accounts. The system administrator creates an account with a known, simple password. When the user logs in for the first time, he/she is asked to change the password to a more secure one.

In addition to users, the "groups" tab in User Manager allows you to manage group creation, deletion, and membership changes (Figure 3.7). To add a new group, just select the "Add Group" button and input a name for the new group. You can also specify a custom group id number if necessary. Once a group is created, you'll need to add members to it. Select the group name from the list in the "Groups" tab and click on the "Properties" button. The window shown on the right will be displayed. Click on the checkbox next to each user that should be added as a member and then click OK. Your new group is now ready to be used.

Command-line user administration

The graphical interface of User Manager is very easy to use and could be used for virtually all user administration tasks; however, what can you do if that package isn't available or you are working on a system remotely over a dial-up connection? In these cases, the command-line-only terminal interface is the best option. The good news is that, on Unix, everything has a command-line equivalent. In fact, many graphical tools on Unix are just frontends to collect data from the user, run a command-line program and display the results.

The useradd, usermod, and userdel commands can be used in place of most of the user administration tasks in User Manager. Like several of the other commands we've discussed in this chapter, these commands have different capabilities depending on which operating system you are working on. The versions that are included with CentOS have a few advanced features that we could take advantage of, but we will demonstrate the features that are available across multiple platforms.

In this example, we will create a new user with the username "fred" and a home directory (-d) of "/home/fred." We will also save their full name in the comment field of the password file (-c "Fred Flintstone").

```
[root@sunshine ~]# useradd -c "Fred Flintstone" -m -d "/home/fred" fred
[root@sunshine ~]# ls -laF /home/fred
total 28
drwx------.  4 fred fred 4096 May   4 19:48 .
drwxr-xr-x.  9 root root 4096 May   4 19:48 ../
-rw-r--r--.  1 fred fred   18 May 10  2012 .bash_logout
-rw-r--r--.  1 fred fred  176 May 10  2012 .bash_profile
-rw-r--r--.  1 fred fred  124 May 10  2012 .bashrc
drwxr-xr-x.  2 fred fred 4096 Nov 11  2010 .gnome2/
drwxr-xr-x.  4 fred fred 4096 Jan 22 18:48 .mozilla/
```

Before the new user can login to the account, we'll need to set a password. When you use the useradd command, it leaves the password field blank, which effectively locks the account until a password is set. The passwd command allows you to set the password on an account to which you have the appropriate permissions to do so. While the example below shows the password, in practice, for security reasons, the password is not displayed. Also, since you will probably need to write the password down (on paper or in a email/file) to give it to the new user, you should require the user to change their password during their first login. In CentOS, you do this with the "-e" flag to the passwd command:

```
[root@sunshine ~]# passwd fred
Changing password for user fred.
New password: NewPasswordGoesHere
Retype new password: NewPasswordGoesHere
passwd: all authentication tokens updated successfully.
[root@sunshine ~]# passwd -e fred
Expiring password for user fred.
```

The user "fred" can now log into the system and access his files. Along with the "-e" flag, there are several useful access controls that the passwd command allows, such as locking (-l) and unlocking (-u) an account and setting the minimum (-n) and maximum (-x) password ages.

```
[root@sunshine ~]# passwd -l fred
Locking password for user fred.
[root@sunshine ~]# passwd -u fred
Unlocking password for user fred.
[root@sunshine ~]# passwd -n 1 -x 180  fred
Adjusting aging data for user fred.
```

To add the user as a member to existing groups, you can use the usermod command with the "-aG" flags and a comma-separated list of groups.

```
[root@sunshine ~]# groups fred
fred : fred
[root@sunshine ~]# usermod -a -G
coll_fine_arts_grp,vp_academic_aff_grp fred
[root@sunshine ~]# groups fred
fred : fred vp_academic_aff_grp coll_fine_arts_grp
```

You can also use the usermod command to modify several other options on the account, such as an expiration date (-e) and move their home directory (-md):

```
[root@sunshine ~]# usermod -e 2013-08-01 -md "/home/flintstone" fred
[root@sunshine ~]# ls -laF /home/flintstone
total 28
drwx------. 4 fred fred 4096 May  4 19:48 .
drwxr-xr-x. 9 root root 4096 May  4 19:48 ../
-rw-r--r--. 1 fred fred   18 May 10  2012 .bash_logout
-rw-r--r--. 1 fred fred  176 May 10  2012 .bash_profile
-rw-r--r--. 1 fred fred  124 May 10  2012 .bashrc
drwxr-xr-x. 2 fred fred 4096 Nov 11  2010 .gnome2/
drwxr-xr-x. 4 fred fred 4096 Jan 22 18:48 .mozilla/
```

Finally, userdel deletes a user account. By default, the user's home directory is not removed, but to remove it, add the "-r" flag.

```
[root@sunshine ~]# userdel -r fred
[root@sunshine ~]# ls -laF /home/flintstone
ls: cannot access /home/flintsone: No such file or directory
[root@sunshine ~]# groups fred
groups: fred: No such user
```

Group management

Along with the useradd, usermod, userdel commands, there are matching groupadd, groupmod, and groupdel commands for group management. Because groups have very few configurable options, these commands have fewer switches that are used. Groupadd and groupdel do not typically need any extra parameters other than the group to work on and the only option for usermod is for renaming (-n) a group. Group membership can be managed with groupmems, which includes switch for adding (-a), removing (-d), and listing all (-l) members of a group.

```
[root@sunshine ~]# groupadd new_group
[root@sunshine ~]# groupmems -a alice -g new_group
[root@sunshine ~]# groupmems -a bob -g new_group
[root@sunshine ~]# groupmems -l -g new_group
alice  bob
[root@sunshine ~]# man groupmod
[root@sunshine ~]# groupmod -n improved_group new_group
[root@sunshine ~]# groupmems -l -g improved_group
alice  bob
[root@sunshine ~]# groupmems -l -g new_group
groupmems: group 'new_group' does not exist in /etc/group
[root@sunshine ~]# groupdel improved_group
```

Example case – Northwest Florida State College

In October 2012, it was announced that personal information of over 300,000 people had been stolen from Northwest Florida State College. The institution, formerly a community college, serves about 17,000 students annually. Since its founding in 1963, the college has awarded almost 30,000 degrees.[13]

The affected population includes almost 200,000 people who may have had no connection to the college. Others affected include over 75,000 former or current students, and 3,200 current or retired employees. The 200,000 people unaffiliated with the institution are students who were eligible for Bright Futures scholarships in the school years beginning in 2005 and 2006. The compromised data included names, Social Security numbers (SSN), birthdates, gender, and ethnicity. In the case of employees, stolen data also included direct deposit routing and account numbers. At the time of the announcement, the school acknowledged that approximately 50 employees, including the college president, had reported issues with identity theft.

According to the college's investigations, conducted with the assistance of an outside consultant and an Okaloosa County Sheriff's Office cybercrimes expert, the breach occurred between May 21 and September 24, 2012. The college speculated that the breach was a "professional, coordinated attack by one or more hackers."

The breach included a folder from the school's main server that included several files. While the institution had ensured that no one file had a complete set of personal information regarding individuals, once the hackers had access to the single server containing the files, they were able to piece together all the required information for at least 50 college employees.

The attackers used the stolen identities to take out payday loans from PayDayMax, Inc., as well as Discount Advance Loans (iGotit.com, Inc.), and used the stolen bank credentials to repay those loans. Both payday loan services are located in Canada. In addition, the stolen data were also used to apply for Home Depot credit cards under the employees' names.

---

[13] As of the latest fact-book at the time of this writing (2010–2011)

REFERENCES

Ragan, S. "Northwest Florida State College says clever attackers were successful in data breach," *SecurityWeek*, October 10, 2012.

Bolkan, J. "Northwest Florida State College data breach compromises 300,000 students and employees," *Campus Technology*, October 17, 2012.

SUMMARY

This chapter demonstrated many of the basic utilities used by system administrators. Reasonable familiarity with these utilities is a prerequisite for professional success in the information security field. It provided concrete examples of the system administration tasks discussed in the last chapter.

The goal of this chapter was to provide a good understanding of Unix administration in general and the CentOS Linux distribution in particular. This knowledge will be the foundation of the technical discussions used throughout the rest of this course.

CHAPTER REVIEW QUESTIONS

1. What is the function of the kernel?

2. What is the shell? What shell program is present in all versions of UNIX? What is a shell prompt?

3. What is the top of a filesystem hierarchy called? How is it represented in UNIX systems?

4. What is a **path**? What is the difference between a **relative** and **absolute** path?

5. What is the pwd UNIX command used for? What are some useful options with the command?

6. What is the cd UNIX command used for? What are some useful options with the command?

7. What is the ls UNIX command used for? What are some useful options with the command?

8. What is the rm UNIX command used for? What are some useful options with the command?

9. What is the mkdir UNIX command used for? What are some useful options with the command?

10. List two commands you could use to change back to your home directory.

11. What are wildcards (file name expansions)? Provide an example of how you may use one.

12. What is recursion in the context of file operations? How is it helpful? Why should you be specially careful when using recursion in file commands?

13. What would be a useful way to use the tail command to view log files?

14. How would you use the find command to search for the "messages" folder, which you know exists in the /var folder?

15. Given the following ls –l output, what do you know about the ownership and access permissions for the accounting folder?

    ```
    drwxr-xr-x.  2  root  accounting_grp
    4096 Jan 28 19:07 accounting/
    ```

16. Given the ls output above, how can you use the chmod command to give write permissions to all members of "accounting_grp" to the "accounting" folder?

17. What are access control lists? How are they used?

18. What is the setfacl command used for?

19. What is the getfacl command used for?

20. Why is working knowledge of the vi editor important for IT administrators?

21. Describe how a **setuid** executable file behaves when running.

22. What would the owner of the .bashrc file have to do in order to be able to edit the file if its current permissions are 444?

23. What is a software package? What are some common formats in which software packages are distributed?

24. How can you search for all installed software packages on your system?

25. How can you use the yum command to update all the software on your system?

EXAMPLE CASE QUESTIONS

1. The college maintains a link to a web page detailing the college's ongoing response to the breach on its home page at http://www.nwfsc.edu/.[14] Based on that information, what facts can you add to those detailed in the case description provided here?

2. If your identity is compromised, what damage is possible to your personal life?

3. What are the recommendations of the Federal Trade Commission (FTC) regarding the steps you should follow if your personal information has been compromised?

4. What in your opinion are the three most important steps you can take to prevent identity theft in the first place?

HANDS-ON ACTIVITY – BASIC LINUX SYSTEM ADMINISTRATION

These activities are included to demonstrate your knowledge of the commands learned in this chapter. Using the Linux virtual machine you configured in Chapter 2, open a terminal window by selecting the "System Tools" panel under the "Applications" menu. After completing each exercise, submit the deliverables listed to your instructor.

1. **Exercise 1**

   1.1. Change directories to /opt/book/system-admin

   1.2. List all directory contents (including hidden files)

Deliverable: Take a screenshot of the directory contents

2. **Exercise 2**

   2.1. Change directories to /opt/book/system-admin/ex2

   2.2. Rename jeklyll.txt to hyde.txt

   2.3. Make a copy of prince.txt named pauper.txt

   2.4. Delete the directory Jacob.marley and all of its contents

Deliverable: Take a screenshot of the directory's contents

3. **Exercise 3**

   3.1. Find the file named gettysburg.txt

   3.2. Display the last three lines of text in gettysburg.txt

   3.3. Find the file named declaration.txt

   3.4. Display the first five lines of declaration.txt

Deliverable: Take a screenshot that contains the requested lines from gettysburg.txt and declaration.txt

4. **Exercise 4**

   4.1. Create three new users:

   - Name: Thomas Jefferson

   - Username: thomas

   - Password: Monticello

   - Name: Abraham Lincoln

   - Username: abe

   - Password: 4score&7years

   - Name: Benjamin Franklin

   - Username: ben

   - Password: Early2bedEarly2rise

   4.2. Create three new groups:

   - presidents (members: thomas, abe)

   - continental_congress (members: thomas, ben)

   - us_currency (members: thomas, ben, abe)

   4.3. Make thomas the owner of the declaration.txt file from the previous exercise

   4.4. Make abe the owner of the gettysburg.txt file from the previous exercise

   4.5. Change the group ownership of declaration.txt to the continental_congress group and make it writable by that group. It should also be readable by all users

Deliverable: Take a screenshot of the owner/group file permissions for both files

---

[14] Last verified, 02/22/2013

5.   **Exercise 5**

5.1.   Install the "xorg-x11-apps" package, a collection of common GUI tools

5.2.   Run the command "xclock"

5.3.   Open a new terminal window and run the command "yum list xorg-x11-apps"

Deliverable: Take a screenshot of the terminal and xclock windows

6.   **Exercise 6**

6.1.   Update all the RPM packages currently installed on the system

Deliverable: Take a screenshot of the first line from /etc/issue

CRITICAL THINKING EXERCISE – OFFENSIVE CYBER EFFECTS OPERATIONS (OCEO)

Among the documents that Edward Snowden, the contractor working at the NSA, released after quitting the agency was Presidential Policy Directive 20 (PPD20), issued on October 2012. Among other things, 18-page top-secret memo defined the role of "offensive cyber effects operations" (OCEO). OCEO was defined as *"Operations and related programs or activities other than network defense, cyber collection, or DCEO – conducted by or on behalf of the United States Government, in or through cyberspace, that are intended to enable or produce cyber effects outside United States Government networks."*

The description of OCEO in PPD 20 states the following:

OCEO can offer unique and unconventional capabilities to advance US national objectives around the world with little or no warning to the adversary or target and with potential effects ranging from subtle to severely damaging. The development and sustainment of OCEO capabilities, however, may require considerable time and effort if access and tools for a specific target do not already exist.

The United States Government shall identify potential targets of national importance where OCEO can offer a favorable balance of effectiveness and risk as compared with other instruments of national power, establish and maintain OCEO capabilities integrated as appropriate with other US offensive capabilities, and execute those capabilities in a manner consistent with the provisions of this directive.

You are entering into the professional world operating in this environment.

REFERENCES

Bruce Schneier's Cryptogram, July 15, 2013

Schneier, B. "Has U.S. started an Internet war?", *CNN*, 2013, http://www.cnn.com/2013/06/18/opinion/schneier-cyberwar-policy (accessed 07/16/2013)

The Guardian, "Obama tells intelligence chiefs to draw up cyber target list – full document text", 2013.

CRITICAL THINKING QUESTIONS

1.   In plain terms, what is OCEO?

2.   What are some activities that may constitute OCEO?

3.   What are some likely repercussions to information security professionals working within the United States (and probably also outside the United States), now that everyone is aware of PPD20?

DESIGN CASE

You are called to take a look at a professor's Linux workstation. The machine is brand new, with a fast processor and lots of memory, but it has been running extremely slow the past week or so.

One of the first things you know to do when looking at performance issues on a UNIX box is to run a **ps** command, which stands for "processor status." The command output lists all the processes running on the workstation and some additional information about their status.

The output of the ps command lists all the standard operating system processes you expect to see running, but you also see a few more processes look a bit out of the ordinary:

- **/home/taylor/.sh**, running as root

- **/home/taylor/. . ./ncftpd**, using up a lot of CPU and disk I/O

The /home/taylor directory is the home directory of the professor, Dr. Taylor. Here is some additional information you gathered during your investigation:

- Permissions on /home/taylor/.sh are set to **7551**

- The file is owned by root

- It's "MD5 hash" is identical to **/bin/bash**, which means the files are the exactly same.

- The **/home/taylor/. . .** directory contains two files:

  - the **ncftpd** file you found running previously with the **ps** command

  - **general.cf** file, owned by taylor, permission 644

  - **domain.cf** file, owned by taylor, permission 644

- The **general.cf** file contained, among other lines:

  - log-xfers = yes

  - port = 80

- The **domain.cf** file led you to a log file. Here is the output of the "**head -7**" command on the log file:

```
2012-04-20 23:30:59 ### | S,/var/tmp/pub/
StarWars.avi, ...
2012-04-20 23:35:59 ### | S,/var/tmp/pub/
Conan.avi, ...
2012-04-20 23:37:59 ### | S,/var/tmp/pub/
Avatar.avi, ...
2012-04-21 00:37:59 ### | R,/var/tmp/pub/
Avatar.avi, ...
```

```
2012-04-21 00:37:59 ### | R,/var/tmp/pub/
Avatar.avi, ...
2012-04-21 01:37:59 ### | R,/var/tmp/pub/
Avatar.avi, ...
2012-04-21 02:35:59 ### | R,/var/tmp/pub/
Conan.avi, ...
```

Write a report on what you believe was the issue with the workstation and suggested steps to resolve the problem, based on what you know.

Guiding questions

The workstation was definitely hacked. Dr. Taylor claims he has no idea who put the programs there. There are two different issues with what you found. One affects the performance of the machine. The other is a bit more serious and should impact your final advice on what to do with the box.

- Discuss the **.sh** program you found in his home directory.

- What happens when a "standard" user such as taylor runs that program.

- Is a non-administrator user able to change the ownership of a file to root?

- Is a non-administrator user able to change the permission of a file to add setuid?

- What does that say about the user who put the file there in the first place?

- What is the ncftpd program? Do some research on the web if you have to.

- What do you think was the purpose of the program?

- Do you have an educated guess as to when the program was installed or started its operations?

- Based on what you know, what should be done with this workstation, and why?

And the bonus questions:

- What does the port 80 line in the configuration file mean?

- Why was it set that way?

## CHAPTER 4

The Basic Information Security Model

Who is in charge of the security of the Internet? How do I know?

– Cuckoo's Egg

Overview

This chapter introduces the basic framework used to implement information security. This framework consists of four elements – assets, vulnerabilities, threats, and controls. We define each of these terms, provide examples for each, and describe how they are related to each other. At the end of this chapter, you should know:

- The elements of the basic information security model
- The relationships between the elements of the basic information security model
- The common classification of information security controls

Introduction

The previous chapters have highlighted the importance of information security. In most organizations, system administrators take on the bulk of the responsibilities of maintaining information security. In anticipation of your continued interest in information security, these chapters have therefore also introduced you to the basic tasks performed by system administrators and the skills required to complete these tasks. In subsequent chapters, you will continue to build on these technical skills.

Information security is a very wide subject area because most information security incidents exploit some new weakness in an organization. Maintaining information security therefore requires attention to almost every aspect of the organization. To provide structure to these efforts, it is useful to organize all the activities associated with maintaining information security into a framework or model. In this book, we call this framework the basic information security model. It is shown in Figure 4.1.

Components of the basic information security model

A model is a representation of the real world. Models are useful in drawing attention to the essential elements of a problem. *A model for information security includes the core components of information security, shows the relationship of these components to each other, and excludes everything else.* The basic information security model we use in this book is shown in Figure 4.1. The

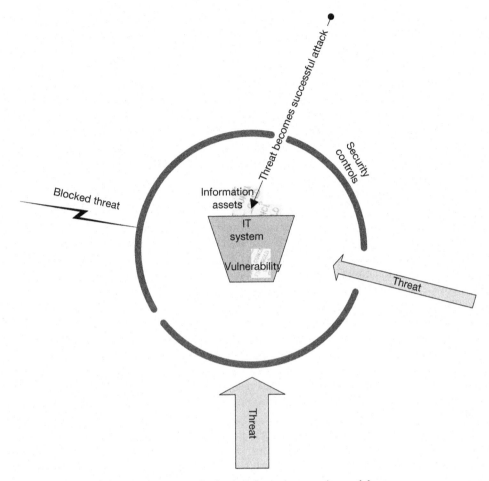

FIGURE 4.1   The basic information security model

model has four components – (1) assets, (2) vulnerabilities, (3) threats, and (4) controls. Every activity related to information security falls into one of these components.

Assets

At the center of the figure are assets. In the context of information security, *an asset is defined as a resource or information that is to be protected*. All security scenarios, whether related to information security or simply related to securing one's home, start with an asset that is considered valuable enough for you to put forth special efforts on protecting it from harm. Information security is no different. If some information or related resource is valuable to the organization, the organization needs to put forth special effort to secure the information.

There are, however, two important differences between conventional assets and information assets – invisibility and duplicability. In most security scenarios that you are likely to be familiar with, the items to be protected can be seen and felt. For example, you lock your cars to prevent theft. You install home alarm systems to prevent break-ins into your home. In both cases, the assets are visible to the naked eye. The damage is also visible. If someone breaks into your car or home, the damage is immediately visible. If there are closed-circuit cameras in the vicinity, they will capture the act of vandalism.

But information security is different. The assets in information security are not tangible artifacts that can be seen and felt. Instead, they are data and information stored as 0s and 1s on computers, tapes, phones, and other devices. While the hard drives and other devices are themselves visible, the valuable data stored on these devices is invisible. If the data is stolen over the network, the transfer of data is not visible to cameras or other conventional security devices. The thieves will typically operate from another country, thousands of miles away, safe from the scrutiny of conventional security agencies.

The second important difference between conventional assets and information assets is duplicability. Continuing with the car example, if your car is stolen, you will notice the missing car in the morning. This is because the car can only exist in one place at any given time. However, information can be duplicated perfectly. If your data is stolen, you will not notice the theft until it is brought to your notice. For example, if someone finds your laptop unattended, emails a copy of your assignment to himself and submits the copied assignment as his own work, you will have no idea of the act of plagiarism if the instructor does not bring it to your notice.

These two differences between conventional assets and information assets – invisibility and duplicability – make information security a considerably different challenge than conventional security. Conventional security methods such as locks and guards are not very effective at maintaining information security. For example, conventional locks will do little to prevent the theft of data over the network. A stolen conventional asset such as gold can be recovered and restored to its owner. But stolen data may be copied to a hundred locations and even if a few of these copies are destroyed, it is almost impossible to deny the thief the benefit of having access to the data. Information security controls therefore have to try to prevent the theft in the first place, and detect and block thefts as they occur through constant monitoring.

Gold has been the standard measure for value for centuries. Accordingly, to denote the value of information, information assets are shown in our basic model (Figure 4.1) as gold bars (though for many organizations, the information in their possession may actually be more valuable than gold!).

In the most common scenario you will encounter, the information assets are stored in an IT system. Paper-based systems simply cannot provide the density of information storage required by modern organizations. *An IT system is defined as an assembly of computer hardware, software and firmware, configured for the purpose of processing, storing or forwarding information.* In a small family-owned business, this IT system may be as simple as an Excel spreadsheet. In a slightly larger business, the IT system may be dedicated software such as QuickBooks and in the largest businesses, the IT system would be an enterprise application such as an ERP system. The IT system is shown in Figure 4.1 as the bucket holding the assets.

Vulnerabilities

Information security becomes important because all systems have vulnerabilities. *A vulnerability is a weakness in an information system that gives a threat the opportunity to compromise an asset.*[1] In the case of the Excel-based IT system discussed above, such vulnerabilities include unauthorized access which may cause loss of confidentiality or integrity and hard drive failures which may cause loss of availability. If we reached some state of utopia where no vulnerabilities existed in IT systems, we would not have to study information security and would not need a cadre of professionals dedicated to information security. However, modern software products are large. For example, Windows Vista had around 50 million lines of code.[2] It is difficult to anticipate and eliminate all possible vulnerabilities in such large products. Additional vulnerabilities are created in the interactions between products. Even if all software vulnerabilities are eradicated, user-created vulnerabilities can remain. For example, many users do not protect their administrative accounts with good passwords.

To deal with vulnerabilities, the software industry in collaboration with the federal government has invested considerable resources to create an inventory of known software vulnerabilities. This is the Common Vulnerabilities and Exposures (CVE) list. The CVE list aims to provide common names and identifiers for all publicly known software vulnerabilities. The list is maintained by Mitre, a non-profit federally funded research and development organization. An example vulnerability in the CVE list (the most recent entry at the time of this writing) is shown in Figure 4.2.[3]

> Considering the spreadsheet based small-business accounting system described above, what in your opinion is its greatest information security vulnerability?

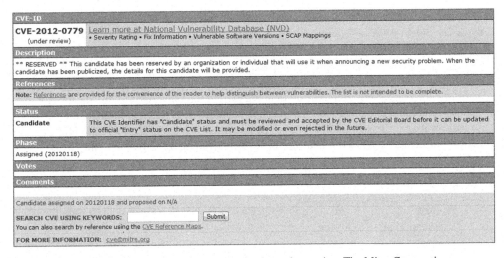

FIGURE 4.2   Example CVE listing at the time of reporting. The Mitre Corporation

---

[1]This is a simplified version of the definition in technical documents. For example, RFC 2828, the Internet security glossary defines a vulnerability as "*a flaw or weakness in a system's design, implementation, or operation and management that could be exploited to violate the system's security policy.*"

[2]http://www.nytimes.com/2006/03/27/technology/27soft.html?pagewanted = all

[3]http://www.cve.mitre.org/cgi-bin/cvename.cgi?name = CVE-2012-0779

Vulnerability Summary for CVE-2012-0779

Original release date: 05/04/2012

Last revised: 05/04/2012

Source: US-CERT/NIST

This vulnerability is currently undergoing analysis and not all information is available.

Please check back soon to view the completed vulnerability summary.

Overview

Adobe Flash Player before 10.3.183.19 and 11.x before 11.2.202.235 on Windows, Mac OS X, and Linux; before 11.1.111.9 on Android 2.x and 3.x; and before 11.1.115.8 on Android 4.x allows remote attackers to execute arbitrary code via a crafted file, related to an "object confusion vulnerability," as exploited in the wild in May 2012.

References to Advisories, Solutions, and Tools

By selecting these links, you will be leaving NIST webspace. We have provided these links to other websites because they may have information that would be of interest to you. No inferences should be drawn on account of other sites being referenced, or not, from this page. There may be other websites that are more appropriate for your purpose. NIST does not necessarily endorse the views expressed, or concur with the facts presented on these sites. Further, NIST does not endorse any commercial products that may be mentioned on these sites. Please address comments about this page to nvd@nist.gov.

External Source: CONFIRM

Name: http://www.adobe.com/support/security/bulletins/apsb12-09.html

Hyperlink: http://www.adobe.com/support/security/bulletins/apsb12-09.html

FIGURE 4.3   NVD entry[4] for the CVE listing

While the community is interested in being alerted to vulnerabilities, most users are more interested in learning about the likely impacts of vulnerabilities and recommended measures to remove the vulnerability. This information is maintained in a parallel effort called the National Vulnerabilities Database (NVD). You can see the link from the CVE listing to the NVD entry in Figure 4.2. Figure 4.3 shows the NVD entry corresponding to the listing in Figure 4.2.

	New vulnerabilities	Attacks
2010	6,253	3 billion
2011	4,989	5.5 billion

Source: Symantec

Some features of the above entry are notable. The vulnerability was added to the database after it was announced on the web. The announcement was made by the vendor of the software. More information about the vulnerability could be found at the vendor's website by following the link on the CVE listing. The CVE list and NVD database are not whistleblowers. They essentially act as a central repository of all vulnerabilities reported publicly, and the vulnerability is often first reported by the vendor of the software itself.

---

[4]http://web.nvd.nist.gov/view/vuln/detail?vulnId = CVE-2012-0779

Given the large number of software products in use and the increasing size of modern software, it should not be surprising that the NVD database is very active. As of May 2012, it was averaging 11 reported vulnerabilities per day. On May 4, apart from the vulnerability reported above, there were vulnerabilities reported by VMWare and IBM. All eight vulnerabilities reported that day were first announced by the vendor firms themselves.

Further, each year, the industry publishes the top 25 most dangerous software errors from this database.[5] This publication is exhaustive and for the convenience of developers, it provides code samples and suggested solutions for each of the identified vulnerabilities. Code samples from this publication are used later in this chapter.

The efforts by the industry seem to be paying off. According to Symantec, the company that develops many popular information security products, 4,989 new vulnerabilities were discovered in 2011 compared to 6,253 in 2010, a drop of about 20%.[6,7]

Threats

The vulnerability of an asset creates threats. *A threat is defined as the capabilities, intentions and attack methods of adversaries to exploit or cause harm to assets.* In the Excel example, a worker may want to exploit the lack of password protection on the file and modify their hourly rate. These threats are shown in the framework of Figure 4.1 as arrows.

The nature of threats has changed dramatically in recent years. In the early days of the Internet, the threats were mostly pranks such as those perpetrated by the gang of 414's. In the early 2000s, these threats became more disruptive (e.g., the ILOVEYOU virus) and widespread. The software industry and user community responded by reducing software vulnerabilities and improving user training. As of 2011, trends indicate that the remaining threats are highly directed and commercially driven.

A popular tool developed by the industry to visualize the important threats facing organizations is ATLAS.[8] ATLAS uses sensors deployed at ISPs around the world to gather real-time information about threats being faced by organizations. This information is then processed and displayed on the web. System administrators can quickly identify the dominant attacks and ensure that they have the necessary defenses in place to counter these attacks. The ATLAS web interface is shown in Figure 4.4.

Symantec released its threat report for 2011 in April 2012. The company's products blocked 5.5 billion attacks in 2011, compared to 3 billion attacks in 2010, an increase of over 80%. Therefore paradoxically, while software is becoming more and more secure and the number of vulnerabilities is decreasing, the number of attacks is increasing.

This paradox has been facilitated by the industrialization of the "attack industry." Integrated development environments (IDEs) and toolkits have emerged (e.g., Zeus, Spyeye) to help attackers quickly create new attacks and to exploit existing vulnerabilities more efficiently. Less expertise is needed to create successful attacks using these toolkits than using first principles, so threats are becoming accessible to a wider population to exploit. This may explain to some extent the rise in attacks driven by political motivations. This is the information security environment we live in today.

---

[5] http://www.sans.org/top25-software-errors/

[6] Symantec Internet Security Threat Report, Trends for 2010.

[7] Symantec Internet Security Threat Report, 2011 Trends.

[8] http://atlas.arbor.net/about/

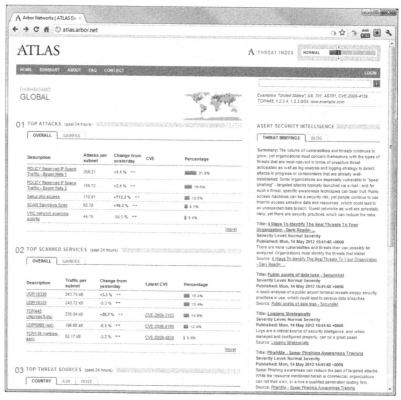

FIGURE 4.4 ATLAS web interface. This information was obtained from Arbor Networks' ATLAS Initiative on May 12, 2012 and permission to republish has been obtained. ATLAS initiative data is dynamic and therefore, the information may have changed since the date of publication of the data. © Arbor Networks, Inc. ALL RIGHTS RESERVED. Atlas is a trademark of Arbor Networks, Inc.

Controls

All IT systems will be vulnerable for the foreseeable future. Also in this timeframe, there will be dedicated attackers threatening to exploit these vulnerabilities for personal gain or other motives. What does a system administrator do to defend the computers in his charge?

The role of information security is to minimize the impact of these threats. This is done by deploying security controls around the vulnerable IT system. *Security controls are safeguards used to minimize the impact of threats.* In our framework of Figure 4.1, these controls are shown as the ring around the IT system. In Figure 4.1 the width of the arrows indicate the relative frequencies of the different categories of threats seen by a typical organization. Most threats are blocked by the controls commonly adopted by organizations. For example, most operating systems now come with a firewall configured with some default settings and encourage users to use a strong password to secure the administrative user account on their computers. Commercially, even the smallest businesses backup their important files on external hard drives or other Internet services and keep their computers locked to prevent unauthorized access.

> What in your opinion, is your best defense against the vulnerability you identified in the spreadsheet-based accounting system?

Even rudimentary controls such as those listed above can successfully block a large majority of the threats facing organizations. These are shown by the wide arrow at the bottom of Figure 4.1.

However as shown in Figure 4.1, even the best security controls have holes. For example, users often prefer memorable passwords over secure passwords. They are also often irregular in backing up their data even if they have spent hundreds or thousands of dollars to purchase backup systems. Threats exploit these weaknesses in security controls to reach the vulnerable IT systems. These threats are shown by the arrow on the right, which has breached the controls and reached the IT system. Fortunately, many of these threats may yet do no harm, as shown by the inability of the arrow on the right of Figure 4.1 to reach the IT system.

Returning to our Excel-based IT system, one such threat is a theft of the laptop in which the business keeps its records. In many such cases, the thieves are just interested in selling the laptop for money, and the buyer may simply reinstall the operating system on the machine for performance. In this case, while the information was vulnerable to the threat of being stolen, no compromise on confidentiality was eventually done. If the firm had good backups, there will also be no loss of availability.

A very small fraction of the threats will cause real damage to the organization. These threats will succeed in getting past any security controls and exploiting vulnerabilities to compromise the information of interest. These threats are shown by the arrow at the top of Figure 4.1. An example in our Excel-based system would be an employee being able to reach the laptop when the manager is not around and successfully manipulate the number of hours worked to increase his compensation.

The information security profession revolves around systematically identifying the information assets, vulnerabilities, threats, and controls and deploying controls appropriately so that the money spent on these controls delivers the greatest possible benefits to the organization. The rest of this book focuses on each of these components in detail. The rest of this chapter surveys the important vulnerabilities, threats, and controls. It may be seen as an exercise in building your vocabulary on information security.

The popular literature on information security often uses the words "vulnerability," "threat," and "risk" interchangeably. This is unfortunate. Risks involve both a potential for loss and a measure of the loss if the loss in fact occurs. Vulnerabilities are related to the first half of risk – they create a potential for loss. Threats are related to the second half of risk – if successful, threats can lead to losses. Managers are interested in mitigating risk. Threats and vulnerabilities become risks only when they put valuable information assets at risk.

An example is "A taxonomy of operational cyber security risks" from the SEI at CMU. The risks identified in the document such as "actions of people," would generally be classified as vulnerabilities.[9]

In our spreadsheet-based accounting system for example, a risk may be the inability of the business to repay business loans due to manipulation of data on an unprotected computer by a disgruntled employee. The vulnerability in this example is the unprotected computer and the threat is the disgruntled employee.

We cover risk management in detail in Chapter 14. In that chapter, we will write a few risk statements to clearly distinguish between the three. It is hoped that readers of this book will distinguish between "vulnerabilities," "threats," and "risks" and use the correct terms as appropriate.

---

[9] http://www.cert.org/archive/pdf/10tn028.pdf (accessed 07/22/2013).

Common vulnerabilities, threats, and controls

As we proceed through the chapters, we will look at the important information security controls in more detail. At this time, it is useful to introduce the most common vulnerabilities, threats, and controls so that you can start thinking about the different dimensions of the information security challenge.

Vulnerabilities

Vulnerabilities are exploitable weaknesses in information systems. Innumerable vulnerabilities exist and new ones are being discovered every day. A convenient way to understand these vulnerabilities is to classify them in some manner. In fact, many vulnerability classification systems exist. For example, one system classifies vulnerabilities based on the stage at which they are introduced in the software development life cycle (SDLC). Another set of classification schemes organizes vulnerabilities based on the threats they create. Unfortunately, all these classification schemes suffer from one weakness or the other. For example, a weakness of the SDLC-based systems is that in large systems, it is difficult to precisely identify the stage at which a vulnerability was introduced. A weakness of the threat-enumeration systems is that the classification mechanism is necessarily incomplete because new kinds of threats are discovered all the time.[10]

For our purposes, we should find it convenient to broadly classify vulnerabilities into software vulnerabilities and procedural vulnerabilities.

Software vulnerabilities

A software vulnerability is an error in the specification, development or configuration of software such that its execution can violate the security policy.[11] Some of the most common software vulnerabilities include the following.

Lack of input validation: *The input validation vulnerability refers to a situation where user input is used in the software without confirming its validity.* A common use of software, particularly web software, is to access data from databases. Examples include retrieving lists of movies at sites such as sonypictures.com, or webpage text from content management systems (CMS) at sites such as PBS Frontline and HB Gary, a computer security firm, providing expert solutions for several government agencies. Users of these sites typically use the search box or other user input fields to specify their information needs, and the software running the site processes this user input to generate the appropriate response. If the user input is not properly validated, users can access information they were not supposed to get access to. A source code example is given below. In this example, the software uses a simple SQL query to return items matching a username and itemname. If the user input is not validated for correctness, the user can obtain all items in the items table.[12]

```
query = "SELECT * FROM items WHERE itemname = '" + ItemName.Text + "'";

// expected user input for ItemName: pencil;
```

---

[10]Meunier, P. Classes of vulnerabilities and attacks (download). In: Handbook of Science and Technology for Homeland Security, Wiley, 2007.

[11]Krsul, I. "Software vulnerability analysis," unpublished PhD dissertation, Purdue University, 1988.

[12]http://cwe.mitre.org/top25/index.html#CWE-89

```
// actual user input for ItemName: pencil OR 'a'='a';

// query result is:
SELECT * FROM items WHERE itemname = pencils OR 'a'='a';

// which translates to:
SELECT * FROM items;
```

A common factor among the sites listed here (PBS Frontline, HB Gary Federal, and Sony Pictures) is that they were compromised in embarrassing fashion in 2011 due to improper input validation in their web software.

The specific form of the input validation vulnerability shown in the example above is called the SQL injection vulnerability. *The SQL injection vulnerability refers to the use of unvalidated SQL input in applications.*

Unrestricted uploads: *The unrestricted uploads vulnerability occurs when files are accepted by software without verifying that the file follows strict specifications.* For example, many e-commerce websites encourage users to upload photographs of their use of products sold by the website. If these sites do not check that the uploaded photographs are indeed .jpg or .gif or other similar file formats, it is possible for an attacker to upload software programs to the site instead of images. These programs may then attempt to compromise the site, for example, by stealing usernames and passwords.

To prevent such attacks from taking place, it is recommended that all files uploaded by users should be treated as malicious and all such files should be searched for malicious code. This search is not trivial since some file types (e.g., .gif files) have comment fields that may be used by attackers to hide malicious code.

Cross-site scripting: *The cross-site scripting vulnerability occurs when user-supplied input is used without verification as part of the output served to other users.* The vulnerability gets its name because the most common way in which it is exploited is by attackers getting their victims, who are browsing on one website, to supply malicious JavaScript code (scripting) as input to another, targeted website (cross-site). The following example from the top 25 software errors database demonstrates the vulnerability.

Consider a simple webpage written in php as follows:

```
$username = $_GET['username'];
echo '<div class="header"> Welcome, ' . $username . '<\div>';
```

This intention of this page is to gather the user's name from a web form on the previous page or a URL ending in "?username = John" to create a welcome message such as "Welcome, John" for the user. However, an attacker can enter some scripting code in the username textfield:

```
http://trustedSite.example.com/welcome.php?username=<Script
Language="Javascript"> alert ("You've been attacked!");<\Script>
```

This will display an alert dialog to the user. To have the same dialog box displayed to another user, the attacker can send an email to the victim with the appropriate URL. When the victim clicks on the email, the alert dialog will be displayed to the victim.

The above example is innocuous. However, a real attacker can exploit this vulnerability to get victims to activate more damaging scripts. Cross-site scripting is one of the most common vulnerabilities of web applications, so much so that it has an abbreviation of its own – XSS. This vulnerability has been present in one form or the other on most of the popular websites, including such well-known names as Facebook, Barracuda Spam Firewall, Mediawiki (the software behind Wikipedia), etc.

Buffer overflow: *The buffer overflow vulnerability refers to the situation where a program puts more data into a storage location than it can hold.* This is one of the most common software vulnerabilities. Normally, such a situation should only lead to a software crash. However, an attacker with detailed knowledge of the program can inject custom-created input such that the overflowed contents compromise the computer in predictable ways. The compromise usually allows the attacker to connect to the computer remotely and steal information.

Buffer overflows are common in programs written in unmanaged languages such as C and C++. Managed languages such as Java and C# manage memory and data such that buffer overflows are not possible in programs written in these languages. However, most software programs (including modern browsers such as Chrome and Firefox) are written in C/C++ for cross-platform compatibility.[13] Therefore, eliminating buffer overflows in most modern applications requires extremely careful programming practices.

Missing authorization: *The missing authorization vulnerability happens when a software program allows users access to privileged parts of the program without verifying the credentials of the user.* Attackers are always trying to find parts of financial information systems that they can reach without credentials. If such a part is found, it is likely to be exploited to steal financially sensitive information. Many large data thefts are indeed the result of a missing authorization vulnerability. For example, according to the "top 25 dangerous errors" publication, hundreds of thousands of bank accounts were compromised in May 2011 at Citigroup as a result of a missing authorization vulnerability.

Unencrypted data: *An unencrypted data vulnerability occurs when sensitive data is stored locally or transmitted over a network without proper encryption.* Sensitive data includes user credentials and other private information. Unencrypted data flowing over a network can be read easily using software called sniffers. Unencrypted data stored in a database can be stolen if missing authorization or unvalidated input allows users to read the data. Unencrypted data is often an element of major data thefts.

Procedural vulnerabilities

A procedural vulnerability is a weakness in an organization's operational methods, which can be exploited to violate the security policy. Procedural vulnerabilities can compromise information even if all software vulnerabilities have been removed. The most important kinds of procedural vulnerabilities are the following.

Password procedures: The standard procedure used to minimize the impact of many software vulnerabilities including "missing authorization," "invalid input," and "unrestricted uploads" is password protection. Users are required to create passwords that are known only to themselves and to provide these passwords before they are allowed to access sensitive information. However, these passwords may not provide adequate security if the organization is not careful about its password procedures.

For example, if passwords are very short (e.g., "abcd"), easily guessable (e.g., "password" or "admin"), use words found in the dictionary (e.g., "computer"), or use parts of user

---

[13]The interested student may browse the Chrome browser source code at http://src.chromium.org/viewvc/chrome/trunk/src/chrome/browser/?sortby = file

---

Password tips

Using good passwords is also advisable in personal life. Tips for good passwords include:[14]

1. Length: Use at least eight characters.
2. Complexity: Use numbers, letters, symbols, and punctuations. Long and complex passwords are difficult to compromise.
3. Variation: Change passwords regularly so that even if a password is compromised, the vulnerability is eventually removed.
4. Variety: Use a different password for every site. At the very least, use two passwords – one for sensitive sites (e.g., banks, online stores) and another for web forums, chat rooms, and other less-sensitive sites. Attackers commonly steal credentials from these less-sensitive sites (which are often less carefully developed) and try them on sensitive sites such as banks and online stores. For an interesting and detailed account of one such incident, read the experience of James Fallows, a national correspondent for The Atlantic magazine and a former speechwriter for President Jimmy Carter.[15]

---

information (e.g., "john"), they do not provide much protection. Attackers usually try various combinations of these passwords when challenged to provide a password.

Since this is such a widespread concern, most software vendors allow system administrators to specify password procedures to prevent the use of weak passwords.

Training procedures: As software gets increasingly secure, attackers are sharpening their focus on the gullibility of end users. They may send emails that appear to arrive from the organization's chief executive, but which in fact use XSS (cross-site scripting) and other methods to get user credentials. These credentials can then be used to bypass password protections and access sensitive information. At the very least, organizations must make it very clear that they will never send any unsolicited email to users, asking them for their password or other credentials. Such requests will always be made more formally, e.g., by a letter in the mail, or by a memo sent through the organizational hierarchy, etc.

Minimal information security training procedure

Organizations must maintain a policy of never asking employees for sensitive information such as usernames or passwords in an unsolicited email or phone call. Employees at all levels of the organization must know this policy. Employees should know that they can safely trash such emails no matter what the source and no matter what the situation are.

Threats

A discussion of all information security threats could fill an entire book. However, some threats have become famous for the havoc they have created over the years and have earned a place in the information security "Hall of Fame." As a professional in this field, it is advisable that you be aware of them. These are briefly described below.

---

[14]http://www.microsoft.com/security/online-privacy/passwords-create.aspx

[15]http://www.theatlantic.com/magazine/archive/2011/11/hacked/8673/

Viruses/worms: Most people are familiar with viruses and worms, and most computers sold today come with trial versions of antivirus software. *Viruses and worms are computer programs that adversely affect computers and propagate through the network without the user's consent.* The difference between the two is that a virus uses other programs (e.g., the user's email client) to spread, whereas the worm can propagate all by itself. Since the authors of worms and viruses know that most users use antivirus software, modern-day worms and viruses are designed to cause all possible damage within minutes of release. For example, the Slammer worm, which was released on Saturday, January 25, 2003, exploited a buffer overflow vulnerability in Microsoft's SQL Server. The vulnerability had been discovered in July 2002 and Microsoft had released an update to patch the vulnerability soon thereafter. Only unpatched hosts were vulnerable and the worm reached 90% of these vulnerable targets in less than 10 minutes,[16] infecting at least 75,000 hosts. The interesting story of the ILOVEYOU virus is described in the example case.

Denial of service (DOS): *Denial of service is the unauthorized prevention of access to resources or the delaying of time-critical operations.* This is usually accomplished by making a large number of unnecessary requests of an information system. The resources of the target system are then preoccupied with responding to these unnecessary requests, which prevents the system from being able to respond to legitimate requests in a timely manner. The impact of a DOS attack can be strengthened by deploying multiple computers to make these unauthorized requests. Such attacks are called distributed denial of service (DDoS) attacks. *Distributed denial-of-service (DDoS) is the use of many compromised systems to cause denial of service for users of the targeted system.* Fortunately, it is relatively easy to recognize the flood of incoming requests to a single target as a DOS attack and most ISPs can easily block these requests. For an absolutely hilarious but very informative and detailed investigation of a DOS attack, read Steve Gibson's report on the DOS attack against his company.[17]

Phishing: *Attempting to compromise a user by masquerading as a trustworthy entity in electronic communication is called phishing.* Early phishing attacks attempted to acquire information such as usernames, passwords, and credit card details. Most people receive at least one or two of these emails every week. An example is shown in Figure 4.5. The emails appear to originate from banks and lead users to visit a website that looks like the bank's website. At the website, users are asked to provide their username and password in order to make some correction at the bank. While the emails and target website appear to be legitimate, they really aren't. A careful look at the URL will show that the website has been hosted at a compromised server. In Figure 4.5 for example, the website has been hosted at a school district in Alabama.

More recently, phishing is used in combination with social engineering and zero-day exploits to initiate advanced persistent threats. The RSA attack of 2011 discussed with zero-day exploits later in this section is an example.

Malware: Malware (<u>mal</u>icious soft<u>ware</u>) is a general term used to describe *software or code specifically designed to exploit a computer, or the data it contains, without the user's consent.* A very common way for malware to reach computers is via free downloads where the malware author creates a computer software that appears to be very useful and

---

[16]Moore, D., Paxson, V., Savage, S., Shannon, C., Staniford, S., and Weaver, N. "Inside the Slammer worm," IEEE Security and Privacy, July/ August 2003.

[17]Gibson, S. "The strange tale of the denial of service attacks against GRC.com," http://www.crime-research.org/library/grc-dos.pdf (accessed 01/13/2012).

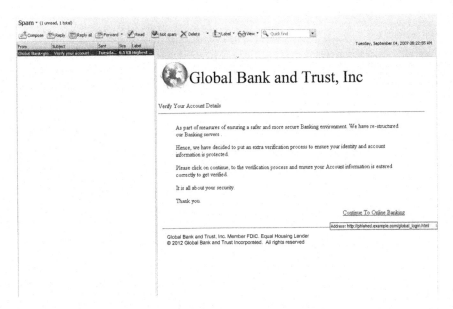

FIGURE 4.5 Phishing example

distributes it for free. When unsuspecting users download and install this apparently useful software, the malware is installed along with it. This is called the Trojan horse technique. There are many kinds of malware including key loggers, zombie clients, and root kits. *Key loggers track (log) the keys struck on a keyboard, typically trying to gather usernames and passwords.* The *zombie client is software that takes directions from a remote computer and uses the infected computer to perform malicious tasks as directed.* The infected computer is called a zombie. Zombies are usually used to send email spam, launch denial of service attacks, and compromise computers at sensitive installations such as banks and the military. Zombies, or robots (bots), get their name because they blindly comply with instructions from their master.

Rootkits: *Rootkits are collections of software programs used to hide the existence of malicious software on computer systems.* The term "rootkit" refers to a software toolkit that gives an unauthorized user root access (root is the administrative account on UNIX systems), while hiding the actions of the unauthorized user. Typically, rootkits replace existing system tools (such as those used to list processes (top) and folder contents (ls)) such that the modified versions conceal the existence of the unauthorized user. One of the goals of malware programs is to install a rootkit on the victim machine.

Rootkits are generally used by intruders to hide the existence of other malware such as zombie clients so that the owner of the computer is not even aware that this computer has been compromised and is being used to send spam or launch denial of service attacks.

Of all software threats, rootkits are particularly insidious because of their ability to subvert standard operating system protections. For this reason, it can be almost impossible to remove rootkits from a compromised machine and it may be advisable to completely reinstall the operating system.

Zero-day exploits: *A zero-day exploit compromises a previously unknown vulnerability in computer software.* The term implies that developers had zero days to address the exploited

FIGURE 4.6   Adobe Flash zero-day exploit launched on February 28, 2011

vulnerability. Though developers are not aware of the vulnerability at the time of the attack, someone is aware of it and has had the opportunity to identify a way to successfully exploit the vulnerability.[18]

One famous zero-day exploit relates to RSA, one of the leading vendors of SecureID tokens. This technology is used for 2-factor authentication in corporate environments. On March 17, 2011, the company reported that its IT system responsible for generating the tokens had been compromised, potentially compromising the security of its customers. Industry experts believe that the compromise was the result of a zero-day exploit involving Adobe's flash technology.[19] Interestingly, 18 days earlier, on February 28, 2011, an attacker with the Twitter handle @yuange1975 had announced the launch of a zero-day Adobe Flash exploit (Figure 4.6), suspected to be the exploit used in the incident.[20]

Zombies: *A zombie is a computer connected to the Internet that has been compromised in such a way that it performs malicious tasks at the direction of a remote controller.* Their unquestioning compliance with remote directions gives them the name of zombies. Zombies are sometimes also called bots. The owners of zombie computers are generally unaware of the compromise until they are informed by their system administrators. Botnets are quite affordable. Twenty-four-hour rental rates for 100,000–2,000,000 zombies are approximately $200.[21] Zombies are generally used to perform three kinds of activities – send spam, launch denial of service attacks, and perform dictionary attacks to break passwords. The vignette of Oleg Nikolaenko and the Mega-D botnet sheds some light into this world.[22]

---

[18]There is a market for such exploits. Greenberg, A. "Shopping for zero-days: a price list for hackers' secret software exploits," http://www.forbes.com/sites/andygreenberg/2012/03/23/shopping-for-zero-days-an-price-list-for-hackers-secret-software-exploits/ (accessed 07/22/2013).

[19]http://blogs.rsa.com/rivner/anatomy-of-an-attack/

[20]http://jeffreycarr.blogspot.com/2011/06/18-days-from-0day-to-8k-rsa-attack.html

[21]Ollman, G. "How criminals build botnets for profit," Damballa, US Department of Defense Cybercrime Conference 2011, Atlanta, GA.

[22]http://en.wikipedia.org/wiki/Oleg_Nikolaenko

> ### Mega-D botnet
>
> As of 2011, there is a mini-industry around installing Trojan horses on hundreds of thousands of computers and renting the processing capability of these computers to spammers and hackers. The collection of compromised computers is called a botnet. An example is the Mega-D botnet. It was a network of about 500,000 infected zombie computers, which was responsible for sending over 30% of all spam in 2008. The bot net was run by Oleg Nikolaenko, a young Russian national, who was paid $459,000 for his services by Lance Atkinson, a convicted spammer from New Zealand. Oleg was arrested by federal agents at the Bellagio hotel in Las Vegas on November 4, 2010, for violating provisions of the CAN-SPAM Act of 2003.

Packet sniffing: *Packet sniffing is the act of intercepting and monitoring data passing through a computer network.* Packet sniffing is an important threat to wireless networks because unencrypted data sent through wireless networks may be read easily using freely available software (Wireshark) and standard computer equipment such as a laptop. Attackers are on the lookout for such unencrypted wireless access points at stores and other business establishments to steal user credentials for later exploitation. One of the best-known information security incidents of recent times, the T.J.Maxx incident, was the result of password theft through packet sniffing of an unencrypted wireless access point.

Password guessing: *Password guessing is the act of repeatedly trying different passwords associated with a user account until the correct password is found.* Sensitive computers are constantly being probed to guess passwords. The attacker tries different passwords until the correct password is found. This attack is so prevalent that most systems ignore repeated failed login attempts originating in quick succession from the same machine. However, occasionally a system administrator may omit the protection leading to compromise. For example, in early 2009, an 18-year-old student ran a password guessing program all-night and discovered that a system administrator at Twitter with username "Crystal" used a password of "happiness."[23] Several other threats related to passwords are discussed later in the book.

> In the example above, normally, the system should have found it unusual for a user to try different passwords at the rate of perhaps one new password per second for 8–10 hours. Upon detection, the user should have been blocked. This would be one of the technical controls, discussed in the next section.

Social engineering: *Social engineering is the art of manipulating people into performing desired actions.* Social engineering exploits the human desire to be helpful and the natural human instinct to be trusting. As the technologies become increasingly secure, social engineering is becoming ever more important to hackers as a way to get into systems of interest.

Social engineering is commonly used to initiate other attacks. Since around 2010, a common mechanism is to send a customized email to a small group of unsuspecting victims, usually at modest levels of the organizational hierarchy. The emails contain attachments containing

---

[23] http://www.theregister.co.uk/2009/01/07/twitter_hack_explained/

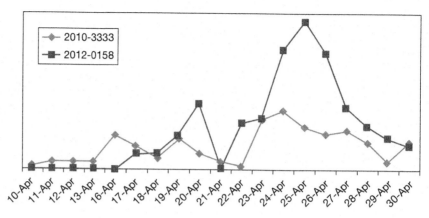

FIGURE 4.7 Exploit usage

zero-day exploits. When any user opens the attachment, the exploit installs some kind of scanning software on the victim's computer. This software passes on information to a remote controller and can also act in response to commands received from the controller. The RSA attack of March 2011 followed this methodology.

Advanced persistent threat (APT): *An advanced persistent threat is a sustained, human intensive attack that leverages the full range of computer intrusion techniques.* APTs are designed to breach organizations even when they are protected by well-designed and well-maintained information security controls. For this reason, APTs require a high degree of target-specific customization, which usually implies that a well-funded group of attackers is responsible for the threat. Since no two APTs are alike, the term APT generally refers to the team behind the attack rather than the attack itself. The most common goal of an APT is to use the attack to obtain and maintain a foothold within the organization for ongoing use and control.

Figure 4.7 is a plot of the usage frequency in April 2011 of two popular vulnerabilities commonly used in APTs. Both are vulnerabilities in MS Word, highlighting the fact that vulnerabilities in popular software are particularly dangerous. The vulnerability discovered in 2010 continued to be used a year after being announced, demonstrating the fondness of attackers to use time-tested exploits and the widespread slackness in applying updates. Figure 4.7 also demonstrates the swift adoption of new exploits, indicating the importance of quick application of updates.[24]

Controls

Information security controls are the safeguards used to minimize the impacts of information security threats. In modern IT systems, implementing appropriate and cost-effective controls is one of the most important tasks of a system administrator. The rest of this book is almost exclusively devoted to describing the various controls and their uses. This section provides a quick overview of the different controls available.

As in the case of vulnerabilities, there are many popular schemes used to classify the various controls available. One scheme, popular in the industry, is to classify controls as physical, procedural, and technical.

---

[24]http://blog.trendmicro.com/snapshot-of-exploit-documents-for-april-2012/

Physical controls: *Physical controls use traditional non-technical methods of preventing harm.* Typically, they prevent unauthorized users from being able to enter technical facilities. Examples of such controls include locks, fire extinguishers, background checks, and doors.

Procedural controls: *Procedural controls are prescribed plans of action that govern the use of computer resources.* Procedural controls follow two established principles of security:

1. Enforce personal accountability: When people know that they are liable for their actions, and that actions can be traced back to them, they are generally vigilant about their actions.

2. Require cooperation of more than one person to commit a fraud: *"When thieves fall out honest men get their dues."*[25] Experience suggests that there is usually a fallout over the spoils of crime, and the right procedural controls can use this human weakness to enhance security. This is the rationale for the standard accounting procedure of double-entry book-keeping.

Examples of procedural controls include the procedures for obtaining computer accounts, procedures for escalating privileges, procedures for modifying programs, procedures for hiring, and requirements that users change their passwords periodically.

> As organizations get larger and larger and the core information technologies become increasingly secure, the primary challenge for information security is to ensure that the most important weaknesses have been eliminated from the organization. The most effective way to do this is to develop effective procedures and then to consistently apply these procedures. On a day-to-day basis, therefore, information security professionals are most focused on procedural controls.

Technical controls: *Technical controls are the security measures built into the information system itself.* Common examples include passwords, firewalls, intrusion detection systems, system updates, and antivirus software. The rest of this book largely focuses on these technical controls in detail.

> Most information security controls straddle multiple categories. For example, passwords may be seen as either procedural controls (procedure to access resources) or technical controls (controls built into the information technology itself). In sensitive industries (e.g., banking), most employees are required to go through extensive background checks. These checks could be considered as physical (non-technical and designed to control physical access) or procedural (procedures followed to control access) controls.
>
> This is one of the weaknesses of most classification schemes in the information security domain – many items can easily fall into multiple categories.

Example case – ILOVEYOU virus

On May 5, 2000, many users received strange emails from people they knew. The subject lines of the emails were "ILOVEYOU." The emails contained a virus. If users opened the emails,

---

[25]The complete quote is "When thieves fall out honest men get their dues, but when honest men fall out lawyers get their fees," http://en.wikipedia.org/wiki/Lying_Jim_Townsend

the virus corrupted image files on the hard disk and sent itself as an email to users in the victim's contact list. Given the interesting subject line, the email has also entered the information security folklore as the "love bug" virus. The virus affected an estimated 50 million computers worldwide.

The legal follow up to the virus was interesting and highlights the limitations of law enforcement in dealing with cybercrimes. The FBI quickly identified Manila, Philippines, as the source of the virus and a recent college student, Onel de Guzman, as the author of the virus. However, virus dissemination was not a crime in the Philippines at the time. Therefore, De Guzman could neither be prosecuted in the Philippines nor be extradited to the United States for prosecution under US laws for the act of creating the virus.

Under heavy international pressure, De Guzman was charged with theft and credit card fraud in June 2000. However, on August 21, 2000, all charges were dismissed for lack of evidence.

Philippines eventually created a law criminalizing virus dissemination, but it is relatively weak. The maximum punishment is 2 weeks imprisonment and a fine equivalent to $100.

REFERENCES

Arnold, W. "Philippines to drop charges on e-mail virus," *New York Times*, August 22, 2000

Brenner, S.W. "Cybercrime jurisdiction," *Crime, Law and Social Change*, 2006, 46: 189–206

SUMMARY

This chapter described the essential information security environment and described the four components of the environment – the information assets, system vulnerabilities, threats, and security controls. Prominent examples of each of these components highlighted the issues you are likely to confront in your careers.

In this and the previous chapters, you have been introduced to the important issues faced by organizations and systems administrators. You have also been introduced to some basic technical skills to perform common system administration tasks. The remaining chapters in this book focus on helping you apply these technical skills to implement the common technical controls.

CHAPTER REVIEW QUESTIONS

1. Briefly describe the information security model shown in Figure 4.1.

2. What is an information asset? Give some examples from your personal life (it is enough to list some categories of assets, please do not violate your own privacy while responding to questions).

3. What are some important differences between conventional assets (e.g., gold, real estate) and information assets? How do these differences impact information security?

4. What are vulnerabilities? List some vulnerabilities to the assets identified in question 2.

5. What is the National Vulnerability Database (NVD)? Why is it useful?

6. What is the latest vulnerability recorded by the NVD? (to answer this question, visit the NVD at http://nvd.nist.gov/, click on the link to the "vulnerability search engine" and click "search," leaving default values in all fields.)

7. What are threats? List some threats to the assets identified to the assets identified in question 2

8. Visit the ATLAS threat index site (atlas.arbor.net as of 05/21/12). What is the top attack on the day of your visit?

9. What are controls? What are some important controls you can implement to minimize the impact of the threats in the previous question.

10. Briefly describe the "lack of input validation" vulnerability. Why is it dangerous?

11. Briefly describe the "unrestricted upload" vulnerability. What harms can this vulnerability cause?

12. Briefly describe the "buffer overflow" vulnerability.

13. Briefly describe the "missing authorization" vulnerability. In what industries is this vulnerability particularly harmful?

14. What are procedural vulnerabilities?

15. What are the recommendations for creating good passwords?

16. What are viruses and worms? What is the primary difference between them?

17. Provide a brief summary of the ILOVEYOU virus and its impacts.

18. What is phishing?

19. What is malware?

20. What are rootkits? Why are they dangerous?

21. What are zombies? What are they commonly used for?

22. What is social engineering? Why is it an increasingly important threat?

23. What are physical controls? Why are they important?

24. What are procedural controls? Why are they important?

25. What are technical controls? Give some examples of technical controls.

EXAMPLE CASE QUESTIONS

1. What was de Guzman's motivation for releasing the ILOVEYOU virus?

2. What is the penalty for creating and/or disseminating a virus in your country?

3. Laws typically allow judges considerable latitude in awarding sentences based on the facts of the case. Based on your response to question 2 above, what penalty would you award de Guzman?

4. Why did you choose this penalty?

HANDS-ON ACTIVITY – WEB SERVER SECURITY

As part of a website redesign at Sunshine State University, a directory search application was developed. It allows anyone to search for Sunshine State students, staff, and faculty names and email addresses. Before the website is released to the public, you have been asked to work with the team evaluating the security.

1. Using the Linux virtual machine you configured in Chapter 2, open a web browser by clicking on the Firefox icon in the bar at the top of the screen (Figure 4.8).

2. In the address bar, type in http://www.sunshine.edu/ directory

3. In the *First Name* field, type in **william** and click *Submit*.

4. Click the "*Back*" button to return to the search screen.

5. Type the following into the *First Name* field:

```
william!' OR 'a'='a
```

QUESTIONS

1. How many search results were returned in the first search?

2. Are there more search results after changing the input?

3. Write a brief (one to two paragraphs) summary of your findings that could be presented to the administration of Sunshine State University. Make sure to include:

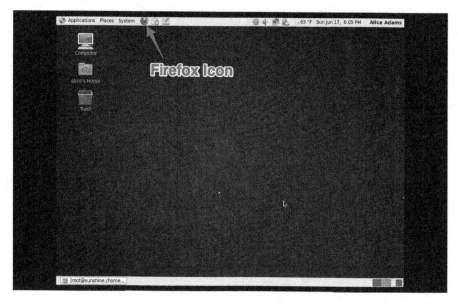

FIGURE 4.8   Using a browser on the VM

a. What vulnerability or vulnerabilities this application suffers from?

b. Reasons that you feel this vulnerability is present.

c. Possible harm that could come from this vulnerability.

CRITICAL THINKING EXERCISE – THE INTERNET, "AMERICAN VALUES," AND SECURITY

In conventional thinking, one of the big reasons for our information security problems is that the designers of the Internet did not build security in the underlying Internet technologies such as TCP and IP. If only TCP and IP also incorporated security, we would have a much more secure information infrastructure.

However, writing for the IEEE Security and Privacy magazine in 2011, Dan Geer, Chief Information Security officer for In-Q-Tel, a non-profit venture capital firm for technologies that support the CIA, stated that the developers of the Internet embedded their interpretations of "American values" in the underlying Internet technologies. This is why IP, the Internet technology that transfers data across the Internet, is "open, non-hierarchical, and self-organizing." Once the data leaves your computer, you have no control over how it is delivered to the destination. The protocol provides no mechanisms for governments to impose restrictions on the flow of information on the Internet, other than restricting user access to the Internet. Dan suggests that the Internet may also be a very successful American cultural export, bringing openness and freedom of information wherever it is adopted.

Adopting this view, Dan believes that the lack of security in the underlying Internet protocols is a strength, not a weakness. The Internet requires end users to take responsibility for their own security, instead of relying on security provided by the fabric of the Internet. An Internet that does not take responsibility for security also does not restrict any user from connecting to any other user, protecting the users' rights to freedom of association. A secure Internet could curtail this freedom in the name of security, requiring permission from the Internet provider for access to a desired resource.

Reference

Geer, D.E. Jr. "A time for choosing," *IEEE Security and Privacy*, January/ February 2011, 96–95

CRITICAL THINKING QUESTIONS

1. How could our information infrastructure been more secure if the underlying Internet incorporated security technologies such as encryption?

2. How could the usability of the Internet been crippled if the underlying Internet technologies had incorporated more security?

3. Based on your responses to these two questions, do you agree with Dan Geer's assessment that leaving security to be the responsibility of end users is a good idea?

DESIGN CASE

The MIS Department of the Sunshine University asked you to drop by for a visit. They are concerned about overall data security in the department and would like an outside opinion on (1) any glaring, major problems found and (2) what could be done to lessen their exposure.

Here are some of the things you found during your visit:

1. The "server room" is a janitorial closet with one UPS in the corner, with seven rack-mounted servers.

2. Three of these servers have only one network card. The other four servers have their network cable plugged in to the same network switch.

3. The UPS seems to be running at 80% capacity. Local techs estimate a 5-minute uptime before it fails.

4. Many research professors house their own server in their offices.

5. Desktop Support techs use the same admin password to access all workstations in the department.

List a minimum of five threats you can find in the list above. Then, suggest five controls that can be added to diminish the threats. Be as complete as possible.

## CHAPTER 5

Asset Identification and Characterization

Overview

We have seen that information security is associated with identified assets. All activities related to information security – security controls, disaster recovery and business continuity programs, and risk assessments, should revolve around protecting the confidentiality, integrity, and availability of the assets of the organization. Unsatisfactory asset identification can leave valuable assets unprotected while the organization spends time on protecting low value resources. Identifying and classifying assets is therefore the foundation of an information security program.

This chapter will describe the important assets in organizations. We will then examine how these assets can be identified and classified. Later chapters will discuss how these assets can be protected. At the end of the chapter you will:

- Be familiar with some of the issues involved in maintaining IT assets
- Have a basic understanding of the mission of the organization
- Know how to classify assets based on their alignment to the organization's mission
- Be aware of asset management issues including life cycle and ownership

Assets overview

The goal of asset identification and classification is to proactively gather all necessary information about an organization's assets that can be useful in responding to a threat affecting that asset. Asset identification should lead to the deployment of required monitoring mechanisms so that the organization can become aware of attacks and take necessary actions. In the absence of effective asset identification and classification, an organization may not even become aware of a threat. In fact, the 2012 Verizon data breach investigations report stated that 92% of all information security incidents were identified by third parties, often weeks or months after the damage had been done.[1] It is useful to identify assets yourself, before your adversaries identify them for you.

In Chapter 4, we defined assets as resources or information to be protected. But how do you know what needs to be protected? What is worthy of protection in one organization may not be considered important in another organization. For example, your music collection might be one of your most treasured assets, but your employer may not care so much for it. Asset identification and classification is therefore fairly unique to each organization.

While no simple checklist can be developed to identify assets, procedures to do so may be developed. Over the years, industry experts have published their collective experiences on

---

[1] Verizon (2012). 2012 Data breach investigations report, (p. 3).

securing information assets as various information security industry standards. ISO 27002 (formerly known as ISO 17799) is the information security standard published by the International Organization for Standardization (ISO). It outlines procedures for maintaining security, including recommendations for identifying and classifying assets. Control Objectives for Information and Related Technology (COBIT) is a similar framework commonly used by auditors which also addresses classification of IT assets. In this chapter, we will develop a procedure for identifying and classifying assets by synthesizing from these guidelines.

At a high level, asset identification and classification involves listing all IT assets in the organization, and characterizing the importance of each asset to the organization's information security, paying attention to the IT systems within which each asset operates.

Broadly speaking, all assets may be classified into two kinds – general and idiosyncratic. *General assets are assets that are found in most organizations.* An example of a general asset is email. Virtually every organization uses email as its primary form of communication and virtually every such organization will consider its emails as an asset worth protecting. You may be able to develop checklists for such general assets without any special knowledge about an organization, based on prior experience, discussions with colleagues or Internet searches.

On the other hand, an example of an idiosyncratic asset is student transcripts. Universities and other educational institutions consider these as vital assets because alumni are entitled to ask for transcripts anytime in their lives. Alumni may potentially sue if they miss out on a job opportunity as a result of the failure of their alma mater to produce a transcript on demand. However, companies are not likely to place such a premium on employee transcripts. Except for some regulated industries (e.g., medicine, accounting), once a person has put in a few years on the job, his career depends upon present performance rather than a college transcript. Therefore, once an employee is hired, employers may not care to save their transcripts. Student transcripts are therefore an idiosyncratic asset. *Idiosyncratic assets are assets that are distinct to an organization.* It can take considerable effort and attention to detail to identify idiosyncratic assets in an organization correctly.

As an employee or analyst, determining idiosyncratic assets requires a determination of the processes, procedures, and activities, which ensure that the organization works to its optimal ability. Such determination starts with one fundamental question: what exactly does this organization do? The answer to this question can appear simple enough, such as "this company sells cars" or "this business cuts hair." However, to identify all the assets relevant to the business, the security analyst needs to dig deeper and determine what is important to the owners, customers, and employees of the organization.

Determining assets that are important to the organization

Two common approaches to identify the idiosyncratic assets important to the organization are the bottom-up approach and the top-down approach.

Bottom-up approach: talking to coworkers

The bottom-up approach is normally what happens when someone is hired. It is also often referred to as the "learning curve," the period of time a new employee has to get acclimated to the work habits and needs of the organization. The employee is either handed a lot of documentation to read and understand, or is paired with an experienced peer to teach her the ropes. This time is the perfect opportunity for the new employee to determine the importance of specific processes to the company. It is also the opportunity to start determining the dependence of lesser-known items to the achievement of the company's goal. While the employee is likely to know what makes the organization relevant to customers, now is the opportunity to find out what is important to the company's operations and tie the needs of the organization and the needs of the customers together.

No one knows the inner work of a workplace as well as the folks that deal with issues on a day-to-day basis. For example, current employees can bring to the new recruit's attention the fact that a simple DNS server failure may bring down a $2 million-dollar application that is critical to the operation of the company.

Top-down approach: understanding the goals of the organization

In addition to looking at the organization from the bottom-up, through conversations with operational staff, understanding the goals of the organization from the point of view of executive leaders is also very important. This can be done even without direct access to the top executives of the organization. Annual Reports and the "About Us" sections of an organization's website are important sources of information about the organization. Top management uses these places to communicate their personal priorities to the world. Other sources of top-down information gathering are Vision Statements and Mission Statements. These are statements used by the organization's leaders to clearly convey the values and priorities of the organization under their leadership.

A Mission Statement is a short (preferably one or two sentences long) expression of an organization's services, its target market, and its competitive advantages. The Mission Statement serves to inform stakeholders (e.g., employees, customers, suppliers) about the priorities of the organization and remind the leadership team on how success will be measured in the organization. *Vision Statements articulate the organization's aspirations.* Vision Statements also define the organization's purpose. However, Vision Statements speak only to employees and communicate the values and beliefs of the organization. Vision statements establish expectations of performance and behavior by employees in the organization. Vision Statements can communicate to customers the work philosophy of the organization, describing what to expect when dealing with the organization.

Since Mission Statements, annual reports, and other such documents make a conscious effort to distinguish the organization from its competition, a scrutiny of these documents can reveal what is important to the organization. While these statements are often dismissed as lofty and generic, efforts should be made to get an insight on what organization leaders believe is uniquely important to the organization. A few examples of recent information security incidents and the mission statements of the associated organizations follow.

British Aerospace Electronic Systems

BAE Systems is a leading British company providing defense and security products, from cyber services and military support, to mission critical electronic systems and protection equipment.

According to its website,[2] the company's mission is "To deliver sustainable growth in shareholder value through our commitment to Total Performance." This is not particularly distinctive. We turn to its Vision Statement, which is to be "the premier global defense, aerospace, and security company."

---

[2]http://www.baesystems.com/our-company-rzz/about-us/our-culture

Listed in the Report under Strategic Actions, you will find:[3]

+ Improve profit and cash generation
+ Grow our Cyber Intelligence and Security business
+ Grow Electronic Systems
+ Drive value from our Platforms and Services positions
+ Increase our international business

These statements suggest that cyber intelligence, security, and electronic systems are the company's core businesses. Data in these areas is likely to be idiosyncratic to the company. Indeed, in 2007, BAE was a victim[4] of an Advanced Persistent Threat (APT). APTs are highly sophisticated penetrations that remain hidden in an organization network, leaking information to outside hackers. APTs are usually deployed by government agencies to spy in other countries' technological developments. The APT was used to steal design documents related to the F-35 Strike Fighter aircraft, for which BAE was a contractor. BAE's leaked data allegedly helped the Chinese government to develop the J-20 Fighter depicted in Figure 5.1.

Yahoo

Yahoo was founded in 1994 by Stanford Ph.D. students David Filo and Jerry Yang. It has since evolved into a major Internet brand with search, content verticals, and other web services. In the past few years, the company has struggled to compete in a market largely dominated by giants such as Google and Microsoft. In January 2012, Yahoo brought in a new CEO to try to "reignite innovation and drive growth." After only 6 months on the job, Yahoo changed direction again and brought in former Google employee number 20, Marissa Mayer.

According to information made available to its shareholders on its website,[5] Yahoo's mission statement is that "Yahoo is the premier digital media company." Its vision statement is that "Yahoo creates deeply personal digital experiences that keep more than half a billion people connected to what matters most to them, across devices and around the globe. That's how we deliver your world, your way. And Yahoo's unique combination of Science + Art + Scale connects advertisers to the consumers who build their businesses."

Again, while these statements appear generic, they suggest that the company's idiosyncratic features will include knowledge of the user preferences of a significant share of the online population in the world, making it an attractive target for attackers trying to harvest user credentials. In July 2012, a simple security misstep in the design of one of its services, Yahoo Voice, led to the leakage of nearly 400,000 online credentials[6] from Yahoo! servers.

[3] BAE Systems Annual Report, http://www.baesystems.com/cs/groups/public/documents/document/mdaw/mdu2/~edisp/baes_045566.pdf

[4] After latest F-35 hack, Lockheed Martin, BAE Systems, Elbit under multiple cyber-attacks. . ..right now, http://theaviationist.com/2012/03/14/f35-anonymous-attack/

[5] Yahoo Investor FAQ, http://yhoo.client.shareholder.com/faq.cfm

[6] How the Yahoo! Voices breach went down, http://blog.imperva.com/2012/07/how-the-yahoo-voices-breach-went-down.html

Color China Photo/ChinaOut/Associated Press

FIGURE 5.1 J-20 fighter

University of Nebraska – Lincoln

UNL, the University of Nebraska-Lincoln, was chartered in 1869. Today, the University of Nebraska–Lincoln is one of the nation's leading teaching institutions, and a research leader with a wide array of grant-funded projects aimed at broadening knowledge in the sciences and humanities. Its enrolment as of Fall 2011 was near 25,000 students.

According to its web pages, UNL's three primary missions are teaching, research, and service. The same page[7] outlines the following values for the university:

Learning that prepares students for lifetime success and leadership;

Excellence pursued without compromise; Achievement supported by a climate that celebrates each person's success;

Diversity of ideas and people;

Engagement with academic, business, and civic communities throughout Nebraska and the world;

Research and creative activity that inform teaching, foster discovery, and contribute to economic prosperity and our quality of life;

Stewardship of the human, financial, and physical resources committed to our care.

Again, these statements appear relatively generic for a university. However, they suggest that the most idiosyncratic information in possession of the university is course material and student information. Loss of this information may be damaging to the university. In May 2012, a breach in UNL's Student Information System[8] lead to the potential leakage of 654,000 students' Personal Identifiable Information including Social Security Numbers. The number

---

[7]UNL Roles and Mission, http://www.unl.edu/ucomm/aboutunl/roleandmission.shtml

[8]UNL Breach http://nebraska.edu/security

(654,000) vastly exceeds the student enrolment at the university because the university maintains records of all alumni. In addition, many universities maintain at least some information regarding all applicants to the university. Further, most universities also attract large numbers of students through non-degree programs such as summer enrichment programs.

As these examples show, organizations are likely to be targets for the most idiosyncratic information in their possession. While not an exact science, an examination of the organization's guiding principles can help to identify such information.

Asset types

As you work on identifying assets in your organization, it helps to know what to look for. What are the different types of assets in an organization? While some organizations may have very unique assets, the most important assets you are likely to encounter in information security are the following. These assets are present in all organizations in one form or another, and we will look at each of these:

- Information assets
- Personnel assets
- Hardware assets
- Software assets
- Legal assets

Information assets

An information asset is a digitally stored content owned by an individual or organization. This is usually the most important asset in an organization from the information security point of view. All deliberate information security attacks on organizations involve attempts to steal data. The most painful accidents with information security implications (crashed hard drives for example) involve loss of data. Therefore, an important component of asset identification involves searching for data and information important to the organization.

Informational assets include individual files such as images, photos, videos, and text files. They also include other digital content such as data in a database. These assets are stored either on a device owned by the organization ("locally") or on devices accessed in the cloud, often as part of a service offered by a third party and governed by a contact with the organization.

Examples of general information assets include payroll data, cash flow data, customer contacts, credit card information, accounts payable, accounts receivable, tax returns, and email. In addition to such raw information, general information assets also include process information such as system documentation, user training manuals, operational documents that ensure regulatory compliance, and business continuity information.

Idiosyncratic information assets include intellectual property such as product designs and product test results. *Intellectual property (IP) refers to creations of the mind (inventions, literary and artistic works, and symbols, names, images, and designs) that can be used for profit.*[9]

---

[9] http://www.wipo.int/about-ip/en/

In the context of a university, examples of idiosyncratic information include student grades, student test scores, and student transcripts.

While data is pervasive, executive leaders are often only aware of the security implications of information that has attracted recent negative media attention or that is included in matters of legal compliance. For example, most executives are aware of the security implications of credit card data. This is because there have been many incidents of credit card theft in the recent past and as a result the issue is discussed at all industry events. This is a classic example of a well-known cognitive bias, the recency bias, where the mind pays unusual attention to recent observations.

The challenge for security professionals is to identify information assets before the loss of such information hurts the organization. Consider the BYOD example below.

Bring your own device (BYOD)

In case you haven't heard about it yet, the latest acronym craze in enterprise IT is BYOD, or "Bring Your Own Device." This is a reflection of the fact that organizations, with all their firewalls and security equipment, have not been able to contain the proliferation of user-owned devices accessing their network and, more importantly, their data. After initially resisting such devices, many organizations have begun to welcome such devices. Sometimes, the motivation is just cost savings – if with some effort, employees can be allowed to use their personal equipment to complete work-related tasks, organizations can save the costs of providing this equipment to employees. For example, a cell phone plan can cost as much as $100/month, or almost $1,000 per employee per year. For approximately every 50 employees that use their personal cell phones at work instead of an employer-issued phone, the organization can save one entry-level professional job. The economics of BYOD are very real.

From a security perspective, it is important to note that BYOD creates challenges in information asset management. The organization's data is now distributed to many personal devices. A theft of any of these devices can compromise information assets of the organization.

For this reason, most organizations insist that they be able to completely wipe out BYODs by remote control in case of theft, mischief, or other concerns.

Personnel assets

Programmers, developers, and, yes, even managers are important organizational assets. It takes a long time to find an employee with the right set of skills who is willing to work at the salary your organization can afford. After the employee is hired, the organization invests a considerable amount on training the employee. Even if such training is not formal, only involving methods such as following another employee for a few days to learn the ropes, or spending days in the office reading user documentation, it creates costs for the organization. Later, as the employee develops professionally, learns the lay of the land, builds his social network within the company, he may find himself being the expert on a particular area. For instance, the employee may evolve to become the person who best understands something that may be a key operation to your department, such as string manipulation in Perl, or MySQL tuning for high-performance operation, or optimization of firewall rules. As an information security analyst, one of your responsibilities is to identify such individuals and manage the risks associated with their uniqueness. One way is to make management aware of the importance of these individuals, so that management can make extra efforts to keep them on-board. Another mechanism is to cross-train other individuals in the organization to take on some of these critical responsibilities.

Personnel assets are also documented from the perspective of disaster response. When an asset comes under threat, you should know how to contact the individuals who can respond to the threat. This documentation takes the form of collecting phone numbers, home addresses, email addresses, and any other applicable forms of contact information.

Hardware assets

Hardware assets include the physical pieces of machinery and associated systems directly or indirectly involved in the support of the mission of the business. It is usually "stuff" purchased with revenue, student fees, grant money, etc. Often, hardware is the medium in which the data exists and, therefore, without hardware there can be no data to secure, and hence no need for information security. Such hardware is as critical to the department as the data it contains.

In addition to the above well-understood role of hardware as a general-purpose asset, hardware may also be idiosyncratic to the firm in the form of a prototype of a new device, or a new patent. Prototypes are usually a form of Intellectual Property. Prototypes are often the foundation of new business opportunities pursued by the firm and so companies guard prototypes very carefully. To protect the commercial opportunities associated with the prototype, release of any information related to the prototype is protected by contracts called *Non-Disclosure Agreements (NDA)*.

An example of a security breach involving a hardware prototype happened in 2010, when an Apple employee forgot a prototype iPhone 4S in a bar in California. The prototype was found and sold to the editors of Gizmodo.com for $5,000. Gizmodo proceeded to publish a detailed story with pictures on their website. In October 2011, the two men involved in the sale of the device were sentenced to 1 year of probation, 40 hours of community service, and will have to pay $250 each in restitution to Apple.

Tracking attributes

What should the organization be recording for hardware assets? This exercise is the foundation to many other security-related activities, from disaster recovery planning to risk assessments. Ideally you would like the information to be as complete as possible so that if a particular device is lost, you'd be able to replace it with little effort. Table 5.1 is an example of attribute tracking for a PC/laptop.

You should notice at this point that the table actually includes more than just the physical description of the machine.

- **Purchase cost and EOL estimate** – The purchase cost will give you a benchmark to use when you are looking into insurance and replacement cost in case of loss. You would need about $1,000 to replace this piece of equipment. The EOL estimate will help you in terms of budget. You should plan on replacing this laptop in about 3 years. At that time, you will need about $1,000.

- **Asset delivery and production date** – These dates will give you a glimpse of how efficient IT was preparing the machine for use. It includes the installation of OS and applications, configuration, and final delivery to the end user. The time span between these dates may increase at the end of the fiscal year, when traditionally departments are making their discretionary purchases. An abnormal increase may indicate additional complexities in the process or the need for more personnel dedicated to preparation of the computers.

Table 5.1   Tracking attributes example

Type	Laptop
Tag Number or Unique Identifier	6000-724872-001
Manufacturer	ASUS
Model #	U46BAL5
Serial Number	7128347-JHF-B7
MAC Address	00-08-CA-84-40-79
Service Tag (if applicable)	URG647
Description	14″ laptop, silver case
CPU	Core i7, 2.7 GHz
Purchase Cost	$958.00
Purchase/Lease Date	5/1/2012
Estimated End of Life	3 years
Asset Delivered to IT	5/15/2012
Production Date	5/20/2012
Primary User	Dr. Jane Davis
Location	PHY Building, 475A
Last Serviced By	Elmer Livingstone
Network jack	PHY475A-B
Date of Service	5/16/2012
Disposal Data	
Disposal Reason	
Special Guidelines for Disposal (Compliance)	Laptop contains export-controlled research data and must be wiped immediately upon receipt by IT personnel, according to DoD guidelines.

You may have noticed that this "machine bio" would actually be useful to multiple departments within IT, and different folks should be able to contribute information. The networking folks, for instance, should be able to tell you which jack number that box is plugged into. They should also confirm the physical location. Desktop support should be able to update the last date of service, and compliance folks can use that date to come up with a list of when the computer was last checked by IT personnel.

Stolen Laptops, machine bio, and network connectivity

At the University of South Florida, University Police (UP) is constantly involved with the search for stolen laptops. Students will go to the Library and "step away to go to the restroom." When they come back, their laptop is gone.

When students register for wireless on campus, we keep a record that ties the user's physical device with his or her identity. When UP contacts IT, we put a trace on the physical device and wait to see if they again appear in the network.

They often do.

Asset discovery

Managing an asset through its life cycle is the gold standard. But realistically the majority of organizations, especially small and medium-sized organizations, do not have formal procedure to follow their hardware assets through the life cycle. Servers get replaced when they break down or when they are too old to operate and their lack of performance starts affecting the business bottom line. In universities, desktops get passed on from faculty members to administrative assistants. Equipment gets purchased by grant money and magically "appears" on the network one day. In most departments, no one really knows (1) what hardware assets the department has or even (2) where these assets are located.

Network scans can be used to come up with a list of such devices. Unfortunately, scanning is not reliable because portable devices may not be connected to the network during the time of the scan. Even multiple scans, performed at different times, may not pick up all devices. To deal with this issue, many organizations institute policies requiring a periodic review of all equipment taken by off-site employees.

Most companies and government entities have guidelines in which only assets above a certain cost threshold are tracked. However, those are usually guidelines based on financial reasons only. An information security analyst has technical reasons to track equipment, even though they may be under the financial threshold required by the organization.

Software assets

Software assets are the software tools needed to manipulate the organization's information to accomplish the organization's mission. Software assets need to be protected in order to ensure that the data within the organization is readily usable so that the organization can maintain high levels of productivity. These assets have many of the same properties of hardware assets. General software assets include user applications such as Microsoft Office, enterprise applications such as PeopleSoft (used for maintaining personnel data), development tools, software version tracking systems, and security related software. Protection of software assets entails activities such as ensuring that the most current versions of the software is available and that the versions of software available are compatible with the versions of hardware deployed in the organization. General software assets are typically purchased.

Idiosyncratic software assets are typically software developed in-house, either to support local operations or to sell as an output of the organization.

Legal assets

IT-related legal assets are the contractual arrangements that guide the use of hardware and software assets within the organization. Examples of such assets include technical support agreements, software licenses, revenue sources, and funding streams. In the flow of day-to-day operations, these assets can be forgotten until they lead to disruption.

One well-known incident that demonstrates the importance of legal IT assets relates to Comair, a subsidiary of Delta airlines.[10] In 2004, the airline was using a crew scheduling system

---

[10]http://www.cio.com/article/112103/Comair_s_Christmas_Disaster_Bound_To_Fail

Table 5.2 Example of assets

Asset	Asset type
Laptop	Hardware Asset
Student Grades	Informational Asset
John Doe – Security Analyst	Personnel Asset
Microsoft Office Suite	Software Asset
Microsoft Office License	Legal Asset

acquired in 1986. Airline safety regulations specify strict guidelines on crew hours to ensure their alertness and the crew scheduling system ensured compliance with these guidelines. Forgotten was the fact that the airline had acquired licenses for a maximum of 32,000 changes in any given month. An unusually extreme winter in December 2004 caused the airline to reach that limit for the first time on Christmas Eve. Without the software, the airline could not operate, though all its aircraft were fully functional. The incident led to over 200,000 stranded customers on Christmas 2004, a loss of $20 million (compared to a profit of $25 million in the previous quarter) and the departure of the airline's CEO. All it would have taken to avoid the incident was an awareness of the licensing constraint and a purchase of the required number of additional licenses. The incident also served as the subject of a very readable book on IT risk management.[11]

Asset identification – an example from a typical university

Now that we have enumerated the important asset classes, we can move on to identifying these assets in any given organization. General assets are easier to identify since general-purpose checklists can be drawn up to itemize them. Idiosyncratic assets are more elusive since the identification of these assets requires deep knowledge of the firm and its industry. To deal with this issue, most guidelines recommend a combination of bottom-up and top-down approaches to identifying assets. Identifying what is important to the organization can help locate assets idiosyncratic to the organization. Table 5.2 is an example of some representative assets you may find at a university.

Asset characterization

Now that all the assets have been identified, with the system profiled so that we know its dependencies, we are ready to start characterizing those assets. The two parameters used to characterize assets are sensitivity and criticality. Asset characterization helps us dedicate resources appropriately toward protecting assets. Ineffective characterization can result in large investments protecting insignificant assets, while leaving the organization vulnerable to common problems.

Asset sensitivity

Sensitivity describes how much damage a breach of confidentiality or violation of integrity of an asset would cause to the organization. We can examine sensitivity based on the following example.

---

[11] Westerman, G. and Hunter R. IT Risk: Turning Business Threats into Competitive Advantage (Hardcover). Boston, MA, Harvard Business School Press.

Given the following assets, which one do you think would be the most sensitive?

+ Dr. Jameson's research files, residing on an ITAR Compliant (International Traffic in Arms Regulations) desktop due to the fact that it involves research of materials under the control of the US Armed Forces.
+ Jane Pauling's email, freshman student in the College of Business
+ Robert Thompson's calendar.

Hopefully you picked option 1. Not because he is a faculty member. If an unauthorized person gained access to Dr. Jameson's research, not only would the US Armed Forces personnel would be potentially put in danger, the university could face serious consequences in terms of grants. And Dr. Jameson himself could go to jail. In fact something similar happened with Prof. John Reece Roth. In July 2009, Roth received a 4-year prison sentence for illegally exporting military technology, in large part due to his work with graduate students from Iran and China.[12]

There are different guidelines on classifying the sensitivity of assets. Some organizations use a scale from 0 to 5. Others go from low to high. For the purposes of this book, we will use a simple binary scheme and classify assets in one of two categories: ***restricted*** or ***unrestricted***.

Restricted asset

A restricted asset is an asset in which disclosure or alteration would have adverse consequences for the organization. It is up to the organization to make the determination on the threshold itself. Some consequences may be acceptable when compared to the cost required to secure the asset. This determination is called risk acceptance and will be discussed again in later chapters.

Take your grades, for instance. Your grades are a highly restricted asset to your university. Not even your parents are allowed to see them without your consent, even if they are paying your tuition in full. That does not happen necessarily because the university is one of the good guys. Universities are required to protect your grades and other data in order to be complaint to the Family Educational Rights and Privacy Act of 1974 ("FERPA"). FERPA is what is known as a "Spending Clause" statute: "No funds shall be made available under any applicable program. . ." unless statutory requirements are met.[13] Unless the university complies with it, no federal funds would be allocated to the university (including student financial aid).

Quite a few of the assets you will find that are considered "restricted" are due to some sort of compliance. Some examples are Payment Card Industry (PCI) compliance, guidelines issued by banks to protect credit card information, the Health Insurance Portability and Accountability Act (HIPPA), and the Sarbanes–Oxley Act (SOX), which sets new or enhanced accounting standards for all US public company boards, management, and public accounting firms.

There are also other assets that may be considered restricted as a matter of choice by the organization. System Characterization reports, for instance, specify exactly what systems the organization consider critical for operations. They also may show vulnerabilities a person could exploit to gain access to the system (remember the unsecured channels on email?). So, System Characterization should be considered restricted. Other examples could include personnel salary, budget spreadsheets, internal audit reports, and others.

---

[12]Prison Time and Export Controls, http://www.governmentcontractslawblog.com/2011/10/articles/itar/prison-time-and-export-controls-university-professors-case-illustrates-dangers-of-ignoring-export-compliance/

[13]Legislative History of Major FERPA Provisions, http://www2.ed.gov/policy/gen/guid/fpco/ferpa/leg-history.html

Unrestricted asset

Unrestricted assets are assets not classified as restricted. It is the data that, if leaked or viewed by someone, would not cause problems for the organization.

We saw that your grades are considered restricted information. In contrast, your university also has something called **Directory Information**, which is information about you that could be posted publicly. Normally, the following information is considered Directory Information and, therefore, unrestricted data: Student Name, Local Address and Telephone, Permanent Address and Telephone, Email Address, Place of Birth, Major Field of Study, Dates of Attendance, Full or Part Time Enrolment Status, Year in School (Class), Degree(S) Received, Scholastic Honors and Awards Received, Other Educational Institutions Attended, Visual Image, Weight and Height of Athletic Team Members.

If you are surprised and are wondering what your university considers Directory Information, look it up. Universities are also required to provide mechanisms to turn your unrestricted data into restricted data. There is usually a privacy form you can fill out with the Registrar's Office that allows you to keep the university from being able to release, for instance, your address.

Information posted on public websites is usually unrestricted information. Marketing information assets, a university's class catalog, and nutrition facts on a food or beverage are also examples.

Asset criticality

Asset criticality is a measure of the importance of an asset to the immediate survival of an organization. The level of criticality of an asset is usually tied with the availability of an asset within the CIA principles of security. Criticality asks the question: how long can my organization survive without this resource? The more critical an asset is, the bigger measures an organization has to take in order to make sure it is redundant, backed up, and protected for failure.

When trying to determine the level of criticality of an asset, you will find that it is largely in the eye of the beholder. It will vary from department to department within your organization, especially when an asset is only perceived to have benefits to their own organization. Some assets are clearly serving the entire enterprise and are often referred as Enterprise Business Systems (EBS). For example, the systems handling HR and payroll functions are usually considered EBS systems. In the university environment, the system handling student grades is considered an EBS. However, an email system handling only the College of Medicine would not be considered EBS, as it only works with that college. It is, however, critical to the College of Medicine operations. EBS systems are generally considered critical, while non-EBS systems are not.

Consider the following when trying to assign a level of criticality to an asset:

What is your point of view?
Will administrators be able to recover the data in case of a disaster?
How long will the recovery process take?
will be the effect of the loss of availability, including the loss of public standing?

Various classes of criticality are defined in the industry. A basic classification system categorizes assets as essential, required, and deferred.

Essential asset

An asset should be considered essential if the loss of availability would cause immediate severe repercussions for the organization. This implies that the organization needs to determine its definition of severe. As far as the duration, an essential asset would be missed even if its absence lasts only a brief period of time.

Take the wheels in a car, for instance. If you are driving your car down the highway, wheels are essential. A blowout could spell major disaster for you and your passengers. Other examples may include a purchasing system for a web-based vendor, electrical power for a hospital, and lifeboats for the Titanic.

One common flaw in information security is that essential assets are sometimes not protected properly and their availability is often taken for granted. We will review this issue further in when we discuss Disaster Recovery in Chapter 11.

Required asset

An asset is considered required when it is important to the organization but the organization would be able to continue to operate for a period of time even if the asset is not available.

Let's think of our car analogy again. This will also illustrate the time-dependency of the criticality level. The wheels are clearly considered essential if you are driving down the road. But what if you get home and later in the evening find that you have a flat? At that point in time, assuming you don't have anywhere to go, the wheels could be considered an essential asset: they are important but not critical. They may again be critical the next day when you have to leave for work, but until then you would have a chance to rectify the problem. One of the ways to rectify things is to activate your Disaster Recovery plan: get the jack, install the spare tire, and take the bad one to be fixed. Downtime: about 20 minutes.

Deferrable asset

A deferrable asset is an asset that is needed for optimal operation of the organization but whose loss of availability would not cause major issues to the organization in the near term. If an asset is described in terms similar to "well, eventually we would like to have it back but we could do without it for now," you know that the asset is a deferrable asset.

These assets are items that would maybe make the organization run smoother, more efficiently, but could be rebuilt it needed. Take something simple, like the pen you are using in class. If you lose the pen you may have difficulty taking notes in this class, but you could simply find a pencil in your backpack and it would work just as well.

Here's another. Imagine you have a 10-item list of to do chores around the house. One of them is to vacuum your room. But in order to do that you have to use the vacuum, but your sister is currently vacuuming her room. Of course you always have the option of going and doing a hostile takeover of the asset if you consider it required at this time. Or you could do the other tasks first and defer the need for this asset at this time in the hopes that she will be done by the time you are done.

Deferrable assets are also those information assets that can be re-created without major impact. Your professor writes your grades on a sheet of paper before entering them on your university's Student Information System. If the computer he is using suddenly crashes and he loses the data he was entering, no worries. He still has that sheet of paper and can reenter the missing data.

Criticality levels may also vary from time to time. Assets may have a lifetime associated with them: they may be critical today while a particular project is going on, but once the project is delivered, the asset may not even be needed.

The elements of asset characterization are shown in Figure 5.2.

Table 5.3 builds up on the example assets by characterizing them. Some definitions are clear-cut. Others require a bit more thinking and perhaps even negotiations within the organization. Take the MS Office Suite, for instance. The software itself, the DVD with the application, can be considered an unrestricted asset because to get the application to run, you need a Product Key. As long as the Product Key is restricted, the MS Office Suite can be considered Unrestricted.

This completes the essentials of asset identification and characterization. However, in practice, an exercise in asset identification and classification requires the analyst to be aware of

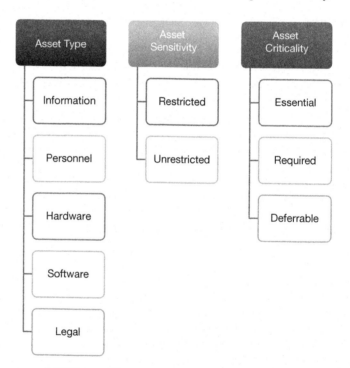

FIGURE 5.2 The elements of asset characterization

Table 5.3 Characterization of example assets from the university's perspective

Asset	Asset type	Asset sensitivity	Asset criticality
Faculty Laptop	Hardware Asset	Restricted	Required
Student Grades	Informational Asset	Restricted	Essential (time dependent)
Security Analyst Position	Personnel Asset	Restricted	Required
Microsoft Office Suite	Software Asset	Unrestricted	Deferrable
Microsoft Office License	Financial Asset	Unrestricted	Required

the environment within which the assets operate. The environment may be characterized along four dimensions – life-cycle stage, system dependencies, ownership, and responsibilities. The prototype case is when a department is considering the purchase of an IT asset with its own budget. The people deciding on the purchase are likely to be business people, with limited awareness of the impacts of the purchase on other IT systems. As an information security analyst with an awareness of the asset life cycle, system dependencies, ownership, and responsibilities, you can be better positioned to guide the introduction of the asset into the organization. We cover these issues in the remaining part of this chapter.

IT asset life cycle and asset identification

Assets have long lives. During their usable lifetimes, assets pass through many stages. While most discussion of information security revolves around assets in operational use, asset identification requires a scrutiny of assets in all stages of the life cycle in order to minimize the likelihood of security issues arising from the use of the asset. This section introduces the asset life cycle and provides examples of potential hazards arising from oversights at each stage of the asset life cycle.

Figure 5.3 shows a generic IT asset life cycle. In the industry, the management of IT assets over their life cycles is called IT Asset Life Cycle Management (ITALM).

The IT asset life cycle in Figure 5.3 shows the high-level stages of an asset. It includes the following stages: planning, acquisition, deployment, management, and retirement.

Planning stage

Assets don't just "show up" in a business. They are usually acquired for a particular purpose, answering a requirement, a project, or an initiative. For instance, when a new employee is hired, one would imagine that the first step would be a change in the work environment in some form, either increased load on existing personnel performing a task, or the need to track and maintain compliance with a new law, or the unveiling of a new product. The cost of the asset will also be considered at this stage.

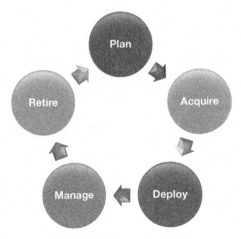

FIGURE 5.3 Generic IT asset life cycle

One of the tools used at the planning stage is the **Request for Information**. The RFI is commonly used when the company is not capable of providing specific product requirements, specifications, or purchase options. RFIs clearly spell out to vendors that a contract will not automatically follow.

The planning stage is also the best time to evaluate the organization's processes to try to leverage the new asset to help with multiple initiatives. For example, a planning exercise may be initiated to acquire software that will encrypt data within a database. The driving force to acquire the asset may be the need for compliance at the state level, with laws requiring Social Security Numbers to be encrypted whenever stored within a Student Information System. However, with appropriate planning, the same software license could also cover credit card numbers stored by the local computer store, or copies of tax returns stored by Financial Aid.

Perhaps the best known example of an oversight at the planning stage relates to the lack of security features built into the Internet. In the planning stages, no one had anticipated the extent to which the technology would be used for commercial transactions worldwide. The planners were mainly concerned with reliable data delivery. This omission is responsible at least in part to the security issues we face today on the Internet.

Another interesting example of an oversight at the planning stage relates to the lack of security features in Windows 95. The technology was developed to help users communicate over small networks in controlled environments, e.g., within homes and small offices. The focus was on user convenience. No one anticipated the wide adoption of the Internet and the use of Windows 95 to access the Internet. Without protections, these PCs became ready targets for attackers. In fact, at least some security experts believe that the information security industry owes its existence to the widespread deployment of insecure Windows 95 computers on an equally insecure Internet.[14]

Finally, consider the average lifetime of the asset and the potential need for a replacement at End of Life (EOL) during the planning phase as well. What will happen to the asset when it reaches its EOL for a particular project? Will the organization be able to reuse it for another project? For instance, a workstation used for 3D gaming development initially dedicated to a game designer may be assigned to an administrative assistant after a year, increasing the overall lifetime of the asset for the company.

Acquiring stage

After the planning stage comes the acquisition of the asset. The prime concerns during this stage are associated with the viability of the vendor, compliance with regulations and internal organizational procedures, and operational viability of the asset and ethics. This could involve a variety of methods and potential complications. Most companies require a series of approvals to ensure that the new asset satisfies these conditions. Some procedures used in this phase of the asset life cycle include:

- **Invitation to Negotiate** (ITN) – The ITN is a statement issued by a company indicating a willingness to look into a product or service. An advertisement, for instance, is considered an ITN. A company has a product and is willing to sell that product at a certain price. Keep in

---

[14]Dan Geer, talk at Tampa Bay ISSA chapter annual meeting, 2011.

mind that a response to an ITN is different than an actual offer and could never, on itself, lead to a contract. ITNs are often used by government agencies when the criteria for purchase are more than just low price alone.

- **Request for Proposal** (RFP) – The RFP is issued when the goals of an initiative or project are known, but the company doesn't really care about how they are done. There may be several methods that could be used to accomplish the task and the company will consider all available options. Detailed instructions identify the elements of information or documentation to be submitted for evaluation purposes. An RFP usually will contain a description of the company issuing the RFP, explain the current condition, project, or challenge facing the organization, layout budget and time frame, and a set of open ended questions to be answered by the vendor.

- **Invitation to Bid** (ITB) – An ITB is used when the requirements for the purchase of the asset or service are very well defined and specific. An invitation to bid is generally structured in such a way that a respondent provides minimal documentation to support their qualifications to provide the goods or services. Examples of documentation required may include licenses, permits, insurance, proof of agreement from product source, references, available equipment, years, and experience performing the services sought. Once the respondent has passed the minimum requirements test, the award is recommended to the respondent with the lowest bid.

An example of improper acquisition is the documented failure of New York City's CityTime payroll system project. Apart from cost overruns, the project led to a criminal probe into an alleged kickback scheme involving former employees of systems integrator SAIC and a subcontractor, TechnoDyne. Compared to an initial $63 million budget, costs reached an estimated $760 million. SAIC agreed to pay $500.4 million to settle the case.[15]

Deploying stage

Deploying is the stage where the asset is made available to organizational employees. The primary concerns at this stage involve compatibility of the new asset with existing organizational assets, integration with other organization systems, avoiding data loss, and minimizing downtime. The complexity of the deployment of new assets will vary greatly from asset to asset. One of the primary differentiators is whether the asset is a new product, software, or initiative versus an update to an existing one.

A simple deployment example would involve the deployment of a new desktop computer to a staff member. While this appears simple, let's think about this situation for a bit. To simplify maintenance, most organizations have minimum requirements for new machines, whether they are published or not. The desktop will come licensed with a specific version of the operating system, say, Windows 7 Home, but the organization is licensed and supports Windows 7 Professional. So, prior to doing anything else, the computer has to be wiped and the operating system reinstalled. Next we would install applications such as Microsoft Office and Adobe Acrobat. If there is an Active Directory domain, the computer would have

[15] http://www.washingtonpost.com/business/capitalbusiness/citytime-fallout-continues-for-saic/2012/04/13/gIQA71QtJT_story.html

to join the domain. Resources such as shared drives and printers are made available to the new machine. Since this is a security class, we also have to mention that antivirus software would be one of the top priorities. Ensure that the AV software is installed and updated **prior** to handing it off to the end user.

To minimize user downtime due to the upgrade (remember the CIA triad, confidentiality, integrity, and **availability**), the final step is to transfer the data files, including images and bookmarks, to the new machine. During this time, the user will not be able to work on either computer, old or new. The switch may have to be scheduled after hours to reduce the impact, or if the user is high enough up on the food chain that disruptions are not seen in a favorable light.

Are we done yet? Not really. The deployment should not be considered complete until the end user has a chance to sit down and test the new machine. This stage is known as the User Acceptance Test or UAT. Missing applications would have to be installed. Read and write access to shared drives confirmed. Only then the deployment phase is complete.

In 2011, a new Student Orientation system was deployed at the University of South Florida. Because the system was brand new and was not replacing any existing application, there was no concern about the lack of availability or downtime. The new SO had to be properly integrated with the application that stored student data, the Student Information System. Students had to be able to access the web front-end to manage their orientation data, and advisors had to be able to login to enter information for the students. Both of these operations required integration with the university's central authentication system.

User Acceptance started with a pilot of 100 students and their advisors. Once that phase was concluded and all integration issues resolved, the software was rolled out to the remaining student population and considered "deployed."

This is an example of a simple deployment. In the light of this example, consider the deployment of a new SCADA (Supervisory Control and Data Acquisition) system for control of a hydroelectric plant. Although very complex and seemingly daunting, the tasks are very similar. If you work for the company selling the SCADA system, the engineers who will be working with the system are your users. Keeping the lights on at people's homes is your goal, installing the new system with minimum impact to the home utility users. For the sake of simplicity, we can assume that the plant has a fully redundant system that can be brought online while work is done on the production system. Finally, testing will be extremely important. Are the controls working as designed? Are the fail-safe mechanisms in place to avoid catastrophic failures? Did the operational test, the nuts and bolts of the system, proceed without failure? Did the functional tests succeed as well?

Managing stage

Managing is the stage where the asset is in use. Once the asset is deployed, it is important to ensure that the asset does not introduce new vulnerabilities into the organization. For starters, let's again start small and focus on the desktop that was just installed. The staff member was absolutely thrilled with the IT desktop service performance, shook hands, and the employee said the usual "if you have any problems, give the help desk a call and we'll come take a look at it" and moved on to the next challenge. Even though the face-to-face support may have ended for the time being, there are many things happening in the background that are often times invisible to the user.

One thing we would like to do is to make sure we track where the desktop was deployed, who is the primary user, if applicable, and the MAC address of the new device (so we can track it on the network). This helps asset tracking, discussed later in this chapter. There are many ways to do this, from a simple spreadsheet for small organizations to large, automated tracking software that is normally deployed with the machine.

From the security perspective, there is one key element that must be done periodically in order to keep the desktop and the organization's computing environment safe: patches and security updates. We will discuss these at length in later chapters but for the time being it suffices to say that operating system, applications, and antivirus signatures must be patched.

The harsh reality for many IT assets is that, even though they may have been initially planned to have a End of Life of, say, 3 years, budgetary constraints will lead to an extension of that life within the organization. More often than not, the "if it ain't broke don't fix it" principle applies to these assets and organizations find themselves managing severely outdated devices. Especially in this situation, it is important to keep up with software and hardware maintenance contracts for as long as possible. It will come a time in which maintenance costs will outweigh the cost of a new device. That is the clear point to alert management and retire the existing, old device for a new one.

Retiring stage

Retiring is the stage when an asset that is no longer contributing to the mission of the organization is removed from use. "Retirement" does not always happen because something is obsolete. A common reason for retirement is when it becomes cheaper to remove an asset than to continue using it. Another possibility is the utilization of a newer, better asset, with improved features.

The primary concerns in the retiring stage are protection of the organization's intellectual property and performance of fiduciary duties. Retired equipment will typically contain data and some of it can be restricted. It is important to ensure that such data cannot be recovered from the retired equipment. For example, the desktop deployed in a college will reach a point where it can no longer provide the minimum level of service the dean and the students consider "adequate." This desktop will then need to be retired. Over the course of its deployment, users are likely to have recorded student data, credit card, and other sensitive data on the machine. As part of its retirement, all such data should be wiped clean.

In later chapters, we will discuss the disposal of equipment. Donation is always an option. Make sure the disk is wiped clean before donating any equipment. If your company has a contract with another company for disposal of the material, make sure there is a privacy clause on the contract and assurances that devices containing data will be appropriately destroyed, and not simply repurposed or thrown on a landfill.

When is the "retirement" line written in stone? Assume the case in which a professor in the College of Engineering brings in 100 million dollars in grant money to the university. His research is vital to the college. However, the instrumentation he uses requires a network connection and runs on an old Windows 2000 computer. Microsoft no longer issues patches to the machine. Is it time to declare the machine obsolete and remove it from the network?

Answer: The truth is that there is nothing written in stone. Decisions such as the one that needs to be made on this case sometimes goes beyond the purely technical, they straddle the political line and **should not** be made at the technical level. The job of a good security analyst is to provide the information so that managers can make an educated decision based on facts and the balance of technical, legal, political, and even media-related repercussions.

Take the example discussed in Chapter 2. Sunshine University was planning to replace its existing student email system with a brand new, cloud-based system that offered stability, redundancy, and new features to the user community, while at the same time allowing Sunshine to repurpose its personnel assets into other new ways to support its mission. Later we will also be discussing the potential impact of continued use of EOL equipment within the university and analyzing the risks versus the benefits of such support.

As an example of what can happen as a result of weaknesses in retirement procedures, it was reported in 2009 that a hard drive purchased from eBay was found to have originated from Lockheed Martin, a defense contractor, and contained details of a US missile defense system.

System profiling

In the previous examples we looked at assets in isolation: a laptop, a server, and a specific data set. This was done for simplicity during the introduction to the topic. However, when evaluating criticality and sensitivity in practice, it is necessary to look at assets in the context of the systems within which they are used. An asset that may be considered "essential" in isolation may be classified as "required" in practice if the organization has invested adequately in redundancy. Similarly, an asset that may be considered "deferrable" in isolation may actually be "essential" when viewed within the context of the system (the license for the scheduling system in an airline for example). Or, a collection of individual assets that by themselves may be considered "deferrable" could come together to form a system that is "critical." This section provides a brief introduction to system profiling.

System profiling is a bit more complex than a simple inventory of computers. Identifying all the components of a system and the dependencies between them may be as much an art as a science. *System profiling is the act of putting together all the assets inventoried, grouping them by function, and understanding the dependencies between these assets.* It is creating a big picture view of a particular system or process.

According to the National Institute of Standards and Technology guidelines for IT risk management, NIST SP800-30 – Risk Management Guide for IT Systems,[16] while performing system profiling, organizations will provide the hardware, software, system interfaces, data, personnel, and the mission of the system. As a result, the system boundaries will be clearly defined, together with function, criticality, and sensitivity.

Think again about your university environment, and some of the IT systems the university has in place in order to run the academic and the business sides of the learning

---

[16]NIST SP800-30, http://csrc.nist.gov/publications/nistpubs/800-30/sp800-30.pdf

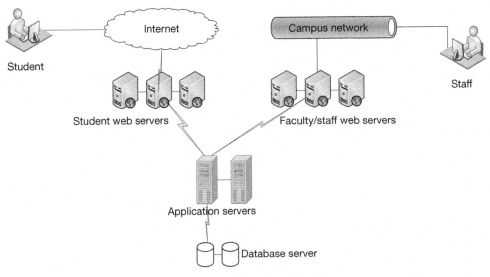

FIGURE 5.4   Student Information System

environment. One core system is the Student Information System (SIS), shown at a high level in Figure 5.4.

Student Information System

The SIS does what the name implies: it stores student information such as financial aid, grades, address, social security number, advising data, and class schedule. It is a vital part of the operations of a university. Figure 5.4 gives us a sample of what a SIS system normally looks like. Students view their information using a web browser interface. Advisors, professors, and other administrators have a deeper view of the data, often using a desktop interface.

Following SP800-30, we can characterize the system in the following manner.

Hardware

Redundant student web servers handle the student interface. Each server on its own is a *deferrable* asset: they can fail and all the end user would see is a performance hit, a slight delay in loading the pages. Together, however, they become *required*: if somehow they lose their connection with the Internet, students may not be able to access them. During registration periods, they become *essential*: if they all somehow lose their network connection, no one is able to register.

Similar analysis can be made on all elements of the system, even separating them into subsystems with differing levels of criticality and sensitivity.

Software

SIS is usually one of those systems too complex to be developed in-house. There are both commercial and open source systems available, such as Ellucian's Banner and OpenSIS. The application has many complex pieces and often includes a database backend where all the information is stored. The student interface is usually web based, but the faculty/staff interface could also have a dedicated client. Typically, all software and the associated licenses will be considered essential assets.

Data

What type of data will be stored in the SIS? A couple of them stand out and must be treated as restricted data: grades and social security numbers. Grades are non-directory information protected by FERPA, as seen previously in this chapter. SSNs are also protected by FERPA in addition to other State and Federal regulations, together with other Personal Identifiable Information (PII). As a whole, due to the type of data it contains, SIS systems are classified as restricted.

System interfaces

The interfaces specify how data is entered and extracted from the system. Consider the following inputs:

- Admissions: how is the student admitted to the university?

- Applicants: is there a separate interface used for applicants?

- Financial aid: is there any reporting requirement on financial aid? Tax considerations?

- Scholarships: how are scholarships awarded and reported.

- Compliance: are there requirements for reporting on the number of students, average GPA, or any other type of information to the Department of Education?

- Grades: how are grades entered? Manually? Automatically from the Leaning Management System?

- Classes: how is add/drop communicated to the LMS so that it has up-to-date information on who is enrolled and authorized to access which class?

All of these interfaces contain data that is exchanged between the SIS and another system. If the data is considered restricted, then this exchange, or at least the restricted data, should be encrypted. Credentials for accessing the system must be protected, especially those with privileged access.

System profiling can also involve an awareness of recent developments in software tools. For example, in October 2010, Eric Butler, a web application and software developer, launched a Firefox plugin called *Firesheep*. Firesheep's primary function is to "listen" to network traffic on shared media, like public Internet access points, for unencrypted data. From Eric's website:[17]

> *It's extremely common for websites to protect your password by encrypting the initial login, but surprisingly uncommon for websites to encrypt everything else. This leaves the cookie (and the user) vulnerable. HTTP session hijacking (sometimes called "sidejacking") is when an attacker gets a hold of a user's cookie, allowing them to do anything the user can do on a particular website. On an open wireless network, cookies are basically shouted through the air, making these attacks extremely easy.*

Eric's tool is nothing new. It is a variation of something known as a "sniffer."
One of the services vulnerable to Eric's tool? Facebook.

---

[17]http://codebutler.com/firesheep

In this manner, the goal of system profiling is to describe the system with all of its dependencies so that we can make decisions on what to modify (user access through unsecure means, for instance), determine single points of failure, and other concerns.

> Another important IT system, particularly found in research-intensive universities, is a high-performance computing system. This system is usually composed of clusters of servers, rackmounted, operating together, sharing processor, and memory resources to work on a single problem. It is not uncommon to have hundreds of servers configured in this manner. In such a setup, each individual server is in itself designed to be a deferrable asset. When it fails, there is a minor hit in performance but the job keeps moving forward. The overall system is designed to allow for a certain percentage of these servers to be down at any given moment and yet continue to operate.

Asset ownership and operational responsibilities

Recall from the beginning of this chapter that the goal of asset identification and classification is to proactively gather all necessary information about an organization's assets that can be useful in responding to a threat affecting that asset. So far, we have gathered all the technical information necessary for this purpose – what are the assets (asset identification), and how important are these assets (asset characterization). But we have missed an important element of responding to threats facing an asset – who should respond to a specific threat facing an asset?

For this reason, as part of the characterization of an asset, it is essential to also determine individual responsibility for the asset. In your home network, this is simple – you are responsible for everything within your home and your ISP is responsible for anything happening with your connection to the ISP. In enterprise networks, however, this is more complex. There are two specific problems you are likely to encounter. The first is that different people or units are likely to be responsible for different functions related to an asset. The second is that in spite of your best attempts, you are not likely to be able to anticipate everything that can go wrong with an asset.

Operational responsibilities are the responsibility of an individual or entity for a specific function related to the use of an asset. Operational responsibilities clarify the roles of organizational members for all well-defined functions related to an asset. *The owner of the asset is the individual or unit with operational responsibility for all unanticipated functions involved in securing an asset.*

You may notice that the above definition of the owner of an asset makes no reference to the entity that pays for the purchase of the asset. This is because while budgetary contributions and asset ownership may sometimes be shared, they can also be separated. This may be clarified from the example below.

> ### Unanticipated risks – a true story
>
> In 2004, a faculty member at a research university requested his department chair to purchase a few computers to set up a department lab. The computer was housed in a room in the department, and the professor and some graduate students, funded by the department, configured the lab and its software.

Thus, all expenses related to the asset were borne by the academic department. The university IT unit had no role to play in setting up the lab and, in fact, was not even involved in the process.

That summer, however, one of the computers in the lab was compromised and was used as part of a botnet to run a dictionary attack (password guess) on the computers of a classified federal agency. The lab computer became part of an FBI investigation and the university received a formal subpoena from the FBI to produce a disk image of the computer. The university's general counsel forwarded the subpoena to the IT unit of the university. Since the academic department did not have the expertise or resources to make a disk image, university IT performed the required tasks and provided the necessary information to the FBI.

It should be clear from the example that while the department paid for the asset, the professor had operational responsibility for all anticipated aspects of the asset – including functions such as software installation, software updates, data backups, and user account management. It should also be clear from the example that the FBI subpoena was a completely unexpected scenario, which was eventually handled by USF IT. As a matter of fact, in this example, the university's IT department was involved in the lab for the first time only when the subpoena was received. Who would you consider to be the owner of the asset – the academic department, the professor, or university IT?

Because the operation of IT assets requires specialized skills, IT organizations are often responsible for all residual functions related to IT assets. However, since most IT assets are purchased by business units from their own budgets, IT is often not considered to be the owners of the asset. A security analyst needs to be aware of this dynamic and its consequences because the owners of the asset are those responsible for coordinating their efforts in order to ensure the security of an asset. A clear understanding of this aspect of asset characterization can be helpful in planning responses to threats on assets.

As another example, let's look at a particular type of information asset common to Universities – "institutional data." The University of South Florida defines institutional data as:

Institutional data is defined as all data elements created, maintained, received, or transmitted as a result of business, educational, or research activities of a USF System unit and may include one or more of the following characteristics:

-*Relevant to the operations, planning, controlling, or auditing of business functions of both administrative and academic units.*

-*Generally referenced or required between more than one administrative and academic unit. Included in an officially published USF System report.*

-*Generated or derived by any entity of the USF System or employee, or an affiliate or agent of the USF System.*

-*Classified and constrained in accordance with USF System, state, and federal laws and policies."*

It is easy to see that this kind of data can be distributed across the university, with a diverse set of owners. It is important to establish clear lines of responsibilities around users handling this type of data. This is where information asset ownership and information asset operational responsibilities come into play.

While the actual data ownership is held by the university, someone must be able to make decisions regarding the use of the data. That being the case, the university delegates the authority and ultimate responsibility for the security of the institutional data to specific individuals within the organization. These individuals are knows as the information asset owners.

Users who have operational responsibilities for maintaining data security but do not own the data are called data custodians. An example of a data custodian is a student advisor in an academic department who has access to student transcripts to help students register for the most suitable courses in order to graduate on time. The advisor has the fiduciary responsibility to maintain the confidentiality of such data but is not the owner of the data.

Incomplete contracts, ownership, and residual responsibilities

There is a theoretical basis for assigning ownership of an asset to the party responsible for handling all unanticipated issues facing an asset. This is the "theory of incomplete contracts." Participants in a transaction can generally not write a contract that anticipates all eventualities and responses appropriate to each of these eventualities. Contracts are therefore necessarily incomplete and it is useful to develop a mechanism that deals with unanticipated issues as they occur.

Economists Sanford Grossman and Oliver Hart developed the idea of "residual rights of control" as a possible mechanism to deal with these gaps. A residual right of control is the right to use an asset as desired, except in the ways in which usage rights have been explicitly given away in a contract. Grossman and Hart suggest that ownership is synonymous with residual rights of control.

The theory of incomplete contracts is used to suggest that ownership (i.e., residual rights) should be assigned to the party whose effort makes the greatest impact on the productivity of an asset. This is because residual rights powerfully motivate parties to invest in improving the productivity of an asset.

What about security responsibilities? The theory of incomplete contracts suggests that the party responsible for making the residual investments necessary to keep an asset useful to the organization should also be assigned ownership of the asset. This will motivate the party to make the right investments in the asset, including information security investments.

The IT organization can be seen as the provider of all unanticipated IT support services within an organization. As such, the determination of the ownership of an asset should require IT involvement in the planning stages of all projects requiring IT operational support. This participation leads to a document known as a *Service Level Agreement* or *SLA. The SLA is the document that delineates what and how IT will deliver and manage the expectations of the customer or system owner.*

References

Grossman, S.J. and Hart, O.D. "The costs and benefits of ownership: a theory of vertical and lateral integration," *The Journal of Political Economy*, 1986, 94(4): 691–719.

Hart, O.D. "Incomplete contracts and the theory of the firm," *Journal of Law, Economics and Organization*, 1988, 4(1): 119–139.

With this background, we can update our asset characterization table to include ownership and responsibilities as given in Table 5.4.

Table 5.4 Asset characterization, ownership, and responsibilities

Asset	Type	Sensitivity	Criticality	Owner	Responsibilities
Faculty Laptop	Hardware	Restricted	Required	Faculty	Deployment – IT; Backup – IT; Patching – Faculty
Student Grades	Informational	Restricted	Essential	RegistrarFinancial AidController's Office	IT
Security Analyst Position	Personnel	Restricted	Required	IT	IT
Microsoft Office Suite	Software	Unrestricted	Deferrable	End User	IT
Microsoft Office License	Legal	Unrestricted	Required	IT	IT

Example case – Stuxnet

The nuclear enrichment facility at Natanz is one of Iran's most critical and sensitive assets. Approximately 5,000 centrifuges work to enrich uranium to weapons grade so the country can develop a nuclear bomb on its own. Alongside these centrifuges are computers used to monitor and control these centrifuges.

Many countries, including the United States, are concerned about Iran's program. After considering all available options, these countries identified the computers controlling the centrifuges as the best assets to leverage to slow down Iran's progress. The result was a sophisticated computer worm, widely known as "Stuxnet." At the peak of its effectiveness, Stuxnet is reported to have taken out 1,000 of the 5,000 centrifuges operating at Natanz, setting back Iran by an estimated 18 months.

Stuxnet was designed to spread from one target machine to another automatically, do its job, and destroy itself, leaving no trace behind. However, the targeted computers were heavily guarded. For added protection, they were not physically connected to the Internet, meaning no Internet-based attack could reach the facility. From the perspective of the attackers, however, the people working at the facility were very useful assets. If one person could be persuaded to carry an infected USB thumb drive to the facility, the worm could begin doing its job. We can only presume that this is exactly what happened.

Stuxnet is now considered the world's first "weaponized" computer worm.

REFERENCES

Sanger, D.E. "Obama order sped up wave of cyberattacks against Iran," New York Times, June 1, 2012.

Ed Barnes, "Mystery surrounds cyber missile that crippled Iran's nuclear weapons ambitions," Fox News, November 26, 2010, http://www.foxnews.com/tech/2010/11/26/secret-agent-crippled-irans-nuclear-ambitions/ (accessed 2/4/2013).

SUMMARY

In this chapter, we looked at the identification and characterization of IT assets in an organization. Assets may be general or idiosyncratic and identification requires close attention to the unique needs of the organization and the IT resources necessary for the organization to succeed in its mission. Identified assets are characterized in order to gather all information necessary to protect the assets in times of war and peace. Characterization involves classifying assets by sensitivity and criticality. Individual responsibilities must be assigned for all known and unknown information security issues that may arise during the use of the asset.

CHAPTER REVIEW QUESTIONS

1. What is an asset from the perspective of an information security professional?

2. While identifying assets, why is it important to start by identifying what is important to the organization?

3. What are the two common ways of finding out what is important to an organization?

4. What are general assets? Idiosyncratic assets? How are they different in terms of the effort required to identify them correctly?

5. What is a checklist? Why are checklists useful in business in general?[18] Why are they not so useful for asset identification?

6. What is the purpose of the Mission Statement? The Vision Statement? How are they different?

7. What is an information asset? Provide some examples.

8. What is a personnel asset? Provide some examples.

9. What is a hardware asset? Provide some examples.

10. What is a software asset? Provide some examples.

11. What is a legal asset? Provide some examples.

12. What are some important items of information tracked for hardware assets? What is the goal of such tracking?

13. What is asset characterization? Why is it useful?

14. What is asset sensitivity? What are the different classes of sensitivity commonly used to characterize assets?

15. What is asset criticality? What are the different classes of criticality commonly used to characterize assets?

16. What is the IT asset life cycle? What are the stages in the life cycle?

17. What are the information security concerns during the "plan" stage of the IT asset life cycle?

18. What are the information security concerns during the "acquire" stage of the IT asset life cycle?

19. What are the information security concerns during the "deploy" stage of the IT asset life cycle?

20. What are the information security concerns during the "manage" stage of the IT asset life cycle?

21. What are the information security concerns during the "retire" stage of the IT asset life cycle?

22. What is system profiling? How does it affect information security?

23. Who is the owner of an asset?

24. What is operational responsibility for an asset?

25. Provide an example of a situation where the owner of an asset may not have operational responsibilities for the asset.

EXAMPLE CASE QUESTIONS

1. What assets were targeted by Stuxnet and the team behind the worm?

2. Classify each of these assets using the asset classification scheme developed in this chapter.

3. Based on the information in the articles referenced in the case, Iran seems to have taken great care to identify and protect its assets at Natanz. What additional precautions could it have taken?

---

[18] A highly recommended website and book on the topic: http://gawande.com/the-checklist-manifesto

HANDS-ON ACTIVITY – COURSE ASSET IDENTIFICATION

In this section, we will use you as a student in this class. Submit your responses to the numbered items.

Determine goal

1. What is your goal for this class? It could be as simple as "getting a passing grade" or more strict, "pass this class with an A."

External forces shaping your goal

2. Are there any outside restrictions that may be shaping your goal for this class? For instance,

   - Do you have a scholarship that requires that you keep a certain GPA? These are very similar to the laws and regulations many organizations must comply with in order to do business.

   - Are your parents helping you pay for college and ask that you do not drop any classes? Your parents are like the shareholders of a company, making sure you perform at a certain target level.

   - Do you have to take this class and pass it this semester so that you can graduate within a certain time frame?

Discuss/discover assets with classmates

Much like discussing your job with others at work, talking to your fellow students may bring to light assets you had not thought about.

3. What assets can you think of that contribute to your goal? Here are some examples:

   - A laptop

   - A ride you get to class every day

   - This textbook

   - Your professor

   Try to think outside the box and come up with things that you would not normally consider off the top of your head.

Classifying the assets

4. Classify your assets as information, personnel, hardware, software, or legal.

Record each asset sensitivity and criticality

5. How sensitive are your assets? Some factors to consider include:

   - Is there a risk if someone else looks at it?

   - Are you being graded on this hands-on assignment?

   - What happens if someone copies your answers and turns it in?

   - What is the impact to your grades if you lose the assignment and cannot turn it in on time?

   - What happens if you miss your ride to class on a quiz day?

   Try to anticipate the worst-case scenario while considering these or similar issues.

Determine ownership of the assets and assign custodianship

6. Are you the owner and the custodian of your listed assets? Or are you, for instance, borrowing your laptop from someone else? Does the fact that you are not the "owner" of your professor affect your goal in any manner?

Pick three assets and describe life cycles

7. Take your textbook, for instance. How much planning did it involve? Did you have the opportunity to buy a used copy? Did you buy laptop for this class? Will you sell it after the class is done?

8. In the context of this class, what is your professor's life cycle?

CRITICAL THINKING EXERCISE – USES OF A HACKED PC

We have seen in this chapter that attackers are always looking for ways to obtain control of a computer connected to the Internet. Brian Krebs, author of the popular information security blog, krebsonsecurity, has plotted the possible uses of a compromised PC[19] (Figure 5.5).

---

[19] http://krebsonsecurity.com/wp-content/uploads/2012/07/valueofhackedpc.png

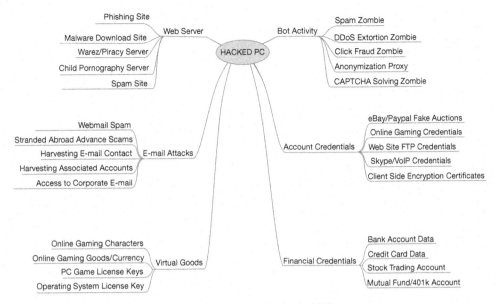

FIGURE 5.5   Uses of a hacked PC

Critical thinking questions

1. If your PC were compromised, provide a brief description of how your PC could be used by an attacker to perform any three of the above activities.

DESIGN CASE

For this chapter's security design case, we head back to Sunshine University used in Chapters 1 and 2. If you recall on Chapter 2, the dean of students asked that we put together a preliminary comparison between maintaining the email service for the students' in-house, use a IaaS cloud provider to support the hardware, or use a SaaS solution and totally outsource the service. That comparison was primarily made on the basis of availability of services and a quick look at services offered.

Now that we took a closer look at assets one thing you can clearly see is that there will be a huge difference in the assets needed to support each option. And these assets are not only limited to hardware assets. They also include the potential creation of new information assets such as calendars and documents. Will these support the goals of the university?

For the purposes of this design, consider the following assets:

- Student Email Data

- Email Server Software

- Email Server Hardware

- External Storage

- Server Hardware Maintenance Agreement

- Email Server Software Maintenance and Technical Support Agreement

- 20 work-hours a week from an Administrator for Server Support

A description of the equipment supporting email for students can be found on the IS design case at the end of Chapter 2. Assume:

- The hardware is fully owned by the Student Services department.

- Sendmail, the email software, was purchased as the application that handles incoming and outgoing email. It has a yearly contract that covers maintenance upgrades, patches, and technical support.

- IaaS solutions are usually priced using two parameters: (1) the amount of network bandwidth used by the system and (2) the amount of storage used by the system.

- Student email is deleted 7 days after they graduate.

DESIGN CASE QUESTIONS

You are required to turn in a new report. In your report, include the following items. A template for listing the assets is shown below:

1. Classify existing assets supporting local email in terms of informational, personnel, software, hardware, or financial asset.

Asset	Class	Sensitivity	Criticality	Local	IaaS	SaaS
Student Email Data	Informational			x	x	x
Email Software						
Server Hardware						
External Storage						
Hardware Maintenance Agreement						
Email Software Technical Support Agreement						
Personnel Hours per Week				20		

2. Can you determine the "primary" asset in your list? Which asset is central to the system, with all other assets supporting its existence?

3. What stage of the IT life cycle is the email server? What type of asset will be needed if a decision is made to keep email on-site?

4. Determine and indicate in the report which of these assets would not be required if student email is moved to an IaaS solution. Repeat the same exercise for the SaaS solution. Are local backup copies of the email data feasible with the IaaS/SaaS solutions? Why? Consider the cost impacts.

5. Will there be a learning curve with the adoption of a new off-site email system?

6. Determine and indicate in the report any other "hidden" assets that are needed to support the current, on-site configuration. How will these assets change by moving to an off-site solution? Examples include the following

   a. If you have a problem with your email account at your university, who do you call first?

   b. How does an email "leave" the sender and "arrive" at the recipient?

   c. If a student accidently deletes their entire Inbox, how is it recovered?

7. Classify each asset according to your view on their sensitivity and criticality. Justify.

8. Are there differences in criticality between the mailboxes of different students?

9. Discuss in the report the possible timing of a switch to an off-site solution.

Threats and Vulnerabilities

## CHAPTER 6

Overview

After the initial chapters that provided an overview of the risk landscape, in Chapter 4, we took an initial look at the components of the information security landscape – assets, threats, vulnerabilities, and controls. We then began a deeper look at these components. In Chapter 5, we looked at assets, including asset types, their classifications, and characterizations.

In this chapter, we will take a close look at threats. At the end of this chapter, you should have a clear understanding of the different aspects of threats including:

- Threat models, integrating the components of a threat
- The forces that could act upon an asset (agents)
- The methods by which these agents could affect an asset (actions)
- Vulnerabilities and their relevance to threats

Introduction

We have defined threats as the *capabilities, intentions, and attack methods of adversaries to exploit or cause harm to assets.* This is consistent with the NIST 800-30 definition of a threat as "any circumstance or event with the potential to adversely impact organizational operations and assets, individuals, other organizations or the nation through an information system via unauthorized access, destruction, disclosure or modification of information, and/ or denial of service."[1] Once the organization has identified and characterized its assets, the next step in the analysis of its information security requirements is an analysis of the threats faced by the organization. We saw in the last chapter how many of our daily actions revolve around the availability of assets, and how we take those assets for granted. What happens if access to these assets suddenly goes away?

As an information security analyst, you will routinely be asked to estimate the importance of emerging threats. Is the fact that Microsoft just found out that Internet Explorer is vulnerable to cross-site scripting attacks a serious-enough threat that all computers in the organization must be forced to upgrade within the next 24 hours? This is analogous to the estimation that Florida residents like us have to make every time we read about a hurricane developing in the Atlantic – is the threat this time serious enough that we should finally buy a generator in case the power fails for an extended period?

---

[1] http://csrc.nist.gov/publications/nistpubs/800-30-rev1/sp800_30_r1.pdf. While the NIST definition is more comprehensive, we believe our definition is more memorable and captures the essential elements of a threat.

Threat models

Threats arise from motivated people (agents) taking specific actions to exploit assets. *The interactions between relevant agents, actions, and assets constitute the threat model facing an organization.* This is represented in Figure 6.1. In the rest of this chapter, we use part of the VERIS[2] incident classification model, the piece dealing with threat, as the basis for discussion. While some of the specific agents and actions discussed in this chapter are based on VERIS, the idea of threats being the actions of agents on assets is quite generic. We have already discussed assets. In this chapter, we focus on the remaining components of a threat – agents and actions.

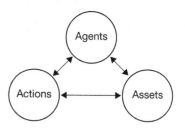

FIGURE 6.1   Threat model

Sidebar – Microsoft STRIDE threat model[3]

VERIS is one of many threat models that can help classify a threat. Another model is the Microsoft STRIDE model, named after the six classes it uses to categorize a particular threat.

$\underline{S}$poofing an identity. An example of identity spoofing is illegally accessing and then using another user's authentication information, such as username and password.

$\underline{T}$ampering with data. Data tampering involves the malicious modification of data. Examples include unauthorized changes made to persistent data such as that held in a database or alteration of data as it flows between two computers over an open network such as the Internet.

$\underline{R}$epudiation. Repudiation threats are associated with users who deny performing an action without other parties having any way to prove otherwise – for example, a user performs an illegal operation in a system that lacks the ability to trace the prohibited operations. Non-repudiation refers to the ability of a system to counter repudiation threats. For example, a user who purchases an item might have to sign for the item upon receipt. The vendor can then use the signed receipt as evidence that the user did receive the package.

$\underline{I}$nformation disclosure. Information disclosure threats involve the exposure of information to individuals who are not supposed to have access to it – for example, the ability of users to read a file that they were not granted access to, or the ability of an intruder to read data in transit between two computers.

$\underline{D}$enial of service. A Denial of Service (DoS) attack forces the system under attack to reject service to valid users – for example, by making a Web server temporarily unavailable or unusable. You must protect against certain types of DoS threats simply to improve system availability and reliability.

$\underline{E}$levation of privilege. In this type of threat, an unprivileged user gains privileged access and thereby has sufficient access to compromise or destroy the entire system. Elevation of privilege threat includes those situations in which an attacker has effectively penetrated all system defenses and become part of the trusted system itself, a dangerous situation indeed.

---

[2] VERIS ≡ Verizon enterprise risk and incident sharing metrics framework. The VERIS model also includes a fourth element – attribute, which describes how the asset was affected. Outcome of threats are studied as part of risk analysis and are covered in the chapter on risk management

[3] The STRIDE Threat Model – Microsoft Corporation: Software (n.d.). Retrieved from http://msdn.microsoft.com/en-US/library/ee823878(v = CS.20).aspx

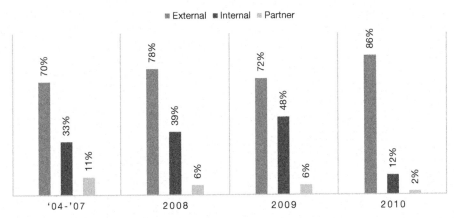

THREAT AGENTS OVER TIME BY PERCENT OF BREACHES

■ External ■ Internal ▫ Partner

FIGURE 6.2   Threat agents over time by percent of breaches

The VERIS model is more general, allowing any threat including threats not yet discovered, to be modeled within the framework. It is also aligned with the academic literature on the topic as well as with standard risk models we consider later in the book. Hence our use of the VERIS threat model.

Threat agent

A threat agent is the individual, organization, or group that originates a particular threat action. Threat agents can be classified into three different types, each with different motivations, to initiate a threat:

- External agents
- Internal agents
- Partners

Figure 6.2 shows how the relative frequencies of the different threat agents classified by the VERIS system have evolved since 2004.[4] It is clear that the number of internal attacks has reduced considerably since 2009 while external threat agents have increased during the same period.

External agents

As the name suggests, external agents are agents outside the organization, with no link to the organization itself. According to the VERIS 2012 Data Breach Report,[5] 98% of the attacks in 2012 originated from an external agent. We look at the important external agents below. A quick list is given in Figures 6.3.

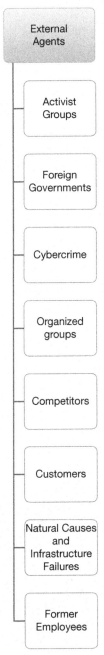

FIGURE 6.3
External agents

---

[4]The numbers do not add up to 100 since many incidents have more than one agent type involved
[5]http://www.verizonbusiness.com/resources/reports/rp_data-breach-investigations-report-2012_en_xg.pdf

Activist groups

The Anonymous group has become popular in the last few years as a *"hacktivist"* organization, groups that mix political activism with hacking activities. A loosely formed group composed of hackers and other Internet enthusiasts, Anonymous members portray themselves as individuals who oppose all types of perceived oppression, Internet censorship, and surveillance by government agencies around the world. A brief listing of their latest exploits is included here.

Recent Anonymous exploits

August 2012: A group associated with Anonymous brought down several government sites in Uganda. This was done in protest to pending bills considered oppressive to members of the gay and lesbian communities in that country. They left the following message: "Anonymous will continue to target Ugandan government sites and communications until the government of Uganda treats all people including LGBT people equally."

September 2012: Anonymous claimed responsibility for taking down the GoDaddy Domain Name Servers, which affected many businesses, from small community websites to larger companies such as JHill's Staffing Services, a recruitment & career consulting firm.

October 2012: Anonymous threatens to go after targets in Sweden in retaliation to the raiding of the ISP web host PRQ, which hosted *The Pirate Bay* and the *Wikileaks* site.

Foreign governments

According to a report issued by the Office of the National Counterintelligence Executive in October 2011,[6] "sensitive US economic information and technology are targeted by intelligence services, private sector companies, academic and research institutions, and citizens of dozens of countries." One well-publicized incident involved the suspected theft of the designs of military aircraft (Figures 6.4a and 6.4b).

FIGURE 6.4A   Chinese J-20 jet

Color China Photo/ChinaOut/Associated Press

FIGURE 6.4B   Lockheed F-22 jet

© Michael Ainsworth/Dallas MorningNews/Corbis

---

[6]http://www.ncix.gov/publications/reports/fecie_all/Foreign_Economic_Collection_2011.pdf

According to the report, China is at the top of the list, with Chinese hackers attacking US private sector firms repeatedly. Russia's intelligence service also actively conducts cyber espionage against US targets to collect economic and technology information.

Mandiant report on APTs from China's PLA

On February 18, 2013, security analyst firm Mandiant released a report identifying a unit of the Chinese People's Liberation Army (PLA) it calls APT1, to be the source of some of the most damaging cyber-attacks on US government and corporate networks. Mandiant's investigations suggest that APT1 has operated since at least 2006 and has targeted a wide array of targets.

At the time of the report, Mandiant had analyzed APT1's intrusions against nearly 150 victims. Mandiant was able to confirm that APT1 was located in Shanghai and could recognize various elements of its tools, tactics, and procedures. The report revealed three identities within APT1 in order to convince readers that APT1 was populated by people, and was not a bot-network. Mandiant believes that these identities are soldiers, simply following orders given to them by superiors.

The existence of the organization for over 7 years suggests to Mandiant that APT1 is a government-sponsored entity, sustained by direct government support. Further investigations suggest that PLA Unit 61398 could be APT1, given the similarities between APT1 and unit 61398 and their locations. Mandiant reports that APT1 is likely to be housed in a 130,663 square foot 12-story high facility built in 2007.

Mandiant has identified 141 companies in 20 major industries that have been compromised by APT1. APT1 steals large volumes of valuable intellectual property from the companies it compromises, tracking the companies' network over several years. The average duration of an attack was 356 days, with the longest observed attack lasting 1,764 days, or 4 years and 10 months. APT1's focus seems to be to steal intellectual property, including technology blueprints, manufacturing processes, and business plans. In one case, Mandiant has observed APT1 stealing 6.5 terabytes of compressed data from a single organization over a 10-month time period. APT1's targets are companies in industries identified by China as strategic to their growth.

APT1 requires that its personnel be trained in computer security and be proficient in English. It recruits heavily from the Science and Engineering departments of universities such as Harbin Institute of Technology and Zhejiang University School of Computer Science and Technology.

But that's not all. Even US allies and partners use their access to US institutions to access information using a multitude of threat actions. Loss estimates from economic espionage range so widely as to be meaningless – $2-400 billion or more a year.

Industrial espionage

In December 2010, David Yen Lee was sentenced to 15 months in jail and ordered to pay more than $30,000 in restitution to Valspar, a maker of paints and industrial coatings. After returning from a trip to China, Lee, former technical director of new product development for Valspar's architectural group, quit the company. When Valspar workers examined the company laptop computer and BlackBerry device he turned in when he resigned they noticed traces of activities that suggested Lee was trying to cover his tracks on laptop usage. Closer examination unveiled Valspar trade secrets downloaded to the laptop.

Government involvement is widespread and not limited to attacks against the United States. The US government is involved in cyberwarfare as well. The New York Times[7] claims that President Obama secretly ordered increased cyber-attacks against the computer infrastructure of Iranian nuclear facilities weeks after he assumed office. The same article alleges that US and Israel were involved in the deployment of Stuxnet, which temporarily took out 20% of the centrifuges operating in Iranian facilities.

DARPA's PLAN X

In 1958, the Defense Advanced Research Projects Agency (DARPA) was established to prevent strategic surprise from negatively impacting US national security and create strategic surprise for US adversaries by maintaining the technological superiority of the US military. Recently, DARPA released information on the start of "Plan X." According to the agency, it seeks innovative research in four key areas, in support of Plan X. This is something many of you may like to follow as these guidelines can impact hiring plans for many military establishments and defense contractors:

Understanding the cyber battlespace: This area focuses on developing automated analysis techniques to assist human operators in planning cyber operations. Specifically, analyzing large-scale logical network topology characteristics of nodes (i.e., edge count, dynamic vs. static links, usage) and edges (i.e., latency, bandwidth, and periodicity).

Automatically constructing verifiable and quantifiable cyber operations: This area focuses on developing high-level mission plans and automatically synthesizing a mission script that is executed through a human-on-the-loop interface, similar to the autopilot function in modern aircraft. This process will leverage formal methods to quantify the potential battle damage from each synthesized mission plan.

Developing operating systems and platforms designed to operate in dynamic, contested, and hostile network environments: This area focuses on building hardened "battle units" that can perform cyberwarfare functions such as battle damage monitoring, communication relay, weapon deployment, and adaptive defense.

Visualizing and interacting with large-scale cyber battlespaces: This area focuses on developing intuitive views and overall user experience. Coordinated views of the cyber battlespace will provide cyberwarfare functions of planning, operation, situational awareness, and war gaming.

Cybercrime

In the late 1990s, when the commercial Internet was in its infancy, hackers were primarily "script kiddies:" usually a teenager who found an exploit script somewhere and decided to deface a web page just to show that the hacker was capable of modifying a website. Many of these scripts recklessly destroyed data on affected machines simply as proofs of concept.

Somewhere down the line, the script kiddies got smart. Why destroy machines when you can make money out of the user of that machine? Why replace a web page when you can sit at home and monitor all activity until you see something you like? Enter what we now call cybercrime. Cybercrime is an incredibly lucrative business, offering a higher profit with a lower probability of being identified and prosecuted than traditional crime such as bank robberies.

---

[7]http://www.nytimes.com/2012/06/01/world/middleeast/obama-ordered-wave-of-cyberattacks-against-iran.html

One popular cybercrime threat agents are the hackers involved with the Nigerian Scam, also known as the "419 Nigerian Scam" referring to an article in the Nigerian Criminal Code dealing with fraud. What follows is a sample email.

LAGOS, NIGERIA.

ATTENTION: THE PRESIDENT/CEO

DEAR SIR,

CONFIDENTIAL BUSINESS PROPOSAL

HAVING CONSULTED WITH MY COLLEAGUES AND BASED ON THE INFORMATION GATHERED FROM THE NIGERIAN CHAMBERS OF COMMERCE AND INDUSTRY, I HAVE THE PRIVILEGE TO REQUEST FOR YOUR ASSISTANCE TO TRANSFER THE SUM OF $47,500,000.00 (FORTY SEVEN MILLION, FIVE HUNDRED THOUSAND UNITED STATES DOLLARS) INTO YOUR ACCOUNTS. THE ABOVE SUM RESULTED FROM AN OVER-INVOICED CONTRACT, EXECUTED COMMISSIONED AND PAID FOR ABOUT FIVE YEARS (5) AGO BY A FOREIGN CONTRACTOR. THIS ACTION WAS HOWEVER INTENTIONAL AND SINCE THEN THE FUND HAS BEEN IN A SUSPENSE ACCOUNT AT THE CENTRAL BANK OF NIGERIA APEX BANK.

WE ARE NOW READY TO TRANSFER THE FUND OVERSEAS AND THAT IS WHERE YOU COME IN. IT IS IMPORTANT TO INFORM YOU THAT AS CIVIL SERVANTS, WE ARE FORBIDDEN TO OPERATE A FOREIGN ACCOUNT; THAT IS WHY WE REQUIRE YOUR ASSISTANCE. THE TOTAL SUM WILL BE SHARED AS FOLLOWS: 70% FOR US, 25% FOR YOU AND 5% FOR LOCAL AND INTERNATIONAL EXPENSES INCIDENT TO THE TRANSFER.

THE TRANSFER IS RISK FREE ON BOTH SIDES. I AM AN ACCOUNTANT WITH THE NIGERIAN NATIONAL PETROLEUM CORPORATION (NNPC). IF YOU FIND THIS PROPOSAL ACCEPTABLE, WE SHALL REQUIRE THE FOLLOWING DOCUMENTS:

(A) YOUR BANKER'S NAME, TELEPHONE, ACCOUNT AND FAX NUMBERS.

(B) YOUR PRIVATE TELEPHONE AND FAX NUMBERS – FOR CONFIDENTIALITY AND EASY COMMUNICATION.

(C) YOUR LETTER-HEADED PAPER STAMPED AND SIGNED.

ALTERNATIVELY WE WILL FURNISH YOU WITH THE TEXT OF WHAT TO TYPE INTO YOUR LETTER-HEADED PAPER, ALONG WITH A BREAKDOWN EXPLAINING, COMPREHENSIVELY WHAT WE REQUIRE OF YOU. THE BUSINESS WILL TAKE US THIRTY (30) WORKING DAYS TO ACCOMPLISH.

PLEASE REPLY URGENTLY.

BEST REGARDS

Thousands of emails would be sent out at a time. Inevitably, the fraudsters would receive a couple of responses.

In Nigeria, cyber cafes dedicate a number of their systems specifically to individuals intending to engage in fraudulent activities. They are known as "Yahoo Boys," after the fact that these users create phony yahoo accounts to use for their schemes.

Government efforts to prevent financial cybercrime continue. In Nigeria, notices are pasted on walls of cafe owners, warning users of possible arrests for scammers who send fraudulent emails. But, generally speaking, users are learning to pay attention to the adage: "if it sounds too good to be true, it probably is."

Defining cybercrime in the Philippines

A new cybercrime law in the Philippines that could see people jailed for 12 years is generating outrage among citizens and rights groups. The stated aim of the wide-ranging law is to tackle a multiplicity of online crimes, including pornography, hacking, identity theft, and spamming. It is the politician's response to police complaints stating they did not have the legal tools needed to follow up on complaints.

The problem is that this new law also includes a provision that puts the country's criminal libel law into force. Users posting comments online that would later be considered libelous by the courts would face a maximum prison sentence of 12 years and a sanction of $24,000. This in comparison with printed media libel fines of half of that amount and a prison term of 4 years.

And that's not all. The Cybercrime Act would allow law enforcement agencies in the Philippines to collect data and monitor all cyber communications without a warrant.

Organized groups

Some threats require the cooperation of multiple agents acting together. The organization of certain cybercrime groups is remarkable. For instance, websites exist that coordinate the sale and purchase of restricted information such as credit cards, social security numbers, bank account info, and more. These sites usually employ a large number of individuals, each with their own job duties.

- Admins: Run the escrow service and control membership

- Global Moderators: Supervise content and arbitrate any disputes

- Moderators: Monitor individual topic areas

- Reviewers: Evaluate quality of vendor products

- Vendors: Have permission to sell goods and services to forum members

- Members (fraudsters): Purchase the goods

In order to become a vendor you have to provide a set of credit card numbers to a reviewer. This person goes out and makes purchases using those numbers. If the cards are mostly valid, you are accepted as a vendor (Figure 6.5). Below is an example of a vendor being rated:

> *Review Results: Zo0mer's dumps. Within 24hrs, I received a total of 50 dumps. . . . 41 accepted, 9 declined – however he will replace declines if notified within 48hrs I also done a store test on 4 cards . . . 3 was accepted £500, £1.2K and £1.8K, US card decline Product: 9/10 Service 9.5/10*

One example of such site was CarderPlanet. CarderPlanet was a criminal organization founded in 2001. It operated and maintained the website www.carderplanet.com for its criminal activities. By August 2004, the site had attracted more than 7,000 members. Although most of the postings on the forum were in Russian, and most of the CarderPlanet members were from Eastern Europe and Russia, the forum had a significant English-speaking component.[8]

The organization was set up in a manner similar to the mafia with the highest ranking members, or "the family," having titles such as the Godfather and "capo di capi" (or boss of all bosses). It was shutdown in 2004 after the arrest of some of its senior members. According to the US Secret Service, "the network created by the founders of CarderPlanet . . . remains one of the most sophisticated organizations of online financial criminals in the world. This network has been repeatedly linked to nearly every significant intrusion of financial information reported to the international law enforcement community."[9]

Competitors

Competitors are always interested in gaining advantage over the competition. This is true not only in private industry but also in politics. In 2003, internal memos from Democrat minority leaders were distributed to GOP-friendly media. "At first, the Republican majority denied any G.O.P. complicity after the memos were leaked and published. The documents detailed how Democratic senators had strategized and consulted outside interest groups dedicated to opposing some of President Bush's more conservative judicial nominees. But after the police moved in last week, Senator Orrin Hatch, the Utah Republican who is the Judiciary Committee's chairman, reversed himself and announced that he had been 'shocked' to find out that it was a member of his own staff who had hacked into the minority's computer files."[10]

Customers

Customers can easily be agents as well, internal or external, depending on where you draw the boundaries of your service. With the Student Information System, for instance, IT has the student users as well as the administrators of the different modules of the SIS application: Financial Aid, Accounts Payable, Financial Aid, etc. These are normally known as "Functional Users." As customers, these users at times also require functionality and privileges that, while

---

[8]CarderPlanet also posted elaborate advertisements that now can be found copied on the F-Secure website:
- http://www.f-secure.com/weblog/archives/planet.swf
- http://www.f-secure.com/weblog/archives/carderplanet.swf
- http://www.f-secure.com/weblog/archives/555.swf

[9]http://www.fbi.gov/atlanta/press-releases/2010/at081110.htm

[10]http://www.nytimes.com/2003/12/05/opinion/partisan-hacking-in-congress.html

could make their job easier, could also put the University at risk. Someone from Financial Aid, for instance, with access to student Social Security Numbers, could feel tempted to sell a list of those in the hacker market.

Natural causes and infrastructure failures

In the United States we have wild fires and earthquakes in the west. Tornadoes in the Midwest. Hurricanes and flash floods on the East Coast and along the Gulf States. Practically no area of the country is 100% safe. And you still have the human intervention: leaky pipes, accidental building fires, etc. All of these are external, natural disasters that could affect a business' IT infrastructure. When the IT infrastructure fails the financial damage can be considerable. That's what happened with Sears in 2013. ". . . the five-hour failure, in the rush just after the holidays, cost Sears $1.58 million in profit, according to the lawsuit. (Sears did $12.3 billion in sales during the fourth quarter but lost $489 million.) The server farm ran on generators for eight days, burning through $189,000 in diesel fuel."[11]

Former employees

Disgruntled employees are a particularly dangerous type of agent, since they oftentimes have insight on the internal workings of the company, and they are capable of using internally known vulnerabilities to gain access and damage the business.

In May 2013, a criminal complaint was unsealed on Thursday in federal court in the Eastern District of New York charging Michael Meneses – who was arrested earlier that day in Smithtown, Long Island – with hacking into the computer network of a company that manufactures high-voltage power supplies, causing the company over $90,000 in damage. "He employed various high-tech methods to hack into the victim company's network and steal his former colleagues' security credentials, including writing a program that captured user log-in names and passwords. He then used the security credentials of at least one former colleague to remotely access the network via a virtual private network (VPN) from his home and from a hotel located near his new employer, corrupting the network."[12]

Internal agents

Internal agents are people linked to the organization, often as employees. They include your expected agents, the sys admins, the Help Desk assistants, the software developers. But other unexpected individuals such as janitorial staff can also be threat agents (Figure 6.5).

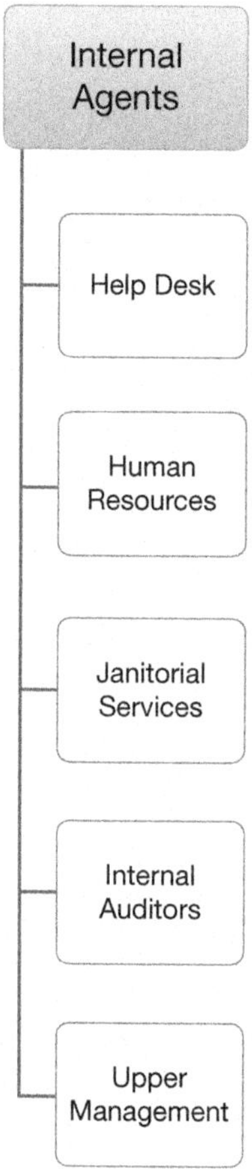

Help Desk

Help Desk employees may be assigned certain privileges that, either through error or misuse, could affect the operations of a company. It is not uncommon to allow Help Desk employees the ability to change passwords for users, after checking their identities. This privilege opens the door for potential bribery and blackmail of the employee, especially when the activity goes unchecked.

Internal Agents

Help Desk

Human Resources

Janitorial Services

Internal Auditors

Upper Management

FIGURE 6.5
Internal agents

---

[11] http://www.chicagobusiness.com/article/20130604/BLOGS11/130609948/the-price-of-failure-data-center-power-outage-cost-sears-2-2m-in-profit#ixzz2X4M39BKI

[12] http://www.net-security.org/secworld.php?id = 14861

Human resources

The hiring and termination of personnel in an organization, normally handled by the HR department, kicks off a number of activities potentially including the assignment and removal of privileges in IT systems. These actions are usually known as onboarding and offboarding. If these are performed automatically, the consequences could be disastrous.

In 2005 a small community bank in the State of Florida had to retrieve all of its employees' emails from backup tapes after an entry error in the HR system laid off all of its employees and all their email accounts were deprovisioned.

Janitorial services

Server rooms and datacenters are normally off limits to anyone without a need to be there. However, not all servers go in server rooms. It is not uncommon in an University environment to have servers in common offices, without physical protection or redundancy.

Back in 2003 a helpful janitor at the University of South Florida, after noticing that a particular office was a bit dirty, decided to vacuum the room. He unplugged the UPS to plug in the vacuum cleaner and neglected to plug it back in when he was done. The UPS ran out of power and the College was left without email until the next day, when the local administrator came back into the office.

Internal auditors

Auditors come in a variety of different flavors. Some are willing to work with administrators and understand different priorities, resource allocation, and how IT processes fit in the overall mission of the organization. Others are simply interested in pointing out the perceived failures of the IT department. Some are fully prepared to discuss database schemas and network routing, as well as cash collection and financial aid. Some in the industry consider auditor to be the consummate generalist, the proverbial Jack of all trades, but not necessarily the master of any.

The primary concern of auditors is compliance. IT systems must be compliant with local, state, and federal laws. They also must ensure that all official policies and procedures adopted by the organization are followed. With that in mind, it is necessary to emphasize that compliance is different from security. And it is this difference that at times may turn an auditor into a threat agent.

For instance, assume your organization has a policy stating, "all employee ID numbers will be encrypted when stored electronically." IDs are stored on a database server, which, for the sake of argument, is only turned on when data is needed. The server is inside an access-controlled facility, and you are the only person with access to the box. From your perspective, the risk of a leak or data loss is extremely small. However, as we will see in future chapters, regulatory compliance, federal and state laws established with the intent to protect users' privacy, are often single minded in their purpose and do not consider the overall system security as a whole, instead focusing simply on the piece it needs to protect. Therefore, any auditor, internal or external, will insist that the data still must be encrypted or the policy amended if the organization is assuming the risk. Even if your organization will have to spend thousands of dollars in order to encrypt the data.

Auditors may also affect IT operations. In the State of Florida, if your server room is not up to code because power is stringed through the use of extension cords, Fire Marshalls are authorized to disconnect the power immediately, even if critical processes are brought down because of the disconnection.

Upper management

Managers can be considered a threat agent in multiple ways. But perhaps the most threatening would be top management's lack of support for IT in general and lack of understanding of security concerns.

IT systems are ubiquitous to organizations nowadays, and yet people do not realize the dependency that creates. In a university, faculty paychecks, registration, transcripts, and financial aid, all depend on the fact that IT systems are available and operating properly.

Most of IT operates in a world where "no news is good news." While that is nice from the operational point of view, it creates a disconnect with users. It is difficult to justify the expenses associated with purchasing a new server if, from the end user's perspective, services are still being offered with no impact on performance. In the long run, IT's success could potentially create its own downfall if management is not reminded constantly of the business dependency on services IT provides.

New University: Florida Polytechnic

In 2012, Florida State Officials approved the creation of a new accredited State University, Florida Polytechnic, or FPU. FPU was previously part of the University of South Florida System. This decision by the state government of this new entity created challenges for IT, providing an example by which top management decisions create trickle-down problems that could potentially have adverse effects on the overall security of an organization:

Every software license had to be reviewed since computers and servers were now owned by a new University and not the University of South Florida. Failure to do so could result in severe legal issues.

IT personnel had to be reallocated to provide support and move content from the FPU servers to other servers owned by USF, leaving certain areas thinly supported.

While some employees were transferred to the system, many were laid off. This created the perfect potential scenario for a disgruntled employee to become a threat agent by committing fraud.

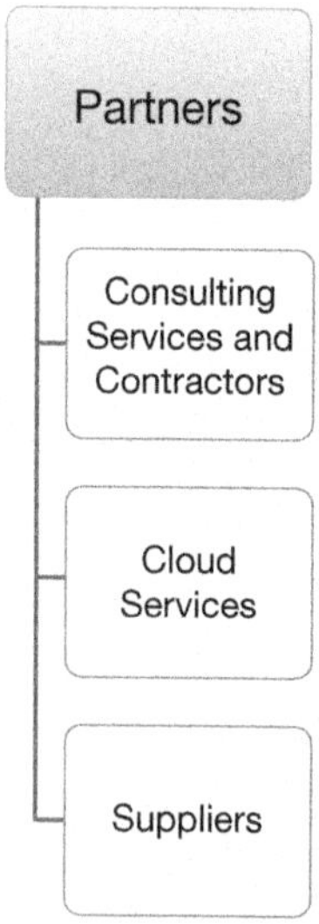

Partners

Partners

Consulting
Services and
Contractors

Partners include any third party sharing a business relationship with the organization. This includes suppliers, vendors, hosting providers, outsourced IT support, etc. Some level of trust and privilege is usually implied between business partners (Figure 6.6).

Consulting services and contractors

Cloud
Services

This category also includes installation services and maintenance services. These are services paid for by an organization in order to perform a specific job or to augment local staff.

Consulting organizations do their best to comply with any special requirements of their clients. However, clients with special needs may get blindsided if an overlooked detail is extremely important to the client. Consider the recent case of the security leak at the National Security Agency (NSA) involving Edward Snowden. Mr. Snowden was an employee of Booz-Allen Hamilton, a contractor that did a lot of technology work for the NSA and other sensitive federal agencies.

Suppliers

FIGURE 6.6
Partners

From June 5 to June 21, 2013, the Guardian newspaper revealed extremely confidential orders permitting the NSA to gather information about US citizens. Lawmakers and the public were surprised by the revelations. Reactions ranged from calling Mr. Snowden a hero for bringing the activity to light, to calling him a traitor for revealing security procedures that have kept America safe. At the time of this writing, his eventual fate is unknown. The US Govt. is working to have him brought to the US for trial (Figure 6.7).

However, from an information security perspective, the incident brought several things to attention. Given the nature of the institution, it is impossible to assert how Mr. Snowden got his data out of the NSA, until it is revealed in a court trial, federal testimony, or other similar outlet. However, it has been speculated that Mr. Snowden used a USB thumb-drive to save his data. Sensitive organizations typically disable these ports on computers to prevent such leakage. So, many experts are surprised at this possibility at the NSA. It is also remarkable how an employee of a partner had access to such sensitive documents.

In the early 2000s, Sun Microsystems was responsible for the installation of several high-performance systems at the University of South Florida. In order to facilitate their work, maintenance engineers from Sun would set up all boxes, including ones set up in other organizations, with the same administrator login and passwords. And to add to the lapse in security, that password was based on a dictionary word.

Cloud services

Cloud services are a very large class of services. NIST[13] lists five essential characteristics of cloud computing: on-demand self-service, broad network access, resource pooling, rapid elasticity or expansion, and measured service. It also lists three "service models" (software, platform, and infrastructure), and four "deployment models" (private, community, public, and hybrid) that together categorize ways to deliver cloud services.

2013 The Guardian/Getty Images

FIGURE 6.7   Edward Snowden

---

[13]http://csrc.nist.gov/publications/PubsSPs.html#800-145

These services were all considered "outsourcing" at one point in time. But since the word outsourcing is linked with people losing their jobs, the industry reinvented itself and was rebranded as services "in the Cloud."

Normally when a company moves some of its services to the cloud there is an assumption of improved redundancy, reliability, with multiple servers hosting failover applications in multiple geographic locations. While that is the case in most situations, it is not always the case. Businesses should never make that assumption. When services are moved, here are a few things to check:

- Does the datacenter have the required security certifications?

- Where are the Center's geographic locations?

- What controls are positioned to protect the data?

It is also crucial to have an exit strategy from the get-go. Establish the methods by which, in an emergency, the data could be moved to another location. A failure in any of these points could move the outsourced service provider from a partner to a threat agent.

Examples of issues with Cloud providers

Dropbox

In July 2011, the cloud data storage company made sweeping changes to its terms and license agreements as a result of an earlier issue involving a software bug in its authentication system. *"By submitting your stuff to the Services, you grant us and those we work with to provide the Services worldwide, non-exclusive, royalty-free, sublicenseable rights to use, copy, distribute, prepare derivative works (such as translations or format conversions) of, perform, or publicly display that stuff to the extent reasonably necessary for the Service."* Dropbox quickly reversed its position once the customers started refusing the agreement and pulling their data back.

Salesforce.com

Salesforce is known for its Customer Relation Management (CRM) software, as well as its cloud offerings: the Sales Cloud, for sales managements, and the Service Cloud, a call center-type service. However, Salesforce does not have its own datacenters. It uses another company, Equinox, and its DR structure to maintain its services.

In July 2012, a brief, one-minute power outage in one of Equinox's Data Center locations in California caused a cascade of problems that eventually took out the entire Salesforce network for nearly 6 hours.

Outsourcing your server room infrastructure is a popular thing to do. It gets the physical worries out of the way and allows organizations to worry about the important part of their business. This is particularly true for news blog sites and certain social media venues.

In October 2012, Hurricane Sandy slammed the East Coast near Atlantic City. Readers woke up the next day disappointed that some of their favorite news sites were brought down, including The Huffington Post and Gawker. These sites used the ISP *Datagram* as their primary platform. Datagram's datacenter was flooded, and fuel lines feeding the generators failed, bringing the entire datacenter down (Figure 6.8).

FIGURE 6.8   Datagram ISP goes down with Hurricane Sandy

Vendors and suppliers

When vendors or suppliers are not able to provide needed resources, or do not exercise proper quality control on devices, or do not properly evaluate the business relationships they maintain, the effect to a business may be considerable.

> In May 2013, Nokia won an injunction against HTC in the Netherlands, related to the sale of HTC One android phone; HTC was apparently using a microphone in the HTC One which is developed by STMicroelectronics, and Nokia apparently has exclusive rights for the use of this microphone in its devices.

Threat action

The agent is the first part of the threat, but until an agent performs some actions to hurt an asset, no threat is created. The action is the activity performed by the agent in order to affect the confidentiality, integrity, or availability of the asset. Creating an exhaustive list of actions is futile since new threat actions are limited only by the ingenuity of the agents. However, most common threat actions may be classified into the following categories:

- Malware

- Hacking

- Social engineering

- Physical

- Error

- Environment

Malware

Malware is short for "malicious software." It is software specifically designed to damage, disrupt, steal, or in general inflict some other "bad" or illegitimate action on computers. Viruses, worms, Trojans, and bots are all examples of malware.

The number of malware in the wild has increased tremendously, going from 1,300 in 1990 to 50,000 in 2000, then to more than 200 million in 2010.

Viruses

Viruses propagate with the use of a "host" file that requires human interaction for it to activate. The infected file itself may reside on a computer's hard drive, but the machine would not be infected until the file is executed. A virus propagates when someone transfers that infected file to a new machine and the file is executed on the new host.

The first piece of code considered to be a virus was created in 1971 by an employee of the so-called BBN, now Raytheon BBN. BBN built packet switching networks for ARPANET, the precursor for the Internet. The software called Creeper was designed as a proof of concept for a self-replicating software. It would jump to from one server to another, installing itself, then removing the previous copy and displaying the message "I am Creeper, catch me if you can" on the screen of the new host.

The Melissa Virus outbreak was the one of the first viruses to impair corporate networks. Melissa was different from other viruses because of the speed with which it spread. It disguised itself as an email with the subject "An Important Message From <someone you know>." The email carried a Microsoft Word document with a macro virus, a virus that would execute automatically when the file was opened.

Machines infected with the Melissa Virus would present a couple of symptoms:

- Unexplained shutdown with the error message shown on Figure 6.9

- Word documents opened while the machine was infected would display quotes from episodes of the TV show "The Simpsons"

- Random files would be selected to be emailed out as the carriers of the virus to 50 users present in the computer's address book.

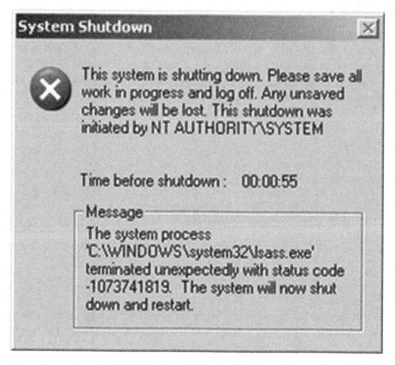

FIGURE 6.9   Melissa error message

Besides the end user–centered problems, Melissa caused severe problems to the email infrastructure of corporations due to the load infected machines imposed on email servers. The author of Melissa virus was caught and sentenced to 20 months in prison and $5,000 in fines.

Worms

While infection and propagation of viruses depends on human intervention, worms use operating system or application vulnerabilities to infect and network access to exploit the same vulnerability on other machines.

The first Internet worm was the Morris Worm, released in 1988. Although like the Creeper virus this worm was intended to be a proof of concept, due to a coding error the software had a fixed chance to spawn multiple copies of itself on the infected machine, causing the host's load to increase and sometimes eventually crash.

The SQL Slammer worm, released in January 2003, is to date one of the fastest spreading worms in history, taking advantage of a buffer overflow vulnerability in Microsoft SQL Server 2000 to replicate. Results of SQL Slammer infections around the world were particularly visible:

- Many ATM Machines from Bank of America were unavailable when the Slammer virus hit.

- Continental Airlines had cancelled and delayed flights because ticketing counters were infected.

- The City of Seattle 911 system was inoperable.

The biggest culprit was not the infection itself, but the alarming rate at which the worm tried to propagate. A single infected machine had the ability to flood the network within minutes, effectively creating a Denial of Service Attack by using up all the network bandwidth available. Estimates are that 90% of all vulnerable servers on the Internet were infected within 10 minutes of the worm's release.

Bots

One of the latest botnets discovered by the security industry is known as ZeroAccess. As of September 2012, it is estimated that the ZeroAccess malware has been installed about 9 million times. Bots are general use software programs, empty husks, which contact a Command and Control server for their orders. The ZeroAccess bot uses a peer-to-peer like network to download plugins from the C&C servers. These plugins carry out tasks designed to generate revenue for the botnet operators. It accomplishes this task with two primary methods: *Click Fraud* and *Bitcoin Mining*.

Click fraud happens in connection with a business using Pay Per Click (PPC) advertising model. The motivation varies. Often hackers are hired to try to drain out competitors' advertising budget. The most frequent perpetrators of click fraud, though, are publishers themselves, many of whom run successful pay per click scams.[14]

Bitcoin is touted to be the new virtual currency to replace cash in the Internet. Much like the Federal Reserve is in charge of regulating our currency, regulation of Bitcoins is delegated to a peer-to-peer network composed of computers running a Bitcoin client, or a Bitcoin Miner. When you install a Bitcoin Miner on your computer, your machine essentially works as a Bitcoin bank, issuing

---

[14]What is Click Fraud? – Internet Marketing Services By (n.d.). Retrieved from http://www.optimum7.com/internet-marketing /ppc/what-is-click-fraud.html

the currency, validating transactions, etc. Individuals usually become part of a "mining pool" and receive payout bitcoins as part of their payment. Obviously, botnets are perfect for this activity.

Hacking

According to the VERIS Data Breach Report for 2011, 81% of the breaches in 2011 involved some type of hacking action. Some of the methods used to gain access to a computer are also used by malware code. The primary difference between a hacking breach and a malware infection is that malware infections propagate automatically, without intervention from a human. Although they both may use the same methods of penetration, a hacking breach is an attack targeted towards a specific host or organization, directed by a hacker.

Brute-force attack

Brute force is a method by which a hacker tries to gain access to an account on the target system by trying to "guess" the correct password. Usually this is an automated process that may take hours to complete.

Although the "made for TV" versions of this attack sound a bit far-fetched, with the hacker simply trying a few passwords and easily accessing to the computer, it is not too far from the truth. An analysis of the 450,000 passwords leaked with the Yahoo attack mentioned previously in this chapter brought up the following pearls of wisdom:

- 160 Yahoo accounts had the password "111111"

- "password" was used as the password 780 times

- "ninja" was used 333 times (not as "ninja" as they'd like it to be)

What follows is a sample of inadequate passwords, the 25 worst passwords of 2011 (Table 6.1) as extracted by antivirus vendor ESET:[15]

Default credentials attacks

Appliances designed to be connected to a network usually come from the factory with a default password. So do certain software applications and databases. Default Credential attacks refer to incidents in which a hacker gains access to the system or software protected by standard preset (and therefore widely known) usernames and passwords.

There are many websites that collect lists of default passwords. CIRT.net, for instance, maintains a database with 1937 default passwords, from 467 vendors like Microsoft and Verizon.

Table 6.1 25 worst passwords, 2011

password	12345	letmein	michael	2000
123456	dragon	monkey	shadow	jordan
12345678	pussy	696969	master	superman
1234	baseball	abc123	jennifer	harley
qwerty	football	mustang	111111	1234567

---

[15] http://blog.eset.com/2012/06/07/passwords-and-pins-the-worst-choices

Microsoft's SQL Server 2000 install will complete and leave a database administrator account "sa" with no password needed.

In July 2012, a major ISP from Holland discovered that costumer accounts were vulnerable due to default credentials. Their user id were set to be their zip code + their street address, and the initial login password was "welkom01." When they performed a security check on the accounts they discovered that 140,000 customers never bothered changing the initial default password.

A slight variation on the theme is a Wireless Access Point (WAP), like the one you probably have at home. In order to associate with your home router and gain wireless network access, all you need is the SID (the name of the network), which is usually broadcasted and discoverable by your computer, and the router password. There are two popular passwords for WAPs as delivered by your Internet Service Provider: either the MAC address of the router or another hexadecimal value. Both can easily be found written on the underside of the WAP. All a hacker would need is quick access to your network, during a get together or a party, and voila, instant access.

Jailbreaking iPhones

In 2010 universities around the world started observing a new rash of port scans targeting port 22, a port dedicated to the encrypted console daemon SSHd. When the IPs were tracked down, all belonged to jailbroken iPhones.

The term "jailbroken" refers to the fact that the iPhone IOS Operating System had been replaced by another Operating System by the iPhone user. Jailbreaking a device is easy and removes certain limitations Apple imposes to app developers. But, as it turns out, it also adds a SSH server to the iPhone, with the default "root" account and a default password of "alpine." A quick scan of the network and users with jailbroken iPhones with default passwords were "owned" by a hacker.

Buffer overflow attacks

Let's start with an analogy. A buffer overflow is like dumping 1 gallon of water in a container that only holds one cup. The water will eventually overflow and use other spaces where it was not supposed to go. Usually the spill is wasted. But in the computer world, a precisely formed spill can yield the keys to the kingdom.

In computing, a buffer overflow happens when a program buffer or container is not dimensioned properly, and the content that was supposed to fit in the memory "spills over" other parts of the computer memory. If the contents of the spillover are crafted properly, the computer may be "tricked" into believing that the spillover is actually part of the program that needs to be run.

Hello World on the PS Vita

Among hackers, Sony's PSP is a favorite for its ease of penetration. The portable console can be altered to play custom games and programs (known as homebrews). With the unveiling of its new portable, the PS Vita, Sony hoped that the days of the hacked portable were gone. Alas, they were wrong.

> A Japanese hacker going by the handle Wololo posted the first Hello World on the PS Vita. Using a buffer overflow, he has found a way into the PS Vita, and with many PSP Game exploits still around and not published for the whole homebrew and hacking community this means that in the short term homebrew is here on the PS Vita.

The Code Red worm used a buffer overflow by connecting to a vulnerable Microsoft IIS Server and sending it a large string of N's (capital letter N). At the end of this string, it would send a snippet of code to be executed by the web server. Simple and efficient!

> Compiler protection against known buffer overflow problems
>
> New compilers will warn users when they try to compile programs containing dangerous function calls prone to be exposed to BOs:

```
user@server ~/user $ gcc simple.c -o simple
/tmp/ccECXQAX.o: In function 'main':
simple.c:(.text+0x17): warning: the 'gets' function is dangerous
and should not be used.
```

Cross-site scripting (XSS) attacks

XSS is one of the most common web-based attacks. It occurs when a website allows a malicious user to enter information with malicious content in it. The content is usually javascript code executed on the client when other users are visiting that site. Common targets for these attacks are web-based forums. The software powering these sites often do not validate the user input, allowing users to enter html or java code. The code is then published on the forum for other users to see and execute (Figure 6.10).

According to Accunetix,[16] a company that specializes in web-based vulnerability assessment tools, exploited XSS sites are commonly used to perform the following malicious activities:

- Identity theft
- Accessing sensitive or restricted information
- Gaining free access to otherwise paid-for content
- Spying on user's web browsing habits
- Altering browser functionality
- Public defamation of an individual or corporation
- Web application defacement
- Denial of Service attacks

---

[16]http://www.acunetix.com/websitesecurity/xss.htm

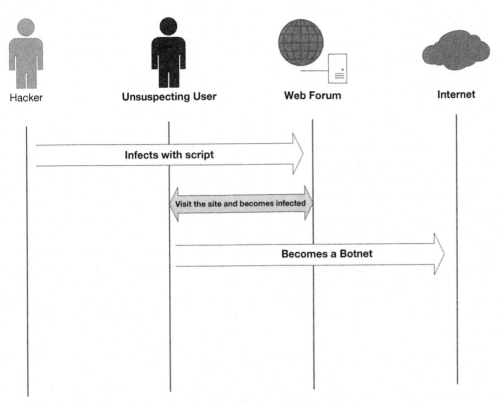

FIGURE 6.10   High level XSS attack

Below is a basic example of an XSS attack. Start with the code below for an ordinary web page that gets a variable from the URL that "should" be a name, then displays a warm introduction message to the screen.

```
<?php
$name = $_GET['name'];
echo "My name is $name<br>";
echo "<a href="http://xssattackexamples.com/">Click to Download</
a>";
?>
```

A malicious hacker could craft the following URL to

```
index.php?name=guest<script>alert('owned')</script>
```

This is a non-persistent XSS vulnerability, and it is by far the most common type of attack. It happens when the data provided by a web client is used by server-side scripts to generate a page of results for that user, without validating the request.[17]

---

[17] You can see an example of non-persistent XSS on the website https://www.insecurelabs.org. The site owners specifically designed the site to be vulnerable to XSS attacks. Select one of the agenda items and paste the <script> above. If your web browser has Javascript enabled, you will see the "owned" message pop up on the screen.

SQL injection attack

SQL injection is an attack technique used to exploit how web pages communicate with back-end databases. An attacker can issue commands (in the form of specially crafted SQL statements) to a database using input fields on a website.[18] As you can see, SQL injection is remarkably similar to an XSS. The primary difference being that an XSS attack is executed at the web front end, whereas the SQL attack is executed at the server. The problem in both cases is that user input was never validated properly.

As an example, let's assume a website that allows you to enter your last name in a text box, hit submit, and then displays your first name and your phone number. The query the web server sends to the back-end database may look something like this:

```
SELECT fname, phone FROM contacts WHERE lname = 'doe'
```

But what if we entered the following in the text box:

```
doe' OR '1=1';
```

Since the '1 = 1' condition is always true, the database would return all of its contents. But it gets worse.

```
doe'  exec master.dbo.xp_cmdshell 'iisreset/Stop'
```

If the database server allows shell escapes (commands could be executed outside the database environment, on the actual operating system itself), the above input would stop the IIS web server on the machine.

In October 2012, the hacktivist group Anonymous used SQL Injection attacks against vulnerable web front ends to disclose information stored in database servers of 50 universities around the world, including Princeton, John Hopkins, and Rutgers.[19]

Misuse

Misuse involves the unauthorized use of assets. In most cases, misuse is a result of the absence of a common security principle known as "need-to-know." With the need-to-know principle, an individual only has access to an asset if he or she needs access to that asset in order to perform his job. And that principle applies independently of the position the person has in the organization.

Abuse of privileges

Abuse of privileges occurs when an employee uses his or her position and/or access to assets in an improper manner, causing damage to the asset and/or the organization.

---

[18] Verizon's Data Breach Investigations Report (n.d.). Retrieved from http://www.slideshare.net/cloudrunnertom/verizon-dbir
[19] http://pastebin.com/AQWhu8Ek

As an IT person, the first thing that comes to mind is a systems administrator misusing their privileges. Take IT contractor Steven Barnes, for example. Steve worked for Blue Falcon Networks, now known as Akimbo Systems. In 2008, Steven was ordered, by a court in California, to pay $54,000 restitution to Akimbo and spend 1 year and 1 day in jail. The reason? Steven used his access to log in to Akimbo's Exchange email server and remove restrictions set up on that server keeping spammers from using it as a spam proxy. The result was the equivalent of a Denial of Service attacks, with Akimbo's email system going down as soon as spammers found the opening. According to Steven, he opened the flood gates as retaliation after coworkers from Blue Falcon Networks, now known as Akimbo Systems, came to his home and took away his personal computers by force in 2003.[20]

Fraud and embezzlement

The Counterfeit Access Device and Computer Fraud and Abuse Act (18 U.S.C.A. § 1030), passed by Congress in 1984, was the first attempt by the Federal government to deal with the issue of fraud in the IT arena. The act also criminalizes the use of computers to inflict damage to computer systems, including their hardware and software and was primarily tailored towards hackers. Since then, the CFAA has been used to prosecute employees who use their position and access to assets to defraud and embezzle money from organizations and their customers.

Fraud and embezzlement cases using IT resources are abundant, especially when individuals find themselves in financial hardship. This has led companies to require a credit check for those employees with access to assets that could potentially lead to fraud.

In August 2012, a Knoxville woman began to serve 5 years on probation after admitting she committed computer fraud while working as a retail operations manager for SunTrust Bank.[21] Her job was to ensure branches in her region followed internal security practices, according to prosecutors. She had access to the financial records of SunTrust's customers through her work computer, according to the US attorney. Below are some more examples of computer fraud:

- Sending hoax emails intended to scare people (*scareware* or *ransomware*)

- Illegally using someone else's computer or "posing" as someone else on the Internet

- Using any type of malware or emails to gather information from an organization or a company with the intent of using it for financial gains

- Using the computer to solicit minors into sexual alliances

- Violating copyright laws by downloading and sharing copyrighted material without the owner's permission

- Using a computer to change information, such as grades, work reports, etc.

Use of unapproved software

Employees may become threat agents when they go against company policy and install software application on their computers. Software installed in desktops or smartphones may provide hackers a way into restricted company assets.

---

[20] http://valleywag.com/5076432/angry-angry-it-guy-goes-to-jail

[21] Former SunTrust bank employee sentenced in computer fraud (n.d.). Retrieved from http://www.knoxnews.com/news/2012/apr/04/former-suntrust-bank-employee-sentenced

Allowing users to install software on their desktops is a particularly problematic issue for universities. By default, universities are supposed to be open, unrestricted, places where curiosity and research come together to foster innovation. On the other hand, that same openness could end up exposing research data and other information assets to threat agents with dire consequences to the department as well as to the individual.

In the late 1990s, a perfect example of the issues associated with these installations was Bonzi Buddy. The Bonzi purple gorilla was cute and adorable, a favorite of many university users on campus. It roamed around their desktops and kept users entertained. Unfortunately, it also gathered information about the user's surfing habits, store preferences (spyware), and displayed related advertisement on the screen (adware). Finally, it used up so much power from the CPU that all other applications would slow down to a crawl (Figure 6.11).

Because of their openness, most universities do not have a policy prohibiting users to install software on their computer, but many other organizations do. In August 2012, the US District Court for the Western District of Oklahoma held that an employee who downloaded shareware from the Internet in violation of company policy may be liable under the CFAA for using the downloaded software to obtain confidential company documents. In Musket Corp. v. Star Fuel of Oklahoma LLC, the court held that anyone who is authorized to use a computer for certain purposes but goes past those limitations is considered to have "exceeded authorized access" under the CFAA.

Threat shifting is the response of hackers to controls, in which they change some characteristic of their intent/targeting in order to avoid and/or overcome those safeguards/countermeasures.[22]

Social engineering

Social attacks involve conversations, a dialog with users convincing them to do something they would not ordinarily do. Even savvy computer users may be susceptible to social engineering attacks given the correct circumstances.

Pretexting

Pretexting is a technique in which the attacker uses a fictitious scenario to manipulate someone into performing an action or divulging information. Pretexting is also known outside the technical area as "con game" or "scam."

One type of pretexting is *phishing*, in which the attacker uses an email to try to get the recipient to divulge information. Phishing emails can be made terribly convincing, visually appealing, and the senders can

I Talk!

I E-Mail!

I Browse!

I Search!

I Sing!

I Laugh!

I Download!

I Tell Facts!

I Schedule!

Bonzi.com

FIGURE 6.11 Bonzi buddy

[22] Guide for Conducting Risk Assessments – #2fishygirl on Scribd (n.d.). Retrieved from http://www.scribd.com/doc/65740364/Guide-for-Conducting-Risk-Assessments

pose as a figure of authority or someone the user knows. Phishing is normally coupled with *spamming*, where the attacker sends thousands and thousands of emails in the hopes that a small percentage of the recipients will be convinced and open a file infected with malware or reply with an account number or password.

Successful spear phishing at the Financial Times

On May 29, 2013, the Financial Times reported a successful spear phishing attack that caught knowledgeable reporters at the venerable newspaper by surprise. The emails were highly customized and targeted to the organization. Hackers calling themselves the Syrian Electronic Army (SEA), perhaps after the ongoing events in Syria at that time, were able to get access to the email account of many veteran reporters. For more details, read the details reported by the newspaper at the link in the reference below.

One interesting feature of the report is that it indicates that many organizations are now very comfortable acknowledging being the victims of attacks and laying out how other organizations, including their competitors, can save themselves the ignominy of being victims of similar attacks. This is a major development from some years prior when organizations would rarely acknowledge such attacks so publicly.

Reference

1. Betts, A. "A sobering day," Financial Times labs, http://labs.ft.com/2013/05/a-sobering-day/ (accessed 07/16/2013)

With the move phone communication is making towards *Voice Over IP* (VOIP), a new method of delivery for the pretexting attack is appearing. Spam over Internet Protocol or SPIT is bulk dialed prerecorded calls using a breached VOIP network. They usually instruct the person answering the call to "stay on the line" or answer to questions that will be recorded and passed on to hackers. Contrary to email delivery, where available controls stop most of the spam received by a user, there are no means to control the calls a person's phone will receive. While some carriers have "black lists" available for customers (for a small fee), the situation would be unmanageable when the source of the calls change periodically.

Physical

A physical action involves the tangible or palpable aspect of an asset. Unfortunately, many organizations do not consider the physical threat action enough of an issue to warrant the expense of protecting against it.

Unauthorized access

This is a common threat. Many organizations require to have certain areas protected by card access mechanisms. However, in an effort to be cordial and polite, employees in these organizations will hold the door open if they see someone else running to use the opportunity to enter the building without searching for their access badge. Employees will often not challenge other individuals if they handle themselves with certainty and conviction, with that air of "I am supposed to be walking around here without my badge."

In an age where terrorism went from a relatively unknown threat agent to a serious concern, control of unauthorized access to areas and systems relating to the country's infrastructure, such as airports, power plants, and even electrical substations serving a limited region have become a critical issue. While fences and other access controls were initially primarily designed to keep people from gaining access and getting hurt by electrocuting themselves, now the concern is that unauthorized access will lead to serious shortage in critical infrastructure services. Organizations are reviewing their guidelines and standards for protection of assets, such as the *Institute of Electrical and Electronics Engineers* (IEEE) and their *Standard for Physical Security of Electrical Power Stations*,[23] focusing on these new and previously ignored threat agents.

Barnes and Nobles

In October 2012, customers of the giant bookstore Barnes and Nobles had their debit card numbers and PINs stolen when entry pads from 63 stores were apparently tampered (another physical threat action) to record information from all customers that used them for payment. Tampered PIN pads were discovered in multiple locations throughout the United States, and all indication point to individuals with unauthorized access to these data entry points.

Theft

Walk around campus, go to your university library or another study area. You will notice how easy it would be to take someone's laptop when they step out quickly to go to the restroom. That's plenty of time to close the lid, unplug the power and take off with the new device.

AvMed theft

In 2009, two laptops containing 1.2 million records from AvMed customers were stolen from AvMed Health Plans' Gainesville office in Florida. It took 3 months for AvMed to comprehend the extent of the breach and notify affected customers. The records stored in the laptops contained AvMed members' names, home addresses, phone numbers, Social Security Numbers, as well as other highly sensitive medical history data such as diagnosis information, medical procedure, and prescription information. A class action lawsuit was filed in 2010 on behalf of customers.

Error

The error category of threat agents includes everything done incorrectly and unintentionally. It includes omissions, accidents, trips, hardware and software malfunctions, etc. Errors do not include things left undone or done incorrectly but intentionally.

Data entry error

Data entry errors come in two varieties: omission or commission. With errors of omission, a value is not entered in the appropriate manner. Errors of commission refer to the integrity of the data entry.

---

[23] http://standards.ieee.org/develop/project/1402.html

Data entry errors are unfortunately common, but particularly dangerous in the Health area. Electronic Health Records are being put in place in hospitals and doctor offices around the country with the intent to facilitate the exchange of data between medical practices and other points of care. However, sharing data in this manner would also share any entry error on the data itself. While technology itself may be important, appropriate training and usability tests are equality critical to the proper operation of these systems.

Misconfiguration

Special care must be taken by system administrators when dealing with servers containing Personally Identifiable Information. Unfortunately, often hardware and software upgrades are done under tremendous pressure to bring systems back online, and the integrity of the system suffers because of it.

The most common incident involving misconfiguration seems to be related to these upgrades. In 2012, the University of North Carolina at Charlotte inadvertently exposed PII of more than 350,000 people due to the failure of administrators to properly migrate security settings from an old server being decommissioned to a new server. The same happened with the Northwest College in Florida just a few months later.

Environment

Threat actions in the environment category include:

- Natural disasters such as hurricanes, tornados, and flood

- Failures of environmental controls dedicated to supporting the IT asset, such as power failures, water leaks, air conditioning failures, etc.

Sidebar – Agents for natural disasters

The question may arise: so, who or what is the agent for a natural disaster? These agents are usually geographical, related to the area where the asset is located. For instance, in the Midwest of the United States, organizations may have to deal with tornadoes. Hurricanes are a concern on the Pacific and Atlantic coasts. West Coast organizations also must be wary of earthquakes.

Air conditioning failure

Level3 is a large, multinational telecommunications company based in Colorado. It provides network transport for data, voice, and content delivery for most large telecom carriers in the United States and abroad.

In 2011, the company suffered an AC failure at one of its datacenters located in France. Since real state in a datacenter is a premium, companies tend to pack as many servers as possible to minimize the support cost. As a result, keeping the air cool is a must. After a few hours, the ambient temperature in the server room reached 131°F. When the ambient temperature reaches that point, motherboard and integrated circuits start failing. Hard drives may still function after the temperature is back to normal, but problems with brittle heads or plates can lurk in the background for months before they show up in any diagnostic.

The culprit was clear. Air conditioning systems use a supply of chilled water to work. Earlier in the day, the line supplying cooled water to the AC systems of the French datacenter ruptured. Without a redundant source of chilled water, the AC systems could not operate and were shut down.

Hurricanes

We're on the 10th and 11th floor of a corporate high rise on Poydras Ave., right near St. Charles. We have generators and tons of food and water. It is five of us total. I am not sure how the Internet connection will be affected. I have a camera and my gun. Sustained winds are 175, gusts to 215. The real danger is not the wind, it's the storm surge the wind will be pushing into the city from the Gulf through the lake. The city might never recover. Honestly, this thing could be biblical.[24]

The entry was posted by Michael Barnett, former Green Beret and consultant to Intercosmos Media Group, parent company of the web host company zipa.com. Barnett was hired specifically as a crisis manager for the approaching Hurricane Katrina. He was holed up with his girlfriend in the datacenter to protect the assets and hopefully ride out the storm.

Katrina proved to be a monster, with millions of dollars in damage. From his perch on the 10th floor, Barnett documented the mayhem, looting, and his struggle to keep operations going with dwindling resources. Unfortunately, this will not be the last hurricane. Every year, from June through September, organizations housed near vulnerable areas prepare for the winds and the floods generally associated with hurricanes. They are one of the most devastating threats to face datacenters and the assets they house.[25]

Vulnerabilities

We have defined vulnerabilities as weaknesses in information systems that give threats the opportunity to compromise assets. Both terms, vulnerabilities and threats, are often used interchangeably in the industry, especially by vendors. However, it is particularly relevant to distinguish the two. By itself, a vulnerability does not present a risk to an asset. In the same manner, a threat does not present a risk unless there is a vulnerability in the system that can be exploited by the threat.

Not every vulnerability presents a threat to a network. Not all vulnerabilities need to be patched immediately. Only a vulnerability that can be exploited is a threat to business operations and information assets. It's common for administrative teams to receive reports of vulnerabilities with requests for immediate action to eliminate them. One source of these requests is an organization's internal audit team. Another common source of fix-it-now-because-the-press/vendor-says-it's-critical messages is management, including many IS Directors. But should all vulnerabilities be considered emergencies? Are all vulnerabilities worthy of your security budget dollars?[26]

---

[24] http://www.baselinemag.com/c/a/Business-Intelligence/Diary-of-Disaster-Riding-Out-Katrina-in-the-Data-Center

[25] Please see this article for some very good example of threat statements: Adam L. Pineberg, "I challenged hackers to investigate me and what they found is chilling," http://pandodaily.com/2013/10/26/i-challenged-hackers-to-investigate-me-and-what-they-found-out-is-chilling/

[26] A Practical Approach – Adventures in Security – Home (n.d.). Retrieved from http://adventuresinsecurity.com/blog/wp-content/uploads/2006/03/A_Practical_Appr

Side Quote: A "zero-day threat" is a threat developed by a threat agent before a solution to eliminate the vulnerability was found and made public.

Threat agents use their knowledge of vulnerabilities to produce new threats against an asset. For information assets, the modifications to existing software code that will resolve vulnerability is known as a "security patch." The Department of Homeland Security's National Vulnerability Database (NVD)[27] reported 3532 vulnerabilities in 2011, about 10 new vulnerabilities being discovered every day. This is actually an improvement compared with the figures from 2009 and 2010 (Figure 6.12).

NVD database hacked

The NVD database maintained by NIST was taken offline on March 8, 2013, when administrators observed suspicious activity and discovered malware on two of its web servers. The servers were believed to have been compromised for at least two months. A vulnerability in Adobe's ColdFusion software was held responsible for the compromise.

Source:

1. www.theregister.co.uk/2013/03/14/adobe_coldfusion_vulns_compromise_us_malware_catalog/
2. http://www.dslreports.com/forum/r28102110-US-National-Vulnerability-Database-Hacked

Operating system vulnerabilities

Operating system vulnerabilities are those problems with the operating system which could grant a hacker access to operating system functions and accounts. Because the OS is the basic building block for all applications running on a system, administrators are usually required to apply OS security patches.

Microsoft issues their patches on the second Tuesday of every month. The date is known as *Patch Tuesday* or *Black Tuesday*, as an acknowledgment to the fact that administrators should

Vendor	# of vulnerabilities (2011)	# of HIGH vulnerabilities	# of MEDIUM vulnerabilities	# of LOW vulnerabilities
Google	299	173	125	1
Oracle	262	46	163	53
Apple	246	139	89	18
Microsoft	244	195	46	3
Adobe	189	153	36	0

FIGURE 6.12 Top vendor vulnerability breakdown

[27] http://nvd.nist.gov/

ideally apply the patch on a test server and analyze its effects prior to applying the patch on production server. If a patch is deemed to be critical, Microsoft will release a security patch between Tuesdays. This type of patch is known as an *Out of Band Patch*.

Among the top 10 external vulnerabilities listed by the security vendor Qualys for August 2012, the following are Microsoft internal operating system vulnerabilities. Internal vulnerabilities are those that can be exploited once the hacker has a foothold on the vulnerable computer, usually through a compromised, non-admin account. Hackers then use these vulnerabilities to gain administrative access and control over the computer.

Microsoft XML core services remote code execution vulnerability (MS12-043 and KB2719615)

Microsoft XML Core Services 3.0, 4.0, 5.0, and 6.0 accesses uninitialized memory locations, allowing remote attackers to execute arbitrary code or cause a Denial of Service via a crafted website.

A remote code execution vulnerability exists in the way that Microsoft XML Core Services handles objects in memory. The vulnerability could allow remote code execution if a user views a website that contains specially crafted content. An attacker who successfully exploited this vulnerability could take complete control of an affected system. An attacker could then install programs; view, change, or delete data; or create new accounts with full user rights. Users whose accounts are configured to have fewer user rights on the system could be less impacted than users who operate with administrative user rights.[28]

Microsoft Windows unauthorized digital certificates spoofing vulnerability (KB2728973)

Unauthorized digital certificates could allow spoofing. Certificates were issued irregularly by a Microsoft Certificate Authority and used to sign parts of the "Flame" malware. Flame is a malware apparently designed to target espionage much like one of its predecessors, Stuxnet. The malware was discovered by Kaspersky Labs in May 2012 but seems to be in the wild since 2010.

Microsoft Windows shell remote code execution vulnerability (MS12-048)

A remote code execution vulnerability exists in the way Windows handles file and directory names. This vulnerability could allow remote code execution if a user opens a file or directory with a specially crafted name. If a user is logged on with administrative user rights, an attacker who successfully exploited this vulnerability could take complete control of an affected system. An attacker could then install programs; view, change, or delete data; or create new accounts with full user rights. Users whose accounts are configured to have fewer user rights on the system could be less impacted than users who operate with administrative user rights.[29]

Microsoft Windows kernel-mode drivers elevation of privilege vulnerability (MS12-047)

An elevation of privilege vulnerability exists in the way that the Windows kernel-mode driver handles specific keyboard layouts. An attacker who successfully exploited this vulnerability

---

[28] http://technet.microsoft.com/en-us/security/bulletin/ms12-043
[29] http://technet.microsoft.com/en-us/security/bulletin/ms12-048

could run arbitrary code in kernel mode. An attacker could then install programs; view, change, or delete data; or create new accounts with full administrative rights.[30]

Microsoft Data Access Components remote code execution vulnerability (MS12-045)

A remote code execution vulnerability exists in the way that Microsoft Data Access Components accesses an object in memory that has been improperly initialized. An attacker who successfully exploited this vulnerability could run arbitrary code on the target system. An attacker could then install programs; view, change, or delete data; or create new accounts with full user rights.[31]

Sidebar – Qualys Laws of Vulnerabilities 2.0 Declarations

Half-life: The half-life of critical vulnerabilities remained at 30 days across all industries. Comparing individual industries, the Service industry has the shortest half-life of 21 days, Finance ranked second with 23 days, Retail ranked third with 24 days, and Manufacturing ranked last with a vulnerability half-life of 51 days.

Prevalence: Sixty percent of the most prevalent and critical vulnerabilities are being replaced by new vulnerabilities on an annual basis. This number has increased from the 2004 research where it was 50%. The top stragglers according to Laws 2.0 are MSFT Office, Windows 2003 SP2, Adobe Acrobat, and Sun Java Plug-in.

Persistence: The Laws 2.0 declared that the lifespan of most, if not all vulnerabilities, is unlimited, and a large percentage of vulnerabilities are never fully fixed. This law was illustrated with data samples from MS08-001, MS08-007, MS08-015, and MS08-021.

Exploitation: Eighty percent of the vulnerability exploits are now available within single-digit days after the vulnerability's public release. In 2008, Qualys Labs logged 56 vulnerabilities with zero-day exploits, including the RPC vulnerability that produced Conficker. In 2009, the first patch released by Microsoft, MS09-001, had an exploit available within 7 days. Microsoft's April Patch Tuesday included known exploits for over 47% of the published vulnerabilities. This law had the most drastic change from the Laws 1.0 in 2004, which provided comfortable 60 days as guidance.[32]

Web application vulnerabilities

Web applications insert yet another point of ingress to the underlying assets it exposes. The Open Web Application Security Project (OWASP) is a non-profit organization with a number of chapters and projects trying to make web-based applications more secure. As part of this effort, OWASP publishes a list of the top vulnerabilities found in web applications. We already discussed a few when we talked about threat actions.

---

[30] http://technet.microsoft.com/en-us/security/bulletin/ms12-047

[31] http://technet.microsoft.com/en-us/security/bulletin/ms12-045

[32] The Laws of Vulnerabilities 2.0 | Qualys, Inc. (n.d.). Retrieved from http://www.qualys.com/research/vulnlaws/

Injection

Injection happens when the mechanism doing the interpretation of the commands sent by a client computer does not validate the commands before passing them to the application to be executed. When input is not validated properly, the web server may attempt to execute commands that should be restricted and never executed. In essence, the fact that the input is not validated gives the attacker a "pseudo shell" into the server and/or its database.

Preventing injection requires keeping data passed by outside sources (such as in a web form) separate from actual back-end commands and queries.

The preferred way to deal with this issue is to use an *Application Programming Interface* or API. With an API, the programmer restricts the type of input accepted from the client. For instance, a programmer may have an API that only accepts single, one-word commands such as READ, WRITE, and MODIFY. Anything other than these key words is ignored.

If this method is not available, the programmer must carefully examine the interpretation and clean any command that would allow a client to break out of the environment. For instance, if the command submitted by the client will be passed as a parameter to a SQL statement, the program should error out if any semicolon is passed by the client.

Attacks using the injection mechanism are the most popular and easy to use, such as SQL Injection or LDAP Injection.

Cross-site scripting (XSS)

XSS flaws occur whenever an application takes untrusted data and sends it to a web browser without proper validation and escaping. XSS allows attackers to execute scripts in the victim's browser, which can hijack user sessions, deface websites, or redirect the user to malicious sites.[33] While the target assets for attacks using injection are servers, the primary targets for attacks using the XSS vulnerability are the clients connecting to a server.

Cross-site request forgery (CSRF)

When you sit down to use your computer, chances are you log in to many different sites: Facebook, MSN, CNN, and others. A hacker using the CSRF vulnerability uses this fact to send "requests" to these login services on your behalf.

While the XSS attack "bounces" the payload on the server back to the client, a CSRF attack simply executes the command on the server on behalf of the client. For instance, behind the scenes, unbeknownst to you, a hacker could send an HTTP request to the server in this fashion:

http://somesite.com/change-password.php&user=jdoe?new-pwd=ilikepie The web server receives this request, confirms "jdoe" is already logged in and changes his password to "ilikepie."

Insufficient transport layer protection

Simply put, this translates to *make sure your web server has appropriate encryption enabled.* Not all web servers may require data encryption. Probably the number one reason for a HTTPS connection would be a website which requires users to login. Unless the login transaction is

---

[33]Top 10 2010-Main – OWASP (n.d.). Retrieved from https://www.owasp.org/index.php/Top_10_2010-Main

encrypted, the entire content of the transfer is visible to a hacker with access, including the user login credentials.

It is also vital to use a valid, current industry-standard algorithm for encryption. We will look at encryption in one of the next chapters.

Finally, a certificate signed by a recognized certificate authority and renewed as needed is essential, especially for production servers. A certificate signed by the CA indicates non-repudiation (the site is what it claims) and that the encryption is trustworthy.

Example case – Gozi

When you think of information security threats, you probably think of smart but crooked people trying to attack your computer for personal gain. But did you realize that there is also a nascent industry developing professional software tools to help novices become industrial-strength for-profit attackers? On January 23, 2013, US prosecutors charged three individuals – Nikita Kuzmin of Russia, Deniss Calovskis of Latvia, and Mihai Paunescu of Romania with creating and distributing the Gozi Trojan. This software was customized for each customer to attack the specific financial institution picked by the customer. All three individuals had been arrested in different parts of the world over the previous 2 years.

The Gozi virus was created in 2005 and distributed as a pdf file. When the file was opened, the virus would secretly install itself, but do nothing malicious, thereby avoiding scrutiny from antivirus software. Eventually, it was installed on over a million computers worldwide, including over 40,000 computers in the United States.

The creators of the Gozi virus were extremely selective about picking customers. When a customer paid the team, select infected machines would be made available to the customer. The customer could then pick a financial firm to target, based on the usage behaviors or the banking preferences of the set of victims made available to him. The Gozi team would then write the customized software for the customer, which intercepted web-banking communications between the victims and their banks, allowing Gozi's customers to harvest account credentials.

To facilitate money transfers, the Gozi team had also lured individuals through envelope-stuffing schemes. These individuals would receive money from banks and mail it to the customers, providing a level of anonymity to the customers.

If convicted, each of the three members behind the Gozi team faces over 60 years in prison.

REFERENCES

http://www.justice.gov/usao/nys/pressreleases/January13/GoziVirusPR.php

http://krebsonsecurity.com/2013/01/three-men-charged-in-connection-with-gozi-trojan/

http://arstechnica.com/security/2013/01/how-the-feds-put-a-bullet-in-a-bulletproof-web-host/

http://krebsonsecurity.com/wp-content/uploads/2013/01/Calovskis-Deniss-S4-Indictment.pdf

http://krebsonsecurity.com/wp-content/uploads/2013/01/Kuzmin-Nikita-Information-1.pdf

http://krebsonsecurity.com/wp-content/uploads/2013/01/Paunescu-Mihai-Ionut-Complaint.pdf

SUMMARY

In this chapter, we saw that a threat is composed of an agent performing an action against an asset. We then looked at the important agents and actions you are likely to encounter in your careers.

CHAPTER REVIEW QUESTIONS

1. What is a threat? Provide some examples.

2. What is a threat model? Why are threat models useful?

3. Consider your laptop as the asset. Draw your threat model for the asset.

4. What are threat agents? Provide some examples.

5. What are the different types of threat agents? How have they evolved in prevalence over time?

6. Describe the typical Nigerian 419 scam.

7. What are hacktivists?

8. In your opinion, which organization in your local area would be the most likely target of a hacktivist attack? Why?

9. What are some known motivations of governments to sponsor or endorse cybercrime?

10. What are internal threat agents? Provide some examples. Which of these do you think is the most dangerous? Why?

11. How can top management be a threat agent from the perspective of information security?

12. What is a threat action? What are some common threat actions?

13. What threat actions can originate from an outsourced IT services provider?

14. What is a brute-force attack? What is the objective of a typical brute-force attack?

15. How can former employees become threats? What can you do to minimize the threat?

16. What is a zero-day threat?

17. What is threat shifting? How does it affect the work of information security professionals?

18. What is a cross-site scripting attack? What is the objective of a typical cross-site scripting attack?

19. What are some threat actions that can originate from the environment?

20. What in your opinion is the most important threat action originating from the environment in your local area?

21. What are vulnerabilities?

22. What is the relationship between vulnerabilities and threats?

23. What does patch Tuesday refer to in the information security profession?

24. What is OWASP? Why is it important to information security professionals?

25. Consider the threat model you developed for the laptop in question 3 above. What in your opinion is the most important threat agent and threat action in your model?

EXAMPLE CASE QUESTIONS

1. Based on the information provided in the case, what suggestions would you offer to a friend to stay safe online?

2. What is "bulletproof" hosting? Why is it valuable to cybercriminals? (you may need to search online)

3. What offenses is each individual in the ring charged with committing?

HANDS-ON ACTIVITY – VULNERABILITY SCANNING

In this exercise, you will install and test the Open Vulnerability Assessment Scanner (OpenVAS) on the Linux virtual machine included with this text. OpenVAS is a collection of tools that allow security administrators to manage the scanning of a large number of systems for network vulnerabilities. For more information, please see the OpenVAS website: http://www.openvas.org.

To install OpenVAS, open a terminal window and 'su' to the root account:

```
[alice@sunshine ~]$ su-
Password: thisisasecret
```

Next, use the YUM package manager to install the required packages:

```
[root@sunshine ~]# yum -y install openvas
Loaded plugins: downloadonly, fastestmirror, refresh-packagekit, security
Loading mirror speeds from cached hostfile
* atomic: www4.atomicorp.com
* base: mirror.flhsi.com
* extras: mirror.cogentco.com
* updates: mirrors.adams.net
Setting up Install Process
Resolving Dependencies
--> Running transaction check
---> Package openvas.noarch 0:1.0-5.el6.
art will be installed
--> Processing Dependency: openvas-administrator for package: openvas-1.0-5.el6.
art.noarch
--> Processing Dependency: wmi for package: openvas-1.0-5.el6.art.noarch
--> Processing Dependency: openvas-scanner for package: openvas-1.0-5.el6.art.
noarch
--> Processing Dependency: wapiti for package: openvas-1.0-5.el6.art.noarch
```

The command will install about 40 new packages on the system. When the installation is complete (this may take some time depending on your Internet connection), run the openvas-setup command to start the OpenVAS configuration process and enter the values below.

```
[root@sunshine ~]# openvas-setup
Openvas Setup, Version: 0.3
```

Step 1: Update NVT's and SCAP data
Please note this step could take some time.
Once completed, NVT's and SCAP data will be updated automatically every 24 hours

```
Updating NVTs....
Updating SCAP data...
[i] This script synchronizes a SCAP data directory with the OpenVAS one.
[i] SCAP dir: /var/lib/openvas/scap-data
[i] Will use rsync
[i] Using rsync: /usr/bin/rsync
[i] Configured SCAP data rsync feed: rsync://feed.openvas.org:/scap-data
OpenVAS feed server - http://openvas.org/
This service is hosted by Intevation GmbH - http://intevation.de/
All transactions are logged.
Please report problems to admin@intevation.de

receiving incremental file list
./
COPYING            1493 100%    1.42MB/s
0:00:00 (xfer#1, to-check=30/32)
COPYING.asc         198 100%   193.36kB/s
0:00:00 (xfer#2, to-check=29/32)
debian.6.0.xml   980140 100%   652.02kB/s
0:00:01 (xfer#3, to-check=28/32)
debian.6.0.xml.asc 198 100%     0.51kB/s
0:00:00 (xfer#4, to-check=27/32)
...
```

Step 2: Configure GSAD
The Greenbone Security Assistant is a Web Based front end
for managing scans. By default it is configured to only allow
connections from localhost.

```
Allow connections from any IP? [Default: yes] no
```

Step 3: Choose the GSAD admin users password.
The admin user is used to configure accounts,
Update NVT's manually, and manage roles.

```
Enter administrator username: openvas-admin
```

Enter Administrator Password: **12345qwert**
Verify Administrator Password: **12345qwert**
ad main:MESSAGE:9806:2013-01-19 14h39.33
EST: No rules file provided, the new user
will have no restrictions.
ad main:MESSAGE:9806:2013-01-19 14h39.33
EST: User openvas-admin has been successfully created.

Step 4: Create a user

Using /var/tmp as a temporary file holder.
Add a new openvassd user

Login: openvas-user
Authentication (pass/cert) [pass] : pass
Login password : secret
Login password (again) : secret

User rules
----

openvassd has a rules system which allows
you to restrict the hosts that openvas-
user has the right to test.
For instance, you may want him to be able
to scan his own host only.

Please see the openvas-adduser(8) man
page for the rules syntax.

Enter the rules for this user, and hit
ctrl-D once you are done:
(the user can have an empty rules set)
Ctrl-D

Login   : openvas-user

Password   : ***********

Rules   :

Is that ok? (y/n) [y] **y**
user added.

Starting openvas-administrator...
Starting openvas-administrator: [OK]

Setup complete, you can now access GSAD
at: https://<IP>:9392

To complete the setup process, you will need to run one more command. Please be aware that this command can take 20 minutes or more to complete, so please be patient.

[root@sunshine tmp]# /opt/book/threats/
scripts/finish_openvas_setup This program completes the OpenVAS configuration
process.
Stage 1: Loading and processing plugins
Processing 57744 plugins. Please be
patient. This will take 15 minutes or
more depending on your hardware.
Starting openvas-scanner: base gpgme-
Message: Setting GnuPG homedir to '/etc/
openvas/gnupg' base gpgme-Message: Using
OpenPGP engine version '2.0.14'

Stage 2: Building the OpenVAS-Manger
database
This will take 10-15 minutes depending on
your hardware.
done.

Stage 3: Starting services
Stopping openvas-manager:
Starting openvas-manager: Stopping
openvas-administrator:
Starting openvas-administrator:

Setup complete. Please open Firefox and
go to https://www.sunshine.edu:9392

Open a web browser window and go to **https://www.sunshine.edu:9392**. You will be presented with the certificate warning. The warning is shown because the certificate was generated during the OpenVAS installation process, so FireFox cannot verify the certificate with an external authority.

Click on the arrow next to "I Understand the Risks" and then click on the "Add Exception . . ." button. The screen shown in Figure 6.13 will be displayed. To accept the certificate, make sure that the "Permanently store this exception" checkbox is check and click on the "Confirm Security Exception" button.

You will be presented with a login screen for "Greenbone Security Assistant" (GSA). GSA is one of the several applications that make up the OpenVAS system. It provides a graphical interface to all of the OpenVAS scanning features. To login, use the **openvas-user** account and password you created above. The main screen for GSA is shown in Figure 6.14:

Select "New Task" from the "Scan Management" menu. The screen in Figure 6.15 will be shown. To create a new scan task, fill in the "Name" field – we've called this sample "myScan", but the exact name isn't that important. Change the "Scan Config" dropdown box to "Full and very deep ultimate"; this enables all of the vulnerability scans included with

FIGURE 6.13   Firefox certificate exception

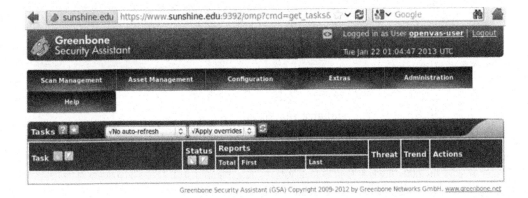

FIGURE 6.14   GSA main screen

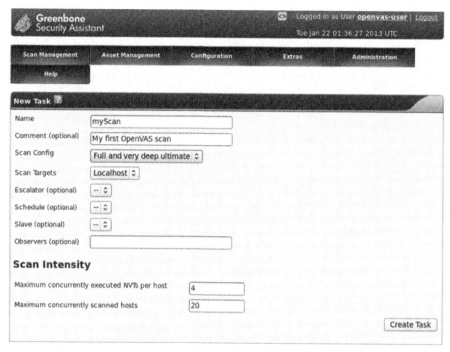

FIGURE 6.15 New Task configuration

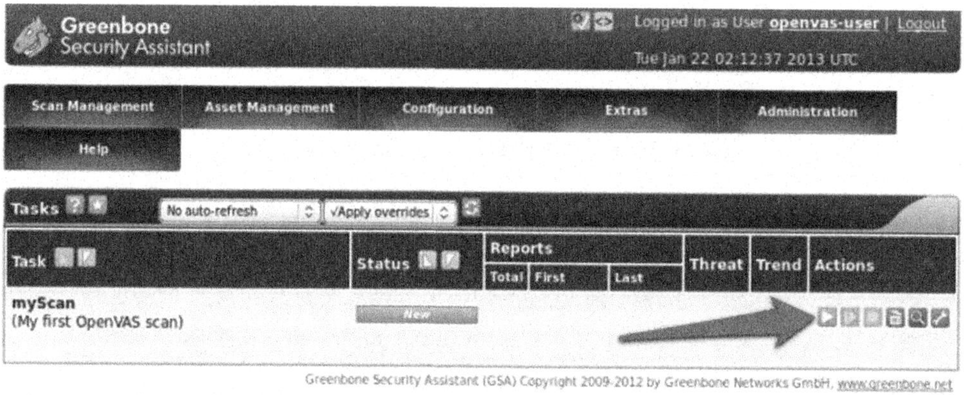

FIGURE 6.16 Starting a new scan

OpenVAS. You can leave the other fields at their default values. Click "Create Task" to complete the configuration.

Once the task is created, you will be presented with the task screen. To begin the scan, click on the start button (see Figure 6.16). The task status will switch from "New" to "Requested." It will take 5–10 minutes to complete the scan, but you can refresh the page in Firefox to check on the current status.

Once the scan is complete, click on the details button (see Figure 6.17).

The scan details page presents you with an overview of scans that have been run and their results. To view the report for the scan that was just completed, click on the details button to open the Report Page. In the Report Page, you can view the results of the scan or download the report in a variety of formats. To download the report, select the file format and click the download button (see Figure 6.18).

Deliverables

Save the full report as openvas_report.pdf and submit it to your instructor.

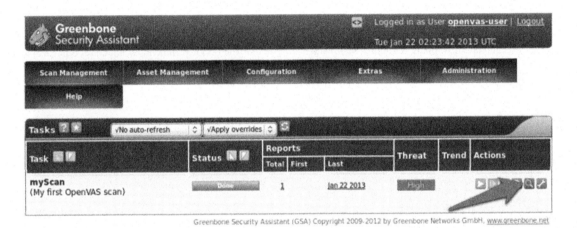

FIGURE 6.17   Viewing scan details

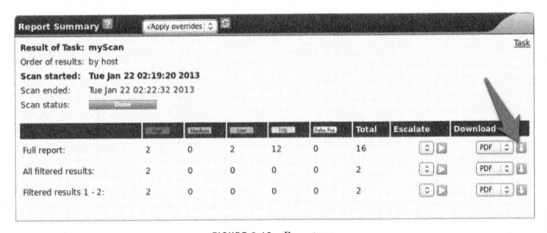

FIGURE 6.18   Report page

CRITICAL THINKING EXERCISE – IRAQ CYBERWAR PLANS IN 2003

In August 2009, the New York Times reported that in 2003, when the US was planning the Iraq war, US Intelligence agencies and the Pentagon developed a plan to launch a cyber-attack with the goal of freezing the bank accounts operated by Saddam Hussein. There were billions of dollars in these accounts, which were used to pay the salaries of army personnel and purchase supplies. If successful, the cyber-attack would incapacitate Saddam Hussein's ability to wage war with kinetic (conventional) weapons.

As the New York Times reported, though the officials involved in developing the plans for cyber-attacks were confident of their ability to execute the attacks, they never got approval to execute on their plans. Officials in President Bush's administration were concerned about collateral damage, i.e., impacts on accounts owned by other individuals,

if any part of the cyber-attack did not go according to plan. This could create financial chaos worldwide, beginning with the Middle East, but likely to spread to Europe and even the United States.

That was 2003. Since then technology has evolved, and cyberwarfare is increasingly becoming part of the military arsenal. Even during the Iraq war in 2003, the military attack included disrupting telephone systems inside Iraq. This temporarily affected civilian telephone services in countries neighboring Iraq. However, this collateral damage was considered acceptable at that time. But the uncertain damage from a cyber-attack gone haywire was not. Since then though, the US Government has felt comfortable using cyber-attacks to advance its goals, best documented in the case of the Stuxnet virus.

REFERENCE

Markoff, J. and Shanker, T. "Halted '03 Iraq plan illustrates U.S. fear of cyberwar risk," New York Times, August 1, 2009

Critical thinking questions

1. What are some ways (however unlikely) in which the proposed cyber-attack on Saddam Hussein's accounts could have harmed you?

2. What are some ways in which a cyber-attack on a military target can harm civilians?

3. One traditional military constraint based on the Geneva conventions and the UN Charter is called proportionality, the idea that a punishment should befit the crime. Given the risks of cyber-attacks identified in the earlier questions, do you think cyber-attacks are more likely to cause disproportional harm to civilians than conventional weapons?

DESIGN CASE

The Help Desk at the College of Engineering at Sunshine University has special privileges. It can fix user access problems bypassing normal access control procedures.

How did this come about, you might wonder? Years ago, an Electrical Engineering professor with considerable prestige in the College was unable to submit a grant proposal because he had accidently locked his Engineering account over the weekend. The Dean of the College and the Department Chair were extremely unhappy. As a "temporary" solution, student workers at the Help Desk were given administrative privileges to the Engineering domain, so they can change passwords and unlock accounts without inconveniencing the faculty and staff. Years later, the so-called "temporary solution" has

become permanent, and quick response over the weekend is expected by all users.

One Saturday morning, Adam, a new student hired as a Help Desk employee decides, against the College's policy, to install a BitTorrent client on his Help Desk computer. Later in the week, an investigation into reports of sluggish computers leads to the discovery of a botnet installation on most of the computers in the College. After days of investigation, the source of the botnet installations is discovered when a keylogger is found on the machine Adam used. He had inadvertently installed malware on the machine together with the BitTorrent installation and the keylogger malware had captured Adam's credentials.

The College Dean has asked you to have an incident report on his desk as soon as possible, including recommendations to prevent such incidents in the future.

1. List the threats and vulnerabilities that allowed this situation to occur.

2. Classify all the events found in 1 above, including:

   a. Asset affected, including asset classification and characterization[34]

   b. Threat agent (including internal, external, or partner)

   c. Threat action (type, etc.)

   d. Vulnerability used

3. What recommendations would you make to the Dean going forward?

4. In your opinion, what should be done with Adam, the student recently hired to the Help Desk position?

---

[34]What the instructor should be looking for at some point is a worst-case scenario situation. A breach of this type could have major consequences. Once the domain admin account is compromised, the agent has access to all information stored in the domain: email, research data, PII, etc.

## CHAPTER 7

Encryption Controls

Overview

Encryption is one of the core operational technologies used in information security. In its essential form, it helps provide confidentiality of information. Through innovative application, encryption can also confirm the integrity of information and the identity of the sender. Every commercial transaction performed over the Internet uses encryption to maintain information security. Encryption ensures that financial information such as credit card numbers sent over the Internet are not stolen during transit. In many cases, encryption is not only appropriate but also required by federal law. Encryption is therefore an essential part of the modern commercial infrastructure. In this chapter, we introduce the fundamentals of encryption technologies. We also discuss the operational challenges in implementing encryption and solutions that have been developed to address these challenges. At the end of this chapter, you should know:

- The three types of encryption commonly used and their most appropriate uses
- The standard, practical implementation of encryption technologies used in information exchange
- The alternate use of encryption technologies to verify identities in the form of certificates
- The infrastructure (PKI) that has been developed to make encryption convenient and practical

Introduction

What do we expect when we send information over the Internet? We certainly want the information to reach the receiver.[1] However, is that enough? What if the message is – "I do not have money to pay the tuition bill this semester. Please transfer $1,000 into my checking account #0000101010 at the credit union, routing number 123456789. In case of any difficulty, the password is 'hello123'."

In the information security world, it is common to use the names Alice and Bob as the sender and receiver of messages when discussing secure communications.[2] In our example above, say, Alice wants to send the message to Bob. What features would Alice desire in the communication? For one, she would like the message to reach Bob. Second, she probably

---

[1] For a brief primer on how information is sent and received on computer networks, see the appendix.

[2] Wikipedia states that these names were first used by Ron Rivest in his paper describing the encryption protocol that bears his name (the RSA protocol). We will have more to talk about RSA later in the chapter (http://en.wikipedia.org/wiki/Alice_and_Bob).

would prefer that only Bob understand the message, even if her friends can see or hear the conversation. (After all, who wants their friends to know they have run out of money?) Upon receipt of the message, Bob is likely to want confirmation that the message came from Alice. Bob may also seek confirmation that the contents of the message are correct. Encryption cannot actually transmit the message, but encryption gives us all the other desired features in the communication between Alice and Bob. Adapting a well-known commercial, there are some things information security cannot do; for everything else, there is encryption.

At a high level of description, encryption converts the message into a form that only the receiver can decode, providing confidentiality. While decoding, the receiver can also detect if the message was modified during transit, providing integrity. Since encryption is so useful, it is used as the information security analog of a Swiss army knife. If information security is involved, chances are: encryption is being in some form or the other.

Encryption basics

Encryption means to crypt and is accomplished through cryptography. Cryptography is a compound word created from the Greek words crypto (κρυπτο) and graphy (γραφη). "Crypto" means hidden and "graphy" means writing, and cryptography is the act of hidden writing. The ATIS telecom glossary, our standard source for definitions, defines *encryption as the cryptographic transformation of data to produce ciphertext*. This definition introduces two new terms – cryptography and ciphertext. We have already seen that cryptography is the act of hidden writing. More formally, based on the ATIS telecom glossary, we can define *cryptography as the art or science of rendering plain information unintelligible, and for restoring encrypted information to intelligible form. Ciphertext is the encrypted text that is unintelligible to the reader.* The etymology of ciphertext is based on the Arabic word *cifr*, meaning nothing. The word cifr was later also used to represent the number 0. At the receiving end, decryption is used to decipher[3] the hidden message.

Figure 7.1 integrates these activities and shows the overall process of secure communication between Alice and Bob.

For all its utility, it is useful to remember that encryption can only do so much. A bolt cutter will break any lock, and a user who is willing to share his password will compromise any encryption scheme.

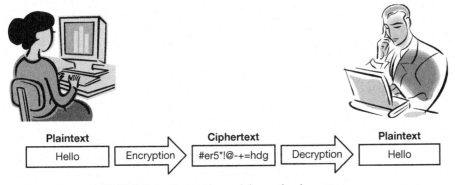

Plaintext **Ciphertext** **Plaintext**

| Hello | Encryption > | #er5*!@-+=hdg | Decryption > | Hello |

FIGURE 7.1   Encryption and decryption in context

---

[3]Do you now see the etymology of this word? De-cipher is to de-zerofy the message, i.e., take an apparently meaningless message and find the meaning in it.

Origins

The first documented instance of encryption was used by Roman Emperor Julius Caesar (100 Bc –44 Bc). Figure 7.2 is an extract from the translated work where the encryption method is described;[4] thus, "*if there was occasion for secrecy, he used the alphabet in such a manner that not a single word could be made out. The way to decipher those epistles was to substitute d for a, and so of the other letters respectively.*"

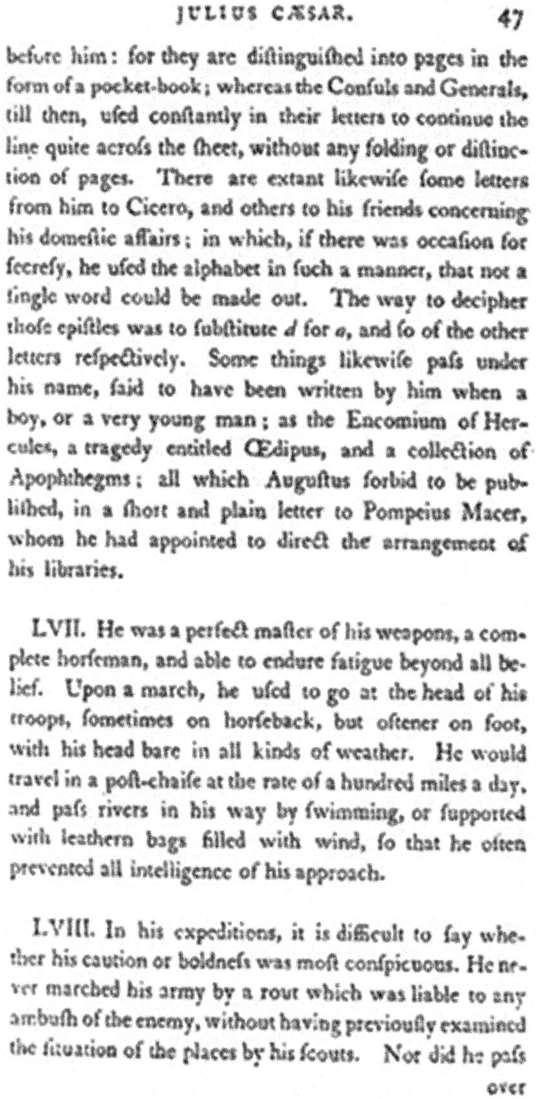

JULIUS CÆSAR. 47

before him: for they are diftinguifhed into pages in the form of a pocket-book; whereas the Confuls and Generals, till then, ufed conftantly in their letters to continue the line quite acrofs the fheet, without any folding or diftinction of pages. There are extant likewife fome letters from him to Cicero, and others to his friends concerning his domeftic affairs; in which, if there was occafion for fecrefy, he ufed the alphabet in fuch a manner, that not a fingle word could be made out. The way to decipher thofe epiftles was to fubftitute *d* for *a*, and fo of the other letters refpectively. Some things likewife pafs under his name, faid to have been written by him when a boy, or a very young man; as the Encomium of Hercules, a tragedy entitled Œdipus, and a collection of Apophthegms; all which Auguftus forbid to be publifhed, in a fhort and plain letter to Pompeius Macer, whom he had appointed to direct the arrangement of his libraries.

LVII. He was a perfect mafter of his weapons, a complete horfeman, and able to endure fatigue beyond all belief. Upon a march, he ufed to go at the head of his troops, fometimes on horfeback, but oftener on foot, with his head bare in all kinds of weather. He would travel in a poft-chaife at the rate of a hundred miles a day, and pafs rivers in his way by fwimming, or fupported with leathern bags filled with wind, fo that he often prevented all intelligence of his approach.

LVIII. In his expeditions, it is difficult to fay whether his caution or boldnefs was moft confpicuous. He never marched his army by a rout which was liable to any ambufh of the enemy, without having previoufly examined the fituation of the places by his fcouts. Nor did he pafs

over

FIGURE 7.2 Reference to Caesar cipher

[4]Alexander Thomson, M.D. (M.DCC.XCVI (1796)). The lives of the first 12 Caesars, translated from the Latin of C. Suetonius Tranquillus: with annotations and a review of the government and literature of the different periods. London, U.K., G.G. and J. Robinson, Paternoster-Row.

Thus, in the Caesar cipher, each letter was replaced by the letter three places to the right of the letter in the alphabet. Thus A → D; B → E, . . . , Q → T, . . . , W → Z, X → A, Y → B, Z → C. While Caesar always used a shift of three letters, we could just as easily use other shifts. For example, a shift of four characters to the right would give us an encryption scheme such as A → E; B → F.

This simple example illustrates an extremely important concept in encryption – keys. We will shortly have more to say about keys and their significance.

In fact, the method can be generalized even further. The letters do not need to be shifted by the same amount. Any mapping from one letter to another letter would work as an encryption scheme. For example, A → H; B → X, C → B . . . would be equally effective. In fact, *this encryption scheme of replacing individual letters with other letters for the purpose of encryption is known in the security literature as mono-alphabetic substitution.*

This example illustrates a very important building block of many encryption technologies – substitution. We will shortly illustrate how substitution is used in modern encryption technologies.

While encryption ensures the confidentiality of the data, this confidentiality is not always desired. There are currently malware in use that will encrypt data in a computer and keep it encrypted until a payment is made to the hacker. This type of malware is known as "ransomware." Encryption poses a problem for security experts engaged in data forensics by obscuring the details of a security incident. It also hinders the use of firewalls and other network devices based on deep packet inspection in order to allow or block a specific data stream. If the data contained in a packet is encrypted, it cannot be inspected.

Encryption requirements analysis

What are the requirements that a good encryption technique should meet? Generally speaking, encryption techniques share many properties with locks and good encryption techniques are similar to good locks in many ways. What do we expect in good locks? First, we expect them to be easy to use for owners. Second, we expect them to be difficult to break for intruders. While most locks can eventually be broken, locks only need to either take long enough to break to draw the attention of onlookers or be too expensive to break to be worth the effort.

Good encryption techniques also share these properties. We expect a good encryption technique to be easy to use for authorized senders and receivers of the information. We also expect that unauthorized users will take so much time to break the encryption that they will either give up or their actions will be noticed before they succeed.

In information security, effort is measured in terms of computational requirements. A good encryption scheme will require minimal computations by authorized users to read and write data, but impossibly large number of computations from unauthorized users.

Creators of encryption techniques have to worry about the fact that intruders can be pretty smart about trying to break encryption schemes. *The art of breaking ciphertext is called cryptanalysis.* For example, if we use mono-alphabetic substitution with the English alphabet, we can use the fact that some letters are known to be more common than others (e.g., e > t > a > I > o > n > s > h > r > d > l > u) to guess the encryption scheme simply from a count of the letters and their relative frequencies. With this knowledge, it is estimated that a mono-alphabetic encryption scheme can be broken with a corpus of only approximately 600 encrypted characters. If we also guess probable words, only about 150 letters are needed. Attackers may even try to send selective plaintext and see how the encryption works. For example, sending "BAT" and "CAT" can indicate how a change in one letter in the plain text affects the encryption outcome, providing hints at breaking the encryption.

Keys

Just as it is not simple to come up with locking mechanisms that are easy and economical for authorized users, but difficult to break for unauthorized users, it is not easy to come up with encryption techniques with similar properties. Look around, how many different kinds of locks are there? There are key locks, combination locks, biometric locks, and perhaps some other types of locks. These few lock types secure all the gates and safes in the world. Similarly, just a few encryption techniques secure all the information in the world.

Returning to the lock analogy, if there are only a few good lock types, how do we use the same lock type to secure all homes in a neighborhood? After all, it wouldn't be very helpful if the method that opened one door also opened all other doors in the neighborhood. This brings us to keys – locks are made unique by keys. The key that opens any given lock is unique to the lock.

The encryption analog to a lock type is a cryptographic algorithm, algorithm for short. *A cryptographic algorithm is a well-defined sequence of steps used to describe cryptographic processes.* Generally, we just call them algorithms. A few good algorithms with all the desired properties have been discovered so far. Each instance of the chosen algorithm is made unique by a unique set of numbers, which are called a key. In the context of encryption, *a key is a sequence of symbols that control the operations of encipherment and decipherment.* Users with the correct key can easily exchange information with each other. Eavesdroppers will take a prohibitively long time guessing the correct key.

What are the properties of a good key? As we have repeatedly stated, a good key should be difficult to guess. In the encryption context, keys are broken by simply trying different keys until the correct one is found. If we use 1-digit keys, we have 10 possible keys (0, 1, . . . , 9). If an intruder takes about 1 second to try one key, he will require at most 10 seconds to guess the correct key. If the process were repeated many times, the average time would be half of this, or 5 seconds. This is because on some occasions the first guess would be right, on others it may be the sixth guess, and so on. To improve security, we could try 2-digit numbers. This increases the number of possible keys to 100 (0–99). At the same rate as before, the intruder would now take 100 seconds at most, and 50 seconds on average. Thus, longer keys improve security.

Since computers can compute and check many hundreds of thousands of keys a second, the keys used in practice are hundreds of digits long.

General algorithm properties

The encryption requirements in the previous paragraphs suggest some important properties of good crypto-algorithms. They may be seen as a process of randomizing input. Input (plaintext) typically has structure in the form of words, images, documents, etc. We have seen that if an intruder can guess any part of the internal structure of the plaintext, that information will be exploited to decode the ciphertext. Therefore, the encryption algorithm must make the ciphertext appear to be a completely random sequence of bits. However, the randomization must be recoverable to the user in possession of the correct key.

Not only should the actual characters in the message appear random, even the length of the ciphertext must appear to be random to an intruder. If not, in certain situations, the intruder might be able to guess the content of the message simply by looking at the length of the message and the context. For example, if you know that in a certain situation, the only two possible messages are "yes" and "no," and you see an encrypted message that reads "!$#," you do not need to decipher the message to know with certainty that the plaintext was "yes."

Finally, another important property of algorithms is that a change in even 1 bit of the input should completely change the ciphertext, changing at least half the bits. This will prevent an intruder from trying to craft selective messages and try to guess the encryption scheme by looking at the ciphertext output.

At this point, we know that encryption involves an algorithm and a key. We also know that there are a few algorithms used universally to encrypt information, which are made unique for each instance by a key unique to that instance. We now turn to the kinds of algorithms in use and their applications.

Encryption types overview

All the known available encryption techniques can be categorized into three types. The categorization is done on the basis of the number of keys used to encrypt and decrypt information. A quick comparison of the three types of encryption is given in Table 7.1. The rest of the chapter discusses each of these three encryption types in detail.

A look at table, one might suggest that Hash functions might be the simplest encryption type to understand. That is probably true too. However, when people talk about encryption, they usually mean the use of secret key cryptography and public-key cryptography. In the sections that follow, therefore, we first discuss secret key cryptography, followed by public-key cryptography. We will talk about hash functions at the end because their use in encryption is less intuitive than the use of the other two encryption types.

Secret key cryptography

Secret key cryptography refers to encryption methods that use one key for both encryption and decryption. Figure 7.3 provides an overview of secret key cryptography.

As seen in the figure, the central feature of secret key cryptography is that the same key is used for both encryption and decryption. Due to this symmetry in the keys used for encryption and decryption, secret key cryptography is sometimes also called symmetric key cryptography, or symmetric key encryption.

The most common use of secret key cryptography is to transmit information securely. If Alice and Bob can both agree on the key, then Alice can encrypt her information with the key and Bob can decrypt the information using the same key. Similarly, Bob can encrypt his information

Table 7.1 Comparison of encryption types

Encryption type	Keys	Applications
Hash function	0	Password protection, data integrity check
Secret key cryptography	1	Secure data storage and transmission
Public-key cryptography	2	Secure key exchange, authentication, digital signatures

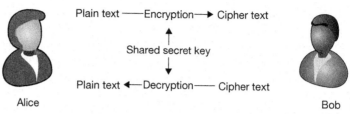

FIGURE 7.3   Secret key cryptography overview

with the shared key and Alice can decrypt the information using the shared key. The information is safe during transmission because only Alice and Bob know the key, and as we have agreed before, it is almost impossible to decrypt the transmitted information without knowledge of the key.

Secret key encryption can also be used to secure information stored in computers. If Bob wants to secure some information, he can select a key and encrypt information on his hard drive using the key. To retrieve the information, Bob simply has to enter his key and decrypt the information. Of course, if Bob forgets his key, he will never be able to retrieve the information on his computer.

The current standard for secret key cryptography is the Advanced Encryption Standard (AES). It was chosen by the National Institute for Standards and Technology (NIST) on November 26, 2001, after a selection process that lasted almost 5 years. The technology used in AES was developed by two Belgian cryptographers. Two technologies, the Data Encryption Standard (DES) and the International Data Encryption Algorithm (IDEA), were predecessor technologies to AES, and you may encounter these terms in the literature on information security. However, since AES is the current standard, we will not talk about DES and IDEA any further in this book. A brief overview of the technology behind AES is provided in the next section.

Public-key cryptography

Public-key cryptography refers to encryption methods that use two keys, one for encryption and another for decryption. The technology is used for two different applications – data transmission and digital signatures. Figure 7.4 provides an overview of public-key cryptography for the purpose of data transmission.

A comparison of Figure 7.3 and 7.4 shows that the unique feature of public-key cryptography is that one key is used for encryption and a different key is used for decryption. Because of this asymmetry in the keys used, public-key cryptography is also called asymmetric key cryptography, or asymmetric key encryption.

As we will see in later sections, when we describe public-key cryptography in greater detail, the receiver's private key is kept confidential. For this reason, it is common to refer to the receiver's private key as the secret key. However, Kaufman et al[5] recommend that the industry must standardize on calling this key the private key, and reserving the phrase "secret key" for the shared secret key used in secret key cryptography. In deference to that advice, we will also strive to avoid calling the private key the secret key.

---

[5] Kaufman, C., R. Perlman and M. Speciner (2002). Network Security: Private Communication in a Public World, Prentice-Hall ISBN 0130460192

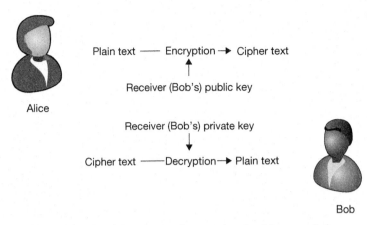

Alice

Plain text ——— Encryption → Cipher text

Receiver (Bob's) public key

Receiver (Bob's) private key

Cipher text ———Decryption→ Plain text

Bob

FIGURE 7.4   Public-key cryptography overview for data transmission

What is public-key cryptography used for? As we will see, public-key cryptography can be seen as a supercharged version of secret key cryptography. As such, it can do anything that secret key cryptography can do, and some more. Why then do we even care about secret key cryptography?

It turns out that public-key cryptography is extremely demanding of computing resources, requiring many millions of times the processing capability required for secret key cryptography. Reckless use of public-key cryptography would bring even the fastest desktop computers to a grinding halt. In practice, therefore, we are extremely selective about when to use public-key cryptography, preferring to use secret key cryptography to the extent possible.

The primary use of public-key cryptography is to exchange keys. While going over the discussion of secret key cryptography in the previous section, did you give some thought on how Alice and Bob might agree on the same shared secret key? You may have noticed that we started with the assumption that Alice and Bob had a shared secret key. This might be possible if Bob and Alice had nearby offices. However, what if Bob was a service provider located in Washington, DC, and Alice was a customer located in Tampa, Florida? Could Alice and Bob possibly have a way of agreeing on a shared secret key that no one else would know? The answer is no. It can in fact be proven that there is no reliable way for Alice and Bob to exchange a secret key securely.[6]

Since there is no trivial way for Alice and Bob to exchange the secret key securely, public-key cryptography is used to do the job. When Alice and Bob are ready to communicate with each other, they first use public-key cryptography to exchange a secret key. Once the secret key has been agreed upon, Alice and Bob switch from using the computing intensive public-key cryptography to the much simpler secret key cryptography.

This is important to remember about public-key cryptography – the private key is known only to the owner of the key. It is not shared with anybody else.

---

[6]In the literature, this scenario is discussed as the two general problems. There is plenty of information available about this well-known problem on the Internet. See, for example, the Wikipedia article http://en.wikipedia.org/wiki/Two_Generals%27_Problem

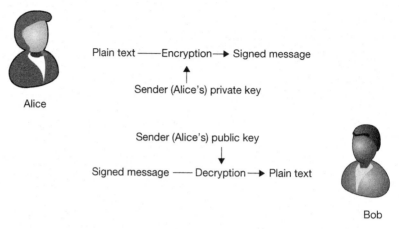

FIGURE 7.5 Using public-key encryption for digital signatures

The second use of public-key cryptography comes from the unique relationship between a public key and its associated private key. It turns out that they exist in pairs. We have seen that information encrypted with the public key can be decrypted by the associated private key. This process also works in reverse. Information encrypted with the private key can be decrypted with the associated public key. This feature is used industrially to create digital signatures. *Digital signatures are defined as cryptographic transformations of data that allow a recipient of the data to prove the source (non-repudiation) and integrity of the data.*

When Alice sends a message to Bob, she can also send an encrypted version of the message, encrypted with her own private key. Bob can try decrypting this information. If the decrypted version matches the sent information, Bob knows not only that Alice sent the message, but also that the message was not modified en route. The process is shown in Figure 7.5.

Public-key encryption can be puzzling for the first time reader. It is also confusing to see two different uses of this puzzling technology. To facilitate learning, we use two approaches in this chapter. The first step is to compare Figures 7.4 and 7.5 and to isolate the differences between them. The second step will be in the next section, where we describe public-key encryption using an example.

Let's look at Figures 7.4 and 7.5.

What keys are used in each case? For data transmission, we used the receiver's keys. For digital signatures, we used the sender's keys. For data transmission, we used the public key for encryption. For digital signatures, we used the private key for encryption. This is summarized in Table 7.2.

What's going on here? Why the differences in the keys used. The critical thing to remember about public-key encryption is that a user only has access to one private key – his own. But everybody has access to everybody's public keys.

Table 7.2 Key comparison for public-key encryption applications

	Data transmission	Digital signature
Key owner	Receiver	Sender
Encryption key type	Public	Private

While transmitting data, we want to make sure the data cannot be read by others during transmission. The best way to accomplish that is to encrypt it in such a way that only the receiver can decrypt the information. How do you do that? What is unique to the receiver?

Well, we know that only the receiver has possession of his or her private key. We also know that if we encrypt some information with the receiver's public key, only the receiver will be able to decrypt the information using his private key. Fortunately, anybody in the world can get any user's public key. So, that is what we will do – encrypt the information with the receiver's public key and send it away. Only the receiver will be able to read the information.

When signing off on letters, privacy is not our concern. For example, Bob would like to be convinced that Alice did indeed send the letter.[7] How can Alice do that? Well, both Alice and Bob know that only Alice is in possession of Alice's private key. If Alice can somehow convince Bob that she is indeed in possession of that key, Bob would be convinced. Fortunately, we have a way of doing that. If Alice encrypts some information with her private key, anybody in the world can decrypt it with her public key. Indeed, Bob does just that. If he succeeds, he is convinced that Alice has the private key she is supposed to have. And since no one else in the world ought to have Alice's private key, the letter must have come from Alice. The public key thus serves as a digital signature.

The way digital signatures are used in practice, we get a bonus feature as well. What message should Alice encrypt and send to Bob to convince him of her identity? We encrypt the message itself. This way, if Bob is able to decrypt successfully, not only is he convinced that the message came from Alice, he is also assured that the message was not modified during transmission.

The above has been simplified in one way compared to what actually happens. The simplification has been done for teaching purposes. In practice, we do not need to encrypt the entire message; we just need to encrypt a hash function of the message. Hash functions are discussed in the next section and we will revisit this issue at the end of the discussion of hash functions.

You may also be thinking – how can Alice keep the message confidential during data transmission if anybody can decrypt it using her public key? Great question. She cannot. Therefore, what we do is to send the message using the data transmission technique discussed above and also send a digital signature along with the message to confirm that the message did indeed come from Alice.

The current technology used to perform public-key cryptography is called RSA. It is named after the three creators of the technology – Ron Rivest, Adi Shamir, and Leonard Adleman. The technology was described in a paper published in 1977.[8]

Hash functions

Hash functions refer to encryption methods that use no keys. These functions are also called one-way transformations because there is no way to retrieve the message encrypted using a

---

[7] Say you receive an unsolicited job offer from the White House. How would you be convinced that the offer was for real?

[8] Rivest, R. Shamir, A. and Adleman, L. "A method for obtaining digital signatures and public-key cryptosystems." Communications of the ACM, 1978, 21(2): 120–126. (The first few pages of the paper should be very interesting for an undergraduate student – the opening line talks about email in future tense.) The paper is also available at http://people.csail. mit.edu/rivest/Rsapaper.pdf (accessed: 10/19/2012).

hash function. Now, that must really get you scratching your heads. Why would you care for an encrypt technology if you can never read the data back? As it turns out, this is actually very useful and, in fact, you have been using this property ever since you have used computers.

Hash functions take a message of any length and convert them to numbers of fixed length, usually 128 or 256 bits long. The length of the hash transform of the number "4" will be the same length as the hash transform of an entire DVD. Hash functions are used with passwords. We will shortly see how in the next paragraph, in the meanwhile, it may be a good exercise for you to think how hash functions may be useful with passwords.

Computers store passwords as the result of a hash transform instead of storing the actual value of the password. This way, the passwords can never be recovered even if the computer is stolen. When a user types in their password, the computer computes the hash of the password and compares the hash with the stored password hash. If the two matches, the computer accepts the provided password, otherwise not. This way, hash functions allow computers to verify passwords without storing a copy of the passwords themselves.

> Hashed passwords are still vulnerable to brute-force and dictionary attacks, as we will see in Chapter 8. If a user selects a weak password, it could still be easily guessed. Hash functions can obscure passwords but cannot prevent them from being guessed.

The other use of passwords is to verify the integrity of information. If the sender sends a message as well as a hash of the message, the receiver can independently compute the hash of the message and compare it to the received hash. If the two hashes match, the receiver can be assured that the message was not modified during transmission. When hashes are used this way, they are called checksums. *A checksum is a value computed on data to detect error or manipulation during transmission.*

You see this commonly during data downloads. Software vendors often provide the checksums to their software downloads to help systems administrators verify that the software was downloaded without errors. Figure 7.6 shows an example from the download site for IBM Application Servers.

```
← → C ⌂   🗋 publib.boulder.ibm.com/wasce/md5/3002/wasce-3.0.0.2.md5

e5943edf209b9da610c353cb0795521d *wasce_ibm60sdk_setup-3.0.0.2-390xlinux.tar.bz2
7b6f822fd58983bd0c515d9367f3d96b *wasce_ibm60sdk_setup-3.0.0.2-ia32linux.tar.bz2
11fe3732c4fd5b36ebb9d88a79f29e4d *wasce_ibm60sdk_setup-3.0.0.2-ia32win.zip
f0bfa0992320afe1f77a43abda82695f *wasce_ibm60sdk_setup-3.0.0.2-ppc64aix.zip
bed57127a2a5a2560665158e18658c86 *wasce_ibm60sdk_setup-3.0.0.2-ppc64linux.tar.bz2
9fa2d5850312698a4807b0f0b4a10135 *wasce_ibm60sdk_setup-3.0.0.2-sparc64solaris.zip
4ddaa95fac2756a0ab86a3325193a2de *wasce_ibm60sdk_setup-3.0.0.2-x86_64linux.tar.bz2
4d9d9837939194119f04f8e4cd35e2b4 *wasce_ibm60sdk_setup-3.0.0.2-x86_64win.zip
69baf09b42e4fbcb495820b496502998 *wasce_ibm70sdk_setup-3.0.0.2-390xlinux.tar.bz2
137f9df15928884be80110279448b1ba *wasce_ibm70sdk_setup-3.0.0.2-ia32linux.tar.bz2
afe7679f636f64cafd6a980ffc0a10a5 *wasce_ibm70sdk_setup-3.0.0.2-ia32win.zip
a6ac0247a621021f4dcc24b77e5cbf6f *wasce_ibm70sdk_setup-3.0.0.2-ppc64aix.zip
0ab7e54a940c95b2d16c92e7e5f20620 *wasce_ibm70sdk_setup-3.0.0.2-ppc64linux.tar.bz2
3e3f5bdb678000fba9190e955c9dc092 *wasce_ibm70sdk_setup-3.0.0.2-sparc64solaris.zip
cf2412a7522ce2c805a080ae7c547c5c *wasce_ibm70sdk_setup-3.0.0.2-x86_64linux.tar.bz2
bf01e274304c8abe2be1568c75bd0f2e *wasce_ibm70sdk_setup-3.0.0.2-x86_64win.zip
b2791cf15dd7f97370783fcbc88c8cd9 *wasce_samples-3.0.0.2.zip
ac591620e85bd9be8acf64c2443e6658 *wasce_setup-3.0.0.2-unix.bin
c359de0e70fce73fd1f2fa3cd65f5113 *wasce_setup-3.0.0.2-win.exe
```

FIGURE 7.6   Checksums example

The most popular hash functions in use today are called MD5 and SHA-2. MD5 stands for version 5 of message digest algorithms. MD5 was universally used since its development by Ron Rivest (the same Ron Rivest who codeveloped RSA) in 1991. However, an array of flaws has been discovered in the algorithm and its use for cryptographic applications has been formally discouraged since December 31, 2008.[9] However, MD5 continues to be popular for low-risk applications such as download verification.

SHA stands for secure hash algorithm and the suffix 2 stands for version 2 of the algorithm. The development of SHA has been facilitated by NIST, the National Institute of Standards and Technology. SHA-2 was published in 2001. Even though there are no known security vulnerabilities in SHA-2, the technology for the next version of SHA, SHA-3 was selected on October 2, 2012.[10] The motivation for the development of the next generation of hash function before any apparent need was to be prepared in case an attack was developed against SHA-2. SHA-3 uses a completely different algorithm compared to SHA-2, so it is highly unlikely that an attack that compromises SHA-2 would also compromise SHA-3. Developers now have the choice of using SHA-2 or SHA-3 depending on their needs.

Encryption types details

The previous section provided an overview of the three types of encryption and their uses. In this section, we look at the primary technologies used in each encryption type in more detail.

Secret key cryptography

Secret key encryption is composed of two procedures – block encryption and cipher block chaining. Encrypting large messages of indefinite size requires enormous computing resources, beyond the capabilities of most end-user computers. Hence, user data is first broken into fixed-size blocks of manageable size. Breaking messages into reasonable-sized blocks offers the best combination of performance and security. *Block encryption is the process of converting a plaintext block into an encrypted block.* Most commercial encryption algorithms use 64- or 128-bit blocks. In particular, the current standard for secret key cryptography, AES, uses 128-bit blocks.

Block encryption

In general, block encryption uses a combination of two activities – substitution and permutation. We have already seen an example of substitution earlier in the chapter – the Caesar cipher and the more generic mono-alphabetic substitution. In the context of secret key cryptography, *substitution specifies the k-bit output for each k-bit input. Permutation specifies the output position of each of the k input bits.* Permutation is a special case of substitution because a specific bit of the input substitutes for a specific bit in the output. The generic operation of block encryption is shown in Figure 7.7.[11]

Figure 7.7, which is based on the DES technology standard, is representative of the operation of secret key encryption technologies. Within each block, the data is further broken into

---

[9] http://www.kb.cert.org/vuls/id/836068

[10] http://csrc.nist.gov/groups/ST/hash/sha-3/index.html

[11] The figure is adapted from FIPS PUB 46-3, Data Encryption Standard (DES), 10/25/99, http://csrc.nist.gov/publications/fips/fips46-3/fips46-3.pdf, (accessed 10/23/12).

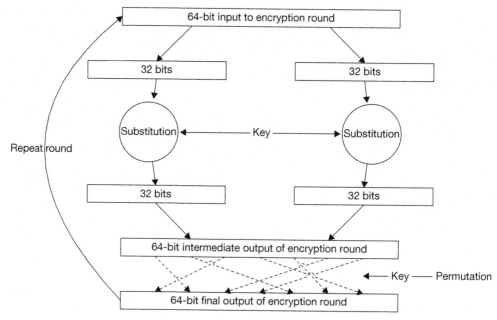

FIGURE 7.7   Generic form of block encryption[25]

two parts. A substitution procedure mangles up all the bits in each part. The two mangled parts are then run through a permutation unit, which shuffles the bits in the block. The process is repeated until the input is satisfactorily encrypted.

> ### Why permutation?
>
> An interested reader might ask – if permutation is just a special form of substitution, why use it at all? Why not just repeat the substitution operations.
>
> The reason for using permutations is to further diffuse the impact of substitution. If you look at Figure 7.7 closely, you will find that if a bit in the left half of the input is changed, the substitution operation only affects the bits in the left half of the output. The same is true for a change in input bits in the right half – substitution only affects the bits in the right half. An adversary could use this property to craft special inputs and break the encryption algorithm. The permutation operation diffuses the impact of a change in a single bit of the input to the overall output of the block.

The substitution–permutation operation is repeated multiple times to ensure that changes in the input are distributed across all bits in the output. In Figure 7.7, a change in 1 bit in the input will impact 32 of the 64 bits in the output of the round (either the left half or the right half, followed by changes in the corresponding 32 bits of the final output of the round). This is not satisfactory. For good encryption, a change in 1 bit of the input should affect all 64 bits in the

---

[25]The figure is adapted from FIPS PUB 46-3, Data Encryption Standard (DES), 10/25/99, http://csrc.nist.gov/publications/fips/fips46-3/fips46-3.pdf, (accessed 10/23/12).

output equally. This is what will make the encryption difficult to break for an intruder. To accomplish this, the rounds are repeated until all output bits are affected by even the slightest change in the input. DES uses 16 rounds. AES uses 10–14 rounds, depending upon the size of the key.

Confusion–diffusion

The substitution–permutation sequence of block encryption algorithms implements Claude Shannon's ideas of confusion and diffusion. Shannon, widely considered the father of information theory, developed the idea that confusion and diffusion provided a good basis for secrecy systems.[12] Confusion is making the relationship between the plaintext and ciphertext as complex as possible. Diffusion is spreading the impact of a change in 1 bit of the plaintext to all bits in the ciphertext.

In block encryption, substitution provides confusion and permutation provides diffusion.

Cipher block chaining

Once the information in a block is encrypted, we need a way to use this mechanism to encrypt input of arbitrary size. The basic idea behind the methods used in practice to accomplish this goal is to collect all the encrypted blocks and aggregate them together suitably to get the encrypted version of the user's input. The simplest method to accomplish this might be to just collect all the blocks as shown in Figure 7.8. This method is very intuitive to understand; however, it is not used in practice for reasons discussed shortly. However, given its conceptual importance, the method is given a name – electronic code book (ECB). *Electronic code book is the process of dividing a message into blocks and encrypting each block separately.*

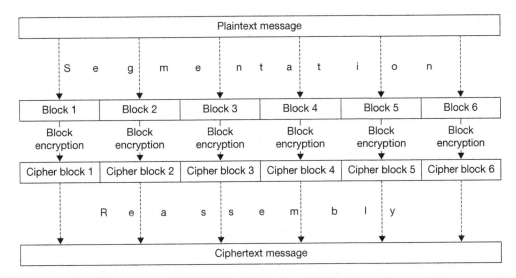

FIGURE 7.8   Electronic code book

---

[12] Shannon, C. "Communication theory of secrecy systems," 1946, http://netlab.cs.ucla.edu/wiki/files/shannon1949.pdf (accessed 10/23/12).

Why is ECB not used in practice? Figure 7.8 shows that there is insufficient diffusion of confusion in the method. If blocks 1 and 3 are identical, cipher blocks 1 and 3 will also be identical and this will be visible in the final encrypted output. This can potentially give an attacker some insight into the information being encrypted. Therefore, in practice, some complexity has to be introduced to diffuse the output adequately. Of these methods, one that is fairly intuitive to understand is called cipher block chaining (CBC). *Cipher block chaining uses information from the previous cipher block while encrypting a cipher block*. The mechanism is shown in Figure 7.9.

The difference between ECB and CBC is that before a block is encrypted, it is mangled with the output of the previous block. The diagonal arrows in the figure show the cipher output of the previous block being used to mangle the input of the next block. The operation commonly used to combine the two inputs is called "exclusive OR," written as XOR, and represented in Figure 7.9 as +. XOR is a bitwise operation where the result is 0 if the 2 input bits are the same and 1 if the two input bits are different. As a result of the chaining of outputs, even if blocks 1 and 3 are the same, cipher blocks 1 and 3 will not be the same.

A randomly chosen initialization vector ensures that even if the same message is sent again, the output will be totally different. The final CBC output is obtained by simply collecting the cipher blocks together, as shown in the lower half of Figure 7.9.

As can be seen from this section, secret key cryptography relies on fairly simple operations. It is therefore computationally very conservative. However, as discussed earlier in the chapter, the challenge in using secret key encryption is key exchange. The sender and receiver have to be able to exchange the key before the encryption begins. Public-key cryptography, discussed in the next section, accomplishes this goal. Public-key cryptography is computationally very intensive, but its greatest virtue is that it allows secret communication over an insecure channel. It is therefore ideally suited for use in key exchange.

Public-key cryptography

Public-key cryptography uses two keys – one for encryption and another for decryption. The encryption key is widely distributed to allow users to send encrypted messages to the owner of the key. The decryption key is used to decrypt messages. Obviously, the owner guards the

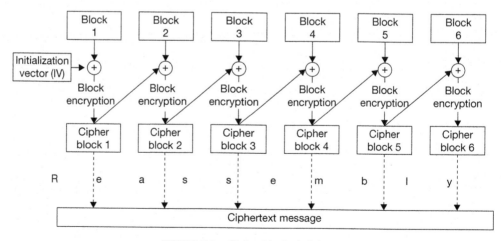

FIGURE 7.9 Cipher block chaining

decryption key carefully. For this reason, a user's encryption key is called his public key and the decryption key, the private key.

To keep the discussion short and as simple as possible, in this section, we provide a simple example of the modular arithmetic that is behind most public-key cryptography algorithms. We then present RSA, the most popular public-key encryption algorithm.

Modular arithmetic used in public-key cryptography

The modulus operation is sometimes also called the "remainder" operation. So, 17 mod 10 = 7, 94 mod 10 = 4, etc. The use of the modulo operation for public-key cryptography may be seen from Table 7.3.[13] The table gives how decimal digits may be encrypted.

To use the table to encrypt data, multiply any number in the table header by 3 and take the modulus with respect to 10. For example, to encrypt 6, we use 6 * 3 mod 10 = 18 mod 10 = 8. Thus, 8 is the ciphertext for the number 6. The first highlighted row in the table shows the ciphertext computed this way for all possible single-digit numbers.

To decrypt, we multiply the ciphertext by 7 and take the modulus with respect to 10. For example, 8 * 7 mod 10 = 56 mod 10 = 6. Note that this gives us the plaintext 6, which had been encrypted to 8. The results for all other numbers are shown in the second highlighted row in the table.

In this example, we may write (3, 10) as the encryption (public) key and (7, 10) as the decryption (private) key. There are two interesting facts about the modulus operation used in this example.

First, data encrypted by the encryption key cannot be decrypted by the encryption key. For example, 8 * 3 mod 10 = 24 mod 10 = 4. But 4 ≠ 6, so an intruder cannot simply exploit his knowledge of the public key to decrypt data encrypted with the same key. Knowledge of the private key is required for decryption.

Second, either key can be used for encryption, and the other key will serve as the decryption key. For example, 6 * 7 mod 10 = 2 (encryption), and 2 * 3 mod 10 = 6 (decryption). This allows public-key cryptography to be used for digital signatures, as mentioned earlier in the chapter.

Table 7.3 Modulo 10 table to demonstrate rudiments of public-key cryptography

Number to encrypt n → (plaintext)		0	1	2	3	4	5	6	7	8	9
Key (multiplier) m	↓										
	0	0	0	0	0	0	0	0	0	0	0
n * m mod 10 →	1	0	1	2	3	4	5	6	7	8	9
n * m mod 10 →	2	0	2	4	6	8	0	2	4	6	8
n * 3 mod 10 = ciphertext c →	3	0	3	6	9	2	5	8	1	4	7
	4	0	4	8	2	6	0	4	8	2	6
	5	0	5	0	5	0	5	0	5	0	5
	6	0	6	2	8	4	0	6	2	8	4
c * 7 mod 10 (plaintext) →	7	0	7	4	1	8	5	2	9	6	3
	8	0	8	6	4	2	0	8	6	4	2
	9	0	9	8	7	6	5	4	3	2	1

---

[13]This table is based on the example in Kaufman, C. Perlman, R. and Speciner, M. 2002. Network Security: Private Communication in a Public World, Prentice-Hall.

The example in Table 7.3 demonstrates the importance of key length in public-key cryptography. It would not take too long for an intruder to guess the private key (7, 10) given knowledge of the public key (3, 10). In practice, therefore, we use extremely large numbers to prevent intruders from guessing the private key in any reasonable amount of time.

RSA

The example in the earlier section uses a simple example to demonstrate the magical properties of public-key cryptography. RSA is the form of public-key cryptography used in practice. The RSA algorithm uses exponentiation instead of multiplication. The algorithm is described here in brief.[14]

1. Start with two large prime numbers, called p and q. Typically these numbers are over 256 bits each (i.e., over 76 decimal digits each).

2. Compute $n = p * q$.

3. Compute $\varphi = (p - 1) * (q - 1)$.

4. Choose a number e that is relatively prime to ϕ, i.e., the two numbers do not share any common factors other than 1 (the letter e stands for encryption, and this number will be used for encryption).

5. Choose a number d that is the multiplicative inverse of e mod ϕ, i.e., a number d such that $d*e - 1$ is divisible by ϕ (the letter d stands for decryption, and this number will be used for decryption).

6. The pair <e, n> is the public key and is used for encryption

7. The pair <d, n> is the private key and is used for decryption

8. The keys are used as follows:

   a. To encrypt message m, compute ciphertext $c = m^e \bmod n$

   b. To decrypt ciphertext c, compute $m = c^d \bmod n$.

A simple example can demonstrate this. We have to be judicious in the numbers we choose since exponentiation very quickly leads to enormous numbers. However $p = 3$ and $q = 11$ work well.[15] With this choice, we have

1. $n = 3 * 11 = 33$

2. $\varphi = (3 - 1) * (11 - 1) = 2 * 10 = 20$

3. Say $e = 3$ since 3, does not share any factors with 20 other than 1.

4. We can choose $d = 7$ since $3 * 7 - 1 = 20$ and 20 divides $\varphi = 20$

5. With these choices:

   a. $c = m^3 \bmod 33$

   b. $m = c^7 \bmod 33$.

---

[14] A method for obtaining digital signatures and public-key cryptosystems, Rivest, R.L., Shamir, A. and Adleman, L. Communications of the ACM, 1978, 21(2): 120–126.

[15] These numbers were also chosen in the book, Tannenbaum, A.S. and Steen, M.v. Distributed Systems: Principles and Paradigms, 2002, Upper Saddle River, NJ, Prentice-Hall, Inc.

Table 7.4   RSA example

Plaintext				Cipher	Plaintext		
	Sender operation				Receiver operation		
Symbol	Numeric representation (m)	m^3	m^3 mod 33	c^7	c^7 mod 33	Symbol
H	8	512	17	410338673	8	H
E	5	125	26	8031810176	5	E
L	12	1728	12	35831808	12	L
O	14	2744	5	78125	14	O
I	9	729	3	2187	9	I
S	19	6859	28	13492928512	19	S
M	13	2197	19	893871739	13	M

Table 7.4 demonstrates the use of these choices in an RSA example. We start by converting plaintext to a numerical form. The example simply uses the position in the alphabet as the numerical representation, i.e., a = 1, b = 2, etc. The encryption and decryption operations may be verified from the table.

Since the public key includes the product n of the two numbers p, q chosen initially, if n could be factored, RSA could be broken. Therefore, the security of RSA depends critically upon the difficulty of factoring large numbers.

RSA also depends critically upon the availability of a large number of large prime numbers. If not, an intruder could simply create a table of all known prime numbers and try product combinations until n was obtained. Fortunately, prime numbers are abundant and it is impractical to store all known prime numbers. Therefore, if used with suitably large prime numbers, RSA is secure at least for now.

Prime number theorem

The probability that a number n is prime is approximately $\frac{1}{\ln(n)}$, where ln represents the natural logarithm. This is also equal to $\frac{1}{2.3\log(n)}$, where log is the logarithm to the base 10. Say n is a 10-digit number. Since $\log(10^{10}) = 10$, the probability that the number is prime $= 1/2.3 * 10 = 1/23$. If n is a 100-digit number, the likelihood becomes 1 in 230.

In other words, if we randomly chose 230 100-digit numbers, we are very likely to find a prime number. Alternately, there are about $10^{100}/230 \approx 10^{97}$ 100-digit prime numbers. All the computer storage in the world amounts to about 10^{20} bytes. It is therefore impractical to store all prime numbers to break RSA using guess-and-check procedures.

Hash functions

Hash functions are used to transform inputs into a fixed-length output. The transformation has two properties: (1) each input has a unique output and (2) it is impossible to guess an input from a given output. This is shown in Figure 7.10. It can be seen that all inputs have a unique

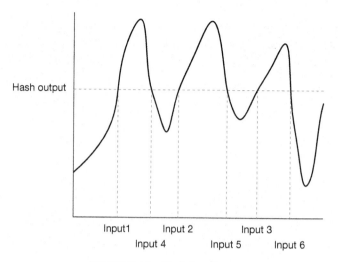

Hash output

Input1   Input 2   Input 3

Input 4   Input 5   Input 6

FIGURE 7.10 Hash functions

output (which is why the transformation is called a function.[16] But inputs 1–6 all transform to the same hash output. Therefore, given a hash output, it is impossible to determine which input led to the given output.

As discussed earlier, hash functions are used to store passwords. If passwords are saved as clear text, data theft could compromise the password. Saving passwords as hashes protects passwords from being stolen.

> A good check to determine whether a website saves passwords in clear-text or as a hash is to ask for the password. If the site can send you your password, you know that the site kept the password in clear text, or it would not be able to send you the password.

Encryption in use

One remaining challenge in using encryption in practice is establishing trust in the public key sent by a user. We have seen that it is fairly simple to generate a public-key–private-key pair. What if an intruder sends you a public key and claims that it is the public key of the Bank of America. How would you detect that it is not? In the remaining sections of this chapter, we will see how public-key encryption is used in commercial technologies such as SSL/TLS and VPNs. We will then discuss the procedures used to establish trust in public keys.

SSL/TLS and VPN

The most common technologies used for encrypting information during network transfer are SSL/TLS (Security Sockets Layer and Transport Layer Security) and VPN (Virtual Private

---

[16]Function: a rule of correspondence between two sets such that there is a unique element in the second set assigned to each element in the first set (Houghton-Mifflin Harcourt eReference).

Network). In SSL/TLS, the transaction with a specific network server, such as a web or database server, is encrypted. In VPN, all communication from the computer is encrypted.

The salient feature of all such encryption technologies used in practice is that they combine the best features of secret key cryptography and public cryptography for a pleasant user experience. Secret key cryptography uses minimal computing power. However, it needs the shared key to be exchanged securely before secret communication can begin. Public key is prohibitively demanding of computing resources and therefore is not very appropriate to encrypt entire conversations particularly on small devices. However, even the simplest devices can use public-key cryptography briefly to exchange the secret key.

Therefore, in commercial practice, secure communication begins with the server providing its public key to the user. The user generates a secret key locally and encrypts the secret key with the server's public key. This ends the use of public-key cryptography for the communication. All subsequent transactions are encrypted with the shared secret key.

Certificates

Real-world encryption critically depends upon the reliability of the public key sent by the server. This is quite analogous to the need for reliability of a driver's license produced as proof of identity in the physical world. In the physical world, we check for the reliability of the license by verifying whether the license was indeed issued by the state DMV. In the Internet world, there are companies called certificate authorities (CAs) that serve as the analogs of DMVs. CAs issue public keys to servers. The public-key exchange process works as shown in Figure 7.11.

Servers interested in participating in eCommerce transactions obtain a public key from one of the well-known public-key providers (certificate authorities). The CA encrypts the web server's public key and IP address with its own private key for use as a certificate. *A certificate*

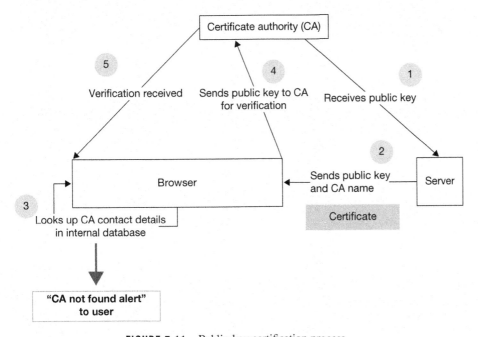

FIGURE 7.11   Public-key certification process

is a bundle of information containing the encrypted public key of the server and the identifica-tion of the key provider. Servers send their certificate to clients to identify themselves before starting a secure connection. The client (browser) comes preloaded with the public keys of all well-known certificate authorities. If the authority is known, the certificate is decrypted using the authority's known public key. The decrypted certificate contains the web server's public key.

To confirm that all is well, the browser also compares the web server's IP address with the IP address of the server it is connected to.[17,18]

PKI

The last missing bit in this process is certificate authorities. What prevents an intruder from masquerading as a certificate authority?

The way we deal with this issue is that browsers come with a preapproved list of cer-tificate authorities. Figure 7.12 shows an example from the Chrome browser. If the certificate provided by the server is from one of these CAs, the browser uses its own information to con-tact the CA and confirm the correctness of the certificate. If the certificate is from some other

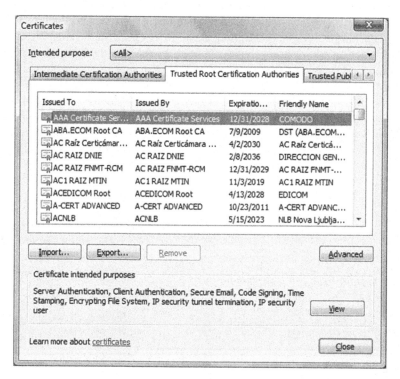

FIGURE 7.12   CAs in browser

---

[17]To see a more detailed explanation, visit http://www.moserware.com/2009/06/first-few-milliseconds-of-https.html (accessed 2/2/13).

[18]For a very interesting example of the encryption-certification process based on Hindu mythology, see the article "Alice and Bob can go on a holiday," by S. Parthasarthy, http://profpartha.webs.com/publications/alicebob.pdf (accessed 07/18/2013). There may be other similar interesting and illustrative culture-specific analogies possible. We would love to hear about them for inclusion in future editions of the book (with attribution, of course).

organization (e.g., the university itself), the browser generally alerts the user about the issue to allow the user to use their personal judgment in trusting the certificate authority. One such alert is shown in Figure 7.13. The certificate in this case was generated on a local web server by Nessus. Since this web server is not one of the well-known CAs, the prudent route for the browser is to ask the user for advice on how to proceed.

The framework established to issue, maintain, and revoke public-key certificates is called the public-key infrastructure (PKI).

Example case – Nation technologies

We have seen in this chapter that the primary way we use encryption is by securing the channel of communication. Technologies such as VPN and SSL allow us to create an encrypted connection between computers, but the content itself remains unencrypted. Other commonly used encryption techniques encrypt the entire hard drive.

A common problem with all these encryption approaches is that though we really aim to encrypt information stored in files, these methods encrypt everything but the files themselves. Once a user is logged into their account, all files are visible. A phishing attack on the currently logged in user can successfully obtain all the files the user is privileged to access. Once a file is emailed, the sender has no control over how the receiver safeguards the information content in the file.

Would it not be convenient to encrypt just the files that need encryption? Better still, leave the files encrypted all the time, only unencrypting them for the duration of reading/editing, and only for designated users?

Such a technology is possible and has been developed by a company called Nation Technologies, founded by Stephen Nation, a former NYPD intelligence officer. The company's product and service allows customers to encrypt files individually. Encrypted files can be exchanged with any number of users. The person who encrypts the file can specify file access permissions for designated users, each identified by email address or other identifier. Receivers can save the file and open it for reading. When they close the file, it reverts back to its encrypted state.

A potential advantage to this approach is that organizations no longer have to worry about stolen secrets. Information is encrypted even when stored.

FIGURE 7.13 Untrusted certificate

SUMMARY

In this chapter, we looked at encryption, in terms of applications, algorithms at a high level and the infrastructure that exists to enable seamless encryption. We looked at the three types of encryption – hash functions, secret key cryptography, and public-key cryptography. The encryption types differ in terms of the number of keys used for encryption.

Technologies used in practice such as SSL and VPN combine secret key cryptography with public-key cryptography. Public-key cryptography is used for the initial key exchange to avoid the computational overhead that would occur if public-key cryptography were used for the entire transaction.

The IT industry has established a set of procedures so that key verification and exchange proceeds smoothly. These procedures are collectively known as the public-key infrastructure. The success of these procedures may be gauged from the relative ignorance of most consumers about the activities taking place in the background to ensure that their eCommerce transactions are secure.

Recommendation

For a very engaging, humorous, and thorough treatment of encryption, the book by Kaufman, Perlman, and Speciner is highly recommended.[19] All missing details in this chapter may be completed by referring to the book. Apart from being some of the most knowledgeable people on the subject, the experts are also extremely gifted writers and have put great effort to make this otherwise technical subject very accessible and personal. The authors have learned a lot about this subject from that resource.

CHAPTER REVIEW QUESTIONS

1. What is encryption?

2. What is encryption used for?

3. Briefly describe the Caser cipher.

4. What are the requirements of a good encryption algorithm?

5. Why do modern encryption algorithms use keys?

6. What is secret key cryptography?

7. Provide a brief overview of the current standard for secret key cryptography. What are some of its applications?

8. What is public-key cryptography?

9. What are some applications of public-key cryptography?

10. What are digital signatures?

11. How is public-key cryptography used to provide digital signatures?

12. What are hash functions? Provide a brief overview of some of the best-known hash functions.

13. What are hash functions used for?

14. What is block encryption? Why is data broken into blocks for secret key cryptography?

15. What is substitution in the context of encryption?

16. What is permutation in the context of encryption? Why is it needed?

17. What is the confusion–diffusion paradigm of cryptography?

18. What is cipher block chaining? Why is it necessary?

19. Provide a brief overview of the RSA algorithm.

20. What is SSL/TLS? What is it used for?

21. What are some differences between SSL and VPNs?

22. What are certificates?

23. What are certificate authorities? What services do they provide?

24. What is PKI?

25. What is the need for PKI?

---

[19] Kaufman, C., Perlman, R. and Speciner, M., 2002, Network Security: Private Communication in a Public World, Prentice-Hall.

EXAMPLE CASE QUESTIONS

1. Visit Nation Technology's website at www.nationtech nologies.com. What are some of the features of the company's product?

2. Describe what in your opinion would be one useful way in which you might use the technology offered by Nation Technologies?

3. Firms in which industry in your opinion would benefit the most from the technology offered by Nation Technologies? Why?

4. What do you think are some of the most important business hazards faced by Nation Technologies?

HANDS-ON ACTIVITY–ENCRYPTION

These activities are included to demonstrate the use of encryption using the Linux virtual machine you configured in Chapter 2. You will perform encryption using hash functions (0 keys), secret key (1 key), and public key (2 keys). Ensure that you have Internet connectivity and open a terminal window to complete these activities.

Password hashes

As was mentioned during the chapter, operating systems store the result of a hashing function instead of storing the actual value of a password. In CentOS Linux, the default hashing function for passwords is now SHA-512 (in the past, DES and MD5 have been used as the default).

- Log in using the "alice" account (password: aisforapple) and open a terminal window

- CentOS includes a program grub_crypt which will allow us to see the result of different hashing functions without changing a user's password:

```
[alice@sunshine    Desktop]$    grub-crypt
--sha-512
Password: aisforapple
Retype password: aisforapple
$6$DqW2UfDcPZjKyQyc$fwQqIAxfEgEuy6
KFAKxEdKP1cWuy0d5vemqNRV2uNAPf1VNaX
hpmZYOIZuW8iitC82MhQMaR2h8EY0DgQb5Z/1
[alice@sunshine    Desktop]$    grub-crypt
--sha-256
Password: aisforapple
Retype password: aisforapple
$5$omu31sk0zLzOVug1$2sbFJlcupATlu6Kw2iTf
qXMMbbgYanXoNtEDjgVH876
```

```
[alice@sunshine Desktop]$ grub-crypt --md5
Password: aisforapple
Retype password: aisforapple
$1$S213Gc1H$sTKjWuHbrSrquDLzy4XT8/
```

The results contain three values separated by dollar signs. They are interpreted as (idsalt$hash):

- Id – a numeric id that identifies which hashing algorithm was used (MD5, SHA-256, SHA-512).[20]

- Salt – random string of characters that is used to increase the length of the input to the function.

- Hash – result of the hashing algorithm on the user's password and the salt.

As you can see, the different algorithms yield vastly different results, even when using the same password as input.

Choose a strong password based on the rules mentioned in Chapter 8 and run grub-crypt with MD5, SHA-256, and SHA-512.

Run grub-crypt multiple times with the same password and encryption algorithm.

Questions

1. Does the command yield the same results every time? Why or why not?

2. Save the output from the previous commands into a text file **/opt/book/encryption/results/ex1. txt**

Deliverable: Submit the contents of ex1.txt to your instructor.

---

[20] See the pam_unix man page (http://linux.die.net/man/8/pam_unix) for full list of supported algorithms.

File hashes (checksum)

In addition to passwords, the other major use for hashing algorithms in Linux is for verifying the integrity of system files. The md5sum command provides an easy way to generate an MD5-based checksum[21] of a file or compare a file to a known-good checksum. If the checksum of the file differs at all from the known-good value, the file has been modified and could mean the system has been compromised. To generate a checksum of a file:

```
[alice@sunshine ~]$ md5sum hello.txt
8ddd8be4b179a529afa5f2ffae4b9858 hello.txt
```

The MD5 checksum is based on the contents of the file, so the file can be copied or renamed without affecting the checksum value, but if the contents are modified in any way, md5sum will return a different value.

```
[alice@sunshine ~]$ cp hello.txt world.txt
[alice@sunshine ~]$ md5sum world.txt
8ddd8be4b179a529afa5f2ffae4b9858  world.
txt
[alice@sunshine ~]$ echo '!' >> world.txt
[alice@sunshine ~]$ md5sum hello.txt world
.txt
8ddd8be4b179a529afa5f2ffae4b9858 hello.txt
c231742ea29c9e53d4956d8fa4dd6d96 world.txt
```

The output from the md5sum command can also be stored as a text file; this is useful if you are generating the checksum for a large number of files. The text file can then be used as input for the –c switch of the md5sum command, which compares the checksums of all the files listed and reports on results.

```
[alice@sunshine ~]$ md5sum *.txt > check-
sums.txt
[alice@sunshine ~]$ cat checksums.txt
8ddd8be4b179a529afa5f2ffae4b9858 hello.txt
c231742ea29c9e53d4956d8fa4dd6d96 world.txt
[alice@sunshine ~]$ echo 'This has been
modified' > hello.txt
[alice@sunshine ~]$ md5sum -c checksums.
txt
hello.txt: FAILED
world.txt: OK
```

```
md5sum: WARNING: 1 of 2 computed check-
sums did NOT match
```

Questions

The file /opt/book/encryption/checksum/check sums.txt contains a list of the MD5 checksums for the files in that directory, validate the integrity of the files.

1. List any files that fail the checksum validation in /opt/book/encryption/results/failed.txt

2. Create a text file that contains all of the checksums for the .png files in this directory and save it as /opt/book/encryption/results/check sum.txt

Deliverable: Submit the contents of failed.txt and checksum.txt to your instructor.

Secret key encryption

Secret key encryption is used extensively in Linux for file encryption. Most modern Linux distributions include support for one or more forms of encrypted filesystem, which encrypt all files as they are written to the disk. Configuring an encrypted filesystem is beyond the scope of this text, but the aescrypt command[22] provides a way to protect individual files with the same form of secret key encryption. The list of command arguments is pretty simple, as given in Table 7.5.

We can use these commands to encrypt and decrypt the file hello.txt, as follows:

```
[alice@sunshine ~]$ cat hello.txt
Hello World!
[alice@sunshine ~]$ aescrypt -e hello.txt
-p 1234qwer -o hello.txt.aes
```

Table 7.5 aescrypt command options

Argument	Function
-e	Encrypt the file
-d	Decrypt the file
-p <password>	Password to use. If this is omitted, the command will prompt the user.
-o <filename>	Output file

---

[21] Commands for generating SHA-based checksums are also available, but MD5 is used more in practice.

[22] Not included in a standard CentOS install, but it is available at http://www.aescrypt.com

```
[alice@sunshine ~]$ head -1 hello.txt.aes
AES^B^@^@^XCREATED BY^@AESCRYPT
3.05^@^@^@^@^@^@^@^@^@^@^@^@^@^@^@^@^@^@^@^
@^@^@^@@^@
[alice@sunshine ~]$ aescrypt -d hello.
txt.aes -p 1234qwer -o
hello.decrypt.txt
[alice@sunshine ~]$ cat hello.decrypt.txt
Hello World!
```

Questions

For this exercise, change directories to `/opt/book/encryption/secret-key`

1. Encrypt the `plans.txt` file using the password **pinky** and save the output to `/opt/book/encryption/results/plans.aes`

2. Decrypt the `encrypted.aes` file using the password **brain** and save the output to `/opt/book/encryption/results/plaintext.txt`

Deliverable: Submit the contents of plans.aes and plaintext.txt to your instructor.

Public-key encryption using GPG[23]

GPG stands for GNU Privacy Guard. It is a free software alternative to PGP (Pretty Good Privacy) and is based on the OpenPGP standard. But that leaves the following question: "What is PGP?"

PGP was developed by Phillip Zimmerman in 1991. It was the first encryption software built upon public-key cryptography algorithms, including the RSA algorithm discussed in the chapter. Due to patenting issues, the OpenPGP standard was created, defining standard data formats for interoperability between encryption software. GPG is one of the most notable programs developed based on this standard. GPG allows you to encrypt data, "sign" it, and send it to others, who will use the public key you provide to them to decrypt the data.

To use public-key encryption, we generate a key pair, share the public key, and use the key pair for encryption and decryption.

Key generation

The first step in any public-key encryption system is to generate your public/private key pair. GPG provides the --gen-key switch that will walk you through the process:

```
[alice@sunshine ~]$ gpg --gen-key
gpg (GnuPG) 2.0.14; Copyright (C) 2009
Free Software Foundation, Inc.
This is free software: you are free to
change and redistribute it.
There is NO WARRANTY, to the extent per-
mitted by law.
```

You will be prompted to choose which type of key you want for digital signatures and encryption. Select the default (RSA and RSA). You will then be asked for the key size. The default is 2048 bits. You can safely select this option. Then, you will choose the length of validity for the key. In real-world situations, this value would be between 1 and 5 years but for these assignments, keys do not need to expire.

```
Please select what kind of key you want:
    (1) RSA and RSA (default)
    (2) DSA and Elgamal
    (3) DSA (sign only)
    (4) RSA (sign only)
Your selection? 1
RSA keys may be between 1024 and 4096 bits
long.
What keysize do you want? (2048) 2048
Requested keysize is 2048 bits
Please specify how long the key should be
valid.
        0 = key does not expire
        <n> = key expires in n days
        <n>w = key expires in n weeks
        <n>m = key expires in n months
        <n>y = key expires in n years
Key is valid for? (0) 0
Key does not expire at all
Is this correct? (y/N) y
```

Following this, you will be prompted to choose a name for the key, email address, and comment. Your real name and email address are both fine to use here. For the comment, you can put whatever company you'd like – e.g., "Sunshine State University." GPG will use this information to create your keypair.

```
GnuPG needs to construct a user ID to
identify your key.
Real name: Alice Adams
Email address: alice@sunshine.edu
```

---

[23]Thanks to Clayton Whitelaw, a junior in Computer Science and member of the Whitehatters student club at USF for creating the first draft of this section

Comment: **Sunshine State University**
You selected this USER-ID:
            "Alice Adams (Sunshine State University) <alice@sunshine.edu>"
Change (N)ame, (C)omment, (E)mail or (O)kay/(Q)uit? **O**

Now, you will need a passphrase. You should see a dialog box similar to Figure 7.13. Enter something that

is reasonably secure, but something that you will remember. Finally, the program will start generating your key. To increase the key's effectiveness, it's a good idea to move your mouse around in random directions or perform some other task on the computer, while the key generation is in progress. This could take seconds or minutes; it varies greatly depending on many factors.

Once this has been completed, then you will have just generated your first keypair.

We need to generate a lot of random bytes. It is a good idea to perform some other action (type on the keyboard, move the mouse, utilize the disks) during the prime generation; this gives the random number generator a better chance to gain enough entropy.

```
gpg: key 9ED0CE35 marked as ultimately
trusted
public and secret key created and signed.
gpg: checking the trustdb
gpg: 3 marginal(s) needed, 1 complete(s)
needed, PGP trust model
gpg: depth: 0 valid: 1 signed: 0 trust:
0-, 0q, 0n, 0m, 0f, 1u
pub   2048R/14382D17 2012-12-01
        Key fingerprint = B317 3F83 705B
889D B414 7DF0 A3C1 B094 7E5B 6F3F
uid          Alice Adams (Sunshine State
University) <alice@sunshine.edu>
sub 2048R/C8761AAB 2012-12-01
```

What we have just done is created a keypair, which is located in a new hidden folder called **.gnupg** in your home directory. This folder, along with some other contents, includes **pubring.gpg**, and **secring.gpg**, which include your public and secret keys, respectively. The files are both stored in a binary format, so you can't read their

contents, but GPG can interpret this file and display the information you need.

Key sharing

To list the public keys stored in GPG's "keyring," type the following command:

```
[alice@sunshine ~]$ gpg --list-keys
/home/alice/.gnupg/pubring.gpg
-----------------------------
pub   2048R/14382D17 2012-12-01
uid          Alice Adams (Sunshine
State University) <alice@sunshine.edu>
sub 2048R/C8761AAB 2012-12-01
```

To list your private keys:

```
[alice@sunshine ~]$ gpg --list-secret-keys
/home/alice/.gnupg/secring.gpg
-----------------------------
sec   2048R/14382D17 2012-12-01
uid          Alice Adams (Sunshine
State University) <alice@sunshine.edu>
ssb   2048R/C8761AAB 2012-12-01
```

Before you can share encrypted data with others, you need to do two things: give them a copy of your public key and import a copy of their public key into GPG. To export your public key as a text file:

```
[alice@sunshine ~]$ gpg -a -o /tmp/alice_
adams.pub --export
[alice@sunshine ~]$ head /tmp/alice_
adams.pub
```

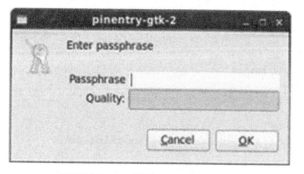

FIGURE 7.14 GPG passphrase dialog

```
-----BEGIN PGP PUBLIC KEY BLOCK-----
Version: GnuPG v2.0.14 (GNU/Linux)

mQENBFC6Q/MBCACjZH9O43XeK8TfDXVWO84xmr2
lgiLsv7drbT9poQiuHmHrnbAm
I/dm+nTIQn4qI8d+qTnOoWUsa9HD+N5sAsAHkYl5
kkmWgg/rtP8NtaH84/qqKSQN
ktmd/zxfyNgJ4fTHhfqJA6RuHoKuFla+MMqKzR4u
+ZSjxgmH14tbSBph2+YgmMp8
```

```
fqLH18i4fSEoG5jZ6VciPw8KAyZvVIsC5TyOfX-
W67UU8QJ7bEZaejxMtrhecF4F/
```

Now that if your key is exported, you will need to give it to the person you want to exchange information with. In the real world, the key would be emailed to the other party or, in extremely high security situations, hand-delivered to the recipient.

Note

If you have multiple keys, such as one for personal use and one for work use, you can specify which key you want to include using **-u <user>** where **<user>** is the email address of the key you want to use.

In our case, the key has already been transferred to another user at Sunshine State University (bob@sunshine. edu) and he has imported the key to his GPG keyring. Bob has also generated his key pair and told us it can be found at **/home/bob/public_html/bob_brown.pub** or **http://www.sunshine.edu/~bob/bob_brown. pub** so we have two options for importing Bob's public key. To import a file from the local filesystem:

```
[alice@sunshine ~]$ gpg --import /home/
bob/public_html/bob_brown.pub
gpg: key 310C3E16: public key "Bob Brown
(Sunshine State University)
<bob@sunshine.edu>" imported
gpg: Total number processed: 1
```

```
gpg:                 imported: 1 (RSA: 1)
```

Or to import a file from a remote webserver:

```
[alice@sunshine ~]$ gpg --fetch-keys
http://www.sunshine.edu/~bob/bob_brown.
pub
gpg: key 310C3E16: public key "Bob Brown
(Sunshine State University)
<bob@sunshine.edu>" imported
gpg: Total number processed: 1
gpg:                 imported: 1 (RSA: 1)
```

Either way, you will now have the public key to use.

Be careful when importing public keys from a remote host, either through the web or email. You must be sure that you are getting the correct public and that it has not been tampered with before using it for any secure communications.

If you run **gpg -- list-keys** again, you will now see the public key for Bob Brown in the list of available keys:

```
[alice@sunshine ~]$ gpg --list-keys
/home/alice/.gnupg/pubring.gpg
------------------------------
pub 2048R/14382D17 2012-12-01
uid                 Alice Adams (Sunshine
State University)
```

```
<alice@sunshine.edu>
sub   2048R/C8761AAB 2012-12-01

pub   2048R/310C3E16 2012-12-01
uid                 Bob Brown (Sunshine State
University)
<bob@sunshine.edu>
sub   2048R/1EA93238 2012-12-01
```

Encryption and decryption

Now that you have a public key, you will now be able to encrypt a message in such a way that it is designed for a particular recipient. To sign and encrypt a file, then save it as a text-based file (the default is a binary format). Use the **-a** and **-e** switches and specify whose public key should be used by using **-r**:

```
[alice@sunshine ~]$ gpg -s -a -r bob@sun-
shine.edu -e hello.txt
you need a passphrase to unlock the secret
key for
user: "Alice   Adams   (Sunshine   State
University) <alice@sunshine.edu>"
2048-bit RSA key, ID 14382D17, created
2012-12-01
```

GPG then displays a dialog box for you to enter the password for Alice's private key. Once it is entered, it then checks its keyring for a public key belonging to bob@sunshine.edu:

```
gpg: 1EA93238: There is no assurance this
key belongs to the named user


pub 2048R/1EA93238 2012-12-01 Bob Brown
(Sunshine    State    University)   <bob@sun-
shine.edu>
Primary key fingerprint: 599F 4790 E781
ADBF 1850 F120 2B51 B871 310C 3E16
Subkey fingerprint: 26BF DCFC 0A62 7224
9D20 5DE5 9734 A6C4 1EA9 3238
```

```
It is NOT certain that the key belongs to
the person named in the user ID. If you
*really* know what you are doing, you may
answer the next question with yes.


Use this key anyway? (y/N) y
```

GPG issues a warning that Bob's key may not be trustworthy because it has just been imported and there is no other data in the GPG keyring that can be used to verify the key's validity. You can safely ignore this message for this exercise, but if you plan on using GPG in a real-world situation, see

the GNU Privacy Handbook[24] for information on building a "Web of Trust" for key management.

```
[alice@sunshine ~]$ cat hello.txt.asc
-----BEGIN PGP MESSAGE-----
Version: GnuPG v2.0.14 (GNU/Linux)
```

```
hQEMA5c0psQeqTI4AQgAgpJ4Z4hiN93q+DdZ2ETg
nm1ib+ciekRGmNtI4C5KMzPm
bCWus0cqmtLWEL6Dj4oM90HBG9Di-
iNKxrxKdjAneh9i/AYVf3/UleyW0Zb2dL/
dC
veCxlkNaGLCtKjV0967ew/
JsHBQbV12jXRnqN61rmp/
edFIQZ1tbXymXlcnfg3vm
aRKnKSsXVa0qOHxPPn0+skP6tFbmT/
q/5F1DfpIf9NY1mVLJDiMNQGpyy2/
ZZyKk
90PWxBsQC90CcWTfJqwjC1wPd4Ck2YOr+q6u36YR
hz8cLwoM9I3MR2xVbtdElTGy
Zd2ogWZImTRBxhKWYV7uVDre095Y4FNIzbzADZ1
KaNLAwgGGslcOrrCI4gpSkGIb
DbvhuIr1r2rKeBRxR3dbQ+xb6Wm9S8v8440VSLDD
D4f3TZFc6+/qULAW7fU9Xu/1
4nqN4nu9NCQLgWmZyLtJr8RIry0tVxHQwhOQl-
2w6t34b0IZJvjLGzkmM589fwWNo
ggE3krRiBvAE17z101Ncqn/zu5bfc6BUD2Okc-
36Qg56NUzvydGM3xgK2FRwgQfhr
7TrsJp/9R+wXV6EGfTuoToA/
p1WY531195212Wrd7e2nwm6umeaKxgzgO4hrC9zS
k5761CUi0cPyhwWBHQdK8UtssmBH1+tt2hEa6H+b
Tf1OIOZptMU64NCG3rWgrI17
NWntq9wwWQT5agqCalthLFM47ni/
mKe51Kay9LckNUmm
5PC8yA4oti5jnpIaW4Jw
xRFvTSoRXH5ARlPc1INoNi+51X+jd8y9AB2096s2
x+BQFuCmG25K/z7E2BoJjsVV
zf/qg6yQTbgPmvG83Jyvev71ykXd7TfKZGs4UlKq
K+grJda8
=BxNI
-----END PGP MESSAGE-----
```

Now that you have encrypted a message for Bob and signed it with your private key, it's time for him to decrypt it. We can switch users to Bob's account and decrypt the file to test it out.

---

[24]http://www.gnupg.org/gph/en/manual.html

```
[alice@sunshine ~]$ su - bob
Password:
[bob@sunshine  ~]$ gpg  -o  hello.txt
--decrypt ~alice/hello.txt.asc
You need a passphrase to unlock the secret
key for
user:  "Bob  Brown  (Sunshine  State
University) <bob@sunshine.edu>"
2048-bit RSA key, ID 1EA93238, created
2012-12-01 (main key ID 310C3E16)
```

You should see the password entry dialog box at this point. Once you've entered the password for Bob's private key (**bisforbanana**), the file will be decrypted; however, you'll receive an error when verifying the signature:

```
gpg: encrypted with 2048-bit RSA key, ID
1EA93238, created 2012-12-01
"Bob Brown (Sunshine State University)
<bob@sunshine.edu>"
gpg: Signature made Sun 02 Dec 2012
10:37:18 AM EST using RSA key ID 14382D17
gpg: Can't check signature: No public key
```

Bob must import Alice's public key before the signature on the file can be verified:

```
[alice@sunshine ~]$ gpg --import /tmp/
alice_adams.pub
gpg:  key  14382D17:  public  key  "Alice
Adams (Sunshine State University) <alice@
sunshine.edu>" imported
gpg: Total number processed: 1
gpg: imported: 1 (RSA: 1)
```

Try the decrypt command again and this time the file will be decrypted and the contents saved to **hello.txt**. GPG will then verify the included signature:

```
gpg: Signature made Sun 02 Dec 2012
10:37:18 AM EST using RSA key ID 14382D17
```

```
gpg:  Good  signature  from  "Alice Adams
(Sunshine State University) <alice@sun-
shine.edu>"
gpg: WARNING:  This key is not certified
with a trusted signature!
gpg:          There is no indication that
the signature belongs to the owner.
Primary key fingerprint: C42E 0E23 08A1
8116 019A AAB3 2D73 7113 1438 2D17
```

Again, GPG issues a warning because Bob's GPG key-ring doesn't have enough information to validate the public key for alice@sunshine.edu. Once the signature has been checked, you can verify that the contents of the decrypted file are correct:

```
[ bob@sunshine ~]$ cat hello.txt
Hello World!
```

Questions

1. Generate a new public/private key pair using your name, email address, and your school as the comment field.

2. Export the public key and save it as **/opt/book/ encryption/results/key.pub**

3. Import the public key stored at **/opt/book/encryp- tion/public-key/eric_pierce.pub**

4. List the public and private keys stored in your GPG keyring and save the output as **/opt/book/encryp- tion/results/public-keyring.txt** and **/ opt/book/encryption/results/private- keyring.txt** respectively.

5. Encrypt and sign **/home/alice/hello.txt** using the public key you just imported and save the output as **/opt/book/encryption/results/ encrypted.asc**

Deliverable: Submit the contents of key.pub, public-keyring. txt, private-keyring.txt, and encrypted.asc to your instructor.

CRITICAL THINKING EXERCISE – ENCRYPTION KEYS EMBED BUSINESS MODELS

We haven't spent much time in this book discussing cloud computing and the risks specifically emanating from putting so much data on the cloud. Do you know where your Gmail data is? Or, where Microsoft saves the files you store on its SkyDrive service?

You probably don't care, and for most people it is the sensible thing to do. The companies have a lot to lose if they abuse the public trust. The current business model essentially seems to be that users trust free cloud service providers with their data with the understanding that the cloud service providers may peek into the contents of the files for limited purposes. Customizing online advertisements seems to be one such accepted purpose. So, the trade-off is free cloud storage service in return for advertising.

However, particularly since the revelations about the collaborations between cloud service providers and the NSA have emerged, some users may be concerned about the privacy of their information. What can they do if they still want to derive the convenience of cloud services?

From what we have read in this chapter, the solution is simple. Currently, the cloud service providers take care of encryption, i.e., the cloud service providers and not the data owners have the encryption keys to the data. This allows the cloud service providers to view your data on demand. Thus, the business model of advertising-for-storage is embedded in the service provider's ownership of the encryption keys.

If you wanted to prevent that, well, you could encrypt your data before you upload the data to the cloud service provider. You would then be responsible for key management because if you lost your decryption keys, you would not be able to read your own data.

REFERENCES

Falkenrath, R. "Op-ed: encryption, not restriction, is the key to safe cloud computing," http://www.nextgov.com/cloud-computing/2012/10/op-ed-encryption-not-restriction-key-safe-cloud-computing/58608/ (accessed 07/18/2013)

Amazon Web Services, "Using client-side encryption," http://docs.aws.amazon.com/AmazonS3/latest/dev/UsingClientSideEncryption.html (accessed 07/18/2013)

Schneier, B. Cryptogram, November 15, 2012

CRITICAL THINKING EXERCISE QUESTIONS

1. Many popular cloud services such as Gmail are currently free because users allow advertisements in return for free service. How do you think the market will evolve if more and more data is encrypted where service providers can no longer monetize your data through advertising?

2. What are some special concerns of regulated organizations such as government agencies when it comes to cloud computing? (The Nextgov op-ed has several examples.)

DESIGN CASE

Sunshine University's Admissions department is extremely active in terms of recruitment of students. It routinely visits local high schools in order to promote the university's programs, frequently gathering Personal Identifiable Information (PII) from high school students in order to help them apply for scholarships, financial aid, and other opportunities.

In order to record all this information, recruiters carry university-issued laptops to their visits. Recently, one of the recruiters' vehicle was broken into and the contents of the car stolen. Luckily, the perpetrator missed the laptop (containing 500 Social Security Numbers) in the trunk of the vehicle.

As an expert in security, the Provost reached out to you in order to ask for your opinion on what could be done to make these laptops safer. In reading your state's statutes you realize that, where whole disk encryption is employed on these laptops, the confidentiality of the information contained would be protected and there would be no need to report the incident.

Write a one-page recommendation to the Provost, covering the information in the previous paragraph and arguing for the purchase of a whole disk encryption solution for the university. In your report, include information on the following.

1. Report on the legal requirements for such encryption in state universities in your state

2. Outline your requirements for the product

3. Do some research on popular product offerings and include a minimum of three vendors

4. Explain the difference between file encryption and whole disk encryption

5. When should one be used versus the other? Consider what each one protects against.

6. Which operating systems are you covering?

7. How will the decryption key be recovered if lost?

Identity and Access Management

## CHAPTER 8

Overview

In this chapter, we will look at some of the most popular mechanisms for identifying users and managing their privileges in enterprise systems. The systems we will discuss share many features in common, but each system has been developed to respond to the unique needs of a popular context. By the end of this chapter, you should know:

- The differences between identity management and access management
- The phases in identity and access management models
- The three categories of user credentials
- The relative strengths and weaknesses of the major authentication technologies

Identity management

Identity management is the processes of identifying individuals and collating all necessary data to grant or revoke privileges for these users to resources. The username and password system you use on your laptop is an example of an identity management system. In larger organizations, formal processes become necessary to manage the churn of users through the system. Using the example of a typical state university, on any given day, hundreds of events such as students joining the university, leaving the university, obtaining on-campus employment, changing on-campus employment occur, each of which affects what information these users are allowed to access. The simple processes that work at a home computer need to be replaced by formal systems to ensure that everyone has timely information in this dynamic environment, without compromising information to which they should not have access. Identity management systems perform the necessary functions to accomplish these goals.

Information about users is stored in a system of record. Based on the US Privacy Act of 1974,[1] we define a *System of Record (SoR) as records from which information is retrieved by the name, identifying number, symbol, or other identifying particular assigned to the individual.* A system of record does not have to be very elaborate. The users panel in your Windows laptop is an example of an SoR. The HR and payroll database would also be considered an SoR. At a large organization, this database may be part of an ERP system, whereas at a small company, it may just be an Excel spreadsheet.

---

[1] http://www.justice.gov/opcl/privstat.htm

Similarly, your university's Student Information System is an example of an SoR for student data. As a general rule, a System of Record is established to store data for a particular purpose or about a particular group of people. For example, information about a student who is employed at her University will be found in both the student and employee SoRs. Thus, it is common for an individual person to have identities in multiple Systems of Record at the same time.

Within the SoR, *an identity is a distinct record stored in a System of Record*. Thus, what we traditionally call a computer user is called an "identity" in the information security world. *An identifier is a string of digits which uniquely identifies an identity in an SoR.*

Identity management systems handle the complexities associated with synchronizing identities across SoRs. They operate in three stages (Figure 8.1) to gather all the information necessary to manage identities – identity discovery, identity reconciliation, and identity enrichment. At the end of the process, we get a person registry with actionable information about users in the organization.

Phase I: identity discovery

Identity management begins with a discovery phase, where all new and updated identities throughout the organization are located. In this phase, the identity management system collects all the new or updated identifiers in each SoR. Name changes, role updates, and corrections to date of birth or identifiers are all common occurrences, and need to be discovered. The complexity of this phase varies greatly depending on the size of the organization. For small organizations with minimal employee turnover, this process can be completely manual – when an employee is hired or terminated, his or her data is updated in the Human Resources database and manually entered into the identity management system. In larger organizations, however, this may involve multiple automated systems collecting thousands of pieces of data from a dozen or more systems several times per day. Regardless of the method, at the end of the identity discovery phase, we obtain a list of new or updated identifiers from all of the organization's Systems of Record. This list is the input data for the next phase of the identity management process – identity reconciliation.

Phase 2: identity reconciliation

Once the list of new or updated identifiers has been compiled, we can perform identity reconciliation. *Identity reconciliation is the process of comparing each discovered identity to a master*

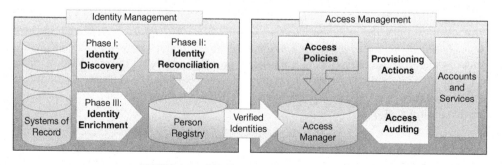

FIGURE 8.1   Identity and access management

record of all individuals in the organization. To demonstrate why reconciliation is necessary, suppose that Sunshine University hires a new faculty member. The following data is entered into the university's Human Resources database:

Identifier	First Name	Last Name	Birth Date	Department
13579	Henry	Jones	03/13/20	Archaeology

After a few years, Dr. Jones decides to take a class in his free time and enrolls in a class in the Biology department. The following data is entered into the Student Information System:

Identifier	First Name	Last Name	Birth Date	Class
24680	Henry	Jones	03/13/20	Biology 101

Without an identity reconciliation process in place, when the identifiers from the various Systems of Record are collected into one place, it is not clear if there are two people with the name Henry Jones, one faculty and one student, or one person with multiple roles:

Identifier	First Name	Last Name	Role
13579	Henry	Jones	Faculty
24680	Henry	Jones	Student

With an identity reconciliation process in place, we can determine that both these records refer to the same Henry Jones, as follows:

Identifier	First Name	Last Name	Student ID	Employee ID	Birth Date
987654	Henry	Jones	24680	13579	03/13/20

Person Registry

As you can see in the example above, Henry Jones was issued an identifier in addition to the Student and Employee identifiers issued by their respective Systems of Record. This third identifier is for the identity management system itself. At the heart of most identity management systems is a database known as the Person Registry. *The Person Registry is the central hub that connects identifiers from all Systems of Records into a single "master" identity and makes the correlation and translation of identity data (such as Student ID to Employee ID) possible.*

What makes up the Person Registry? The registry itself is just a simple database. It issues a unique identifier for each new person that is created. Notice that these identifiers are issued "per person" and not "per identity" as with the Systems of Record. As we've seen in the example above, a single person can have multiple identities in the Systems of Record, but the goal of the Person Registry is to issue a single identifier for each person. The Person Registry stores all the identifiers from the different Systems of Record and a few other important pieces of identity data (name, date of birth, etc.) for each individual in the organization.

Identity reconciliation functions

The identity reconciliation process is itself characterized by three main functions – identity creation, identity matching, and identity merges. In fact, identity reconciliation is sometimes referred to in the industry as the "match/merge" process. *Identity matching is the process of searching the existing Person Registry for one or more records that match a given set of identity data*. Once a matching person record has been found, the *identity merge function combines the new or updated record with data associated with the existing person record*. If a suitable match is not found in the Person Registry, the supplied data is assumed to represent a new person. In this situation, we invoke identity creation, which is *the function that creates a new person record and identifier in the Person Registry*. If the given identity data matches multiple identities, an identity conflict occurs. To resolve an identity conflict, an administrator must evaluate the identity data supplied by the SoR and decide if this is a new identity or manually match it with one of the existing identities. A flow chart of the match/merge process is included in Figure 8.2.

Again, depending on the organization size and the number of Systems of Record, the identity reconciliation phase varies greatly in complexity. In the simplest case – an organization with only one System of Record – reconciliation and the Person Registry are not needed. In any case, after identities are reconciled, we move to the next phase of the identity management process – identity enrichment.

Why not use social security numbers as identifiers everywhere?

A very natural question at this point would be – why not just use social security numbers everywhere? After all, they are issued per person, and not per identity. This would largely eliminate the need for identity reconciliation.

One of the most important reasons for not using social security numbers extensively is that using social security numbers in this manner would create an additional burden upon the organization to maintain the security of these numbers.

Phase 3: identity enrichment

Up to this point in the identity management process, the only data that has been collected from Systems of Record has been related to identifying an individual and distinguishing them from all other individuals in the organization. *The identity enrichment phase collects data about each individual's relationship to the organization*. In our Sunshine State University example, during the identity discovery phase, we collected the identifiers for Henry Jones from the student and Human Resources databases, but not any information about his relationship to the university. During the identity enrichment phase, we would also record that Henry Jones is a faculty member in the Archaeology department and is taking a class in the Biology department. After identity enrichment, Dr. Jones' Person Registry entry would look like this:

Identifier	First Name	Last Name	Student ID	Employee ID	Birth Date	Roles	Primary Role
987654	Henry	Jones	24680	13579	03/13/20	Faculty: Archaeology Student: Biology	Faculty

An individual's relationship to the organization is referred to as their role or affiliation. Individuals can have multiple roles within an organization, and may have roles with multiple organizations concurrently. For instance, the director of Marketing at a company holds both the roles of director in terms of the Marketing organization, and employee in terms of the company as a

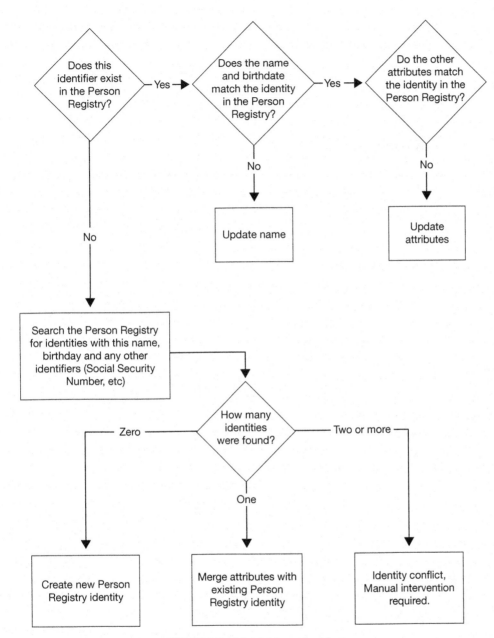

FIGURE 8.2   Match/Merge flowchart

whole. Because of this, in most organizations it is necessary to determine a primary role for each individual. This is accomplished by applying a priority value to each role as part of the identity enrichment process. Once a list of all roles of an individual have been compiled, the list can be sorted by priority value and the primary role selected. In the preceding example, the role of director would receive a higher priority value than employee, so this user's primary role would be recorded as "director." Similarly, Henry Jones would have a primary role of "faculty."

At the completion of the identity enrichment phase, the identity management process is complete. The identity management system has compiled enough information in the Person Registry to be reasonably certain that each individual in the organization is uniquely identified and enough information has been extracted to make intelligent decisions about the access and privileges this individual should receive. The identity is now ready to be used by the access management system, which handles these access decisions and the resulting actions.

Access management

The identity management process established who the individuals are in the organization. We now need to determine what each of these individuals is allowed to do. *The access management system encompasses all of the policies, procedures and applications which take the data from the Person Registry and the Systems of Record to make decisions on granting access to resources.*

Role-based access control

Before granting access to any resources, security administrators and the organization's leadership need to develop policies to govern how access is granted. In most large organizations, these policies use a role-based access control (RBAC) approach to granting access. In an RBAC system, the permissions needed to perform a set of related operations are grouped together as a system role. These system roles are mapped to specific job functions or positions within the organization. *The RBAC system grants individuals in specified job roles the access privileges associated with the corresponding system role.* For example, someone who is employed as a purchasing agent in an organization may be allowed to enter a new purchase order, but not approve payment. The ability to approve payment would be given to a role connected to an individual in a different position, such as in accounting. *A constraint where more than one person is required to complete a task is known as separation of duties.* Separation of duties is a common feature of business systems, especially when monetary transactions are involved.

The goal of an RBAC security system is to make the security policies of an organization mirror the actual business processes in the organization. Each individual in the organization should only be granted the roles that are absolutely necessary to complete their work successfully and each role should only contain the permissions needed to perform its specific tasks. Since the RBAC framework maps directly to the real-world functions of the individuals in an organization, security administrators can work directly with system users and business-process owners to develop policies that will be put in place. This is important because the system users are the subject-area experts; they know what system permissions are needed for a particular job function and what job functions are performed by which position.

Access Registry

The core of the access management process is the Access Registry database. *The access registry provides security administrators with a single view of an individual's accounts and permissions across the entire organization.* Each IT system connected to the access management system is audited on a regular basis for permission and account changes and the data is updated in the access registry. In addition, the access registry includes applications that run periodic access audits. *Access audits determine what access each individual should have based on the data provided by the Person Registry and the current security policies.* By comparing the access audit results with the access data stored in the access registry, security administrators can easily determine what access should be added or removed to ensure the system is in compliance with security policies.

The final step in the access management process is to act on the access changes required by sending/provisioning actions to each affected service or system. Provisioning actions include creating accounts or adding permissions that an individual is lacking or deleting (de-provisioning) accounts or permissions that are no longer needed.

Provisioning standards

The applications used to send provisioning actions have historically been highly specialized and generally have to be written to target a single application or service. However, given its importance, there has been some work to create standard frameworks for sending provisioning data, such as the Service Provisioning Markup Language (SPML)[2] and the System for Cross-Domain Identity Management (SCIM).[3] The specification for SPML was approved in 2007, but it has only seen limited use, mainly in very large enterprises, because of its complexity. SCIM, on the other hand, is relatively new (version 1.0 was released in December 2011) and strives for simplicity. It is still too early to tell if SCIM will become a widely used standard, but it does appear to have broad support from the major cloud service providers.

Once the system administrator has completed the identity management and access management processes, the system is ready to serve the users. The system needs to provide a way for users to prove their identities so that appropriate privileges may be provided. Authentication mechanisms enable users to prove their identities.

Authentication

In computer networks, *authentication is the process that a user goes through to prove that he or she is the owner of the identity that is being used.* When a user enters his username (also known as a security principal), he or she is attempting to use an identity to access the system. To authenticate the user, i.e., verify that the user is indeed the owner of the identity, the most common next step is to ask for credentials. *Credentials are the piece (or pieces) of information used to verify the user's identity.* The most commonly used credentials fall into three broad categories:

- Something you know
- Something you have
- Something you are

Something you know – passwords

A password is the oldest and simplest form of credential. *A password is a secret series of characters that only the owner of the identity knows and uses it to authenticate identity.* If the person attempting to access the account provides the correct password, it is assumed that they

---

[2] https://www.oasis-open.org/committees/tc_home.php?wg_abbrev = provision

[3] http://www.simplecloud.info/

are the owner of the identity and are granted access. You are no doubt familiar with the use of passwords already. They are widely used because they are simple and don't require advanced hardware or software to implement. Although passwords are currently the most widely used form of credential, we have seen earlier that there are many issues with their security, including weak passwords. Also, attackers use two common techniques for guessing passwords:[4]

- Dictionary attacks – trying thousands of passwords from massive dictionaries of common passwords and words from multiple languages

- Brute-force attacks – trying random character combinations until the password is guessed or every possible combination has been tried

Dictionary attacks can guess common passwords very quickly, but are not very effective against passwords containing multiple numbers and symbols in addition to letters. A brute-force attack, on the other hand, will guess any password given enough time. To combat this weakness, most organizations enact password policies to enforce "strong" passwords. Some of the typical rules in use are as follows:

- Passwords must be eight or more characters long.

- Passwords must contain a number, upper- and lowercase letter, and a special character.

- Passwords must not contain a dictionary word.

Password entropy

Unfortunately, these rules generate passwords that are hard to remember, but do not necessarily result in a strong password. In 2006, the National Institute of Standard and Technology (NIST) issued the Special Publication 800-63,[5] which presents a mathematic definition of password strength based on the entropy[6] of the password. The entropy calculation allows you to estimate how long it would take an attacker to guess a given password using a brute-force attack. For example, a password that meets all of the rules above and would be considered strong: *!d3nT1ty* was calculated to have 25 bits of entropy, which represents 2^{25} possible (33 million) passwords. On average, an attacker would have to try over 16 million passwords (half the total number) to guess the correct value. At 1000 attempts per second, it would only take the attacker about 4 hours to guess the password. However, if instead of a single word, you use 3–4 common words together as a passphrase, such as "rock paper scissors" you raise the entropy to 2^{41} – it would increase the amount of time required to guess it to over 8 years.

As you can see, a password with a higher entropy is much more resistant to brute-force attacks.[7]

---

[4]For a readable account of the state of the market, http://www.dailymail.co.uk/sciencetech/article-2331984/Think-strong-password-Hackers-crack-16-character-passwords-hour.html#ixzz2UcKeZwyW (accessed 04/4/2013)

[5]http://csrc.nist.gov/publications/nistpubs/800-63/SP800-63V1_0_2.pdf

[6]A measure of the disorder or randomness in a closed system: Houghton Mufflin Harcourt eReference

[7]An essay on the topic by Bruce Schneier, "Passwords are not broken, but how we choose them sure is," http://www.schneier.com/essay-246.html (accessed 07/18/2013)

Something you have – tokens

Instead of basing authentication on a secret that the user knows and could share (intentionally or otherwise) with someone else, *tokens are physical objects (or in the case of software tokens, stored on a physical object) that must be presented to prove the user's identity.* In nearly all cases, the token must be accompanied with a password ("something you have" and "something you know"), creating a two-factor authentication system. Two-factor authentication is a relatively simple way to establish a high degree of confidence in the identity of the individual accessing the system. Financial institutions have used two-factor authentication (ATM card and PIN) for decades, as have large corporations. However, the rise in phishing and other password-based attacks in recent years have motivated many more organizations to add a second factor to their existing authentication scheme.

Smart cards are credit-card sized hardware tokens that either store an ID number, which uniquely identifies the card, or include a small amount of memory to store a digital certificate which identifies the user themself. Smart cards are used in a wide range of applications, from the SIM cards inside every mobile telephone to the access cards used for physical access to secure areas in government and military installations. An alternative approach to certificate-based authentication is to load the certificate directly on a USB storage device (Figure 8.3). In addition to eliminating the need for a smart card reader, some USB-based authentication tokens also use the certificate and password to secure the onboard storage.

A drawback of the smart card and USB-based authentication tokens is that the user must have physical access to a computer's USB ports or a previously connected card reader. This is not always possible, especially when using a mobile device or logging in from an open-use computer lab or Internet Café. In these environments, a token that does not need to connect directly to a computer is required. Key-chain size hardware tokens from companies like RSA

Julia Malakie/Associated Press

FIGURE 8.3   Smart card in a USB card reader

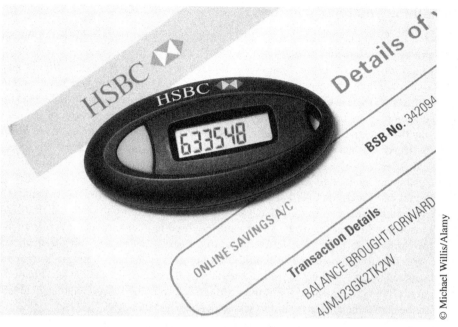

FIGURE 8.4 Hardware token

and Vasco deal with this by generating a string of numbers that is displayed on a small LCD screen on the front of the token. This string is then entered by the user as a one-time password (OTP), a password that can only be used one time and is usually only valid for a limited time. Such hardware tokens (Figure 8.4) have been popular for many years in corporate and government sectors because they are relatively easy to implement, do not require special readers or other accessories to be connected to each computer in the organization and can be used easily in a desktop or mobile environment.

These types of tokens create the one-time passwords by using either time-based or sequence-based methods.

- Time-based tokens generate a new password on a set time interval, usually 30 or 60 seconds.

- Sequence-based tokens use complex algorithms to generate a series of passwords that cannot be guessed based on previous passwords in the series.

Regardless of which type is used, the hardware token is registered with the authentication server before being given to the user, establishing an initial value to start the sequence-based algorithm or synchronizing the internal clock for time-based ones.

In addition to hardware tokens, security vendors such as RSA also offer software tokens, mobile phone applications that function in the same manner as a hardware token but don't require the user to carry a separate device. Since they don't involve delivering a physical device, these tokens have the added benefit of quick, simple deployment – just installing an application. Once the application is installed, the software token functions exactly like the hardware variety – the application generates a one-time password which then can be combined with their password to authenticate to the system. The Google Authenticator is a software token available for iOS and Android smartphones which provides two-factor authentication for Google accounts.[8]

In addition to software token applications, the unique capabilities of modern mobile phones have increased the number of options available for two-factor authentication. SMS text messaging is a simple way to provide a second factor for authentication. During account setup, users register their mobile phone numbers with the authentication service. From that point on, when the user attempts to authenticate, a short passcode is sent in a text message to their phone number. The user then enters the code to prove they are still in possession of the registered phone. One drawback of using SMS as an authentication credential is that many cellular phone companies charge per-message fees.

tiQR (http://tiqr.org) provides an example of another novel approach to authentication that takes advantage of the hardware features found in smartphones. When logging into a site protected by tiQR, the user is presented with a challenge-phrase encoded as a Quick Response (QR) code. The user then takes a picture of the QR code using the tiQR application (as of this writing, Android and iOS versions are available) on their smartphone. The user then enters their password into the tiQR application and submits it to the authentication server along with the decode challenge-phrase. The authentication server validates the user's password and challenge-phrase to verify the user's identity.

Something you are – biometrics

Hardware and software tokens are a great way to add a second factor and increase security, but like any physical object, tokens can be lost or stolen and used by attackers to impersonate users. How can we ensure that the person accessing a system is definitely the owner of the identity? *Biometric devices analyze the minute differences in certain physical traits or behaviors, such as fingerprints or the pattern of blood vessels in an eye, to identify an individual.* In general, biometric devices work by comparing the biometric data captured from the subject against a copy of the person's biometric data previously captured during an enrollment process. If the person accessing the system's biometric data matches the saved data, he or she is assumed to be the same person and authentication is successful.

Observable physical differences among people are called biometric markers. There are many markers that could be used, but the suitability of a particular marker is determined by several factors, including:[9]

- Universality – every person should have the trait or characteristic

- Uniqueness – no two people should be the same in terms of the trait

- Permanence – the trait should not change over time

- Collectability – the trait should be measurable quantitatively

- Performance – resource requirements for accurate measurement should be reasonable

---

[8] http://googleonlinesecurity.blogspot.com/2012/03/improved-google-authenticator-app-to.html

[9] Jain, A.K., Bolle, R., Pankanti, S., eds. *Biometrics: Personal Identification in Networked Society.* Kluwer Academic Publications, 1999

- Acceptability – users' willingness to accept the measurement of the trait
- Circumvention – difficulty of imitating traits of another person[10]

Fingerprints

By far, the most widely known and used biometric marker is the fingerprint. Fingerprints that are made up of the unique pattern of ridges on the fingers or palm of the human hand are truly unique – in over 100 years of crime-scene investigation and millions of prints, no two people have ever been found to have matching fingerprints.

Once common only in highly secure applications, the price and complexity of scanning technology has lowered to the point that fingerprint scanners are commonly included as standard equipment in PC laptops designed for business users. Fingerprint scanners use either *optical sensors that are tiny cameras which take a digital image of the finger*, or *capacitive scanners that generate an image of the user's finger using electrical current*. Instead of comparing the entire print, the scanning software compares the shape and location of dozens of uniquely shaped features (minutiae) (Figure 8.5). By matching up multiple minutiae between the two fingerprints, the software can compute the probability that the two prints are a match. This type of probabilistic matching prevents environment factors (lighting, smudges on the camera, etc.) from affecting the outcome of a fingerprint match. However, it also introduces a weakness in biometric authentication. An attacker doesn't need to get an exact match of a fingerprint to impersonate a target; he only needs to duplicate enough of the minutiae to convince the scanner that he is "probably" the correct person. Although successful attacks against fingerprint scanners have been published,[11] the technology is generally secure and will continue to be the most used form of biometric identification for years to come.

Iris and retinal scanning

Retinal scanners record the unique pattern of blood vessels located in the back of your eye. In addition to the retina, the eye contains another uniquely identifying trait: the iris. *The iris is the thin, circular structure that surrounds the pupil and gives the eye its color.* Like fingerprints, these structures are unique to each individual and can be used for authentication. Retinal and iris scans have long been the stuff of spy movies – in order to enter the secret base, a security system scans the agent's eye and verifies his or her identity. In real life, these systems are used to protect areas as secure as the Pentagon and as mundane as your local gym.

Retinal scanners have been used in the highest security areas for many years. To the user, a retinal scan is much like a test that would be done at an Optometrist's office. He or she looks into a eyepiece and focuses on a point of light for several seconds while the scanner captures an image of the retina and processes the data. Retinal scans are highly accurate, but they are not considered acceptable for general use because they are much more invasive that other technologies and are generally slower than the alternatives.

---

[10]Biometrics was in the news in June 2013 when the US Supreme Court ruled lawful the collection of biometric identification of an arrestee and the use of such biometric identification in the detection of other unrelated crimes. Maryland vs. King, http://www.scotusblog.com/case-files/cases/maryland-v-king/ (Accessed 10/11/13)

[11]Matsumoto, T. et al. *Impact of Artificial "Gummy" Fingers on Fingerprint Systems*. International Society of Optics, 2002

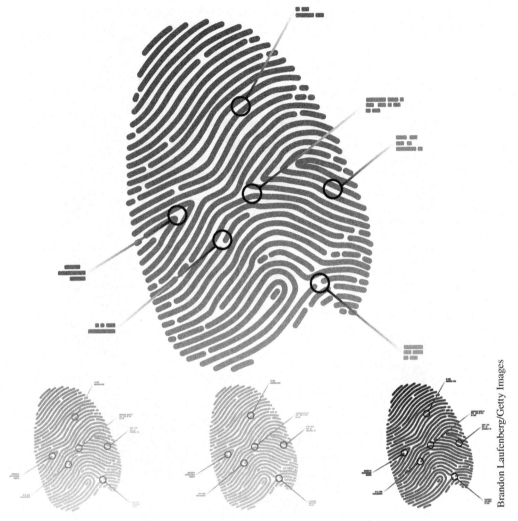

Brandon Laufenberg/Getty Images

FIGURE 8.5 Fingerprint with minutia highlighted

Unlike retinal scanners, iris scanning is quick and painless. An iris scanner is basically a standard digital camera (video or still) fitted with an infrared (IR) filter which allows it to capture an enhanced image of the iris. Although not quite as accurate as a retinal scan, iris scanners are used in many more applications because they are much easier to use. An iris scan is very similar to taking a photograph and does not require the user to be in close proximity to the scanner (up to a few meters away) or to hold still for an extended period of time as the images are captured instantaneously.

In 2001, the United Arab Emirates Ministry of the Interior began a program of scanning all foreign nationals entering the country, looking for people who have been previously ejected from the country for work permit violations (Figure 8.6). The system contains millions

Chuck Stoody/Canadian Press/Associated Press

FIGURE 8.6 Iris scanning in the Dubai Airport

of identities and runs billions of searches per day. To date, the system has caught over 10,000 people with fraudulent travel documents attempting to re-enter the country.[12]

Iris scanning has also begun to move from large government organizations into business applications. For example, Equinox Fitness Clubs has equipped 15 of their locations with iris scanners instead of the traditional card scanners used in other fitness clubs. The scanners allow their VIP members to access exclusive services without having to carry cards or remember a PIN.[13]

---

[12] Daugman, J. *Encyclopedia of Biometrics*. Springer, 2010

[13] "Equinox Fitness Clubs Case Study." *IRIS In Action*. IRISID. Web. 15 May 2013

Biometric system issues

Biometric systems provide a highly secure form of second-factor authentication and can provide a high degree of certainty in the user's identity, however their permanence is actually a drawback. If an attacker steals a user's password or hardware security token, the threat is eliminated once a new password or token is issued. That is not possible when dealing with biometric data. By their nature, biometric markers are permanent – we can't issue someone new fingerprints if their fingerprint data is compromised. That marker can no longer be used as a reliable authentication factor. Either the fingerprint system must be upgraded to remove the flaw that allowed an attacker to imitate a valid user or the entire system must be replaced using a different biometric marker.

> Biometrics may seem new, but they're the oldest form of identification. Tigers recognize each other's scent; penguins recognize calls. Humans recognize each other by sight from across the room, voices on the phone, signatures on contracts, and photographs on driver's licenses. Fingerprints have been used to identify people at crime scenes for more than 100 years.
>
> What is new about biometrics is that computers are now doing the recognizing: thumbprints, retinal scans, voiceprints, and typing patterns.[14]

Single sign-on

Once the user's identity has been established, access is granted to a system or application. If this authentication is for a local account, such as logging into Windows when you start up your computer, the authentication process is complete. The operating system informs all programs on your computer about your identity and there is no need to authenticate again. However, what if the application you need to access is on another system? How would you identify yourself to the remote application? An example would be accessing course information from a learning management system such as Blackboard.

You could repeat the authentication process and supply your username and password plus any other factor (token, biometric, etc.) that is required in your environment. This would work, but quickly becomes tedious, particularly if you are accessing many systems. What is needed is a way to login once to a system and gain access to all connected applications without being prompted for credentials again. This system is referred to as single sign-on (SSO) and can be accomplished in a number of ways. *Single sign-on (SSO) refers to technology that allows a user to authenticate once and then access all the resources the user is authorized to use.*

Generally, the system administrator in a single sign-on environment creates unique and strong user passwords for each resource the user is authorized to access and changes each of these individual resource passwords regularly, as specified by the organization's password policy. The end user is not aware of any of these individual resource passwords. Instead, the user is provided one single password that the user enters when trying to access a resource controlled by the single sign-on technology.

The implementation of single sign-on technology typically uses one central repository for password-based authentication. Once the user authenticates to this repository, the system

---

[14] Bruce Schneier, Crypto-gram, January 15, 2009

looks up the resources which the user is authorized to access. When the user tries to access any of these resources, the SSO system provides the resource password on the user's behalf. Single sign-on is becoming increasingly popular in large organizations such as universities and banks.

SSO benefits and concerns

Before looking at the different SSO technologies, let's look at the advantages and disadvantages of deploying SSO in a system. There are several major benefits that SSO provides immediately to users and the system administrators:

- Better user experience – no one likes entering credentials multiple times.

- Credentials are kept secret – only the user and the SSO server have access to the user's credentials. This eliminates the possibility of an attacker accessing passwords through a compromised service.

- Easier implementation of two-factor authentication – instead of updated all of the services to support token or biometric authentication, only the SSO system needs to be updated.

- Less confusion – users don't have to remember multiple accounts with differing usernames and passwords.

- Fewer help desk calls – users are more likely to remember their password.

- Stronger passwords – since users only need to remember one password, that password can be more complex.

- Centralized auditing – all authentication is logged and can be monitored in one place.

In general, implementing an SSO technology improves the security and user experience, but there are drawbacks as well:

- Compromised credentials are a bigger threat. A single compromised account can access multiple systems or applications.

- Phishing attacks – Having a single login page creates an attractive target for phishers. They can copy the HTML of your login page exactly, making it easier for users to fall for their deception.

- Your SSO system becomes a single point of failure. If it is unavailable, no one can authenticate to any system. A failure of this repository will compromise not only the confidentiality and integrity of all passwords in the repository but also the availability of any system controlled by this repository.

- Adding any type of SSO increases the complexity of the system as a whole. The more complex a solution is, the more things that could go wrong.

Password synchronization

In addition to SSO, some organizations employ a password synchronization authentication scheme. *Password synchronization ensures that the user has the same username and password in all systems.* However unlike SSO, in password synchronization, the user is required to enter the credentials when accessing each system. Password changes on one system are propagated to other resources. This reduces user confusion and may reduce help desk calls for password resets.

Unlike SSO, there is no central repository of passwords in password synchronization. Instead, each synchronized system stores a copy of the user's password and the user authenticates to each system directly. The benefit to the user is that there is only one password to remember. Password synchronization is commonly used when integrating several different types of systems together, for instance the user must be able to access a web-based application, an application running on a mainframe, and a database account using the same credentials.

Since password synchronization has fewer components to implement, it is generally less expensive than SSO. However, password synchronization has its own problems. Since the same password is known to be used on many resources, a compromise of any one of these resources compromises all other resources synchronized with this resource. If password synchronization is used with resources with different security requirements, attackers can compromise less secure resources to gain access to higher security resources, which are likely to be more valuable.

Active directory and Kerberos

In Microsoft Windows networks, Active Directory serves as the single sign-on architecture. Active Directory integrates various network services including DNS and LDAP with Kerberos. *Kerberos is an authentication protocol that allows nodes in an insecure network to securely identify themselves to each other using tokens.* Kerberos is a very popular authentication protocol, and serves as the basis for many other authentication technologies. The Kerberos project was developed in the 1980s by researchers at MIT and released to the public in 1993.[15] Kerberos provides a very high degree of confidence in the identity provided to the protected application by building a trusted relationship based on shared encryption keys between the authentication server, the protected application, and the client.

In a typical Kerberos situation, an actor wishes to use a remote service, such as a printer or file server. Authentication using the Kerberos protocol requires one additional participant, a key distribution center, and requires that all three actors be members of the same Kerberos "realm" (domain in Active Directory):

- A client that is initiating the authentication.

- A Key Distribution Center (KDC), which has two components:

  - Authentication service,

  - Ticket-granting service.

- The service that the client wishes to access.

With this setup, the operation of Kerberos is shown in Figure 8.7.

Before a client can access a "kerberized" service, they must authenticate to the KDC. Client and services first announce their presence on the network by providing their credentials

---

[15] http://www.kerberos.org/about/FAQ.html

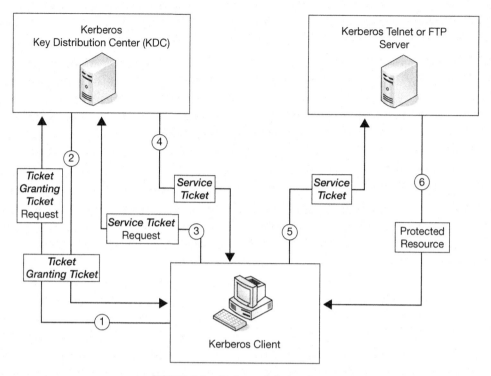

FIGURE 8.7 Kerberos ticket exchange

and requesting a Ticket-Granting-Ticket (TGT) (1). The KDC then issues a TGT encrypted with a secret key known only to the KDC and a session key that future responses from the KDC will be encrypted with (2). The TGT and session key have a lifetime of 10 hours by default and can be renewed by the client at any time.

When the client needs a service, it requests a Service Ticket for the particular service by presenting the TGT to the KDC (3). If the KDC can successfully decrypt the TGT, it issues a new service ticket for both the client and the requested service (4). The client decrypts its portion using the session key sent earlier by the KDC and then sends the other portion to the requested service (5). The service then verifies the ticket using its own long-term session key generated by the KDC and grants access to the user (6).

Kerberos is by far the most popular SSO technology for desktop use. Most large organizations are using Windows desktops and Active Directory to manage user accounts. The Kerberos authentication included with Active Directory allows users to login to their desktop once and mount remote drives and printers or access remote applications without providing their username or password. However, Kerberos and Active Directory are geared towards corporate use – they work when all users are accessing the system on trusted (usually company owned and maintained) computers. Kerberos is not a good fit for applications that are targeted at web users who are accessing the system on their personal computers. In these cases, it is not possible to assume that retailers and consumers would be willing to enter into a trusting relationship with each other to exchange service tickets. The techniques discussed below are designed to work in these wider environments.

		WebSSO			Federation	
	Kerberos	Token	CAS	SAML	OpenID	OAuth
First release	1987	˜1995	2001	2003	2005	2006
Authentication context	Operating system	Web browser	Web browser	Web browser	Web browser	Application
Identity confidence	Very high	Varies by implementation	High	High	Low	Low
Identity providers	Single	Single	Single	Multiple; Federation-defined list	Multiple; User-entered	Multiple; User-entered
Validation method	Secret key(s)	Various (hash or secret key)	SSL Certificate	Public key	Signature	Signature
Message security	Encrypted	None	None	Encrypted and signed	Signed	Signed
Client/Server/ Application validation	Authentication server, application, client	None	Authentication server	Authentication server, application	Application	Application
Implementations	MIT Kerberos Active Directory	Custom; Unique to each deployment	Multiple OpenSource clients	Shibboleth, Microsoft ADFS	Multiple OpenSource clients	Multiple OpenSource clients
Typical usage	Computer login; Desktop applications	Web applications	Internal web applications	External web applications (Google Apps, Office 365)	Public web applications (Facebook, Twitter)	Non-interactive access to web services

Web single sign-on

Kerberos was designed in the 1980s, well before the creation of the World Wide Web. Although the protocol has been updated in the years since, it has never been integrated easily with web-based applications. There are two reasons for this: the first is the requirement that all clients and servers be members of a Kerberos realm; that is not feasible with general web applications. The other reason is browser support – the major web browsers did not support Kerberos authentication until relatively recently and some still require extensive configuration to enable support. Web single sign-on (WebSSO) systems allow users to authenticate to a single web application and access other web applications without entering their username and password again. There are many different types of WebSSO in use. We will look at the broad outlines of authentication technologies used for web single sign-on and then focus on a particular WebSSO protocol that is widely used in education and commercial networks.

Token-based authentication

The simplest form of Web single sign-on is the use of a shared authentication token. *An authentication token is a unique identifier or cryptographic hash that proves the identity of the user in possession of the token.* When a user attempts to access one of the protected web applications for the first time, they are redirected to a token provider service that validates their username and password (and any other required authentication factors) and generates the authentication token (Figure 8.8).

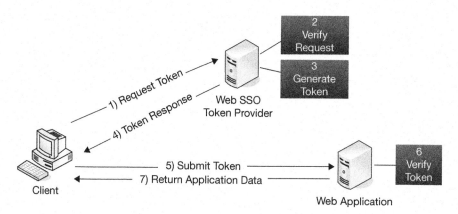

FIGURE 8.8 Token-based authentication

Depending on the specific implementation of the token provider, the authentication token may be generated in a number of different ways. Most commonly, the token is the result of a cryptographic process such as passing the username through a secure hashing algorithm (HMAC-MD5) or secret-key encryption algorithm (AES). Once the token is generated, the user is redirected to the requested service and the token is added to the HTTP request parameters. An alternative to this is to save the token into the user's browser as a session cookie before redirecting the user to the requested service. Session cookies are stored in temporary memory only and are deleted whenever the user closes their browser. In addition to authentication data, applications may store other data such as stored items in a shopping cart or site preferences for the user in the session cookie.

> Sharing authentication tokens in a session cookie is a simple way to enable SSO between multiple web applications, but a major limitation is that web browsers do not allow cookies to be shared between multiple domains. A session cookie saved for *sunshine.edu* can only be used by applications on subdomains of sunshine.edu such as *www.sunshine.edu* and *mail.sunshine.edu*, but not on www.example.com. If SSO is needed between applications on two different domains, session cookies cannot be used.

At the web application, the process to validate an authentication token depends on the method that was used to generate it. In the simplest case, if a symmetric-key algorithm were used, the requested web application would input the token and its copy of the cryptographic key to a decryption algorithm. The resulting data would include at least the username of the person authenticating it, but could also include other data about the person, such as name, or the authentication event, such as timestamp or IP address.

Single sign-on using token-based authentication is relatively easy to implement and, when done correctly and using a strong cryptographic key, is secure. However, there are some drawbacks. The first is that there are no standard protocols or frameworks for authentication tokens, so each organization implements their authentication system differently. This isn't a problem if all of the applications that will be using SSO are written in-house, but can be a major issue when trying to integrate external applications. Another problem is that cryptographic key management is hard to deal with. If you generate a unique key for each application using SSO,

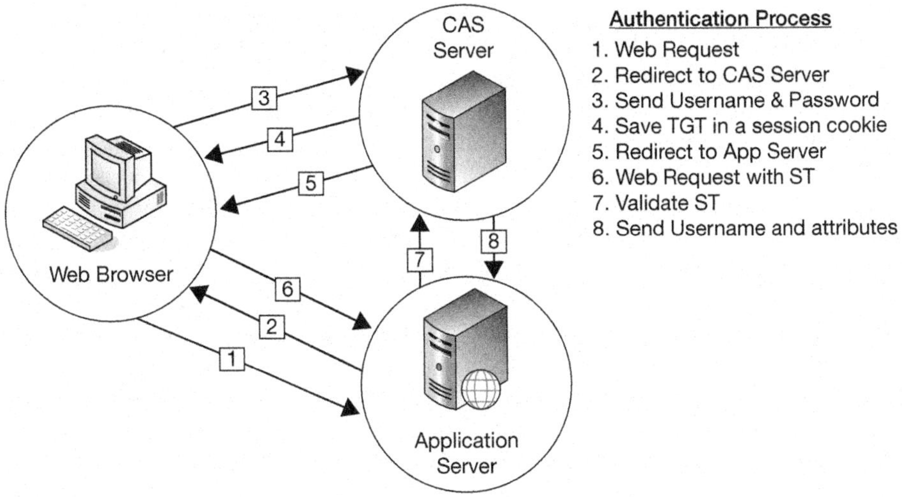

Authentication Process
1. Web Request
2. Redirect to CAS Server
3. Send Username & Password
4. Save TGT in a session cookie
5. Redirect to App Server
6. Web Request with ST
7. Validate ST
8. Send Username and attributes

FIGURE 8.9   Central authentication service

you'll potentially have hundreds of keys to manage. On the other hand if you use a single key for all services, and the key is compromised, all of the services are vulnerable.

Central Authentication Service (CAS)

The Central Authentication Service (CAS) protocol is one of the leading open-source single sign-on technologies, especially in higher education. It was first developed at Yale University in 2001. The CAS protocol combines aspects of token-based authentication with concepts gleaned from Kerberos to develop a Web SSO that is both secure and easy to integrate with most web applications (Figure 8.9). In 2004, ownership of the project was transferred to the Java Architectures Special Interest Group (Jasig), a consortium of education institutions dedicated to developing software primarily for higher education.

Like token-based authentication, when a user attempts to access a web application pro-tected by CAS, they are redirected to an authentication service on the CAS server. Like a Kerberos KDC, this service accepts and validates the user's credentials and then issues a Ticket-Granting-Ticket (TGT). The unique thing about CAS is that this ticket is saved into the user's browser in a session cookie that only the CAS server has access to. On subsequent visits to the authentication service during the CAS login session (2 hours by default), the browser presents the TGT for authentication instead of prompting the user to enter their credentials.

Continuing with the similarity to Kerberos, the browser requests the CAS server to issue a Service Ticket (ST) for the protected web application. A CAS Service Ticket is a random value that is used only as a unique identifier; no user data is stored in the service ticket. Service Tickets are of single use; they can only be verified once and then they are deleted from the CAS server. Also, they are only valid for the URL that the ticket was requested for and are valid for a very short period of time (10 seconds by default). Once the ST is generated, the user is redirected to the application they had originally requested with the ST appended to the HTTP request parameters, similar to the process used by token-based authentication.

Instead of being validating by the web application itself like an authentication token would be, the Service Ticket is submitted back to the CAS server for validation. If the service's URL matches the one the ST was generated for and the ticket has not expired, the CAS server responds with an XML document which contains the authenticated username. Later versions of the CAS server added the ability to return attributes such as name or email address in addition to the username.

The key factors in the success of the CAS server have been its simplicity and flexibility. CAS support can be easily added to virtually any web application, either by using one of the available clients[16] or developing your own client. Unlike token authentication, which requires cryptographic algorithms that can sometimes be difficult to work with, the only requirements to interact with the CAS server are the ability to make a HTTPS connection and parse the CAS server response XML. Every major programming language in use today easily meets both of these criteria, so developing a custom CAS client is not difficult. The CAS server itself is also easy to extend and is designed for flexibility. It supports many different types of user credentials such as LDAP username/password and x.509 certificates. It can even be configured to accept Kerberos tickets, creating a complete SSO solution – users login when their computer starts up in the morning and do not have to re-enter their password, even when accessing web applications.

Federation

Kerberos and some form of Web SSO provide all of the necessary controls for securing applications within an organization, but what if your users need to access applications outside of your organization (such as Google Apps or Office 365) or users from other organizations need to access to some of your applications? The traditional answer was to generate accounts for your users in the external systems and "guest" accounts in your system for all of the external users. Imagine that faculty members at Sunshine State University are collaborating with researchers from a local biotech firm. The only way to give access to the research data to both groups of researchers, all of the biotech personnel would need university credentials and the faculty members would need credentials from the biotech.

Ultimately, this process is unsupportable for a number of reasons; the first of which is it introduces a second set of credentials; eliminating all of the advantages gained by SSO. The most important issue from a security standpoint, however, is that there is no way to know when to revoke privileges from an external user. Access for individuals inside the organization can be revoked as soon as a change in their affiliation (termination, position change, etc.) has been detected by the identity management system. However, this type of information would generally not be available for individuals outside the organization, which makes access control difficult. In addition to the security implications, creating accounts in external organizations normally requires the release of personal data (such as name and email address) for your users, which may introduce serious privacy concerns.

A federation bridges the gap between the authentication systems in separate organizations. Federation is typically implemented by providing a method for an internal application (service provider or SP) to trust the information about an individual (assertion) sent by a external source (identity provider or IdP). In the Sunshine State example above, instead of creating accounts for all of the biotech researchers, the system containing the research data on the Sunshine State campus would verify the identity of the user with the biotech companies' IdP

---

[16]https://wiki.jasig.org/display/CASC/Client + Feature+Matrix

and request enough information about the user to make a decision on whether to grant access. If the authentication succeeds and the information provided by the IdP meets the application's requirements, access would be granted. This information request and access decision is done each time the user attempts to authenticate, allowing Sunshine State to deny access to a user who no longer meets the criteria as soon as the biotech IdP has the information.

Allowing users from more than one identity provider to access a service introduces an interesting challenge. How can the service know which identity providers can authenticate users? The answer is to ask the user which organization they are affiliated with. *A discovery service provides the user with a list of the trusted organizations that they can choose from to authenticate*. Figure 8.10 is an example of the discovery service in one of the popular federation systems – InCommon.

Security Assertion Markup Language (SAML)

The most common federation protocol used in enterprise software is the Security Assertion Markup Language (SAML). SAML is an XML-based protocol that was first developed in 2001 by the OASIS Security Services Technical Committee.[17] The protocol has gone through several revisions, the latest (SAML 2.0) being released in 2005. SAML incorporates several other XML standards for message security, including encryption and signing. Message security is important in the protocol because instead of sending data directly from the IdP to the SP, the parties in a SAML-based transaction communicate by relaying messages through the user's browser in HTML forms. This simplifies the configuration of SAML federations, as network controls don't need to be updated to allow a new IdP or SP to connect to the other members of the federation. However, since the message is passing through an untrusted third party (the user's browser), the XML messages must be cryptographically signed and encrypted to ensure their security and integrity.

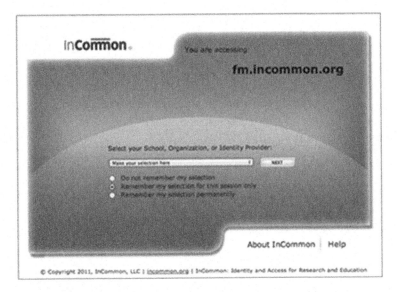

FIGURE 8.10 Discovery service for the InCommon federation

[17]https://www.oasis-open.org/committees/security/

In federations of more than a few identity and service providers, the maintenance of the federation becomes so complex it can be separated into its own organization. *The federation provider is responsible for all of the administrative tasks related to the running of the federation, such as membership management, creating and enforcing federation policies and managing the Public Key Infrastructure (PKI) needed for cryptographic operations.* The federation provider also publishes the federation metadata, *which is an XML document containing a comprehensive list of all federation members and important data, such as organization and contact information, for each identity service provider.* The federation provider is the central point in the network of trust that makes up the federation. The participants of the federation trust the provider to vet new members and uphold a certain level of quality in their identity management processes. In turn, the participants fund the federation provider through membership fees.

Figure 8.11 describes the process of authenticating a user in an SAML federation. When a user attempts to authenticate to an SAML-protected service provider (1), the SP first checks that the requested resource requires authentication (access check). If authentication is required,

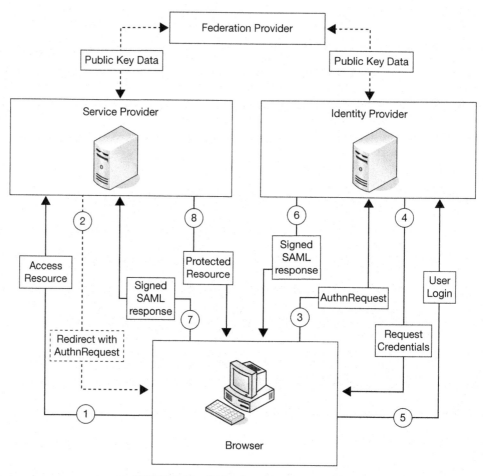

FIGURE 8.11   SSO with a SAML federation

the SP returns a HTML form (2) that contains an AuthnRequest XML document that will be presented (3) to the SSO service on the identity provider. The IdP then requests the user's credentials (4) and validates them (5). If the authentication is successful, the IdP gathers all of the data about this user that should be released to this service provider and generates an SAML response. To protect the data contained in the response, the IdP encrypts the XML with the service provider's public key (retrieved from the federation provider) and signs the document with its own private key. The IdP then sends a HTML form that contains the response data to the user (6). The form is automatically submitted to the service provider (7), which decrypts the XML document and verifies the message signature. Now that the user has been authenticated, the service provider supplies the requested resource to the user (8).

Unlike some of the other SSO protocols that we have covered in this chapter, SAML was not written as part of a server application. The SAML standard defined the details of how the protocol worked, but the actual implantation of those details were left up to application developers. Because of this, there are many different authentication systems that support the SAML protocol both from major commercial software vendors, such as Oracle and Microsoft, and freely available open-source implementations.

Microsoft's implementation of SAML is a portion of their Active Directory Federation Services (ADFS) product. *ADFS is a service that extends the Active Directory system to support federated access to local and external resources using SAML and related protocols.* ADFS is at the heart of many of Microsoft's newest products as they begin to introduce more Software-as-a-service model for software delivery. For instance, using ADFS for federated access to Office 365 allows an organization to use their local credentials (with single sign-on to their desktop computers) to access their cloud-based email and calendar. ADFS' compliance to the SAML standard also allows the organization to federate with non-Microsoft products such as Salesforce.com or Google Apps for business.

Shibboleth is the most popular of the open-source SAML-based authentication server implementations. *Shibboleth is an open-source identity management and federated access control infrastructure based on Security Assertion Markup Language (SAML).* It was developed for web single sign-on by an Internet2 group consisting of developers from several major universities and research organizations. Faculty and researchers from the various organizations needed a way to access shared resources on the various member campuses, each of which used their own unique authentication system. The initial version (1.0) of Shibboleth was released in 2003, with major version upgrades in 2005 (version 1.3) and 2008 (version 2.0) and many smaller point releases have been released since then. Shibboleth is now the most popular authentication system for educational institutions, especially large research universities, and is the basis for many national and international federations.

Shibboleth?

The Merriam-Webster Dictionary defines Shibboleth as "a custom or usage regarded as distinguishing one group from others."[18] The term comes from the Hebrew Bible (Judges 12:5–6) in which correct pronunciation of this word was used to distinguish the Gileadites (who pronounced it correctly) from the Ephraimites (who pronounced it as "Sibboleth").

---

[18] http://www.merriam-webster.com/dictionary/shibboleth

Around the same time the first versions of Shibboleth were being developed, the foundation that runs the networking infrastructure for all Swiss universities, SWITCH, was dealing with the same issues that the members of the Internet2 group working on Shibboleth were facing. In 2003 SWITCH announced a new federation, SWITCHaai[19] that would link all of the universities in Switzerland and all of their research or commercial partners, allowing Swiss students and faculty to access all of the educational resources in the country with a single set of credentials. As of November 2012, SWITCHaai had over 50 educational institutions with identity providers and nearly 100 public sector and corporate partners as service providers.

After the success that SWITCH had with running a large-scale federation, educational networks around the world started to develop their own plans for federation. In 2004, Internet2 announced a national federation, InCommon, to link American universities with government research institutions and corporate partners. InCommon started off with just a handful of members and grew slowly at first, but with the addition of major corporate partners like Microsoft and the release of Shibboleth 2.0 in 2008, membership exploded. By the end of 2012, InCommon included over 300 educational institutions, representing almost 6 million users, and over 150 research and commercial partners.[20] SWITCH and Internet2's counterpart in the United Kingdom, JISC, announced the UK Federation in 2005,[21] which has become one of the largest federations in the world with nearly 1000 participants and hundreds of service providers.

OpenID

SAML-based federations are an excellent solution for enterprise security, such as authenticating employees or business partners, but it requires planning and forethought before adding new federation resources. Each identity and service provider must be registered with the federation before being used for authentication. The registration must be performed by the identity provider's system administrators and, depending on the service provider's requirements, may require configuration changes to the IdP system. In an enterprise situation, this is fine. When a new federated service is identified by employees or other members of the organization, the requirements are reviewed and must be approved before any configuration changes are made. This also means that SAML has distinct disadvantages when applications whose user base includes the general public. Imagine the amount of work required to maintain a federation that contained the millions of services and identity providers that exist on the Internet with hundreds or thousands of new providers created daily. To handle sites with massive user populations from all over the globe, like Twitter and Facebook, a new type of federation is required.

OpenID was originally developed in 2005 for the LiveJournal.com blogging platform. Instead of requiring identity providers (referred to as OpenID Providers) to register with a central federation provider, OpenID uses a distributed model for authentication. The only requirements to becoming an OpenID Provider are having an Internet connection that allows other computers to reach you and a web server running an OpenID-compliant server application. These low barriers for entry meant that extremely security and privacy conscious users could even run their own OpenID Provider, allowing them to set the strength requirements and type of credentials they

---

[19] http://www.switch.ch/aai/about/federation

[20] http://www.incommonfederation.org/participants

[21] http://www.ukfederation.org.uk

use to authenticate themselves. The reason that the protocol succeeded, however, was the benefit to the service providers (Relying Party in the OpenID protocol). The promise of "web applications" was just beginning to appear with sites like Gmail, Flickr, and Facebook, all launching in 2004. Startups were launching new applications all the time and users were frustrated at having to juggle multiple accounts and passwords. Adding OpenID support was relatively easy for the application developers and major email providers such as AOL, Google, and Yahoo were soon on board as OpenID Providers. Thanks to providers such as these, OpenID is in use in thousands of sites and over one billion OpenID URLs are in use on the web.

To authenticate using the OpenID 1.0 protocol, users supply their OpenID URL to the Relying Party instead of a username (1). The OpenID URL is unique to each user and is normally a subdomain of the organization that hosts the OpenID provider, for example, http://jsmith.sunshine.edu. The Relying Party then requests the URL and is redirected to the OpenID provider (2). The OpenID provider responds with a shared secret that will be used to validate the authentication response (3). The Relying Party then redirects the user's browser to the OpenID provider to authenticate. Once the user has supplied their credentials (4) and the OpenID provider verifies that they are valid (5), it generates an authentication response and returns it, along with the shared secret, back to the Relying Party (6). Once the user is authenticated, the OpenID URL is associated with a local account at the Relying Party application and user details necessary for the service (name, email address, etc.) are requested from the user. The process is shown in Figure 8.12.

The final specification for OpenID 2.0[22] was released in late 2007, bringing with it the ability to release attributes about the user in addition to the authentication response (OpenID Attribute Exchange[23]). OpenID 2.0 also added support for "directed identities" which allows users to enter

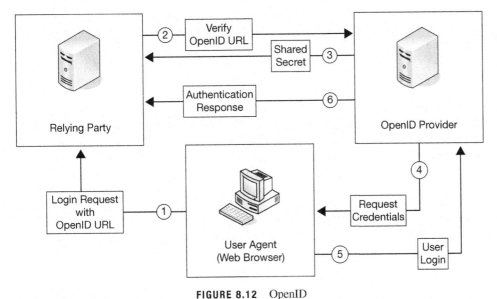

FIGURE 8.12   OpenID

---

[22] http://openid.net/specs/openid-authentication-2_0.html

[23] http://openid.net/specs/openid-attribute-exchange-1_0.html

FIGURE 8.13 OpenID 2.0 provider selection screen.
Source: Janrain

the domain name of their OpenID provider (yahoo.com, for example) or select the provider from a list and a central discovery service at that provider would return the correct OpenID URL for the user. Figure 8.13 shows a typical provider selection screen for an OpenID 2.0 Relying Party. Attribute release was an important feature; it allowed users to bypass forms requesting basic user info such as name and email address by having their OpenID provider assert that information for them. Because the signup and login process was easier for users, Relying Parties saw marked increases in registrations and service usage when using OpenID authentication.[24] The attribute release system in OpenID 2.0 can also be seen as a gain for user's privacy. Before releasing any data to a Relying Party, the OpenID provider seeks the user's permission and allows them to terminate the transaction if they do not wish to release the requested data.

OAuth

The OpenID protocols were designed to fill the typical use case of a web application – a human being sitting in front of a web browser is accessing the service. However, two new use cases appeared shortly after the development of OpenID: web mashups and mobile applications. *A web mashup is a web page or application that combines data from one or more web-based APIs into a new service.* For example, BigHugeLabs (http://bighugelabs.com) uses the image APIs from Flickr to create posters, mosaics, and many other types of new images. There are literally thousands of mashups using the Google Maps API (https://developers.google.com/maps), from finding a Winery tour anywhere in the United States (http://winesandtimes.com) to seeing the current Twitter trends by location (http://trendsmap.com) (Figure 8.14). The APIs used by mashups can't be protected by OpenID because they are not being accessed by a person who can authenticate to the OpenID provider. They are being accessed by the web application combining the data and creating the mashup.

Similarly, applications on mobile devices such as smartphones and tablets access the web-based APIs to retrieve and manipulate data for the user to enhance their native capabilities. A game on a smartphone may allow you to update your status on Twitter or Facebook with your high score, but you would not want to give full access (to update your friend list, for instance) to the game's developer. A protocol was needed that would allow a user to grant an application or service access to specific resources for a limited amount of time without giving out their credentials. The OAuth (open authorization) protocol was developed to meet this need. According to the OAuth technology home page,[25] *OAuth is a mechanism that allows a user to grant access to private resources on one site (the service provider) to another site (the consumer).* Figure 8.15 is an overview of the protocol.

The first thing that you must know about the OAuth protocol is that it is *not* an authentication protocol, although many people mistakenly refer to it as one. OAuth deals strictly with

[24]http://janrain.com/resources/industry-research/consumer-perceptions-of-online-registration-and-social-login

[25]http://oauth.net/about/

FIGURE 8.14   http://trendsmap.com

authorization, it provides a web application (OAuth client) with a way to request access to one or more resources (scope) from a user (resource owner) through an OAuth authorization server and be able to reuse that authorization for an extended period of time and allow the user to revoke access at any time.

Before a client can send requests to an authorization server, the application must register an identifier with the server and receive client credentials, usually in the form of a password or shared secret. When a client needs to access a resource for the first time, it redirects the resource owner's user agent (browser or mobile application) to the authorization server along with the scope of the request and the client identifier (1a & 1b). The Authorization Server authenticates the user (2 & 3) (it may request their credentials directly or, more likely, be part of a federation/SSO network) and presents them with a list of the requested resources and gives them a chance to accept or deny the request.

If the resource owner grants access, the user agent is redirected back to the OAuth client along with an authorization code (4a & 4b). The OAuth client then sends the authorization code and the client credentials previously established with the authorization server (5). The authorization server verifies the client credentials and request and then issues an access token (6) that the client can use to access the protected resource (7). The OAuth client can continue using this access token until it expires or access is revoked by the resource owner.

Most of the major social networking sites including Facebook, Twitter, Foursquare, and Google+ provide access to an OAuth authorization server. If you've ever allowed another application to post to your Facebook timeline or update post to your Twitter account, you've been the resource owner in an OAuth transaction. The major problem with OAuth is that the user authentication is left up to the authorization server, meaning that if a user has clients accessing three different services that use OAuth for authorization, they will likely have to authenticate three separate times. Many developers consider OAuth "good enough" as an authentication system because they feel that if the authorization server issues an authorization code for an OpenID request, the user's identity has been verified and the authentication can be trusted. If

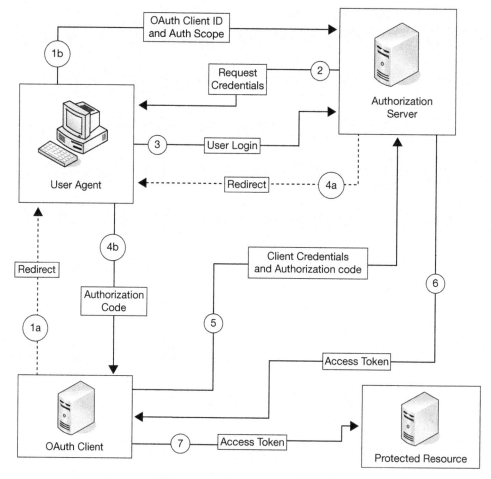

FIGURE 8.15 OAuth token passing

an OAuth access token is used for authentication and authorization, there is the possibility, however, that a rogue or compromised client could misuse the token and impersonate the user at any other site that uses the same authorization service. In most applications that OAuth is in use for today the risk of this type of attack is minimal, as the resources protected by OAuth (social networking, blogs, etc.) aren't particularly valuable. As banking and other financial institutions begin to implement OAuth however, the target becomes much more valuable and more likely to be exploited. A newly proposed protocol, OpenID Connect, combines OAuth for authorization, OpenID for authentication, and elements of the SAML protocol for message security into a single standard.[26] The design of OpenID Connect is still very much in flux and is several years from approaching the popularity of OAuth, but as the successor to OpenID 2.0 it is worth mentioning.

---

[26] http://openid.net/connect

A simple way to see how OAuth is used in practice may be seen by creating a simple MVC 4 application with the Internet template in Visual Studio 2012. MVC 4 introduces the SimpleMembershipProvider mechanism to authenticate users and includes OAuth as one of its features. To implement OAuth, MVC 4 uses a table called webpages_OAuthMembership, whose structure may be seen in Figure 8.16. The Userid column in the table is the primary key to the user's record in the local application. Through the webpages_OAuthMembership table, SimpleMembership associates the local user id to the user's identification information on a remote provider such as Facebook or Twitter. Once the association is made, the user can provide their credentials at the remote provider. The local application will verify it with the remote provider and, if confirmed by the third party, allows the user access into the local application.

The user, not the application, makes the association between the local user id and the id at the third party. The application merely allows the user to make such as association.

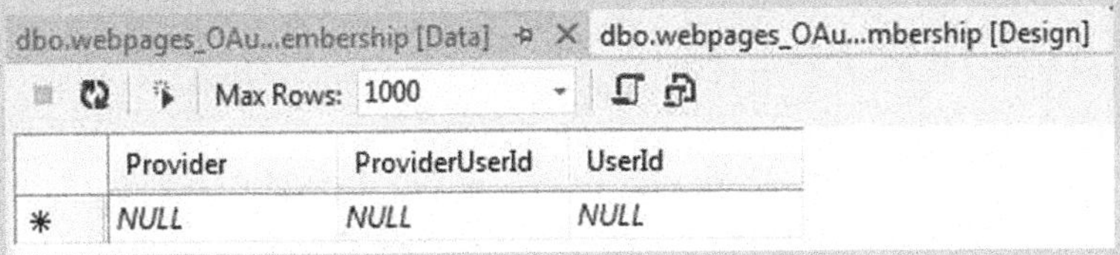

FIGURE 8.16   Application UserId and ProviderUserId

Example case – Markus Hess

Cliff Stoll, an astronomer and amateur IT system administrator used his keen sense of observation to track down a young German intruder, Markus Hess, who successfully entered many US military establishments over a 1 year period during 1986–1987. The intruder sold many of the files he downloaded to the KGB. Apart from the intruder's persistence and skill, in most cases, he was able to enter computers by exploiting weak passwords. The intruder's connection path is shown in Figure 8.17.

Monitoring detailed printouts of the intruder's activity, it turned out that he attempted to enter about 450 computers, using common account names like roof, guest, system, or field and default or common passwords. Using simple utilities such as who or finger that list currently logged users, he could find valid user account names. In about 5% of the machines attempted, default account names and passwords were valid, though the machines were expected to be secure. These default credentials often gave system-manager privileges as well. In other cases, once he entered into a system, he could exploit well-known software vulnerabilities to escalate his privileges to become system manager. In other cases, he took advantage of well-publicized problems in several operating systems, to obtain root or system-manager privileges.

The intruder also cracked encrypted passwords. In those days, the UNIX operating system stored passwords in encrypted form, but in publicly readable locations. Traffic logs showed that he was downloading encrypted password files from compromised systems to his own computer and within about a week, reconnecting to the same computers and logging into existing accounts with correct passwords. Upon investigation, it turned out that the successfully guessed passwords were English words, common names, or place-names, suggesting a dictionary attack

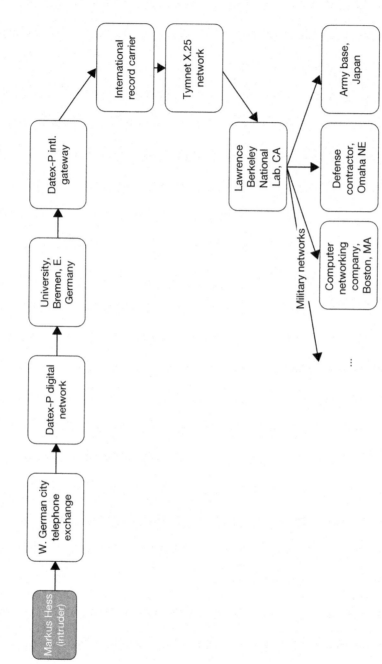

FIGURE 8.17 Intruder's attack path to military establishments

where he would successively encrypt dictionary words and compare the results to the downloaded passwords.

This experience helped investigators appreciate the weaknesses of password security in some versions of UNIX and its implications. These versions of Unix at the time lacked password aging, expiration, and exclusion of dictionary words as passwords. Also, allowing anyone to read passwords, trusting the security of the encryption scheme was improper. The Lawrence Berkeley lab guidelines did not bother to promote good password selection with the result that almost 20% of its users' passwords could be guessed using dictionary words.

REFERENCES

Stoll, C. "Stalking the wily hacker," Communications of the ACM, May 1988, 31(5): 484–497

Stoll, C. "The Cuckoo's egg," Doubleday, http://en.wikipedia.org/wiki/The_Cuckoo's_Egg

SUMMARY

In this chapter, we looked at identity and access management processes, from the start of a user's identity in a System of Record to the mechanics of authentication and authorization. We introduced the phases of identity management – identity discovery, identity reconciliation, and identity enrichment – and how role-based access control policies are used for access management.

Authentication is the process used to validate the identity of an account holder. It requires at least two pieces of information: a principal (username) and a credential. Credentials can be broken up into three broad categories: passwords, tokens, and biometrics. Multifactor authentication requires two or more different types of credentials used together to validate an identity.

Single sign-on systems allow users to access applications on multiple computer systems within a single organization while only authenticating once. Some SSO protocols such as Kerberos are designed for desktop use, while others, like CAS and token-based authentication, are meant to be used by web applications. Federation protocols such as Shibboleth and OpenID allow users from multiple organizations to access shared resources and extend the single sign-on experience outside of a single organization.

CHAPTER REVIEW QUESTIONS

1. What is identity management?

2. Briefly describe the phases of the identity management model.

3. What is a System of Record?

4. Would a person's name be a good identifier for a System of Record? Why or why not?

5. What role does the Person Registry play in the identity management process?

6. What is a role?

7. What is separation of duties?

8. Give an example of role-based access control policy.

9. What do access audits do?

10. What is a credential?

11. What are the three categories of credentials?

12. What is the oldest and simplest form of credential?

13. What is the difference between a dictionary and brute-force password attack?

14. Name one advantage and disadvantage for each of these types of credentials:

   • Password

   • Smart card

- Hardware token

- Mobile phone (SMS) software token

- Biometric comparison

15. What are the seven factors that should be considered when determining the suitability of a biometric marker?

16. Name and briefly describe three advantages and disadvantages to single sign-on.

17. What is the name of Microsoft's single sign-on architecture?

18. What is an authentication token?

19. Name at least one advantage and disadvantage to using:

- Shared tokens

- CAS

- Shibboleth

- OpenID

- OAuth

20. Name at least one similarity in design that CAS and Kerberos share.

21. What is the purpose of a federation?

22. Where was the first of the major SAML federations established? What was it called?

23. Name and briefly describe the four roles in an SAML federation.

24. Describe two ways that the OpenID 2.0 differs from the OpenID 1.0 specification.

25. What is a web mashup? Why are they reliant on OAuth for functionality?

EXAMPLE CASE QUESTIONS

1. What are some of the activities that the Lawrence Berkeley labs are currently engaged in?

2. What in your opinion may be the most valuable items of information an attacker may gain from improperly accessing computers at these labs?

3. What are the steps currently being taken by the labs to reduce the likelihood of such compromises? (you should be able to find this information online)

4. What is the operating system you use the most?

5. How do you view all user accounts and their properties on this operating system?

6. Do you see any default user accounts on your system (guest, administrator, etc.)?

7. If there are any such accounts, do you see any potential vulnerabilities on your computer as a result of these accounts?

8. If you answer yes to the above, what can you do to fix these vulnerabilities?

HANDS-ON ACTIVITY – IDENTITY MATCH AND MERGE

This activity will demonstrate the identity match and merge process used by a Person Registry during the identity reconciliation phase of the identity management process. You will compare the data from two different Sunshine State University Systems of Record and create a single data file.

1. Download the spreadsheet (human_resources.xls) containing the employee identity data from the Human Resources system from the textbook companion website.

2. Download the spreadsheet (student_system.xls) containing the student identity data from the textbook companion website.

3. Download the Person Registry spreadsheet (person_registry.xls) from the textbook companion website.

4. Using the flow chart in Figure 8.2, apply the Match/Merge process to data in the Human Resources and Student spreadsheets.

5. Record the results of the Match/Merge process in the Person Registry spreadsheet.

Deliverable: Submit the contents of the Person Registry spreadsheet to your instructor.

Example

Human Resources data:

Identifier	First Name	Last Name	Birth Date	College	Department	Title	Role
1003455	Susan	Myers	07/05/92	Engineering	Electrical Eng.	Grad. Asst.	Staff
1003456	John	Smith	01/23/88	Arts & Sciences	Chemistry	Professor	Faculty

Student data:

Identifier	First Name	Last Name	Birth Date	College	Department
U8123658	Susan	Myers	07/05/92	Engineering	Computer Science
U7634106	David	Johnson	09/12/90	Fine Arts	Art History

Resulting Person Registry data:

Identifier	First Name	Last Name	Birth Date	Student ID	Employee ID	Primary Role
0000001	Susan	Myers	07/05/92	U8123658	1003455	Staff
0000002	John	Smith	01/23/88		1003456	Faculty
0000003	David	Johnson	09/12/90	U7634106		Student

Two-factor authentication

The next activity will demonstrate the use of two-factor authentication. You will build and install the Google Authenticator authentication module on the Linux virtual machine included with this text. The Google Authenticator is a time-based one-time password (TOTP) application that runs on iOS and Android mobile devices. Although it was originally developed to provide two-factor authentication for web applications written by Google, it can also be used when logging into a Linux system.

To install the Google Authenticator module, open a terminal window and "su" to the root account:

```
[alice@sunshine ~]$ su -
Password: thisisasecret
```

Copy the Google Authenticator install files to a temporary directory, extract the files and build the authentication module.

```
[root@sunshine ~]# cp /opt/book/chptr8/
packages/libpam-google-authenticator-
1.0-source.tar /tmp/.

[root@sunshine ~]# cd /tmp
```

```
[root@sunshine /tmp]# tar xvf libpam-
google-authenticator-1.0-source.tar
```

```
[root@sunshine        /tmp]#        cd
libpam-google-authenticator-1.0-source
[root@sunshine libpam...]# make
```

The make command compiles the module's source code into binary instructions.

Next, run the automated testing suite:

```
[root@sunshine libpam...]# make test
```

and install the module:

```
[root@sunshine libpam...]# make install
```

To enable the module, modify /etc/pam.d/sshd to match the following:

```
#%PAM-1.0
auth        required      pam_sepermit.so
auth    required    pam_google_authenticator
.so nullok
auth        include       password-auth
```

```
account    required       pam_nologin.so
account    include        password-auth
password   include        password-auth
# pam_selinux.so close should be the first
session rule
session    required       pam_selinux.so close
session    required       pam_loginuid.so
# pam_selinux.so open should only be fol-
lowed by sessions to be executed in the
user context
session    required       pam_selinux.so open
env_params
session    optional       pam_keyinit.so
force revoke
session    include        password-auth
```

Restart SSHD:

```
[root@sunshine libpam...]# service sshd
restart
```

Open a new terminal window and use SSH to access another account to insure that users who have not yet configured a Google Authenticator token are not required to enter an authentication code. To test this, we'll login to the bob@sunshine account using SSH:

```
[alice@sunshine Desktop]$ ssh bob@sunshine
The authenticity of host 'sunshine
(127.0.0.1)' can't be established.
```

```
RSA key fingerprint is 5c:40:15:b8:b7:f4:
eb:08:14:cd:1b:c7:d0:4c:76:74.
Are you sure you want to continue con-
necting (yes/no)? yes
Warning: Permanently added 'sunshine'
(RSA) to the list of known hosts.
Password: bisforbanana
Last login: Sun May 12 20:23:01 2013 from
sunshine.edu
[bob@sunshine ~]$
```

Now, let's configure a Google Authenticator for the bob@sunshine account:

```
[bob@sunshine ~]$ google-authenticator
Do you want authentication tokens to be
time-based (y/n) y
https://www.google.com/chart?chs=200x200
&chld=M|0&cht=qr&chl=otpauth://totp/bob@
sunshine.edu%3Fsecret%3DXPE7E73HKJ7S4XB3
Your new secret key is: XPE7E73HKJ7S4XB3
Your verification code is 424105
Your emergency scratch codes are:
  85632437
  55053127
  44712977
  12900353
  82868046
```

Save the URL returned in the response from google-authenticator. You will need it when configuring your mobile device.

```
Do you want me to update your "/home/
bob/.google_authenticator" file (y/n) y

Do you want to disallow multiple uses of
the same authentication
token? This restricts you to one login
about every 30s, but it increases

your chances to notice or even prevent
man-in-the-middle attacks (y/n) y
```

```
By default, tokens are good for 30 sec-
onds and in order to compensate for
possible time-skew between the client and
the server, we allow an extra
token before and after the current time.

If you experience problems with poor
time synchronization, you can increase
the window from its default
size of 1:30min to about 4min. Do you want
to do so (y/n) n
```

If the computer that you are logging into isn't hardened against brute-force
login attempts, you can enable rate-limiting for the authentication module.
By default, this limits attackers to no more than 3 login attempts every 30s.
Do you want to enable rate-limiting (y/n) **y**

The Google Authenticator module is now configured for the bob@sunshine account when logging into the server with SSH. Before testing the module, you'll need to configure the Google Authenticator app for iOS or Android mobile devices or use one of the "emergency scratch codes" provided by `google-authenticator`. The Google Authenticator mobile application uses an innovative configuration method; a QR code contains all of the information required to configure the device. Before configuring your device, open the link returned from `google-authenticator` configuration app in your desktop's browser to view the configuration QR code.

Configuring Google Authenticator on an iOS device

To use the Google Authenticator app, you must have an iPhone 3G or newer running iOS 5 or later.

1. Visit the Apple App Store

2. Search for *Google Authenticator*

3. Download and install the application

4. Open the application

5. Tap the plus icon

6. Tap the "Scan Barcode" button and point your camera at the QR code on your screen (Figure 8.18).

Configuring Google Authenticator on an Android device

To use the Google Authenticator app, you must be running Android 2.1 (Éclair) or later.

1. Visit the Google Play app store

2. Search for *Google Authenticator*

FIGURE 8.18 Configuration QR code

3. Download and install the application

4. Tap the "Add an Account" button

5. Select "Scan account barcode"

6. If the app cannot locate a barcode scanner app on your device, you will be prompted to install one. Press the "Install" button and go through the installation process.

7. Point your camera at the QR code on your screen

Using Google Authenticator with your mobile device

Now that you have configured your device, you can now log into the bob@sunshine account using both a password and the Google Authenticator token using SSH. Open the Google Authenticator app again. The application will present you with a new authentication code every 30 seconds. You can see how much time has elapsed for the current code by watching the circle in the top-left corner.

```
[alice@sunshine Desktop]$ ssh bob@sunshine
Validation    Code:    <enter    Google
Authenticator code>
Password: bisforbanana
Last login: Sun May 12 22:11:03 2013 from
sunshine.edu
[bob@sunshine ~]$
```

As you can see, the login using both the password and code from the Google Authenticator app was successful. All SSH login attempts for the bob@sunshine account will receive the Validation Code prompt from now on. If you wish to stop using two-factor authentication with an account, just remove the `.google_authenticator` file from the home directory.

Using Google Authenticator without a mobile device

What if you lose your mobile device or you're not able to open the Google Authenticator app (dead battery, broken device, etc.)? That is the purpose of the "Emergency Scratch Codes" listed when you ran `google-authenticator`. The scratch codes are special authentication codes that can be used instead of the mobile app. If you ever find yourself without your mobile device, you can use a scratch code. The codes must be used in the order they are listed from top to bottom, and each code can only be used once (Figure 8.19). If you use all five codes, you'll need to run `google-authenticator` again to generate more.

Question

1. Many websites and Internet services such as Google, Twitter, and Facebook have optional two-factor authentication systems. Do you use any services that provide this option? If so, do you use two-factor authentication with that account? Why or why not?

FIGURE 8.19 Google Authenticator (iOS)

CRITICAL THINKING EXERCISE – FEUDALISM THE SECURITY SOLUTION FOR THE INTERNET?

Feudalism: The dominant social system in medieval Europe, in which the nobility held lands from the Crown in exchange for military service, and vassals were in turn tenants of the nobles, while the peasants (villeins or serfs) were obliged to live on their lord's land and give him homage, labor, and a share of the produce, notionally in exchange for military protection.[27]

The critical thinking exercise in Chapter 4 referred to the thinking among the designers of the Internet that security would be the responsibility of end users. How has that turned out? Well, it has been very difficult for end users to keep pace with security requirements.

During the heydays of the desktop, end users took responsibility for computer security. Some ISPs provided free antivirus subscriptions to their subscribers as part of their Internet packages, but the responsibility remained the end users'.

With the proliferation of smartphones and tablets, this model has changed considerably in a short time. End users have always expected security "out of the box." As Bruce Schneier writes on his blog, two technology trends have largely made this a reality: cloud computing and vendor-controlled platforms. As cloud computing rises in popularity, more and more of our information resides on computers

---

[27]http://www.oxforddictionaries.com

owned by companies including Google, Apple, Microsoft (Docs and email), and Facebook (pictures). Vendor-controlled platforms have transferred control over these devices and through them, our data, to the vendors of these platforms. The new smartphones and tablets are almost fully controlled by vendors.

In this world, we get very satisfactory levels of security, someone who knows more than we do takes care of security, but providing us with few, if any, details of such security. We cannot discuss the elements of our security with these vendors or bargain for security features. How is the email in users' Gmail account or photos in a Flickr used? Users generally have no idea. Users cannot view files or control cookies on their iPads. As Bruce writes, users "have so little visibility into the security of Facebook that [they] have no idea what operating system they're using."

Users have shown that they like this trade-off – greater security and convenience in return for limited control over security, with the trust that the security will be done right. From the perspective of security alone, this is probably right. Providers do security far better than most end users can. Automatic backup, malware detection, and automatic updates are all core services provided at almost no cost. Yet, in spite of the huge benefits, users are inherently in a feudal relationship with these cloud providers and vendor-controlled platforms.

Whereas the currency in the medieval feudal era was labor, in the modern version, the currency is data. Users yield to the terms of the service provider with regard to their data and trust that the vendors will provide security. As the services become ever more sophisticated, providing context-aware benefits, there is greater temptation for users to share more of their data with the cloud providers. Not only email, but also calendars and address books. If all this data import and export takes time and we are happy with one provider and platform, we may even be willing to trust one provider entirely.

So, who are today's feudal lords? Google and Apple are canonical examples. Microsoft, Facebook, Amazon, Yahoo, and Verizon are contenders. What defense do users have against arbitrary changes in service terms by these vendors? We now know for example that almost all of these providers shared our data with the government without our consent or notice. Most users know that these providers sell the data for profit, though few if any, know how or to what purpose or what form.

In Medieval Europe, people pledged their allegiance to a feudal lord in exchange for that lord's protection. Today, we volunteer allegiance to a provider for that provider's protection. In Medieval Europe, peasants worked their lord's farms. Today, we toil on their sites, providing data, personal information (search queries, emails, posts, updates, and likes).

REFERENCES

Schneier, B. "Feudal security," http://www.schneier.com/blog/archives/2012/12/feudal_sec.html (accessed 07/14/2013)

Schneier, B. "More on feudal security," http://www.schneier.com/blog/archives/2013/06/more_on_feudal.html (accessed 07/14/2013)

CRITICAL THINKING EXERCISE QUESTIONS

1. Do you agree with the parallels drawn by Bruce Schneier between feudalism in medieval times and the relationship of modern technology users to large providers such as Google and Apple?

2. Bruce Schneier thinks that government intervention is "the only way" to fix the asymmetric power relationship between the large providers and end users in today's technology world. In light of the revelations of the US government's own controversial data monitoring of US citizens, do you agree with this assessment?

3. Do you think the free market can alleviate some of Bruce Schneier's concerns?

DESIGN CASE

At Sunshine University, students have the ability to use their Sunshine login and password to manage their classwork enrollment every semester. Right after the beginning of the Fall semester, after the drop-add period is over, you are called to the Registrar's Office to investigate a case. A student is complaining that all of her classes were dropped from the system, but she claims she did not do it.

1. Research and describe the concept of non-repudiation.

2. How does it apply to electronic authentication, particularly to this situation?

   Upon further investigation, you find out that the student's former boyfriend, upset after the break up, used the student's Sunshine credentials to login to the system and drop all of her classes.

3. How do you think the boyfriend obtained the credentials to the other student's account?

4. How could the system be modified to use biometrics to ensure non-repudiation?

5. Besides biometrics, what other suggestions for authentication methodologies, technical or non-technical, would you offer to help ensure non-repudiation?

6. As universities move more and more towards online courses, what other situations could arise in which a simple login and password would not be enough to ascertain the student's identity and prevent fraud?

7. How could the student have prevented this incident?

Hardware and Software Controls

Overview

In this chapter, we will complete our detailed look at the components of our general information security model, which was introduced in Chapter 4. In Chapter 5, we discussed asset identification and characterization. In Chapter 6, we discussed threats and vulnerabilities. The final component of the general model was controls. We look at some of the most essential and best-known controls in this chapter. At the end of this chapter, you should know about

- Password management
- Firewalls and their capabilities
- Access control lists (ACLs)
- Intrusion detection/prevention systems
- Patching operating systems and applications
- End point protection
- Information security control best practices

The above list is not intended to be comprehensive. This is just a list of the essential controls selected by the authors. A simple example of a control that is not discussed above is antivirus software. Further, once you enter the profession, you will encounter many other information security controls including application-specific controls. The intention of the above list and this chapter is to introduce the best-known controls so that you have an understanding of the basic ideas underlying information security controls. Most of these ideas are generalizable, so they should help you in quickly evaluating the merits of other controls you encounter.

Password management

We have defined passwords as a secret series of characters that only the owner of the identity knows and uses it to authenticate identity. Passwords are designed to be a security mechanism that is simple enough for average users while being secure enough for most applications. Passwords are used to protect data, systems, and networks. A password is typically combined with a username. The username serves as identification. *Identification is the presentation of a user identity for the system.* Authentication establishes confidence in the validity of a claimed identity.[1] Successful

---

[1] We have earlier defined authentication as "the process that a user goes through to prove that he or she is the owner of the identity that is being used."

use of a username and associated password provides a user access to restricted resources such as email, websites, and sensitive data according to the permissions associated with the identity.

Passwords are known by a few different names depending upon the context. *A personal identification number (PIN) is a short (4–6 digits), numerical password.* PINs are used when small keypads are necessary (ATM machines), or when regular passwords could potentially create human safety problems (airport fire suppression systems). Since they are short, PINs can be easily guessed and only provide limited security. In general, the use of PINs assumes the existence of other security mechanisms. These include daily withdrawal limits and security cameras in ATMs and physical security at airports.

Another form of passwords is the passphrase. *A passphrase is a sequence of words that serves as a password.* An example of a passphrase is "Wow!!!thisis#1clasatschooL." The motivation for using passphrases is that though the human brain can only retain up to about seven chunks of information in short-term memory, each chunk can be fairly large.[2] Passphrases can therefore be longer than passwords but easier to remember than an arbitrary sequence of characters. However, it is important to remember that simple passphrases such as "thisisthe#1classatschool" can be predictable and easily guessed by attackers compared to passwords such as "TiT#ˆCaS." A long passphrase is not necessarily more secure than passwords or a shorter passphrase.

The security of passwords depends entirely on the inability of intruders to guess passwords. Earlier, we have discussed two sets of password guidelines. The first guideline is related to the complexity of the password itself. The second is related to the diversity of passwords so that passwords stolen from one resource cannot be used at another resource.

The above is the end user's perspective on passwords – a password gets you access to a secure system. However, as a system administrator or security professional, you are responsible to make the system work. In particular, you are responsible for ensuring that the passwords in your custody are safe. This is accomplished through password management. *Password management is the process of defining, implementing, and maintaining password policies throughout an enterprise.*[3] Effective password management reduces the likelihood that systems using passwords will be compromised.

Password management reintroduces the CIA triad because organizations need to protect the confidentiality, integrity, and availability of passwords. Using the terminology introduced in Chapter 5 on asset management, passwords can be seen as restricted and essential information assets. Passwords are restricted because a loss of confidentiality or integrity of passwords can give intruders improper access to information. Passwords are essential because nonavailability of a password can make the underlying protected resource unavailable.

The National Institute for Standards and Technology (NIST), in furtherance of its responsibilities, has published guidelines for the minimum recommendations regarding password management. We use these minimal guidelines as the basis for the information in this section. Organizations with more stringent security requirements may impose additional requirements, including requiring mechanisms other than passwords for authentication.

Password management begins with the recognition of the ways in which passwords can be compromised and takes actions to minimize the likelihood of these compromises. NIST

---

[2]Miller, G.A. "The magical number seven, plus or minus two: some limits on our capacity for processing information," The Psychological Review, 1956, 63: 81–97, http://www.musanim.com/miller1956/ (accessed 11/1/2012).

[3]NIST Special publication 800-118 (draft), Guide to enterprise password management, http://csrc.nist.gov/publications/drafts/800-118/draft-sp800-118.pdf (accessed 11/1/2012).

recognizes four threats to passwords – password capturing, password guessing and cracking, password replacing, and using compromised passwords.

Password threats

Password capturing is the ability of an attacker to acquire a password from storage, transmission, or user knowledge and behavior. If passwords are stored improperly in memory by an application, or on the hard drive by the operating system, a user with appropriate credentials on the system may be able to steal the password. Similarly, if passwords are not encrypted during transmission, they can be sniffed by anyone on the network. User knowledge and behavior can be exploited in social engineering attacks.

Password guessing is another threat. *In password guessing, an intruder makes repeated attempts to authenticate using possible passwords such as default passwords and dictionary words.* Password guessing can be attempted by any attacker with access to the login prompt on the target system. *Password cracking is the process of generating a character string that matches any existing password string on the targeted system.* Password cracking can only be attempted by an attacker who already has access to encrypted versions of saved passwords. These encrypted versions of passwords are called hashes and will be covered in the chapter on encryption.

Password replacing is the substitution of the user's existing password with a password known to the attacker. This generally happens by exploiting weaknesses in the system's password reset policies using various social engineering techniques.

Compromised passwords are passwords on the system known to unauthorized users. Once such a password is known, it may be exploited to launch other social engineering attacks, changing file permissions on sensitive files, etc. If the compromised password is of a privileged user, say an IT administrator, the attacker may even be able to modify applications and systems for later exploitation. For example, the attacker may be able to create a privileged account for himself (most attackers are indeed men!).

Effective password management attends to these threats. NIST recommendations for minimal measures for password management are creating a password policy, preventing password capture, minimizing password guessing and cracking, implementing password expiration as required.

> Password threats demonstrate the recursive nature of information security threats. We have already discussed threats to assets. Ostensibly, in this chapter, we are trying to develop safeguards against the common threats. But we find that these safeguards may themselves be compromised. For example, passwords are a safeguard, but passwords may themselves be compromised. And therefore, specific measures must be taken to keep the safeguards safe.

Password management recommendations

A password policy is a set of rules for using passwords. For users, the password policy specifies what kinds of passwords are allowed. For example, passwords, length, and complexity rules fall in this category. For administrators, the password policy specifies how passwords may be stored, transmitted issued to new users, and reset as necessary. The password policy must take into account any regulations that are specific to the industry in which the organization operates.

Minimizing password guessing and cracking requires attention to how each technology in the organization stores passwords. Access to files and databases used to store passwords should be tightly restricted. Instead of storing the passwords, it is recommended that password hashes are saved (this is discussed in more detail in Chapter 7). All password exchange should be encrypted so that passwords cannot be read during transmission. The identity of all users who attempt to recover forgotten passwords or reset passwords must be strictly verified. Finally all users must be made aware of password stealing attempts through phishing attacks, shoulder surfing, and other methods.

To prevent password guessing and password cracking, passwords must be made sufficiently complex, and accounts must be locked after many successive failed login attempts. This minimizes the opportunities for hackers to guess a password. Placing strict limitations on access to password files and databases reduces the opportunities for password cracking.

Password expiration specifies the duration for which the password may be used before it is required to be changed. Password expiration reduces the likelihood that a compromised password can be used productively. Often, passwords are collected through automated procedures, and it can be a while before an attacker actually tries to use a compromised password. If the password is changed before the attacker attempts to use it, the password compromise may not be very damaging. However, password expiration has its problems, particularly if the organization requires different passwords for different systems. Users forget passwords, requiring costly IT support to recover forgotten passwords. In general, therefore, password expiration should be used judiciously, with longer durations for systems with lower security needs.

Password limitations

While passwords are ubiquitous in information security, they do have many significant limitations. Users often forget passwords, requiring either expensive help desks to respond to user requests or password reset mechanisms. Password reset mechanisms introduce their own vulnerabilities because the challenge questions may not be strong enough. Users often save passwords in locations where other users can see them. Finally, relatively simple social engineering attacks such as phishing can be remarkably successful at stealing passwords.[4]

For all these reasons, there has been considerable interest in developing alternatives to passwords for authentication. However, coming up with a good alternative is not trivial. Users know how to use passwords and managers are reluctant to ask employees to change work methods unless absolutely necessary. It does not help that there is limited data available on actual losses suffered by organizations due to password theft.

The future of passwords

Various authentication mechanisms have been proposed to replace passwords. One of these is Passfaces, where a user preselects a set of human faces and the user selects a face from this set among those presented during a login attempt. Another is draw-a-secret, where users draw a continuous line across a grid of squares. While passwords are likely to continue to be in use for a while, it would not be surprising if these or other similar mechanisms become more popular in the coming years.

---

[4]Herley, C. van Oorschot, P.C. and Patrick, A.S. "Passwords: if we're so smart, why are we still using them?" Lecture Notes in Computer Science 5628, 2009, Springer-Verlag.

Passwords and the more general concern of managing identities is such an important area of information security in practice that we have an entire chapter on identity and access management later in the book.

Access control[5]

We have earlier defined access control as the act of limiting access to information system resources only to authorized users, programs, processes, or other systems. We deal with access control systems on a day-to-day basis. For example, locks are a form of access control. In computer security, access control is represented using access control models. *Access control models describe the availability of resources in a system.* Useful access control models are able to represent the protection needs of information and resources of any type and at varying levels of granularity. At the same time, execution of the models should not place unreasonable computational burden on the operating system. Two common implementations of access control models are access control lists (ACLs) and role-based access control (RBAC).

Access control lists (ACLs)

An access control list (ACL) is a list of permissions attached to specified objects. ACLs use a simple syntax to specify subjects, objects, and allowed operations. For instance, if the ACL for a network connection says (131.247.93.68, ANY, block), the host 131.247.93.68 should be blocked from passing through the network connection to reach any resource on the network. The operating system checks all incoming resource requests for ACL entries that may prohibit access to the resource.

ACLs are commonly used to defend two kinds of resources – files and network connections. File ACLs specify rights for individual users or groups of users to files and executables. The use of the chmod command in Chapter 3 is an example of a File ACL system. Network ACLs specify rules that determine port numbers and network addresses that may be accessed. Network ACLs are a common way to implement firewalls (discussed later in this chapter). Most modern operating systems come with default ACLs that provide reasonable levels of security for the average user. ACLs are some of the simplest controls to implement and many other security controls depend upon ACLs for their effectiveness. For example, ACLs help maintain the integrity and availability of passwords by preventing attackers from overwriting passwords.

ACLs begin with a basic distinction between subjects and objects. Subjects attempt operations on objects. The operations are permitted if allowed by the ACL. ACLs may be represented as an access matrix which specifies the permissions for each subject on each object. An example is shown in Figure 9.1. Each cell in the figure shows the access permissions for the corresponding subject on the corresponding object.

Subject John is the owner of File 1. He also has read and write permissions on the file. Being the owner, John can assign any permissions to any user on the file. In this case, subject Bob has been given the read permission and subject Alice has been given the Execute permission on the file. Thus, each cell is the access control list for each user on the corresponding object.

---

[5]Tolone, W. Gail-Joon Ahn and Tanusree Pai, "Access control in collaborative systems," ACM Computing Surveys, 37(1): 29–41.

		Objects		
		Host 1	File 1	File 2
Subjects	John	Block	Own Read Write	Read
	Bob	Block	Read	Read
	Alice	Allow	Execute	Own Read Write Execute

FIGURE 9.1   Access matrix example

Limitations

Access control lists are a very simple and effective access control mechanism. They also have some significant limitations. If the permissions for a specific user have to be modified, the permissions for that user must be modified on all the objects to which the user has access. Also, it is not possible to assign permissions based on user responsibilities. If a user changes roles, providing access permissions to the user that are appropriate to their new role requires modifying permissions to the user individually on all applicable objects.

Role-based access control (RBAC)

We have seen that role-based access control assigns permissions to user roles rather than to individual users. Roles are created for job functions and users are assigned roles based on their responsibilities. By defining access permissions for roles, there is a separation between users and access controls. As users evolve within the organization, their roles can be assigned and the access permissions are automatically updated. RBAC therefore reduces the cost and administrative effort required to implement access control in large organizations, compared to ACLs.

Firewalls[6]

A firewall is a form of protection that allows one network to connect to another network while maintaining some amount of protection. One of the most familiar examples of a firewall is the door to a home or office. The door allows residents to get out of the house, while blocking rain and sleet from entering the home. The door also helps residents maintain some degree of confidentiality.

Network firewalls are hardware or software that prevent the dangers originating on one network from spreading to another network. In practice, network firewalls are used to serve multiple purposes including (1) restricting entry and exit from the network to carefully specified locations, (2) limiting incoming Internet traffic to specific application running on specific devices, and (3) blocking outgoing traffic from hosts suspected to have been compromised. Firewalls are not generally intended to defend against specialized attacks. For example, the doors of a retail store are not designed to detect shoppers with explosives, or shoplifters. Those tasks, where necessary (e.g., at airports), are left to more specialized controls such as human inspectors or antitheft technologies. However, firewalls are a very effective and relatively inexpensive first line of defense against a large number of common nuisances.

Figure 9.2 shows the common arrangement of a firewall relative to an organization's internal network and external networks such as the Internet. All traffic between the Internet and

---

[6]An excellent resource on Internet firewalls is "Building Internet firewalls," by Elizabeth D. Zwicky, Simon Cooper and D. Brent Chapman, O' Reilly Media, ISBN 978-1-56592-871-8 (896 pages). A lot of information in this section is based on this resource.

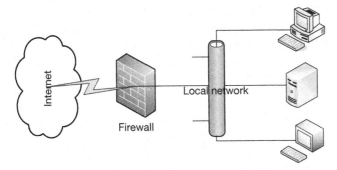

FIGURE 9.2   Typical firewall

the organization's network is directed through the firewall where the organization's traffic rules may be implemented.

Firewall decisions

A firewall chooses one of two possible actions on packets that pass through it – allow or deny. Allowed packets continue on to their intended destination, while denied packets are blocked at the firewall. We begin with the basic stance of the firewall – default deny or default allow. *A firewall with a default allow stance will allow all packets into the network, except those that are explicitly prohibited. A firewall with a default deny stance blocks all packets, except those explicitly allowed.*

Default deny or default allow?

The standard security recommendation is to use the default deny stance. This way, only services known to be safe will be reachable from the Internet. However, users typically prefer the default allow stance, since it allows experimental and other network services to operate.

The default allow stance may be acceptable for novice administrators or students learning how to configure firewalls. For all other uses, the default deny stance should be used.

The basic stance of the firewall is augmented by the administrator who specifies ACL rules to identify allowed packets (assuming a default deny stance). A few representative rules are shown below, using the syntax used by ipfilter, a popular firewall software.

```
pass in quick from 192.168.1.0/24 to 192.168.10.50
pass out quick from 192.168.10.50 to 192.168.1.0/24
pass in log quick from any to any port = 22
pass out log quick from any port = 22 to any
block in all
block out all
```

These rules may be interpreted as follows. The first two rules allow packet to reach and leave from the IP address 192.168.10.50 to any IP address in the 192.168.1.0/24 subnet. 192.168.1.0/24 is a compact way to represent all IP addresses from 192.168.1.0 to 192.168.1.255. This may be useful if, for example, the host 192.168.10.50 is used to provide shared services such as file and printer sharing or a Sharepoint portal to the organization. The second set of rules allows all incoming and outgoing connections to the ssh service (this is a remote login service to UNIX hosts). The SSH rules also specify that all ssh transactions be logged. The organization may like to do this to keep track of all SSH activity. The last two rules specify the default stance of the firewall, which is to deny by default.

Limitations of firewalls

Given their popularity, it is important to know what firewalls cannot do. Some of the important limitations of firewalls include the following:

Insiders and unregulated traffic: Firewalls protect the organization against attacks originating outside the network. If a computer inside the organization is compromised, it can steal data from other computers within the organization without passing through the firewall. Similarly, if a user brings in a flash storage device and copies sensitive data on to that device, there is nothing a firewall can do to prevent such theft because the traffic does not flow through the firewall.

Encrypted traffic: Encrypted data cannot be inspected, and therefore firewalls have limited ability to defend against encrypted data. For example, if a user browses a secure website, the firewall will not be able to examine the encrypted information exchanged between the user and the website.

Configuration: The security and usability afforded by a firewall depends upon its configuration by an administrator. A poorly configured firewall can allow malicious traffic to reach sensitive targets while providing an illusion of security.

Firewall types

There are broadly speaking, two types of firewalls – packet filtering firewalls and deep packet inspection firewalls. *Packet filtering firewalls examine the protocol header fields of packets flowing through the firewall to determine whether to allow the packets to enter the network.* Packet filtering firewalls may inspect fields such as source and destination IP addresses, destination port addresses, and TCP flags. One use of such a firewall would be to block incoming packets from a host or ISP that has a history of sending large volumes of spam messages. The host or ISP would be identified by the source IP address field.

Deep packet inspection firewalls examine the data carried by a packet, in addition to the protocol headers, to decide how to handle the packet. The data carried by the packet can be compared against a database of known malicious payloads. Such comparison can identify attempts to launch buffer overflow or other attacks that depend on carefully crafted payloads.

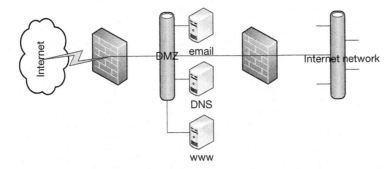

FIGURE 9.3   Perimeter firewalls and demilitarized zones

Firewall organization

Figure 9.2 is a simplified representation of how firewalls are used. Figure 9.3 is a more representative of the standard firewall configuration. It involves a perimeter firewall, a demilitarized zone, an interior firewall, and a militarized zone.

The perimeter firewall is the firewall that lies between the external network and the organization. It allows hosts outside the organization to access public-facing services offered by the organization such as the web, email, and DNS.

The perimeter network, also called the demilitarized zone, is the network that lies between the external network and the organization's internal network. The perimeter network hosts external services such as http, smtp, and DNS.

The internal network, or the militarized zone, is the location of all the organization's information assets.

The interior firewall limits access to the organization's internal network. Generally, access to the internal network is limited to some specific applications for requests originating from specific hosts on the perimeter network. For example, a university could maintain a portal at the demilitarized zone. Resources such as student records are stored on the internal network. These records can only be accessed using requests that originate from the portal. If the portal is compromised, other information inside the university is not at risk of compromise.

Basic firewall recommendations

If you are tasked with setting up a firewall for a small business or department, here are some settings you can start with. Allow users to access to the following services on the Internet:

Web (port 80, 443) to specified hosts running web servers
Email (ports 25, 465, 585, 993, 995) to specified hosts running email servers
DNS (port 53) to specified hosts running the DNS service
Remote desktop connections (port 3389)
SSH (port 22) to specific UNIX hosts

A general rule of thumb is to allow "secure" services. These are services that encrypt transactions and are in popular use. The popularity of a service is important because it ensures that the relevant software is constantly updated when any security flaws are reported. The most common of these services are SSH (for UNIX connections) and remote desktop (for Windows clients). In a typical commercial organization, these services may typically be allowed to connect to any host within or outside the network.

Another set of services are called "safe" services. These are popular services which can only be used as specified but which do not encrypt their transactions. Examples of such services include email and the web. For these reasons, it is recommended that hosts only be allowed to connect to web servers or email servers on designated hosts, which are maintained by trained and responsible system administrators. This ensures that even if a web server is accidentally enabled by a user on their desktop and not updated any further, the risks posed by such servers is limited.

Two services that were very common in the past but which are discouraged today are Telnet and FTP. These services have been replaced by their secure counterpart (SSH) and the software is generally unmaintained, leaving potential vulnerabilities. These services should generally be blocked, unless there is a special reason to enable them (e.g., to allow legacy applications using these services to work).

The figures below show the Windows firewall in action. The column on the left shows that when the firewall blocks incoming http requests (default), a website running on the host is not accessible from the outside world. The column on the right shows the same host but this time, with the Windows firewall configured to allow incoming http requests. The site can now be accessed from the outside world (Figures 9.4 and 9.5).

Intrusion detection/prevention systems

IT systems are under constant attack from various sources. For example, Federal agencies have reported that the number of security incidents that placed sensitive information on Federal systems at risk have increased from 5,503 in 2006 to 41,776 in 2010, an increase of over 650% during this period.[7] To respond effectively to these incidents, system administrators are interested in technology that can detect intrusion attempts in real time and alert administrators so they can respond promptly. This requirement has led to the development of intrusion detection systems.

Intrusion detection systems (IDS) are hardware devices or software applications that monitor IT systems for malicious activity or violations of usage policies established by the system administrator. Intrusion prevention systems build on IDS and attempt to stop potential intrusions. IDSs and to some extent IPSs have now become an integral part of the IT security infrastructure of most organizations.

Broadly speaking, there are two types of intrusion detection systems – network-based and host-based. *Network IDSs (NIDSs) monitor network traffic and application protocol activity*

---

[7]INFORMATION SECURITY: Weaknesses Continue Amid New Federal Efforts to Implement Requirements, United States Government Accountability Office, GAO Report to Congressional Committees, GAO-12-137, October 2011, http://www.gao.gov/assets/590/585570.pdf (accessed 11/23/2012).

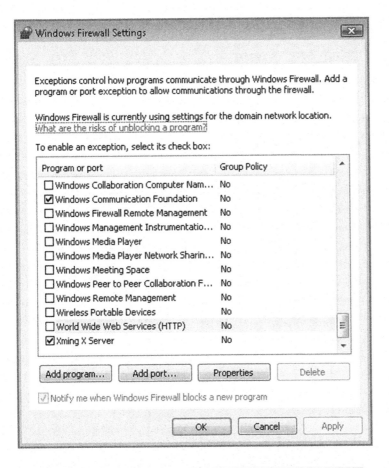

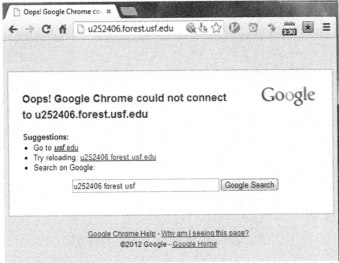

FIGURE 9.4   Windows firewall blocking http

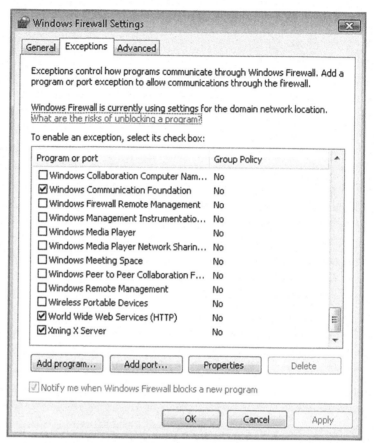

FIGURE 9.5 Windows firewall allowing http

to identify suspicious connections. NIDSs are usually included in routers and firewalls.[8] *Host-based IDSs (HIDSs) are software applications installed on individual hosts that monitor local activity such as file access and system calls for suspicious behavior.* To maximize the probability of detecting intrusion attempts, most enterprise environments employ multiple IDSs, each with its own set of rules, to observe system activity from its own perspective.

One interesting function of an IDS is to raise alarms about impending attacks. This is done by watching for reconnaissance activity – host and port scans to identify targets for subsequent attacks. Such scans often precede large-scale attacks. If the system administrator is notified of such scans, they can take necessary actions to be prepared for any of the following attacks.

Detection methods

Contemporary IDSs are based on three detection methods – signatures, anomalies, and protocol states. Most commercial implementations use a combination of all three to maximize effectiveness.

Signature-based IDS

A signature is a sequence of bytes that is known to be a part of malicious software. Signature-based detection methods compare observed events to a database of signatures to identify possible incidents. An example of a signature is an email with a subject line of "ILOVEYOU" and a file attachment called "LOVE-LETTER-FOR-YOU.txt.vbs." This corresponds to the well-known ILOVEYOU virus released on 5/5/2000 in the Phillipines.

Signature-based detection is very effective against simple well-known threats. It is also computationally very efficient because it uses simple string comparison operations. However, it is not very useful at detecting previously unknown threats, disguised threats, and complex threats. For example, the ILOVEYOU virus would be equally effective if the email subject line read "job offer for you" and the attachment file was called "interview-script.vbs." However, this simple disguise would make it very difficult for a signature-based IDS to detect the virus.

Another limitation of signature-based IDS technologies is that signature matching is limited to the current unit of activity, e.g., an incoming packet or an individual log entry. Signature-based IDSs do not understand the operations of network protocols. As a result, a signature-based IDS cannot detect port scans since every individual probe packet is a well-formed and legitimate packet. Threat detection of a port scan requires an aggregation of information about the current packet with information about packets received in the past – something signature matching of the current packet alone cannot do. More generally, signature-based IDSs cannot detect attacks composed of multiple events if none of the individual events clearly match the signature of a known attack.

---

[8] Karen Scarfone and Peter Mell, NIST Guide to Intrusion detection and prevention systems, special publication 800-94, http://csrc.nist.gov/publications/nistpubs/800-94/SP800-94.pdf (accessed 11/23/2012). The National Institute of Standards and Technology (NIST) includes two other categories of IDS – wireless and network behavior analysis (NBA). For the purposes of this chapter, these categories are considered part of NIDS. This guide is the source of much of the information in the section on IDS/IPS.

Anomaly-based IDS

Anomaly-based detection is the process of detecting deviations between observed events and defined activity patterns. The administrator defines profiles of normal behavior based on users, hosts, network connections, or applications. For example, a profile for an average desktop PC might define that web browsing comprises an average of 20% of network usage during typical workday hours. The IDPS then compares current activity and flags alarms when web activity comprises significantly more bandwidth than expected. Other attributes for which profiles can be created include the number of emails sent by a user and the level of processor usage for a host in a given period of time.

Anomaly-based detection methods are very effective at detecting previously unknown threats. For example, if a computer is infected with a new type of malware that sends out large volumes of spam email, or uses the computer's processing resources to break passwords, the computer's behavior would be significantly different from the established profiles for the computer. An anomaly-based IDS would be able to detect these deviations and alert the system administrator.

One problem with building profiles for anomaly-based IDS is that it can be very challenging to develop accurate baseline profiles. For example, a computer may perform full backups involving large volumes of network data transfer on the last day of the month. If this is not included as part of the baseline profile, normal maintenance traffic will be considered a significant deviation from the baseline profile and will trigger alarms.

Protocol-state-based IDS*

Protocol-state-based IDS compares observed events against defined protocol activity for each protocol state to identify deviations. While anomaly-based detection uses host or network-specific profiles, stateful protocol analysis specifies how particular protocols should and should not be used. For example, a stateful IDS knows that a user in an unauthenticated state should only attempt a limited number of login attempts or should only attempt a small set of commands in the unauthenticated state. Deviations from expected protocol behavior can be detected and flagged by a protocol-state-based IDS. Other abilities of a stateful protocol IDS is the ability to identify unexpected sequences of commands. For example, issuing the same command repeatedly can indicate a brute-force attack. A protocol-state-based IDS can also keep track of the user id used for each session, which is helpful when investigating an incident.

Protocol analysis can include checks for individual commands, such as monitoring the lengths of arguments. If a command typically has a username argument, an argument with a length of 1,000 characters can be considered suspicious. In addition, if the username contains non-text data, it is even more unusual and merits flagging.

The primary limitation of protocol-state-based IDS is that tracking state for many simultaneous sessions can be extremely resource-intensive, requiring significant investments in computer hardware.

IDS/IPS architecture

Enterprise IDS/IPS deployments follow a typical distributed systems architecture. There are many sensor agents deployed throughout the enterprise, collecting network-based and host-based information. These agents send their data to a central management station, which records all received data in a database and performs various signature-based, anomaly-based, and protocol-state-based analyses on the data. System administrators use desktop or web-based consoles to configure agents, monitor alarms, and take appropriate defensive actions.

Limitations of IDS/IPS

IDS/IPS technologies have two well-known limitations – false positives and evasion.

With the current state of technology, IDSs are not completely accurate. Many alarms raised by IDSs do not represent real threats and many real threats are missed. Flagging safe activity as malicious is called a false positive. Failing to identify malicious activity is called a false negative. Reducing one generally increases the other. For example, a very sensitive IDS will detect more real attacks, but it will also flag many benign transactions as malicious. A less sensitive IDS will not raise too many false alarms, but in the process will also miss many real attacks. Since real attacks are very expensive, organizations generally prefer to maximize the probability of detecting malicious traffic, even if it means having to respond to more false alarms. This comes at the cost of the information security group having to devote more resources to sift through all the false alarms to find the really malicious events.

Evasion is the act of conducting malicious activity so that it looks safe. Attackers use evasion procedures to reduce the probability that attacks are detected by IDPS technologies. For example, port scans can be conducted extremely slowly (over many days) and from many different sources to avoid detection. Malware can be sent as parts of file attachments and appear legitimate.

IDS/IPS therefore cannot be trusted to detect all malicious activity. However, like firewalls, they can be very effective as a part of an organization's overall information security deployment.

The NIST guide is an excellent resource for more information on IDS/IPS technologies.

Patch management for operating systems and applications[9]

A patch is a software that corrects security and functionality problems in software and firmware. Patches are also called updates. Patches are usually the most effective way to mitigate software vulnerabilities. While organizations can temporarily address known software vulnerabilities through workarounds (placing vulnerable software behind firewalls for example), patches or updates are the most effective way to deal with known software vulnerabilities.

Patch management is the process of identifying, acquiring, installing, and verifying patches. Patches are important to system administrators because of their effectiveness at removing software vulnerabilities. In fact, many information security frameworks impose patch management requirements. For example, the Payment Card Industry (PCI) Data Security Standard (DSS) requires that critical patches must be installed within 1 month of the release of the patch (PCI DSS 2.0 requirement 6.1.b).

Patch management introduces many challenges. The most important of these is that patches can break existing software, particularly software that has been developed in-house using older technologies. The PCI DSS defines appropriate software patches as "those patches that have been evaluated and tested sufficiently to determine that the patches do not conflict

---

[9] Souppaya, M. and Scarfone, K. Guide to enterprise patch management technologies (draft), NIST special publication 800-40 (accessed 11/24/2012).

with existing security configurations." Effective enterprise-wide patch management addresses these and related challenges, so that system administrators do not spend time fixing preventable problems.

In recent years, automated patch management software has gained popularity to deal with these issues. In a recent survey of IT professionals, automated patch management software products (such as SUS, HFNetChk, BigFix Enterprise Suite, and PatchLink Update) were used by 64% of the respondents for patch management; 18% used Windows update and 17% applied patches manually.[10]

NIST identifies the following challenges with enterprise patch management: timing, prioritization, and testing; configuration; alternative hosts; software inventory; resource overload and implementation verification. Each of these is discussed in brief below.

Timing, prioritization, and testing

Ideally, every patch should be installed as soon as it is released by the vendor to protect systems as quickly as possible. However, if patches are installed without exhaustive testing, there is a real risk that operational system might fail, causing immediate disruptions to the normal course of business of the organization. In the short run, many organizations may perceive such disruptions to be more damaging than any potential harm from not installing the patch. Matters are even more complicated in practice because organizations are often short-staffed. To get maximum benefits from the limited staff-time available for patching, it usually becomes necessary to prioritize which patches should be installed first. Therefore, during patch management, timing, prioritization, and testing are often in conflict.

One response to this challenge is patch bundles. Instead of releasing patches as soon as they are ready, product vendors often release aggregates of many patches as patch bundles at quarterly or other periodic schedules. This reduces patch testing effort at organizations and facilitates deployment. Patch bundling can even eliminate the need for prioritization if testing and deployment efforts are sufficiently reduced by bundling. Even if a software vendor uses patch bundles, if it becomes known that an unpatched vulnerability is being actively exploited, the vendor will issue the appropriate patch immediately, instead of waiting for the release time for the bundle.

While prioritizing patches, it is important to consider the importance of the systems which are to be patched in addition to the importance of the vulnerability itself. Web-facing servers may be more important to patch than desktops located behind militarized zones. Dependencies are another consideration. If the installation of one patch requires that some other patches be installed first, the prerequisite patches will also need to be tested and applied, even if the patched vulnerability is not in itself very important.

Configuration

In enterprises environments, patch testing and deployment are complicated by the fact that there are usually multiple mechanisms for applying patches. For example, some software could have been configured to automatically update itself by the end user, in other cases, users may have manually installed some patches or even installed newer versions of software. While

---

[10]Gerace, T. and Cavusoglu, H. "The critical elements of the patch management process," Communications of the ACM, 52(8), 2009: 117–121.

the preferred method may be to use centralized patch management tool, in some cases, patching may get initiated by tools such as network vulnerability scanners.

These competing patch installation procedures can cause conflicts. Competing methods may try to overwrite patches, remove previously installed patches, or install patches that the organization has decided not to install for operational stability reasons. Organizations should therefore identify all the ways in which patches could be applied and resolve any conflicts among competing patch application methods.

Users are a related concern in patch management configuration. Users, particularly power users, may override or circumvent patch management processes, e.g., by enabling direct updates, disabling patch management software, installing old and unsupported versions of software, or even uninstalling patches. These user actions undermine the effectiveness of the patch management process. Organizations should therefore take steps to prevent users from adversely affecting the organization's patch management technologies.

Alternative hosts

The typical enterprise environment has a wide array of hardware and software deployed. Patch management is greatly simplified when all hosts are identical, fully managed, and running typical applications and operating systems. Diversity in the computing environment generates considerable challenges during patching. Examples of architecture diversity include hosts managed by end users; tele-work laptops which stay outside the enterprise's environment for extended durations and can collect vulnerabilities; non-standard IT components such as Internet-enabled refrigerators or other appliances; personally owned devices such as smart phones over which the organization has no control; and virtualization, which brings up and tears down computer systems on demand, sometimes with obsolete software.

In this list, appliances are a particularly interesting case because often the manufacturers of these appliances are not very familiar with the importance of patch management and may not support automated procedures for testing and deploying patches. Patch management for these devices can easily become a time-consuming and labor-intensive process.

An effective patch management process should carefully consider all alternative host architectures connected to the organization's IT infrastructure.

Software inventory

For effective testing, enterprise patch management requires that the organization maintain a current and complete inventory of all patchable software installed on each host in the organization. This inventory should also include the correct version and patch status of each piece of software.

Resource overload

After testing is completed, the deployment needs to be managed to prevent resources from becoming overloaded. For example, if many hosts start downloading the same large patch at the same time, it can significantly slow the download speed as the hard drives hunt for the different blocks of software for each individual host. In large organizations, network bandwidth can also become a constraint, particularly if the patches are being transmitted across the continent on WAN networks. Organizations should plan to avoid these resource overload situations. Common strategies include sizing the patch management infrastructure to handle expected request volumes and staggering the delivery of patches so that the enterprise patch management system only delivers patches to a limited number of hosts at any given time.

Implementation verification

Another critical issue with patch management is forcing the required changes on the target host so that the patch takes effect. Depending upon the patch and the target hardware and software, this may require no additional step, may require restarting a patched application or service, rebooting the entire operating system, or making other changes to the state of the host. It can be very difficult to examine a host and determine if a particular patch has taken effect.

One mechanism to deal with this challenge is to use other methods of confirming installation, e.g., using a vulnerability scanner that is independent from the patch management system.[11]

End-point protection

End-point protection is the security implemented at the end user device. End user devices are desktops, laptops, and mobile devices used directly by consumers of the IT system. End-point security is typically implemented using specialized software applications that provide services such as antivirus protection, antimalware protection, and intrusion detection. End-point protection serves as the defense of last resort, attempting to pick up security problems missed by network controls such as firewalls and intrusion detection systems.

End-point security can offer security that organization-wide systems cannot provide. For example, end-point security systems can confirm that the versions of the operating system, browser, email client, and other software installed on the device are up-to-date and alert the user if necessary to initiate an update. Network-based security controls cannot generally provide such fine-grained security.

End-point protection also provides protection against other compromised devices internal to the network. For example, if a desktop within the network is compromised and begins scanning ports within the network, the end-point security software on targeted hosts can detect the scans and block any further requests from the computer until the matter is resolved.

Well-known firms offering end-point protection software include Symantec and McAfee. Microsoft also includes Windows Defender as part of its operating system.

Operations

End-point security software recognizes malware and viruses using one of two methods – signatures and reputation. Signature-based detection is the traditional method of detecting malicious software. Reputation-based mechanisms are newer and are computationally more efficient at detecting previously unknown threats.

---

[11] For an overview on how Microsoft manages its security patches, see "Software vulnerability management at Microsoft," at http://go.microsoft.com/?linkid = 9760867 (accessed 07/22/2013).

Signature-based end-point protection

We have seen that a signature is a sequence of bytes that is known to be a part of malicious software. Signatures have been the dominant technique used in end-point protection. Traditional virus and malware detection methods have relied on experts performing detailed analysis of each virus and malware executable to identify sequences of bytes that are unique to the virus or malware. In common parlance, these identifying byte sequences are also called virus definitions. Once such a byte sequence is identified, it is added to the end-point software's database of known malicious software.

The end-point protection software examines all incoming, outgoing, and executing files for the presence of any known virus signature. If such a signature is found, the file is immediately quarantined.

Signature-based virus and malware detection have few well-known problems. The most obvious is that it cannot defend against previously unknown threats. When a virus is newly released, its signature will not be present in the end-point databases, and the end-point protection software will consider the software safe.

Secondly, the inability of signature-based detection to block previously unknown viruses encourages growth in the number of viruses. Conceptually, creators of viruses can modify just 1 byte of malware and thwart the ability of signature-based systems to recognize the malware. This encourages developers to create viruses that modify themselves subtly between infections without any intervention from the developer, resulting in an explosion in the sizes of the signature databases. Since every file has to be scanned against all known signatures, eventually, growth in the size of the signature database causes signature-based detection to slow the system significantly. This arms race between viruses and virus signatures comes at the cost of system performance for the end user.

The state of the market in virus signatures[12]

In 2008, Symantec, a well-known company specializing in end-point protection, discovered over 120 million distinct malware executables. Whereas in 2000, the firm published an average of five new virus signatures each day; in 2008, it published thousands of new virus signatures each day. These new signatures steadily added to the signature detection workload of each computer, taking away computer resources that could be used for more productive tasks.

Reputation-based end-point protection

Reputation-based end-point protection tries to predict the safety of a file based on a reputation score calculated using the file's observable attributes. The influence of each file attribute on the reputation of files is calculated from the observed behaviors of files on user machines. Over time, reputation scores are calculated and periodically updated for every known executable file.[13] When an executable file (computer program) is encountered, a reputation-based end-point

---

[12] http://www.symantec.com/connect/blogs/how-reputation-based-security-transforms-war-malware

[13] It is estimated that there are 10 billion executable files "out there." Source – personal conversation with industry experts at first NSF meeting of principal investigators on Secure and Trustworthy Cyberspace.

protection system can determine the file's safety by looking at its reputation score (if known) or by computing the file's likely reputation from the file's observable attributes.

Since reputation-based end-point protection only needs to look at the file's known attributes (such as file size, age, source), this method eliminates the need to scan every byte of every file for the existence of any of millions of known malware signatures. This greatly speeds up the process of virus and malware scanning, enabling computer resources to be devoted to productive tasks, as opposed to signature detection.

Reputation-based methods have built-in resistance to new viruses. Previously unknown files naturally receive a low reputation score, much like how new borrowers like teenagers begin with a low credit score. As a file is used by more users for longer periods of time with no observed malicious effects, the file keeps improving its reputation score. This is similar to how users improve their credit ratings through responsible borrowing. Reputation-based mechanisms thus place a premium on familiarity and can potentially truncate the growth of malware variants.

Relative security versus absolute security

The controls in this chapter are intended to defend against most general threats and attackers. For example, attackers who just want to install bots on computers, any computers. In these situations, security is generally relative. As long as you are more secure than other organizations within the industry, you should be safe because attackers will focus on the easiest targets. This has indeed been the overall approach to information security.

Advanced persistent threats create a new challenge. These are targeted attacks where the attackers are specifically interested in your organization for whatever reason (intellectual property typically). They will try everything in their arsenal until they succeed at obtaining what they want from you. Security in this case is absolute. Your organization needs to be secure enough not to be compromised by the targeted attempts of the determined attacker.

Example case – AirTight networks

After completing his Ph.D. in Computer Science from the University of Maryland at College Park in 1995, Pravin Bhagwat worked as a lead researcher at AT&T Research and IBM Thomas J. Watson Research Center. By 2003, he was a well-recognized pioneer and researcher in wireless networking, eventually co-authoring 5 patents on various aspects of wireless networking.[14] In the early attempts made in those days, the industry was trying to create a wireless version of Ethernet. The goal was to enable computers to send data without any need for a wire to carry the data. The commercialization of the technology began around 1997, when IEEE published the 802.11 standard for the emerging wireless Ethernet technology. The standard specified data rates of up to 2Mbps and was designed primarily for use by bar code scanners at retail stores and warehouses. In 1999, the 802.11b standard was published, specifying data rates up to 11Mbps. When computer manufacturers recognized that these data rates were comparable to Ethernet data rates of 10Mbps, they considered the technology as capable of being added as an integral part of computer motherboards.

---

[14]http://patft.uspto.gov/netahtml/PTO/search-adv.htm

The integration of wi-fi networks into computers signaled to Pravin that wireless networking would soon become a mainstream technology. He could see that it would soon become commonplace for users to carry computers in briefcases (laptops). Having spent many years in the industry as a technologist, he now began giving serious thought to entrepreneurial opportunities in this sector.

The obvious choice was to get into the business of offering wireless access points. However, by the time Pravin had identified the opportunity, firms such as Aruba, Airespace, Trapeze, Vivato, Airgo and Aerohive had already secured significant levels of funding from marquee investors. Competing in this space would mean competing with well-funded firms with access to the best advisors in the industry. His 3-step framework for entering the technology space was to (1) anticipate a problem, (2) build a superior mousetrap to solve the problem and (3) be ready to serve customers when the anticipated problem manifested itself. Recognizing that others had beat him to this opportunity, he decided to look ahead to figure out what the next opportunity might be in the sector. Not only that, he decided to be prepared with a solution when the opportunity arrived.

Vulnerabilities as a business opportunity

Expertise gained from being involved with technology development from its infancy gave Pravin some unique insights. He realized that the introduction of wireless networking would expose an entire new class of vulnerabilities within organizations. Specifically, until now, businesses never considered their Ethernet (layer 2) cables as a source of threats. Ethernet cables were typically confined within buildings, where traditional physical security procedures would-be attackers from reaching the cables and doing harm. Most security vulnerabilities in this environment therefore occurred at the network layer or above. Since all traffic across organizations passes through a central location, the gateway router, a protecting firewall with well-defined rules was sufficient to handle most attacks in most organizations.

However, this was going to change if wi-fi APs were going to be connected to Ethernet directly. Wireless signals spread in all directions. In a large office complex, signals from one business could be monitored from a neighboring business. It would be possible to unauthorisedly inspect, modify and inject packets and traffic into the network from outside the network through these APs. Or even just by standing in the lobby. This was a completely new vulnerability that would inevitably affect every organization in the world.

Sensing that no one he knew was thinking about the commercial opportunities this vulnerability presented, he decided to work towards developing a solution. He started by putting together what he considered the three essential elements of starting up a company – an idea, a team and the necessary finances to sustain the team until it turns a profit.

But what is a superior mousetrap in information security? An intrusion prevention system? That's a well-known technology. Something that lowers costs? How would you do that? Perhaps by automating something? After much thought he concluded that something that automated key system administration functions could be useful.

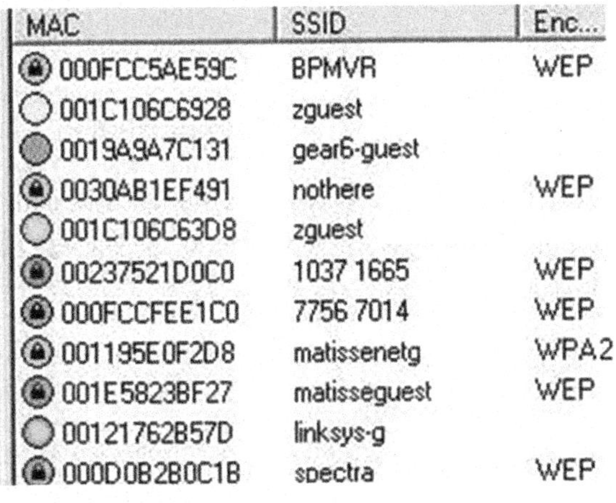

MAC	SSID	Enc...
000FCC5AE59C	BPMVR	WEP
001C106C6928	zguest	
0019A9A7C131	gear6-guest	
0030AB1EF491	nothere	WEP
001C106C63D8	zguest	
00237521D0C0	1037 1665	WEP
000FCCFEE1C0	7756 7014	WEP
001195E0F2D8	matissenetg	WPA2
001E5823BF27	matisseguest	WEP
00121762B57D	linksys-g	
000D0B2B0C1B	spectra	WEP

FIGURE 9.6 Typical competitor console, circa 2003

🔒	RSSI	Name	MAC Address	Channel	Protocol	No. of ...	SSID	Security
▲🔒	ᵢₗₗ	AirTight_A0:82:00	MULTIPLE	MULTI...	a/b/g [...	0	MULTIPLE	802.11i
📶 ᵢₗₗ		AirTight_A0:82:00	00:11:74:A0:8...	36	a [802...	0	anw	802.11i
📶 ᵢₗₗ		AirTight_A0:82:00	00:11:74:A0:8...	1	b/g [80...	0	@NAT	802.11i
🔒 ᵢₗₗ		AirTight_01:00:11	MULTIPLE	52	a [802.1...	20	MULTIPLE	Open
🔒 ᵢₗₗ		AirTight_01:00:21	MULTIPLE	6	b/g [80...	20	MULTIPLE	Open
🔒 ᵢₗₗ		00:CF:5F:33:C4:21	00:CF:5F:33:C...	10	b/g	14	cream_hotspot	Open
🔒 ᵢₗₗ		Cisco-Linksys_06:8...	00:16:B6:06:8...	14	b	0	Test_212	802.11i
🔒 ᵢₗₗ		Cisco-Linksys_10:B...	C0:C1:C0:10:8...	1	b/g	0	choochee-cell	802.11i
🔒 ᵢₗₗ		AirTight_A0:4B:50	00:11:74:A0:4...	11	b/g [80...	0	AA_BGN_1	802.11i
🔒 ᵢₗₗ		D-Link_7F:7A:62	14:D6:4D:7...	6	b/g [80...	0	dlink-bgn	802.11i, ...

FIGURE 9.7   AirTight console, circa 2005

The company therefore focused on automating the detection of rogue access points and wireless network scanning. By the end of 2005, after about two years of intense development, he had a working solution to the problem. Whereas existing solutions listed all available access points on the network (Figure 6), his technology could label each access point in vicinity as internal, external, rogue or misconfigured (Figure 7). His technology allowed a network administrator to clearly identify the access points that needed attention (those in red in Figure 7).

The basic element of Airtight's technology is a hardware box that is added to the network. The box senses the wireless signals in the medium to gather all required information and processes the signals using its proprietary algorithms.

Market catalyst

While the technology was interesting and compelling, he soon ran into another barrier. When he went out to market the technology, potential customers did not recognize the need to take any urgent action. After all, Pravin was trying to get customers to spend money on solving a potential problem that had never existed before and one they had never experienced. It was like he was selling Aspirin to people who hadn't yet experienced a headache. In 2005, wireless security solutions were not a requirement imposed upon companies by either state regulators or industry bodies such as the Payment Card Industry (PCI) consortium. And no one wants to spend money on security unless they absolutely have to. To the extent anyone was interested in wireless security, they were happy with whatever security the access point vendors built into their systems.

The way this was playing out, as of 2007, success was limited to industries where high security was a priority. These included financial institutions, telecom, and government. IT managers in these firms recognized the threat and were willing to invest in technology solutions that added an additional layer of security to their existing wireless networks.

During the years from 2003–2007, the company sustained itself through what Pravin considered the three essentials of sustaining a company after it starts – effort, time and patience, capital. It secured funding from reputed venture capital firms around the world who bought into his vision.

All this changed when Alberto Gonzalez and his activities at T J Maxx became known. Companies became aware of the new threat vector created by wireless networks. In addition, revision 1.1 to the PCI standards introduced a requirement for all companies accepting credit cards to periodically scan their wireless networks for misconfigured access points (there was no such requirement at the time of the TJX incident). Thus Alberto Gonzalez helped educate his customers in a way that he himself could not. Suddenly, companies were experiencing headaches and were looking for the Aspirin that AirTight could provide.

Current status

Airtight products have received numerous industry awards over the years. At the time of writing, the company has 29 patents to its credit, covering different aspects of the technology developed by the firm. In 2012, Gartner MarketScope for wireless LAN intrusion prevention systems ranked Airtight Networks "strong positive," the only company to achieve that rating in a field that included products from industry leaders such as Cisco, Motorola and Aruba Networks. Airtight has leveraged this product advantage with some success, attracting marquee customers such as Citrix, New York City Transit, and Ryder Systems.

Future directions

After dominating the wi-fi security space for several years, AirTight is now looking to expand its footprint by entering into bigger markets. Remember the wireless access market Pravin gave up in the early days of the company for being late in entering the market? AirTight is now looking at that very market after establishing relationships with some large customers through its wireless security offerings. It is projected that revenues in the wireless access market will rise from approx. $ 4bn. in 2013 to about $20 bn. by 2020. AirTight believes that if they can get security right, which is widely recognized as a considerably more difficult technology to master, they will also be able to do access right.

AirTight is making a push into several industries where there are large-scale distributed wireless deployments such as retail, hospitality, healthcare, and education. Organizations in these industries are large, but have modest security needs. It is entering these industries by introducing features that may be of interest to each of these sectors. For example, customers can enable wi-fi access capabilities using deployed security hardware with simple software upgrades. In the higher education sector, it is developing features that allow professors and students study computer networking by examining live, filtered network traffic within the campus.

At the time of writing in mid-2013, AirTight networks has secured key wi-fi access wins in the retail sector. The firm's technology is being deployed at some well-known national retailers, with thousands of locations each. One of the features deployed at retail locations is big data analytical services to help these firms track visitors across stores and offer customized promotions through cell phones. Another feature allows these establishments to securely offer guest wireless access at each location, with minimal configuration within each store.

Also, to address the tight budgets in higher education, it has developed Cloud managed wireless access point solutions, which eliminate one of the most expensive components in a typical campus-wide WLAN deployment. This model allows institutions to simply deploy wireless access point on the network, where they automatically configure themselves. Network administrators manage the access points using a simple web-browser based interface.

Airtight calls these cloud-managed smart edge-APs in comparison to the traditional controller-managed light-weight APs. These architectural changes leverage the developments in computer hardware over the last decade. As CPUs have become faster, RAM has become cheaper and standards have become prevalent, the trade-offs that necessitated the use of central controllers have changed. Inexpensive access-points (APs) can now pack technology that was prohibitively expensive only a decade ago. The wireless access industry that has already gone through two phases of disruptive change[15] in its young life could be in for yet another disruptive change.

---

[15] The phase where access points managed all traffic is considered the first phase and the use of central controllers to manage traffic is considered the second phase

REFERENCES

Wireless Field Day 5 presentation by David King, CEO of AirTight Networks, http://www.youtube.com/watch?v = qxNAUeevfvc&list = PLObjX_zORJMAz0EBXmsQqSS5EOWzb96St&index = 16 (accessed 8/11/13)

Personal conversation with protagonist by one of the authors

CHAPTER REVIEW QUESTIONS

1. What is a password? What is it used for?

2. Briefly describe some alternate forms of passwords.

3. What is password management? Why is it necessary?

4. What are the important threats to passwords?

5. What are the important recommendations for password management?

6. What are some advantages and limitations of passwords?

7. What are firewalls? What are their common uses?

8. Write an example firewall rule using the syntax shown in the chapter. Describe what the rule does.

9. Write a firewall rule that blocks all incoming web requests (port 80) from the 192.168.0.0/16 network.

10. What are some limitations of firewalls?

11. What are deep packet inspection firewalls? What additional capabilities do they offer, compared to packet-filtering firewalls?

12. What are the differences between the perimeter network and the interior network, from the perspective of information security?

13. Draw a diagram of a typical enterprise firewall organization, showing the perimeter firewall, interior firewall, demilitarized zone, and internal network.

14. What are the recommendations for a basic firewall configuration?

15. What are IDS/IPS?

16. What are signature-based IDSs? What are their advantages and limitations?

17. What are anomaly-based IDSs? What are their advantages and limitations?

18. What are protocol-state-based IDSs? What are their advantages and limitations?

19. What is a patch? What is a patch bundle and why is it used?

20. What is patch management?

21. Briefly describe the important challenges in effective patch management.

22. What is end-point protection? Is it necessary in an organization with strong network controls such as firewalls, IDSs, and strong passwords?

23. What are some important services offered by end-point protection?

24. What are some limitations of signature-based malware detection?

25. What is reputation-based malware detection?

EXAMPLE CASE QUESTIONS

1. Provide a summary of the security requirements for wireless networks (an Internet search for "PCI wireless requirements" should point you to some useful resources)

2. You are the CIO of a medium- to large-sized firm. How important would the size of a vendor firm be in your decision to use its products for your organization's information security? Why would size of the vendor matter to you?

3. You are the CIO of a medium- to large-sized firm. How important would the prior existence of a vendor's technology in your firm be in your decision to use its products for your organization's information security? Why would prior experience with the vendor matter to you?

4. You are the CEO of a start-up firm offering a compelling product to improve an organization's information security. How may you address the issues raised in the last two questions?

5. Visit the website of AirTight networks. What are the primary products and services offered by the company?

HANDS-ON ACTIVITY – HOST-BASED IDS (OSSEC)

In this exercise, you will install and test OSSEC, a Open Source Host-based intrusion detection system, on the Linux virtual machine included with this text. OSSEC performs log analysis, file integrity checking, policy monitoring, rootkit detection, real-time alerting, and active response. For more information, see the OSSEC website http://www.ossec.net

To install OSSEC, open a terminal window and "su" to the root account:

```
[alice@sunshine ~]$ su -
Password: thisisasecret
```

Copy the OSSEC install files to a temporary directory, uncompress the file and begin the installation process.

```
[alice@sunshine ~]# cp /opt/book/con-
trols/packages/ossec-hids-2.7.tar.gz /
tmp/.
[alice@sunshine ~]# cd /tmp
[alice@sunshine /tmp]# tar zxvf ossec-
hids-2.7.tar.gz
[alice@sunshine /tmp]# cd ossec-hids-2.7
[alice@sunshine /tmp/ossec-hids-2.7 ]# ./
install.sh
```

```
** Para instalação em português, escolha
   [br].
** 要使用中文进行安装, 请选择[cn].
** Fur eine deutsche Installation wohlen
   Sie [de].
** εια εγκατάστασηστα Ελληνικά, επιλεξτε [el].
** For installation in English, choose
   [en].
** Para instalar en Español , eliga [es].
** Pour une installation en français,
   choisissez [fr]
** A Magyar nyelvü telepítéshez válassza
   [hu].
** Per l'installazione in Italiano, sce-
   gli [it].
```

```
** 日本語でインストールします. 選択して下さい
   [jp].
** Voor installatie in het Nederlands,
   kies [nl].
** Aby instalować w języku Polskim, wybi-
   erz [pl].
** Для инструкций по установке на русском, введите
   [ru].
** Za instalaciju na srpskom, izaberi
   [sr].
** Türkçekurulum için seçin [tr].
(en/br/cn/de/el/es/fr/hu/it/jp/nl/pl/ru/
sr/tr) [en]: en
```

```
OSSEC HIDS v2.7 Installation Script -
http://www.ossec.net
You are about to start the installation
process of the OSSEC HIDS.
You must have a C compiler pre-installed
in your system.
If you have any questions or comments,
please send an e-mail to dcid@ossec.net
(or daniel.cid@gmail.com).
- System: Linux sunshine.edu 2.6.32-
279.2.1.el6.i686
- User: root
- Host: sunshine.edu
-- Press ENTER to continue or Ctrl-C to
abort. --
1- What kind of installation do you want
(server, agent, local, hybrid or help)?
local
- Local installation chosen.
2- Setting up the installation environment.
- Choose where to install the OSSEC HIDS
[/var/ossec]: /var/ossec
- Installation will be made at /var/
ossec .
3- Configuring the OSSEC HIDS.
```

```
3.1- Do you want e-mail notification?
     (y/n) [y]: y
   - What's your e-mail address? root@
     localhost
   - We found your SMTP server as: 127.0.0.1
   - Do you want to use it? (y/n) [y]: y
--- Using SMTP server: 127.0.0.1
3.2- Do you want to run the integrity
     check daemon? (y/n) [y]: y
   - Running syscheck (integrity check
     daemon).
3.3- Do you want to run the rootkit detec-
     tion engine? (y/n) [y]: y
   - Running rootcheck (rootkit detection).
3.4- Active response allows you to exe-
     cute a specific
     command based on the events received.
     For example,
     you can block an IP address or dis-
     able access for
     a specific user.
     More information at:
     http://www.ossec.net/en/manual.
     html#active-response
 - Do you want to enable active response?
   (y/n) [y]: n
   - Active response disabled.
3.6- Setting the configuration to analyze
     the following logs:
-- /var/log/messages
-- /var/log/secure
-- /var/log/maillog
-- /var/log/httpd/error_log (apache log)
-- /var/log/httpd/access_log (apache log)
 - If you want to monitor any other file,
   just change
   the ossec.conf and add a new localfile
   entry.
   Any questions about the configuration
   can be answered
```

```
by visiting us online at http://www.
ossec.net .
--- Press ENTER to continue ---
- System is Redhat Linux.
- Init script modified to start OSSEC
  HIDS during boot.
- Configuration finished properly.
- To start OSSEC HIDS:
     /var/ossec/bin/ossec-control start
- To stop OSSEC HIDS:
     /var/ossec/bin/ossec-control stop
- The configuration can be viewed or mod-
  ified at /var/ossec/etc/ossec.conf
  Thanks for using the OSSEC HIDS.
  If you have any question, suggestion or
  if you find any bug,
  contact us at contact@ossec.net or using
  our public maillist at
  ossec-list@ossec.net
( http://www.ossec.net/main/support/ ).
  More information can be found at http://
  www.ossec.net
--- Press ENTER to finish (maybe more
information below). ---
```

You could now start OSSEC with the command given above, but first there is one configuration option that needs to be adjusted. By default, the OSSEC system checks are run every 22 hours. This is fine for general use; however, we'll want to the processes to run more often for these exercises. You'll need to open /var/ossec/etc/ossec.conf in a text editor and change the value in line 76 from 79200 (22 hours in seconds) to 300 and save your changes. Notice that ossec.conf can only be viewed or modified by root. While logged in as root, modify the file using the Gnome Text Editor (Figure 9.8):

```
[alice@sunshine etc]# gedit /var/ossec/
etc/ossec.conf
```

To enable line numbers in Gedit, select File → Preferences and enable the "Display line numbers" checkbox.

```
<!-- Frequency that syscheck is executed
- default to every 22 hours →
<frequency>300</frequency>
```

This will cause the system checks to run every 5 minutes instead of every 22 hours. With that change in place, you can now start the OSSEC server. Save your changes and exit the Gnome Text editor to return to the terminal prompt.

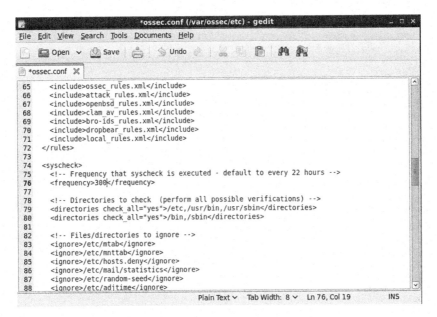

FIGURE 9.8   /var/ossec/etc/ossec.conf (after change)

```
[alice@sunshine  ossec-hids-2.7]#  /var/
ossec/bin/ossec-control start
```

The programs that make up the OSSEC system are now running, you can view the main OSSEC log at /var/ossec/logs/ossec.log. It provides you with details on the files that OSSEC reads during start-up and the results from the execution of OSSEC programs. If OSSEC detects any events that could be significant from a security standpoint, details are logged to /var/ossec/logs/alerts/alerts.conf. However, OSSEC outputs large amounts of information and viewing it by paging though log files is not very easy. The OSSEC-WebUI package is a web-based interface that provides a much easier way to search and view the recorded alerts (Figure 9.9).

Unlike the main OSSEC package, OSSEC-WebUI does not include an installation script and requires slightly more effort to configure.

```
[root@sunshine]#  cd  /home/shared/busi-
ness_finance/information_technology/
website/main
[root@sunshine main]# cp /opt/book/con-
trols/packages/ossec-wui-0.3.tar.gz .
[root@sunshine main]# tar zxvf ossec-wui-
0.3.tar.gz
```

```
[root@sunshine  main]#  mv  ossec-wui-0.3
ossec
[root@sunshine main]# groupmems -g ossec
-a apache
[root@sunshine main]# chmod 777 /tmp
[root@sunshine  main]#  chmod  770  /var/
ossec/tmp
[root@sunshine main]# chgrp apache /var/
ossec/tmp
[root@sunshine  main]#  service  httpd
restart
```

You should now be able to access the OSSEC-WebUI interface by opening a web browser and visiting http://sunshine.edu/ossec.

To test that OSSEC is working correctly, we will now demonstrate some of the ways the OSSEC is used to monitor for possible security incidents.

File integrity monitoring

The file integrity monitoring system in OSSEC detects changes in system files and alerts you when they happen. This could be caused by an attack, misuse by an internal user, or even a typo by an administrator. To simulate an attack that modifies system files, you will modify a file and view the results in OSSEC-WebUI.

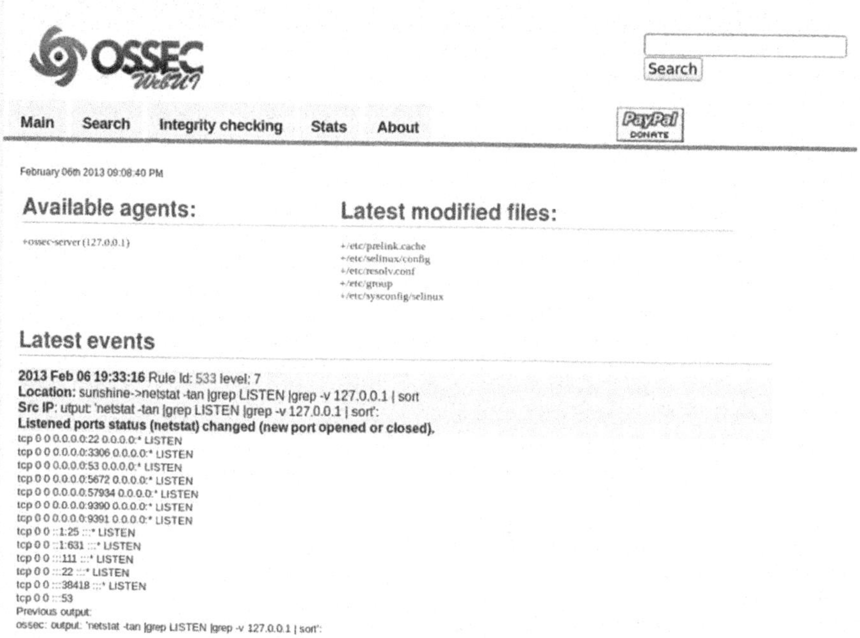

FIGURE 9.9 OSSEC-WebUI

1. Modify the contents of `/etc/hosts` to match this:

```
127.0.0.1 sunshine.edu localhost hacked.
sunshine.edu
::1   sunshine.edu localhost
```

2. Wait 5–10 minutes. The file integrity checks will run every 5 minutes, but they may take a few minutes to complete, so it is best to wait a few more minutes to ensure the full scan has taken place.

3. Open the OSSEC-WebUI and select the "Integrity checking" tab.

4. Click on the plus sign next to /etc/hosts to expand the details about this file.

5. Take a screenshot of this page and submit it to your instructor.

Log monitoring

OSSEC collects, analyzes, and correlates multiple logs throughout your Linux system to let you know what is happening. To demonstrate this, you will do some common system administration tasks that generate audit messages tracked by OSSEC and view the results.

1. Install the `zsh` package using the YUM package manager.

2. Create a new user:

   Username: ossec-sample

   Home Directory: /home/ossec-sample

   Password: oSS3c!

3. Open a new terminal window and run this command:

```
[alice@sunshine ~]$ ssh bob@sunshine.edu
```

4. When prompted for a password, use *bisforbanana*.

5. Open OSSEC-WebUI in a web browser.

6. Wait 5–10 minutes for OSSEC to complete all scanning and processing.

7. Review the recent alerts captured by OSSEC and locate the ones related to the three events above.

8. Copy and paste the data about each event into a Word document.

Deliverable: Submit the document containing the OSSEC results to your instructor.

CRITICAL THINKING EXERCISE – EXTRA-HUMAN SECURITY CONTROLS

Research reported from Australia in November 2012 suggests that security controls are even used in interesting ways outside the human world to deal with the unique problems of surviving in the wild. Horsfield's Bronze-Cuckoos lay their eggs in the nests of Superb Fairy-Wrens, hoping to leave parenting duties to unsuspecting Fairy-Wrens. The eggs of the two species look similar, enabling the ruse.

From the perspective of the Fairy-Wren, the problem is actually much worse. Bronze-Cuckoo eggs hatch 3 days before the Fairy-Wren eggs, 12 days versus 15 days. As soon as they are born, the Bronze-Cuckoo chicks push out the Fairy-Wren eggs from the nest. Without effective detection mechanisms, an aggrieved Fairy-Wren might end up feeding the offending Bronze-Cuckoo chicks, that destroyed her eggs.

While the Wrens are unable to do much to prevent the destruction of their eggs, they have developed a mechanism (control) to avoid feeding the Bronze-Cuckoos. About 10 days after the eggs are laid, the mother begins to sing to her embryos. After birth, the chicks are expected to incorporate the unique notes in the song in their calls for food. If the unique notes are missing, the chicks will be abandoned. The Fairy-Wren embryos

FIGURE 9.10   Superb Fairy-Wrens, 40% success rate with security controls

get 5 days to learn the notes, the Bronze-Cuckoo embryos only get 2 days, insufficient to learn the notes. The test succeeds about 40% of the time in detecting offenders (Figure 9.10).

REFERENCES

Schneier, B. Cryptogram, November 15, 2012

Yong E., "Fairy Wrens teach secret passwords to their unborn chicks to tell them apart from cuckoo impostors," Discover Magazine blog, November 8, 2012, http://blogs.discovermagazine.com/notrocketscience/2012/11/08/fairy-wrens-teach-secret-passwords-to-their-unborn-chicks-to-tell-them-apart-from-cuckoo-impostors (accessed 07/18/2013)

Corbyn, Z. "Wrens teach their eggs to sing," November 8, 2012, http://www.nature.com/news/wrens-teach-their-eggs-to-sing-1.11779 (accessed 07/18/2013)

CRITICAL THINKING EXERCISE QUESTIONS

1. Of the controls discussed in this chapter, which control most closely resembles the control used by Fairy-Wren mothers to detect imposters?

2. The control used by Fairy-Wren mothers seems rather complex. Some simpler controls suggest themselves. Could you name a few?

DESIGN CASE

You are asked to harden a CentOS machine for a faculty member. He is the recipient of a sizeable grant from the federal government, but it requires that he uses CentOS for some of the data analysis. The results are considered restricted data, so access to the computer has to be restricted. You are not sure exactly how to do it, so it will take some research.

After some research on the web, you found the items listed 1 through 6 below. Write down the exact procedure (the command strings and the file details), you used to implement these changes so that you can replicate them on other machines as needed.

1. Change the default port for the sshd daemon from port 22 to port 4444. This minor change will avoid most automated scans to break into the machine using SSH.

2. Add the professors' login id (jamesc) to the wheel group.

3. Disable SSH logins as root, forcing users to use the sudo command instead. This command allows users listed on the wheel group to elevate their privileges and execute commands as the root user.

4. Change password aging parameters for the user jamesc to expire in 60 days.

5. Change password history parameters to remember the last three passwords and password length to a minimum of eight characters.

6. List the firewall rules and keep a hard copy.

   Hint: You may find the following configuration files and commands useful:

   - sshd_config

   - login.defs

   - group

   - chage

   - system-auth

   - iptables

Shell Scripting

## CHAPTER 10

Overview

In previous chapters, we looked at some of the common tasks associated with system administration. Beginning with the introduction to the role of the system administrator in Chapter 2, subsequent chapters have introduced the technical controls used to combat security threats and the efforts required after a security breach has occurred.

In this chapter, we will introduce you to a way to handle the sometimes complex and often repetitive, tasks required for effective system administration. The BASH shell provides a mechanism for creating a **script** – an application constructed from multiple command line applications – to accomplish complex tasks. At the end of this chapter, you should know:

- how to write a simple BASH shell script
- the use of common programming elements (variables, loops, etc)
- how to handle user interaction
- how to use common UNIX tools to parse and manipulate text files

Introduction

Basic knowledge of shell scripting is necessary for anyone wanting to complete common system administration tasks, audit the security of a system, or implement many of the controls we have discussed in the previous chapters. Shell scripts are used for automating processes throughout a Unix system, from starting network services at boot up to configuring the user's shell environment during login. This chapter will just be an introduction to shell scripting. To begin, we will be creating scripts that are intended as examples of common structures and procedures used in all shell scripts. Later in the chapter, we will combine some of these common elements to demonstrate the automation of processes that would be too time-consuming to do manually or need to be repeated in the future.

What exactly is a script and how does it differ from a program written in other programming languages you may be familiar with such as C# or Java? The most important difference between a script and a program written in a language such as Java is that scripts don't have to be compiled into a binary file to be run. The script is interpreted and converted into the necessary binary code at run-time. Since the compilation process is eliminated, developing applications with a scripting language is generally faster than with compiled languages; however, there can be a performance penalty when the code is executed. There are several popular scripting languages in use, including PHP, Python, and Ruby. Unlike scripts written in these languages, shell scripts do not require an interpreter program to convert the script into binary. Shell scripts are interpreted directly by the shell process; BASH in our case, but any of the other popular shells could be used.

Windows Powershell

Since Windows 7, Microsoft has included a new scripting language called Powershell. Powershell provides all of the programming constructs we will be covering in this chapter and much more. Microsoft has integrated Powershell functionality throughout their operating systems, allowing an administrator access virtually to any Windows function both locally and on remote systems.

We will not be covering the use of Powershell in this text, but to learn more about it, visit the Microsoft Script Center at http://technet.microsoft.com/scriptcenter

So, how do we write a shell script? At its most basic, a shell script is a list of commands saved in a text file that we can run by calling the BASH program on the command line:

Listing 1: /opt/book/scripting/backup_v1

```
[alice@sunshine ~]$ cat /opt/book/scripting/backup_v1
mkdir -p /tmp/backups
cp -pr /home/alice/work /tmp/backups
cd /tmp/backups/
zip -qr backup.zip work/
rm -rf /tmp/backups/work

echo "Done Backing up the work directory"
[alice@sunshine ~]$ bash /opt/book/scripting/backup_v1
Done Backing up the work directory
[alice@sunshine ~]$ ls /tmp/backups
backups.zip
```

This saves you the effort of retyping a list of commands each time you need to complete a task. However, by adding a single line to the top of the script and changing the file permissions to make it executable, we can convert this list of commands into a command of its own:

Listing 2: /opt/book/scripting/backup_v2

```
#! /bin/bash
# This is a comment.
# Lines starting with the pound sign (#) are ignored in BASH scripts
#
# This script copies and compresses files in /home/alice/work and
# saves them to /tmp/backups/work
mkdir -p /tmp/backups
cp -pr /home/alice/work /tmp/backups
cd /tmp/backups/
zip -qr backup.zip work/
rm -rf /tmp/backups/work
echo "Done Backing up the work directory"

[alice@sunshine ~]$ chmod 500 /opt/book/scripting/backup_v2
[alice@sunshine ~]$ /opt/book/scripting/backup_v2
Done Backing up the work directory
```

The chmod command sets the executable bit for the owner of the file. All others will not be able to execute the script. The first line of this version of the script (#! /bin/bash) tells the operating system that this file should be sent to the specified program for processing. We have also added a **comment** to the script. Any line that starts with a pound sign (#) is ignored by the BASH interpreter as a comment. Comments help you document how a script works, especially if you are working with complex logic. You can add a comment explaining what a particular statement should be doing and what the expected output is. Comments also allow you to add important information about the script such as the author and last modification date.

Once this line is added to the top of a text file, you can set the permissions to make the file executable and you have created a brand-new custom application. You can use these steps to create a script for any set of commands you need to repeat on a regular basis. Also, the length of the list of commands doesn't matter – you could have a list of a hundred commands or just one. It's often a good idea to create scripts for a single command if multiple command line options are required to accomplish a task, such as with curl or wget.

Output redirection

We've seen how to save multiple programs into a single script file, but there is another way to integrate multiple command line programs to accomplish a complex task. The output from one command can be used as the input for another one, creating what amounts to a script on a single line. This is possible because of the UNIX architecture's use of streams. "A stream is nothing more than a sequence of bytes that can be read or written using library functions that hide the details of an underlying device from the application. The same program can read from, or write to a terminal, file, or network socket in a device-independent way using streams."[1] There are three standard I/O streams:

- Standard Input (stdin) provides input from the keyboard.

- Standard Output (stdout) displays output from commands to the screen.

- Standard Error (stderr) displays error messages to the screen.

These I/O streams can be easily redirected in BASH, allowing you to read input from a file instead of the keyboard, send one (or both) output streams to another program as input, or save the output to a file. The pipe (|) operator connects the stdout stream of one program to stdin of another program. As an example, we'll list all of the commands in /usr/bin that contain the word "gnome" in the filename:

```
[alice@sunshine ~]$ ls -l /usr/bin | grep gnome
```

When you run this command, you will receive about 50 files as a result. What if you just want the first three results? You can pipe the output from grep to another command:

```
[alice@sunshine ~]$ ls -l /usr/bin | grep gnome | head -3
-rwxr-xr-x. 1 root root    37070 Mar 20 2012 gnome-about
-rwxr-xr-x. 1 root root    88944 Jun 25 10:29 gnome-about-me
-rwxr-xr-x. 1 root root   233664 Jun 25 10:29 gnome-appearance-properties
```

---

[1] Shields, I. N.p.. Web. 10 December 2012, <http://www.ibm.com/developerworks/library/l-lpic1-v3-103-2/>

The redirect operator (>) is used to send the output to a file instead of displaying it on screen. You can also append data to an existing file using the >> operator:

```
[alice@sunshine ~]$ ls -l /usr/bin | grep gnome | head -3 > /tmp/exam-
ple.txt
[alice@sunshine ~]$ cat /tmp/example.txt
-rwxr-xr-x. 1 root root   37070 Mar 20 2012 gnome-about
-rwxr-xr-x. 1 root root   88944 Jun 25 10:29 gnome-about-me
-rwxr-xr-x. 1 root root  233664 Jun 25 10:29 gnome-appearance-properties
[alice@sunshine ~]$ ls -l /usr/bin | grep gnome | head -5 >> /tmp/
example.txt
[alice@sunshine ~]$ cat /tmp/example.txt
-rwxr-xr-x. 1 root root   37070 Mar 20 2012 gnome-about
-rwxr-xr-x. 1 root root   88944 Jun 25 10:29 gnome-about-me
-rwxr-xr-x. 1 root root  233664 Jun 25 10:29 gnome-appearance-properties
-rwxr-xr-x. 1 root root   37070 Mar 20 2012 gnome-about
-rwxr-xr-x. 1 root root   88944 Jun 25 10:29 gnome-about-me
-rwxr-xr-x. 1 root root  233664 Jun 25 10:29 gnome-appearance-properties
```

Using multiple small programs in sequence instead of a single, complex application is central to the Unix design. The original developer of the I/O redirection system in Unix, Doug McIlroy, summed it us this way: "This is the Unix philosophy: Write programs that do one thing and do it well. Write programs to work together. Write programs to handle text streams, because that is a universal interface."[2]

Text manipulation

Because the use and manipulation of text streams is so important to writing BASH scripts, we are going to spend a little bit of time on command line applications that specialize in manipulating text streams. Together, these commands are the "swiss-army knife" of text manipulation, providing everything from file sorting to case conversion and are used in virtually every BASH script regardless of size.

Cut

You will often find yourself dealing with columnar data that uses some form of separator, such as a tab or comma, to delimit each column in the data set. The cut command allows you to parse each line of the data file and extract only the column that you need. For this example, we'll be using a Comma-Separated Value (CSV) file exported from Excel that has the following fields: first name, last name, username, and email address. To extract the email address for all users:

```
[alice@sunshine ~]$ head -3 /opt/book/scripting/users.csv
Ian,Cook,ian.cook,ian.cook@sunshine.edu
```

---

[2] Peter, S. A Quarter-Century of Unix, Addison-Wesley, 1994.

```
Christine,Riggs,christine.riggs,christine.riggs@sunshine.edu
Lindsay,Fishbein,lindsay.fishbein,lindsay.fishbein@sunshine.edu
[alice@sunshine ~]$ cut -d, -f4 /opt/book/scripting/users.csv
ian.cook@sunshine.edu
christine.riggs@sunshine.edu
lindsay.fishbein@sunshine.edu
...
```

We can also return multiple columns and filter the output by combining the cut command with grep:

```
[alice@sunshine ~]$ cut -d, -f1,2,4 /opt/book/scripting/users.csv |
grep john
John,Jayavelu,john.jayavelu@sunshine.edu
Jennifer,Johnson,jennifer.johnson@sunshine.edu
John,Altier,john.altier@sunshine.edu
...
```

As you can see, it returned the first, second, and fourth columns and only returned those records that contained the string "john."

Sort

The sort command does exactly what its name implies – it sorts the lines of a text file:

```
[alice@sunshine ~]$ cat /opt/book/scripting/words.txt
eyes
record
explosive
spice
prison
videotape
leg
ice
magnet
printer
[alice@sunshine ~]$ sort /opt/book/scripting/words.txt
explosive
eyes
ice
leg
magnet
printer
prison
record
spice
videotape
```

Be aware that the default sort order assumes text data, therefore the -n switch must be given if you are sorting numerical data:

```
[alice@sunshine ~]$ sort /opt/book/scripting/numbers.txt
1
1002
1234567
356
4
8675309
99
[alice@sunshine ~]$ sort -n /opt/book/scripting/numbers.txt
1
4
99
356
1002
1234567
8675309
```

uniq

Continuing the trend of simple commands that are named after their function, uniq removes duplicate lines from a text file. Uniq only searches adjacent lines to find duplicates, so input must be sorted first:

```
[alice@sunshine ~]$ cat /opt/book/scripting/duplicates.txt
apple
banana
orange
orange
kiwi
banana
kiwi
apple
[alice@sunshine ~]$ sort /opt/book/scripting/duplicates.txt | uniq
apple
banana
kiwi
orange
```

tr

The tr command substitutes the specified list of characters with a second set of characters or deletes (-d) them from the input stream. To substitute x, y, and z for all occurrences of a, b, and c in a text file:

```
[alice@sunshine ~]$ cat /opt/book/scripting/original.txt
The quick brown fox jumps over the lazy dog.
```

```
[alice@sunshine ~]$ cat /opt/book/scripting/original.txt | tr "abc"
"xyz"
The quizk yrown fox jumps over the lxzy dog.
[alice@sunshine ~]$ cat /opt/book/scripting/original.txt | tr -d
"abc"
The quik rown fox jumps over the lzy dog.
```

A more commonly used function of tr is to convert lower case text to uppercase and vise versa:

```
[alice@sunshine ~]$ cat /opt/book/scripting/original.txt | tr "[:lower:]"
"[:upper:]"
THE QUICK BROWN FOX JUMPS OVER THE LAZY DOG.
```

[:lower:] and [:upper:] are *character sets*; they are a quick way to specify all lower and upper case letters, respectively. See the manual page for tr (man tr) for a full list of available character sets.

Variables

A **variable** is a representation of a piece of data (number, filename, text string, etc.) stored in the computer's memory. To create a new variable, you simply need to supply the variable *name* and the data it represents: its *value*

```
[alice@sunshine ~]$ myVariable=20
[alice@sunshine ~]$ echo $myVariable
20
```

No spaces are allowed before or after the = when assigning a value. Therefore, the following assignments will all result in an error:

```
[alice@sunshine ~]$ myVariable = 20
[alice@sunshine ~]$ myVariable =20
[alice@sunshine ~]$ myVariable= 20
```

You can also assign text or even another variable as a variable's value.

```
[alice@sunshine ~]$ hello="Hello World"
[alice@sunshine ~]$ world=$hello
[alice@sunshine ~]$ echo $hello
Hello World
[alice@sunshine ~]$ echo $world
Hello World
```

Finally, you can assign the output from a command as the value of a variable by enclosing the command in $( ), which is known as a **command expansion.**

```
[alice@sunshine ~]$ now=$(date)
[alice@sunshine ~]$ echo $now
Wed Dec 19 10:41:40 EST 2012
```

Table 10.1 Arithmetic operators in BASH

Operator	Description	Example	Result
+	Addition	$((5 + 5))	10
−	Subtraction	$((5 − 1))	4
*	Multiplication	$((3 * 2))	6
/	Division	$((10/2))	5
%	Modulus (Remainder)	$((10 % 3))	1
**	Exponent	$((6 ** 2))	36

You can also do basic arithmetic with integers (whole numbers) in BASH by using the $(( )) construct, which is referred to as an **arithmetic expansion**. A list of arithmetic operations that can be performed by BASH are listed in Table 10.1.

```
[alice@sunshine ~]$ myVariable=20
[alice@sunshine ~]$ myBigVariable=$(( $myVariable * 100 ))
[alice@sunshine ~]$ echo myBigVariable
2000
[alice@sunshine ~]$ echo $(( $myBigVariable + 1 ))
2001
```

Quoting

Enclosing a variable in double quotes (" ") does not affect its use. However, single quotes (' ') will cause the variable name to be used literally instead of substituting the variable's value.

Listing 3: /opt/book/scripting/quoting

```
#! /bin/bash
name=Alice
echo "My name is $name and the date is $(date +%m-%d-%Y)"
echo 'My name is $name date is $(date +%m-%d-%Y)'

[alice@sunshine ~]$ /opt/book/scripting/quoting
My name is Alice and the date is 12-19-2012
My name is $name and the date is $(date +%m-%d-%Y)
```

As you can see, the use of single quotes in the second line printed the literal variable names while the variable substitution took place on the first string. Also, note that the current date was substituted for $(date +%m−%d−%Y) without having to assign a variable name. Commands enclosed in $( ) are run each time they are encountered in a script and the value is determined dynamically.

Environment variables

Some variables are created automatically when you login or start a new terminal window. These **environment variables** hold default values and user preferences for the current terminal session. To view the list of environment variables and their values, use the env command:

```
[alice@sunshine ~]$ env
HOSTNAME=sunshine.edu
SHELL=/bin/bash
USER=alice
PATH=    (/usr/lib/qt-3.3/bin:/usr/local/bin:/usr/bin:/bin:/usr/local/
sbin:/usr/sbin:/sbin:/home/alice/bin
...
PWD=/home/alice
TERM=xterm
```

You will see several screens of data in the results, most of which are application-specific, but there are a few that are worth mentioning (Table 10.2).

These variables can be used in a command line just like regular variables:

```
[alice@sunshine ~]$ echo "My name is $USER and my current directory is
$PWD"
My name is alice and my current directory is /home/alice
```

We can also take advantage of these variables in our shell scripts. For example, look at listing 4.

Listing 4: /opt/book/scripting/env_variable_example

```
#! /bin/bash
echo "Hello $USER"
echo "You are calling this program from $PWD"
echo "Your home directory is $HOME"
```

Since the environment variables are created automatically by BASH, we can have dynamic output based on the user that is executing the script. Here is the output when the user Alice runs this script:

```
[alice@sunshine Desktop]$ /opt/book/scripting/env_variable_example
Hello alice
You are calling this program from /home/alice/Desktop
Your home directory is /home/alice
```

And here is the result when Bob runs it:

```
[bob@sunshine tmp]$ /opt/book/scripting/env_variable_example
Hello bob
You are calling this program from /tmp
Your home directory is /home/bob
```

Table 10.2 Common environment variables

USER	The current user
HOME	Home directory of the current user
PWD	The current directory
PATH	List of directories (colon-separated) that the shell will search through when looking for an application

The PATH variable is different from the other environment variables we have looked at. Instead of being used as part of a command, the value in the PATH variable is used directly by the BASH shell itself. When a user inputs a command, such as firefox to start a web browser, BASH looks for that command sequentially in each directory listed in PATH. You can use the which command to see a demonstration of the search in action:

```
[alice@sunshine ~]$ which firefox
/usr/bin/firefox
[alice@sunshine ~]$ which ThisProgramDoesNotExist
/usr/bin/which: no ThisProgramDoesNotExist in (/usr/lib/qt-
3.3/bin:/usr/local/bin:/usr/bin:/bin:/usr/local/sbin:/usr/sbin:/sbin:/
home/alice/bin)
```

Built-in variables

In addition to environment variables, BASH also defines several variables with useful values; collectively they are referred to as **built-in variables**. The built-in variables provide a wide array of small functions, from reporting on the type of hardware the server is running on to returning the status of the last command issued. There are dozens of built-in variables to choose from (see the BASH man page for a full list), but we will be working with a small subset (Table 10.3).

The script in listing 5 is an example of how these can be used.

Listing 5: /opt/book/scripting/builtin_variable_example

```
#! /bin/bash
echo "This script is executing with process ID: $$"
echo "OS: $OSTYPE Hardware: $MACHTYPE"
echo "This is he current date and time:"
date
echo "The exit value from date was $?"
echo "This command should fail:"
ls -l NoFile
echo "The exit value was $?"
echo "Wait 2 seconds"
sleep 2
echo "Here are 3 random numbers:"
echo $RANDOM
echo $RANDOM
```

Table 10.3 Built-in variables

$?	Returns the exit status of the last command. 0 means success, any other value indicates an error. The meaning of each value is application-specific.
$$	Returns the id number of the currently running script.
$MACHTYPE	Returns the hardware architecture in use.
$OSTYPE	Returns the operating system in use.
$SECONDS	Returns the number of seconds the current script has been running.
$RANDOM	Returns a random number between 0 and 32767.

```
echo $RANDOM
echo "Wait 3 seconds"
sleep 3
echo "This script has run for $SECONDS seconds"

[alice@sunshine ~]$ /opt/book/scripting/builtin_variable_example
This script is executing with process ID: 10380
OS: linux-gnu Hardware: i386-redhat-linux-gnu
This is the current date and time:
Wed Dec 19 11:41:40 EST 2012
The exit value from date was 0
This command should fail:
ls: cannot access NoFile: No such file or directory
The exit value was 2
Wait 2 seconds
Here are 3 random numbers:
10549
319
20535
Wait 3 seconds
This script has run for 5 seconds
```

Conditionals

In the last section, we introduced the $? variable and that it returns the exit value from the last command run. What if you wanted to take one action if the command succeeds ($? equal to 0) and another action if it fails? Like any other programming language, BASH provides constructs that test a set of given conditions and act based on the result of the test.

If/then

The most basic form of conditional is the if/then construct. The if command checks the exit value of a series of comparison statements. If the exit value equals zero, the commands in the then stanza are executed. The entire construct is terminated by the fi command.

```
#! /bin/bash
if [ "$USER" = "alice" ]
then
     echo "Good Morning, Alice!"
fi
```

If the user running this script has the username alice ("$USER" = "alice"), the echo command is executed. If their username is anything else, the script completes without executing any commands.

The syntax of the if/then construct in BASH is a bit different than that of most other programming languages.[3] The most common mistake when writing an if/then statement in BASH is not separating elements with spaces. You must put a space between the if and the square

---

[3] BASH supports multiple syntaxes for if/then. See http://tldp.org/LDP/abs/html/testconstructs.html for more information.

brackets and around the comparison statement inside the brackets. Most other languages are more forgiving in their use of white space. Any of these attempts at an if statement will fail with an error:

```
if["$USER" = "alice"]
if  ["$USER" = "alice"]
if[ "$USER" = "alice" ]
```

Another difference in the use of if/then in BASH compared to other languages is that string comparison such as the example above uses a different operator (=) than a numerical comparison (-eq) would. The following chart has a list of the comparison operators with examples of their use.

Operator	Comparison	Example usage
For the usage examples:		
X = 5		
Y="RED"		
-eq	Is equal to (integer)	if [$X -eq 5]
-ne	Is not equal to (integer)	if [$X -ne 3]
-gt	Greater then (integer)	if [$X -gt 2]
-lt	Less than (integer)	if [$X -lt 10]
-ge	Greater than or equal to (integer)	if [$X -ge 4]
-le	Less than or equal to (integer)	if [$X -le 7]
=	Is equal to (string)	if ["$Y" = "RED"]
!=	Is not equal to (string)	if ["$Y" != "BLUE"]

If/then/else

If you want to take one action if a conditional statement is true and a different action if it is false, you'll use the if/then/else construct. It is identical to the if/then construct except that for the addition commands in the else stanza that will be executed if the conditions were not met. /opt/book/scripting/number_guess_v1 is an example of a basic if/then/else construct. We will be building on this basic example to develop a more complex application over the rest of the chapter.

Listing 6: /opt/book/scripting/number_guess_v1

```
#! /bin/bash
guess=2
number=$(( ( $RANDOM % 100 ) + 1 ))
#Is the guess correct?
if [ $guess -eq $number ]
then
     echo "Correct Guess: The number is $number"
else
     # Is the guess high?
     if [ $number -lt $guess ]
```

```
then
      echo "Guess lower: The number is less than $guess"
fi
      # Is the guess low?
if [ $number -gt $guess ]
then
      echo "Guess higher: The number is greater than $guess"
fi
fi
```

Because guess is equal to 2 and number is 5, the first if/then statement will always be false (we'll add user-supplied guesses later in the chapter), and the program should always execute the code in the else stanza. At this point, the script does something we haven't seen before: a **nested-if statement**.

A nested-if statement is just a normal if/then statement inside another if or else statement.

```
if [ condition1 ]
then
    echo "condition1 is true"
else
    #Nested-if statement
if [ condition2 ]
    then
        echo "condition2 is true"
     else
        echo "Neither condition is true"
     fi
fi
```

If condition1 is true, the else section is skipped, so the nested-if statement is not executed at all and no tests are run on condition2. However, if condition1 is not true, the nested-if is executed and condition2 is checked. In the number guessing script, since guess is less than 5, the first of the two nested-if statements will return true and it should print Guess higher: The number is greater than 2. We can run the script to test the output:

```
[alice@sunshine ~]$ /opt/book/scripting/number_guess_v1
Guess higher: The number is greater than 2
```

If/then/elif

The final construct we'll be looking at is the if/then/elif construct. elif is a contraction of "else if" and is an alternative to nested-if structures. The example from above can be written using elif as follows:

```
if [ condition1 ]
then
    echo "condition1 is true"
elif [ condition2 ]
```

```
then
     echo "condition2 is true"
else
     echo "neither condition is true"
fi
```

Multiple elif stanzas can be added to an if statement if there are more than two conditions to be checked. As an example, we'll update the number guessing script as /opt/book/scripting/number_guess_v2

Listing 7: /opt/book/scripting/number_guess_v2

```
#! /bin/bash
guess=2
number=$(( ( $RANDOM % 100 ) + 1 ))
#Is the guess correct?
if [ $guess -eq $number ]
then
     echo "Correct guess: The number is $number"
# Is the guess high?
elif [ $number -lt $guess ]
then
echo "Guess lower: The number is less than $guess"
# Is the guess low?
elif [ $number -gt $guess ]
then
echo "Guess higher: The number is greater than $guess"
fi
```

The use of elif instead of a nested-if statement makes the code slightly shorter and easier to read. We can run the code to verify that it returns the same results:

```
[alice@sunshine ~]$ /opt/book/scripting/number_guess_v2
Guess higher: The number is greater than 2
```

User input

The values for all of the variables in the scripts we have looked at so far were **hardcoded**. They were defined in the script itself and the only way the values can be changed is by modifying the script. In many cases, this is fine, but you may also want values that are supplied by the user. There are two ways to accept input from the user: command line arguments and the read command.

Command line arguments

Like other commands that you execute in a terminal window, BASH scripts can accept program arguments. The arguments are automatically stored in special variables when the program executes. The variables are named with a number in the order the arguments were given on the command line:

Listing 8: /opt/book/scripting/user_input_ex1

```
#! /bin/bash
echo "The first argument: $1"
echo "The second argument: $2"
echo "The third argument: $3"

[alice@sunshine ~]$ /opt/book/scripting/user_input_ex1 42 "Hello World"
Earth
The first argument: 42
The second argument: Hello World
The third argument: Earth
```

Note that the second argument consists of two words ("Hello World"). The quotation marks around the group of words tells BASH that this is a single argument.

So, now we can accept arguments from the command line, but how can we ensure that the correct number of arguments are entered? BASH includes another special variable, $#, which stores the total number of arguments that were entered. This allows you to test the number of entered arguments against the expected number and print an error message if the test fails.

Listing 9: /opt/book/scripting/user_input_ex2

```
#! /bin/bash
if [ $# -eq 3 ]
then
echo "The first argument: $1"
echo "The second argument: $2"
echo "The third argument: $3"
else
    echo "Three arguments are required!"
fi

[alice@sunshine ~]$ /opt/book/scripting/user_input_ex2 42 Earth
Three arguments are required!
```

Reading user input

The other option for including user input into your scripts is the read command. read pauses the execution of a script until the user enters a value and presses return. To demonstrate the use of read, we will update the the number guessing script:

Listing 10: /opt/book/scripting/number_guess_v3

```
#! /bin/bash
#Prompt for user input
echo "Enter a number between 1 and 100 and press [ENTER]: "
read guess

number=$(( ( $RANDOM % 100 ) + 1 ))
#Is the guess correct?
if [ $guess -eq $number ]
then
    echo "Correct guess: The number is $number"
```

```
# Is the guess high?
elif [ $number -lt $guess ]
then
echo "Guess lower: The number is less than $guess"
# Is the guess low?
elif [ $number -gt $guess ]
then
echo "Guess higher: The number is greater than $guess"
fi

[alice@sunshine ~]$ /opt/book/scripting/number_guess_v3
Enter a number between 1 and 100 and press [ENTER]: 15
Guess lower: The number is less than 15
```

Loops

One of the most useful aspects of BASH scripting (and computer programming in general) is the ability to reduce repetitive tasks down to a few simple commands. Instead of typing the same or similar commands over and over again, a **loop** allows you to write the commands you wish to execute once and then have the shell repeat them. We will be working with two types of loops available in BASH scripts:

1. for loops – These loops repeat the commands using a given list of input items

2. while loops – These loops repeat the commands while a given condition is true

For loops

For loops are the most basic and the most commonly used looping construct in BASH scripts. A for loop iterates over a list of items, executing any commands contained in the loop during each iteration. When the BASH intepretor reaches the keyword "done," it jumps back to the beginning of the loop and begins the next iteration. During each successive pass through the loop, the value of the **loop variable** (var in the following example) is changed to the current element in the list. /opt/book/scripting/for_loop_example1 is an example of a simple for loop:

Listing 11: /opt/book/scripting/for_loop_example

```
#! /bin/bash
for var in "item1" "item2" "item3"
do
    echo "The current item is $var"
#More commands could be added here
done
```

When run, you can see that the value of $var changes with each iteration:

```
[alice@sunshine ~]$ /opt/book/scripting/for_loop_example1
The current item is item1
The current item is item2
The current item is item3
```

In addition to listing each item on the command line, you can also use the output of a command as the list of items to iterate over.

Listing 12: /opt/book/scripting/for_loop_example2

```
#! /bin/bash
for word in $(head -3 /opt/book/scripting/words.txt)
do
    echo "Original word: $word"
    echo "All uppercase: $(echo $word | tr '[:lower:]' '[:upper:]')"
done

[alice@sunshine ~]$ /opt/book/scripting/for_loop_example2
Original word: eyes
All uppercase: EYES
Original word: record
All uppercase: RECORD
Original word: explosive
All uppercase: EXPLOSIVE
```

As you can see, the first three lines in /opt/book/scripting/words.txt (eyes, record, explosive) were used as the list of items to iterate over. The first command in the loop is a simple echo statement, printing the value of $word, but the second command is a little more complex. In this command, we piped the value of the $word variable to tr and converted the lower case characters to upper case (echo $word | tr '[:lower:]' '[:upper:]'), the output of that command is then printed to the screen.

Internal field separator

When reading the output from a command in a for loop, BASH determines the separation between each item by using a special internal variable $IFS, the **internal field separator.** The variable contains a list of characters which are used as field boundaries; when one is found, a new item for the for loop is created. The default values in $IFS are the white space characters (space, tab, and newline), but the list can be modified, for example, to parse a comma-separated list or to ignore one of the defaults as a separator and allow it as part of an item.

Listing 13: /opt/book/scripting/ifs_example1

```
!# /bin/bash
for line in $(tail -3 /etc/passwd)
do
    echo $line
done

[alice@sunshine ~]$ /opt/book/scripting/ifs_example1
russell.dacanay:x:1648:100:"Russell
Dacanay
(Staff-Library)":/home/staff/russell.dacanay:/bin/bash
daniel.saddler:x:1649:100:"Daniel
Saddler
(Staff-Student
```

```
Services)":/home/staff/daniel.saddler:/bin/bash
russell.lavigne:x:1650:100:"Russell
Lavigne
(Staff-Academic
Affairs
VP
Office)":/home/staff/russell.lavigne:/bin/bash
```

As you can see, using the default value for $IFS, the lines from /etc/passwd are broken up in the middle of fifth column because of the space or spaces in the text of that field. To fix this issue, we will set $IFS to contain only the newline character ($'\n').

Listing 14: /opt/book/scripting/ifs_example2

```
!# /bin/bash
#Change IFS to the newline character only
IFS=$'\n'
for line in $(tail -3 /etc/passwd)
do
    echo $line
done
[alice@sunshine ~]$ /opt/book/scripting/ifs_example1
russell.dacanay:x:1648:100:"Russell Dacanay (Staff-Library)": \
/home/staff/russell.dacanay:/bin/bash
daniel.saddler:x:1649:100:"Daniel Saddler (Staff-Student Services)": \
/home/staff/daniel.saddler:/bin/bash
russell.lavigne:x:1650:100:"Russell Lavigne (Staff-Academic Affairs VP
Office)": \
/home/staff/russell.lavigne:/bin/bash
```

Not that the backslash (\) in the output above is a line-continuation character, which is used because the output is too long to be printed on a single line. If you run the script in your Linux virtual machine, you will find the line with the backslash and the one after it are printed as a single line.

Sequences

You will often need to execute an action a specific number of times or use a sequence of numbers as the input for a loop. Since version 3.0,[4] BASH has included a built-in syntax for generating a sequence of numbers as input for a for loop. Number sequences are surrounded by curly braces ({ }) and the arguments are separated by two periods (..). Sequences can be created using either two or three arguments – if two arguments are given, the first is the starting value and the second is the ending value. The loop is then executed using each integer from the starting to the ending value.

---

[4]See the manual page for the seq command for information on generating sequences in earlier versions.

Listing 15: /opt/book/scripting/sequence_example1

```
#!/bin/bash
for number in {1..5}
do
     echo $number
done

[alice@sunshine ~]$ /opt/book/scripting/sequence_example1
1
2
3
4
5
```

You can also increment numbers backward by listing a higher number as the starting value and a lower number as the ending value.

Listing 16: /opt/book/scripting/reverse_sequence

```
#!/bin/bash
for number in {10..1}
do
     echo $number
done

[alice@sunshine ~]$ /opt/book/scripting/reverse_sequence
10
9
8
7
6
5
4
3
2
1
```

If three arguments are given,[5] the third argument determines what the increment between each number in the series should be.

Listing 17: /opt/book/scripting/sequence_example3

```
#!/bin/bash
for number in {1..10..2}
do
    echo $number
done
```

---

[5]BASH version 4.0 or greater required.

```
[alice@sunshine ~]$ /opt/book/scripting/sequence_example3
1
3
5
7
9
```

Note that "10" was not part of the results returned. This is because the number sequence contains all of the numbers that are less than or equal to the ending value. Since the sequence is incrementing by two, the next number in the series would be eleven, but that is greater than our ending value of 10.

Break and continue

Under certain conditions, you may want to stop the processing of a loop or skip ahead to the next iteration of a loop. The break and continue keywords give you this ability. The break keyword stops the processing of a loop, skipping any remaining commands in the current iteration of the loop, and skipping all of the remaining items in the input list. Execution of the script is not interrupted; however, it will continue to execute any commands after the loop.

Listing 18: /opt/book/scripting/break_example

```
#!/bin/bash
for number in {1..5}
do
if [ $number -eq 4 ]
then
    echo "Stop!"
    break
fi
echo "$number"
done
echo "This command runs AFTER the loop is complete."
[alice@sunshine ~]$ /opt/book/scripting/break_example
1
2
3
Stop!
This command runs AFTER the loop is complete.
```

Note that the loop is processed as expected for the first three numbers in the sequence. When the condition in the if statement ($number -eq 4) is met, "Stop!" is printed to the screen, the break keyword is reached, and execution of the loop ends. As another example, we will update the number guessing script to give the user five chances to guess the number and break if the number is guessed early.

Listing 19: /opt/book/scripting/number_guess_v4

```
#! /bin/bash
number=$(( ( $RANDOM % 100 ) + 1 ))
```

```
#Give the user 5 guesses
for loop in {1..5}
do
#Prompt for user input
echo "Enter a number between 1 and 100 and press [ENTER]: "
read guess

echo ""

#Is the guess correct?
if [ $guess -eq $number ]
then
        echo "Correct guess: The number is $number"
        echo "You guessed it in $loop tries"
            break
# Is the guess high?
elif [ $number -lt $guess ]
then
        echo "Guess number $loop"
        echo "Guess lower: The number is less than $guess"
# Is the guess low?
elif [ $number -gt $guess ]
then
   echo "Guess number $loop"
   echo "Guess higher: The number is greater than $guess"
fi
end
[alice@sunshine ~]$ /opt/book/scripting/number_guess_v4
Enter a number between 1 and 100 and press [ENTER]: 15

Guess number 1
Guess lower: The number is lower than 15
Enter a number between 1 and 100 and press [ENTER]: 3

Guess number 2
Guess higher: The number is higher than 3
Enter a number between 1 and 100 and press [ENTER]: 5

Correct guess: The number is 5
You guessed it in 3 tries
```

The continue keyword skips the remaining commands in the current iteration of the loop and begins the next iteration. In the next example, we'll use the same code from listing 13 but replace the break keyword with continue.

Listing 20: /opt/book/scripting/continue_example

```
#!/bin/bash
for number in {1..5}
do
if [ $number -eq 4 ]
then
        echo "Stop!"
        continue
```

```
fi
echo "$number"
done

echo "This command runs AFTER the loop is complete."
[alice@sunshine ~]$ /opt/book/scripting/continue_example
1
2
3
Stop!
5
```

This command runs AFTER the loop is complete.

Note the difference in the output between this script and the script in listing 18. Again, the first three iterations of the loop are processed as expected and the condition of the if statement is met on the fourth iteration. However, instead of exiting from the loop, processing continues with the fifth (and final) iteration of the loop.

While loops

Instead of operating on a list of items like a for loop, while loops will continue running until a specific condition is met. Before starting an iteration of the loop, the condition is tested. If the result is true, the commands inside the loop are executed. If it is false, the loop is skipped and the rest of the script is executed.

Listing 21: /opt/book/scripting/while_loop_example1

```
#! /bin/bash
counter=1
while [ $counter -le 5 ]
do
    echo $counter
    $(( counter=$counter + 1 ))
done

[alice@sunshine ~]$ /opt/book/scripting/while_loop_example1
1
2
3
4
5
```

As you can see, the output from this command is similar to some of the for loop examples that we have looked at previously. However, the script itself has some major differences. The first difference you'll notice is that unlike when using a for loop, we defined the initial value of the counter variable before executing the loop.

When the BASH interpreter reaches the while statement, if the current value of counter is less than or equal to five, the commands inside the loop are executed. During the loop, the current value of counter is printed to the screen and then increased by one ($((counter=$counter + 1))). At this point, the value of counter is tested again and if it is still less than or equal to five, the loop continues.

When writing a script, you may need to create an **infinite loop**: a loop that continues until the user explicitly ends the script. They are typically used when you need to monitor something at regular intervals, such as the size of a file or the number of logged-in users. To create an infinite loop, you'll create a while loop whose test condition always evaluates as true. You can see the use of an infinite loop to monitor the size of a log file (/var/log/httpd/access_log) in listing 14. With each iteration, the time the file was checked and the size of the log file is printed to the screen. The script will loop until the user exits the script, either by pressing the "CTRL" and "C" keys together or closing the terminal window the script is running in.

Listing 22: /opt/book/scripting/while_loop_example2

```
#! /bin/bash
echo "This script will loop forever. Hit Control+C (CTRL+C) to exit."
while [ true ]
do
    sleep 2
    echo ""
    date
    echo " $(wc -l /var/log/httpd/access_log)"
done
[alice@sunshine ~]$ /opt/book/scripting/while_loop_example2
This script will loop forever. Hit Control+C (CTRL+C) to exit.

Fri Jan 4 08:11:00 EST 2013
   7 /var/log/httpd/access_log

Fri Jan 4 08:11:02 EST 2013
   7 /var/log/httpd/access_log

Fri Jan 4 08:11:04 EST 2013
   8 /var/log/httpd/access_log

Fri Jan 4 08:11:06 EST 2013
   9 /var/log/httpd/access_log
```

To test this script, you'll need to open the web browser and visit http://www.sunshine.edu after starting the script. The number of entries in the log file will increase each time you load the web page.

Putting it all together

You've now seen the basic pieces of a shell script; let's look at a script that uses many of these elements to automate a process across all of the users on the system. The Linux virtual machine included with this text has over 1,000 accounts, far too many to support by hand. This script extracts important information for each account and displays it in an easy to read format.

Listing 23: /opt/book/scripting/user_info

```
#! /bin/bash
#This script returns import information about all users on the system

#Example line from /etc/passwd
#alice:x:501:501:Alice Adams:/home/alice:/bin/bash
```

```
for user in $(cut -d: -f1 /etc/passwd)
do
    IFS=$'\n'

    #Grab the line from the password file that
    #contains this user's info. We append the
    #delimiter (:) to ensure we only get results
    #for this username and not similar users
    userinfo=$(grep $user: /etc/passwd)

    comment=$(echo $userinfo | cut -d: -f5)
    home=$(echo $userinfo | cut -d: -f6)
    groups=$(groups $user | cut -d: -f2)

 #We only want this to run on "regular" users,
 #not system accounts. Skip users that do not
 #have '/home' in the path to their home directory
  if [ $(echo "$home" | grep -v '/home/') ]
  then
      continue
  fi

    echo "Username: $user"
    echo "User Info: $comment"
    echo "Home Directory: $home"
    echo "Groups: $groups"

    echo "Disk usage: $(du -sh $home)"

    last=$(last $user | head -1)

    if [ $( echo $last | wc -c ) -gt 1 ]
    then
        echo "Last login: "
        echo "$last"
    else
        echo "User has never logged in!"
    fi
    echo ""
    echo "--"
    echo ""
done
[alice@sunshine ~]$ /opt/book/scripting/user_info
Username: alice
User Info: Alice Adams
Home Directory: /home/alice
Groups: alice sys
Disk Usage: 75M /home/alice
Last login:
alice   pts/3   sunshine.edu   Sun Jan 13 12:22 - 13:00 (0:48)
--
Username: bob
User Info: Bob Brown
Home Directory: /home/bob
```

```
Groups: bob
Disk Usage: 1.1M /home/bob
Last login:
bob  pts/6   sunshine.edu  Sun Jan 6 16:48 - 18:46 (1:58)
--
```

Let's look at this script in depth. In the first few lines, we set up a loop using all of the username on this system. The username is always the first column in /etc/password.

```
for user in $(cut -d: -f1 /etc/passwd)
do
```

For each account, we search the /etc/password file to find the account information for the user.

```
IFS=$'\n'
userinfo=$(grep $user: /etc/passwd)
```

The next section of the script uses cut to separate the columns of the account information into usable variables. It also uses the groups command to get the list of groups the user is a member of and the du command to calculate the amount of storage their home directory is using.

```
comment=$(echo $userinfo | cut -d: -f5)
home=$(echo $userinfo | cut -d: -f6)
groups=$(groups $user | cut -d: -f2)

echo "Username: $user"
echo "User Info: $comment"
echo "Home Directory: $home"
echo "Groups: $groups"
echo "Disk usage: $(du -sh $home)"
```

The final portion of the script uses the last command to get the latest login for this user. If the user has never logged in, the result from last will be a blank line and the script will display an error message. If the user has logged in, the last time the user has logged in and the duration of that login session are displayed.

```
last=$(last $user | head -1)
if [ $( echo $last | wc -c ) -gt 1 ]
then
  echo "Last login:"
  echo $last
else
  echo "User has never logged in!"
fi
```

Example case – Max Butler

In 1998, Max Butler was a 26-year-old computer enthusiast, earning over $100/hour testing the security of corporate clients while also volunteering for the San Francisco office of the FBI. That year, a critical security flaw was found in the most popular open-source DNS server used on the Internet – BIND. BIND was used on virtually all servers to map URLS such as "www.usf.edu" to IP addresses such as 131.247.88.80. The flaw would allow hackers to get complete control of any server running an unprotected version of BIND. In particular, almost all US Department of Defense servers ran BIND. If these servers were to be protected from attackers, they were to be patched before attackers got to them. But the military bureaucracy can be slow. How is a concerned security expert with all the innocence of a 20-year-old to fix the problem asap?

Enter scripting. A script could operate at the speed of a computer and instruct hundreds of computers every second to download a patch and fix themselves. Max Butler did just that, putting together a script that located any server running the unpatched version of BIND and updating it with the specified patch. While he was at it, Max also modified the patch so that it created a backdoor that only Max was aware of. This way, Max thought he was protecting the computers from attackers, while at the same time, giving him unrestricted access to the same computers so he could go in and fix them all by himself the next time a vulnerability was reported. No need to waste time contacting DoD administrators.

The good deed worked, but unfortunately for Max, the backdoor was not seen kindly. When DoD system administrators found about it, they prosecuted Max. On May 21, 2001, Max was sent to prison for 18 months for the deed.

This was not Max's last brush with cybercrime or prison. He later went on to command the majority of illicit online credit card marketplaces. On February 12, 2010, he was sentenced to 13 years in prison for the offense, then the longest sentence ever awarded for computer crime. This was later eclipsed by the sentence awarded to Albert Gonzales for the T.J. Maxx case. Max is currently serving the sentence at the Yankton Federal Prison Camp, a minimum security facility in South Dakota. He is scheduled to be released on 1/1/2019. CNBC produced a case file segment on him, called "American greed."

REFERENCES

http://www.wired.com/techbiz/people/magazine/17-01/ff_max_ butler?currentPage = all

Poulsen, K. "Kingpin: how one hacker took over the billion-dollar cybercrime underground," Random House.

http://www.cnbc.com/id/100000049

SUMMARY

This chapter introduced you to shell scripts and their utility. Scripts are one of the most powerful tools in the arsenal of any IT professional, and especially so for an information security professional. With discipline, a professional can incorporate all their professional experience into their script repertoire for reuse at moment's notice. We have tried to use an interesting use case to introduce the topic and hope you will be inspired to develop your own scripts to automate repetitive tasks in your day-to-day work.

Apple's developer library has a very concise and well-written chapter to introduce shell scripting called Shell scripting primer.[6]

---

[6] http://developer.apple.com/library/mac/#documentation/OpenSource/Conceptual/ShellScripting/Introduction/Introduction.html (accessed 07/19/2013).

CHAPTER REVIEW QUESTIONS

1. What is shell scripting?

2. What is shell scripting used for? Why is this helpful?

3. What is the important difference between scripting languages and other computer languages?

4. What is the first line of every BASH script?

5. What happens when the script file does not have execute permissions for the user attempting to run the script?

6. What is output redirection? Why is it useful?

7. What character redirects the output of one command to be the input of another?

8. How can you send the output of a script to a file? How can this be useful?

9. Would echo "$PATH" and echo '$PATH' result in the same output?

10. What symbol does BASH use for multiplication?

11. What character begins every comment in a BASH script?

12. What does the cut command do?

13. What is the sort command used for?

14. What is the uniq command used for?

15. Which of these variable assignments is correct?

    a. myVariable = 35

    b. myVariable = 35

    c. myVariable= 35

    d. myVariable =35

16. What character reads data from a file and uses it as input for another command?

17. What are environment variables? How are they useful?

18. What are built-in variables? How are they different from environment variables?

19. What should the value of $? be if the last command that was executed completed successfully?

20. How can you collect user input from a script?

21. What variable will return the second argument given to a script on the command line?

22. What is an internal field separator? What is its default value? How can it be modified? Why might you do that?

23. What sequence of numbers would {1..10..3} include?

24. What are loops? Why are they useful?

25. When does a while loop end?

EXAMPLE CASE QUESTIONS

1. What were some establishments affected by Max Butler's script?

2. Max Butler claims that he installed the backdoor on the affected computers as a benign move so that he could fix the computers in the future all by himself. How do you react to this claim, i.e., to what extent do you believe that this claim absolves him of guilt?

HANDS-ON ACTIVITY – BASIC SCRIPTING

These activities are included to demonstrate your knowledge of the commands and scripting techniques learned in this chapter. Using the Linux virtual machine you configured in Chapter 2, open a terminal window by selecting the "System Tools" panel under the "Applications" menu. After completing each exercise, submit a screenshot of the output to your instructor.

1. Save the output of /opt/book/scripting/user_info to a text file. Name it /opt/book/scripting/results/exercise1

2. Write a script (name it /opt/book/scripting/results/exercise2) which:

    2.1 Lists all of the files in the /usr/bin directory whose name contains "my"

    2.2 Save the list of files to /tmp/exercise1.txt

    2.3 Displays the number of files found to the user

3. Write a script (name it /opt/book/scripting/results/exercise3) which:

   3.1 Asks the user for the length and width (in feet) of a rectangular room

   3.2 Calculates the area of the room

   3.3 Displays the result to the user

4. Write a script (name it /opt/book/scripting/results/exercise4) which:

   4.1 Counts backward from 10 to 1

   4.2 Displays the current number

   4.3 Pauses for 1 second between numbers

   4.4 Displays the text "LIFT OFF" after reaching number 1

5. Make a copy of /opt/book/scripting/while_loop_example1 (name it /opt/book/scripting/results/exercise5) and modify it to:

   5.1 Ask the user for a maximum number

   5.2 Display all of the even numbers up to the maximum number

6. Make a copy of /opt/book/scripting/number_guess_v4 (name it /opt/book/scripting/results/exercise6) and update it to give the user as many chances as necessary to guess the number.

7. Make a copy of /opt/book/scripting/user_info (name it /opt/book/scripting/results/exercise7) and update it to:

   7.1 Accept a username as a command line argument

   7.2 Instead of displaying the account information for all accounts, output only the information for this account

   Deliverables: Submit all of the files in the /opt/book/scripting/results directory to your instructor.

CRITICAL THINKING EXERCISE – SCRIPT SECURITY

Scripting is a great utility. But we would be remiss in a book on information security if we did not alert you to important security concerns with scripts. Apple's developer pages have information on shell script security. Highlights include the following:

- If the full (absolute) paths to commands are not specified, the script may end up running malicious code that has the same name as a command invoked from the script.

- If user input is accepted without verification, a knowledgeable user can exploit the script's privileges. Therefore, as far as possible, user input should be used only if matches a set of allowed values.

- Scripts should not have to determine whether a user has the required privileges to execute a script. The user invoking the script can modify environment variables to defeat such checks.

REFERENCE

Apple Corp., "Shell scripting primer," http://developer.apple.com/library/mac/#documentation/OpenSource/Conceptual/ShellScripting/ShellScriptSecurity/ShellScriptSecurity.html#//apple_ref/doc/uid/TP40004268-CH8-SW1 (accessed 07/19/2013)

SHELL SCRIPTING QUESTIONS

1. If scripts are primarily for use by expert system administrators, why should you care about security in the script code?

2. Why is it dangerous to execute scripts as the root user?

DESIGN CASE

You are called to investigate a possible break in on an Ubuntu Linux box. The log file storing ssh login information is of interest. The following is a snippet of the file `auth.log`. The complete file is available on the Linux Virtual Machine as /opt/book/scripting/design_cas/auth.log

```
Feb 17 08:00:08 inigo sshd[7049]: Failed
password for root from
61.136.171.198 port 59146 ssh2
Feb 17 08:00:09 inigo sshd[7049]: Received
disconnect from
61.136.171.198: 11: Bye Bye [preauth]
Feb 17 08:00:16 inigo sshd[7051]: pam_
unix(sshd:auth): authentication
failure; logname= uid=0 euid=0 tty=ssh
ruser= rhost=61.136.171.198
user=root
Feb 17 08:00:18 inigo sshd[7051]: Failed
password for root from
61.136.171.198 port 59877 ssh2
Feb 17 08:00:19 inigo sshd[7051]:
Connection closed by 61.136.171.198
[preauth]
Feb 17 08:17:01 inigo CRON[7296]: pam_
unix(cron:session): session
```

```
opened for user root by (uid=0)
Feb 17 08:17:01 inigo CRON[7296]: pam_
unix(cron:session): session
closed for user root
```

1. Create a script that displays the IP addresses (without duplicates) of all servers that tried to login and failed to login as the user 'root' along with the number of times each server attempted to log in. Sort the results by the number of failed logins.

2. Create a script which displays all of the account names and that were tried that do not exist on this server (Hint: look for the phrase 'Failed password for invalid user') and the IP address that attempt came from. Sort the list alphabetically and do not include duplicate lines.

3. Create a script that will read a file (ip.txt) containing a list of IPs and try to resolve the Fully Qualified Domain Name (FQDN) with the `host` command. The FQDN is the human mnemonic version of the IP address, such as www.google.com or my.usf.edu. The script should store the IP and FQDN (or 'UNKNOWN' if the IP can not be resolved), one set per line, comma-separated, to a file named fqdn.txt.

## CHAPTER 11

Incident Handling

Introduction

In this chapter we will wrap up many of the concepts and ideas we reviewed in the past chapters into the narrative of an incident. Incident handling is an important facet of security, since it involves minimizing the adverse effects of the incident on the assets, implementing controls needed to decrease the exposure of the assets to the existing threats, and ultimately restoring IT services with as little impact to the organization as possible. By the end of the chapter you should be able to:

- Identify the major components of dealing with an incident
- Understand the incident handling lifecycle
- Prepare a basic policy outlining a methodology for the handling of an incident
- Use material seen so far to properly identify and classify an incident
- Judge when to start the process of containment and eradication of the incident
- Report on the incident to improve preparation for a similar incident in the future
- Know the elements of disaster recovery and business continuity planning

Incidents overview

According to NIST 800-61 rev2, *a computer security incident is a violation or imminent threat of violation of computer security policies, acceptable use policies, or standard security practices*. Examples of incidents include:

- An attacker commands a botnet to send high volumes of connection requests to your organization's web server, causing it to crash.

- Some users in your organization are tricked into opening a "quarterly report" sent via email that is actually malware; running the tool has infected their computers and established connections with an external host.

- An attacker obtains sensitive data and threatens your CEO that the details will be released publicly if the organization does not pay a designated sum of money.

- A user provides or exposes sensitive information to others through peer-to-peer file sharing services.

In earlier chapters, we have defined the components of information security concerns including threats, assets, and their characteristics as well as some common measures taken to minimize information security problems. Unfortunately, in spite of your best attempts, intruders are likely to find ways of creating problems for you. We call them incidents. To respond to incidents, it is useful to develop some standard procedures and refine these procedures based on your experience. We introduce the essential elements of incident handling procedures in this chapter.

Incident handling

How does one go about handling an incident? You have seen a preview of the issues encountered in responding to incidents when you faced the student email server issue in the design case in the early part of this book. Looking back, what steps should you have performed to respond to that incident? What about a virus infection, or a web page defacement? Are there any actions common to an appropriate response to all these incidents?

While some of the procedures dealing with each incident may vary, the overall process remains the same. These are described in NIST 800-61 rev.2, and involve 4 basic steps:

1. Preparation

2. Detection and analysis

3. Containment, eradication, and recovery

4. Postincident analysis

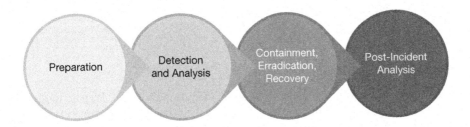

In the most effective organizations, these steps do not stand on their own. Instead, they are part of a cycle that repeats itself every time the organization faces an adverse event.

In the rest of this chapter, we will discuss the elements of handling a typical incident, following the NIST procedure.

Reference example – Incident handling gone bad

These days, with the high degree of professionalism in the IT world, it is difficult to find an example of really bad incident handling. Fortunately for us, on June 26, 2013, the Inspector General for the US Department of Commerce released an audit report of an exceptionally poorly handled incident at the Economic Development Administration (EDA), a relatively small unit in the US Department of Commerce, with an annual budget of about $460 million in 2012.

In summary, on December 6, 2011, the Department of Homeland Security alerted the EDA and the National Oceanic and Atmospheric Administration (NOAA) of potential malware in their IT systems. NOAA fixed its problems and brought back the affected systems into operation by January 12, 2012, i.e., about 35 days after the initial alert.

By contrast, the EDA, fearing widespread infection and potential state-actor involvement, insisted on an assurance of malware removal on all its systems. In this effort, it spent over $2.7 million in remediation expenses, including over $1.5 million in services from an IT contractor. This was more than half the EDA's total IT budget for the year. Even more interestingly, it paid $4,300 to the contractor to physically destroy $170,500 in IT equipment. IT equipment destroyed included printers, TVs, cameras, desktops, mice, and even keyboards.

The wanton destruction only stopped because by August 1, 2012, EDA had exhausted funds for its destructive efforts. The EDA therefore halted the destruction of its remaining IT components, valued at over $3 million. The EDA intended to resume its destructive activity once funds for such destruction became available.

All this, just to remove routine malware that affected two of its approximately 250 IT components (e.g., desktops, laptops, and servers).

This incident is a font of examples for what can go wrong at virtually every stage of the incident handling process. We will use the example throughout the chapter to illustrate what can go wrong. The incident would be funny, if it were not for our own taxes paying for this unhappy outcome.

Reference

1. US Department of Commerce, OIG Final Report, "Economic Development Administration Malware Infections on EDA's Systems Were Overstated and the Disruption of IT Operations Was Unwarranted," OIG-13-027-A, June 26, 2013, http://www.oig.doc.gov/OIGPublications/OIG-13-027-A.pdf (accessed 07/14/2013)

Preparation

Preparation is the first step in the creation of an incident response plan. Preparation involves more than just sitting around trying to think about all the possible threat scenarios that could affect the attributes of a specific asset, and the appropriate response to each of these scenarios. Instead of attempting to be fully prepared to handle all the different types of threat actions against all different assets, it is more productive to identify the basic steps that are common to all events, and plan the execution of each of these steps.

Creating a policy for incident response

Within incident preparation, the first step is to create a policy around incident response and obtain top management's agreement to the policy. *An incident response policy describes the standard methods used by the organization for handling information security incidents.* This may strike many as unnecessary paperwork but it is extremely important to execute in advance. This is because the policy will help you focus on the incident as a whole, from start to finish, without getting diverted by media and organizational pressures, including the possible consequences of any temporary controls you may have to put in place in order to contain or eradicate the threat. For example, if your university's web server is defaced, it is better to have a policy in place that allows IT to bring the website down for as long as necessary to deal with the issue, rather than having to obtain permissions in real time from stakeholders to do so. In fact, most stakeholders, including users of the website will find it more assuring to know that you are following standard procedures than to know that you are figuring out what to do in real time. The discussions involved in developing an incident response policy also provide management with an understanding of the issues they may have to deal with during an actual incident.

"Put it in writing!" This is an important concept in security and is something all managers understand. The difficulties in implementing this policy will vary greatly from organization to organization.

At the University of South Florida, official policies are first written, then vetted by internal IT units and steering committees, moved on to General Counsel for an 8-week vetting process with different entities on campus, from the faculty union group to Human Resources. The advantage of such a drawn out process is that it also helps to publicize the policy and increase security awareness. In other organizations, however, a simple email to an executive may suffice to implement the policy. One common point to both approaches, and a must for any policy, is the support of top management.

And this is why you need to have something in writing: if you have to pull the plug on a server because sensitive data may be leaking due to a hacker, you want to make absolutely sure someone has your back.

The scope is the part of the incident response policy that specifies the targets of the policy. It is recommended that the scope should be narrow and specified as closely as possible to what is achievable. The elements of the scope include (a) which assets are covered by the policy; (b) are there any exclusions to the policy; (c) are there departments within your organization with the autonomy to decline adherence to the policy; (d) can individual departments be more exclusive/stricter with their policy? Universities, for instance, are notoriously decentralized in terms of IT resources. In such organizations, it may even be necessary to try to find agreement on when a local security incident becomes an organization-wide concern.

Having a policy is not enough. Everyone involved must know what is in the policy. In the EDA case, as stated in the OIG report,

"DOC [staff] did not understand that there was a preexisting expectation of specific incident response services, as outlined in the service level agreement (SLA) between the [DOC] and EDA. This agreement clearly states [DOC's] obligated incident response services (e.g., investigation, forensics, and reverse engineering) and defines EDA's incident response responsibilities (e.g., reporting incidents and dealing with quarantined or deleted malware). Since [DOC] staff did not understand this agreement, they inaccurately assumed EDA was capable of performing its own incident analysis activities (e.g., determining the extent of the malware infection)."

Incident response team

Just as organizations have designated employees for specific functions, it is important to have staff designated to respond to incidents. These staff members are called the incident response team. Even though security incidents do not happen every day, the designated incident response staff develop experience into the expectations of the organization during incidents. The primary goal of the incident response team is to protect the overall computing infrastructure of the organization, and hence its members need to be aware of the overall IT architecture of the organization. The team is responsible for the overall incident handling cycle, including:

- quickly identifying threats to the campus data infrastructure,
- assessing the level of risk,

- immediately taking steps to mitigate the risks considered critical and harmful to the integrity of university information system resources,

- notifying management of the event and associated risk,

- notifying local personnel of any incident involving their resources,

- issuing a final report as needed, including lessons learned.

The incident response team (IRT) has multiple roles before, during, and after an incident. The roles of each member of the IRT must be part of the incident response policy. Often, membership to the IRT will cross departmental boundaries, and managers have to understand and agree that, when called upon, IRT members will be pulled from their current projects and allocated to the IRT, especially when it comes to the containment phase of the incident.

In a large organization, there may be a need to have multiple IRTs, one within each division of the organization. If such a framework is necessary, it is important that a central group be in charge of making security decisions when events start crossing the boundaries of the original affected division. For instance, a malware infection initially localized to computers in the College of Arts may threaten the integrity of the overall network if other campus areas are also infected. Containment of the infection at the college by interrupting the access of the college to the rest of the university network is something that falls under the jurisdiction of a central IRT group.

At the University of South Florida, individual units and departments are required by policy to alert the IRT as soon as any asset classified "restricted" is involved in an adverse event. Members of the incident response team should be brought together as soon as an incident is detected within the university. After normal operations are restored, a report must be presented to all members of the IRT and local system administrators, clearly outlining the extent of the breach, and the steps taken to avoid future incidents. These incidents will be reviewed by the head of the IT Security department as part of the continuous risk assessment program (risk assessment is discussed in Chapter 14).

The IRT will have one chair, usually a senior security analyst. This person will coordinate and help other IRT members to perform their functions when dealing with the incident, from communication with management, users, other IT personnel, vendors, ISP, etc. The chair of the IRT controls the situation as it evolves, especially from a technical perspective. As such, it is vital that this individual have high credibility within the organization for their competence, excellent communication skills, both oral and in writing, enough technical background to understand the situation, and to be able to make split-second, educated decisions based on the status updates given to him or her by the other members of the team.

Technical members of the IRT are selected depending on the threat action. For example, if an Oracle database was breached due to a compromised administrator account on the operating system, the IRT may include the following members:

- A person familiar with the OS to look at the OS system and logs, or at least extract them for analysis by someone familiar with data forensics.

- A database administrator to examine the Oracle database, contents, and logs to try to determine if anything was altered.

- A network engineer to review firewall and/or netflow logs to try to observe any traffic out of the ordinary.

- Desktop services personnel may be called if desktop machines provided the vector for the admin account to be compromised.

The IRT needs to be competent and the organization needs to invest as necessary to help the IRT maintain its competence. When the tide turns ugly, the IRT is the primary line of defense. In the EDA example, the OIG report has this to say about the Department of Commerce's (DOC) IRT:

"DOC CIRT's inexperienced staff and inadequate knowledge of EDA's incident response capabilities24 hindered its ability to provide adequate incident response services. DOC CIRT's incident handler managing EDA's initial incident response activities had minimal incident response experience, no incident response training, and did not have adequate skills to provide incident response services. The lack of experience, training, and skills led the incident handler to request the wrong network logging information (i.e., perform the wrong incident analysis), which led EDA to believe it had a widespread malware infection, and deviate from manda-tory incident response procedures. The Department's Office of the Chief Information Officer should have ensured that all DOC CIRT staff met the Department's minimum incident response qualifications."

Supporting team

During an incident, there is much more happening than technical sleuthing. Communication is an important aspect of the duties of the IRT. One of the special features of incidents relative to routine IT operations is the extreme interest among different constituencies for information. Often these information needs are inconsistent with each other. End users are greatly interested in knowing when their services will be restored. Compliance officers are interested in know-ing whether any information has been compromised. If there is any possibility of wider public interest in the incident, the media is immediately interested in the comments of the sen-ior-most executives of the organization before the next news show. When you receive these queries, often you will not have enough information to respond satisfactorily (Figure 11.1).

Managing information flow is important in these circum-stances. It is especially important to resist the temptation of conveying speculation as informed "expert" opinion. While it is useful to acknowledge incidents, particularly those that affect end users, it is advisable to follow the concept of "need-to-know." *Need-to-know is an information management principle where a person is only provided the information that is necessary to per-form their job.*

Need-to-know does not imply that events are supposed to be kept secret. Instead, consistent adoption of need-to-know decreases unnecessary calls to IT personnel from managers

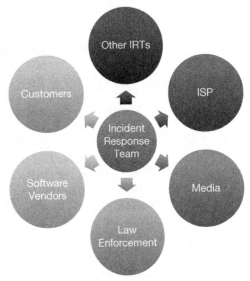

FIGURE 11.1 IRT interactions

seeking "privileged" information. Information seekers can be directed to websites or other channels specified in the incident response policy. Before updating such information, the IRT should consider the intervention of the legal department to decide on what will be disclosed, and how it will be disclosed. In terms of communication with the general public, three entities should be considered:

- **Media Relations**: if the organization has such a department, any and all information with the community outside the organization should be routed through this department. They have the know-how and experience on how to deal with an event.

- **Legal Counsel**: the legal department will verify if any federal or state disclosure laws apply to a particular event, especially when it involves problems with data confidentiality. Unintended disclosure may have severe financial and public relation consequences to the organization.

- **Law Enforcement**: universities have a local University Police. No outside law enforcement agency is allowed to enter a campus, not even the CIA or FBI, without the knowledge of both the Universal Police and General Counsel.

These steps minimize the possibilities of rumor-mongering, ill-informed publicity, and general disorder during incident response.

> Need-to-know is common in military and espionage settings as a way to keep personnel safe. If the enemy knows that a soldier or spy has no privileged information, the enemy is less likely to invest in the effort required to capture the soldier or spy.

Communication

Let's take a look at communication, since it is a key part of the response to an incident (Figure 11.2).

Reporting an incident for follow up   Incidents may come to the IRT attention in a variety of ways.

On a ***Direct Report***, the asset owner or custodian may report the incident himself. For instance, say you cultivate the healthy habit of looking up your Social Security Number on Google from time to time. One day, presto, you get a hit. It looks like the number was found on a word document from a class you took a long time ago at your previous university. As a knowledgeable user, you look up the IT person responsible for security immediately and report that your SSN is exposed.

Another possibility is an ***Anonymous Report***. Organizations usually maintain processes by which someone can report an issue anonymously and not be afraid of reprisal. One such example could be allegations that a high-ranking university official is printing material of pornographic nature on university printers. This allegation would ring all sorts of bells at the university, from public relations risk to sexual harassment and inappropriate use of tax dollars. Understandably, assuming the allegation is true, an employee would not desire to see his or her name linked to such an allegation in fear of losing his or her job.

FIGURE 11.2 IRT communications

The **Help Desk** may be involved in the reporting as well. Maybe, during the process of resolving a problem, the help desk employee stumbled on to something. A misconfiguration of shared network drives, for instance, allowing too much access to users without need-to-know. Perhaps the Help Desk received a report from a user who found something. The reason we should consider the Help Desk as a separate reporting entity is because normally help desks have trouble tickets, which themselves may be visible to a large group of people. Consider how much detail would you like to see on a Help Desk ticket? It goes back to controlling the message and need-to-know.

Finally, **Self-Audit** methods such as periodical vulnerability assessment and log analysis may bring to surface breaches that must be handled. One common example is that of an administrator who discovers a breach because the computer CPU load was too high, causing availability issue. Once the administrator is called to analyze the problem it is quickly apparent that a runaway FTP process is the guilty party. This FTP site stores mp3 files for hackers to share with each other and it is heavily used, causing the high CPU load. Unfortunately, this is an all too common scenario.

Notifications More often than not, as soon as an incident becomes problematic, people in the organization will start asking questions. This is especially true for those folks affected by the event. If the event is affecting managers and other executive leaders, the pressure for quick communication and resolution will be even greater.

IT Personnel and the IT Help Desk should be maintained informed, especially when the event affects the availability of the asset. Users will quickly overwhelm the Help Desk with calls if the event involves an asset which criticality to the organization has been deemed "essential." On a decentralized IT environment, like many large research universities across the United States, other IT organizations should also be informed to be in the lookout. For instance, if the event is a Denial of Service attack made possible thanks to an unpatched vulnerability, other units may wish to perform an emergency patching session before they also suffer the consequences of the DoS attack.

Management must be kept updated. It is a good idea to inform managers and other executives periodically, even if nothing has changed. This will keep phones from ringing, even those direct calls to engineers who are supposed to be dedicating 100% of their effort to the containment and eradication of the problem. Quick text messages and brief email messages with status updates are very useful in this situation.

End users and **customers** also get very edgy when they don't know what is going on. There are always two questions that are asked during an outage: when will the system be back, and what happened. At times they are both difficult to answer. In December 2013, Facebook

FIGURE 11.3   DollSays

suffered a massive outage throughout the Internet due to DNS problems. Even though the service itself was down for only 15–25 minutes, users around the globe were frustrated and confused, as one of the thousands of tweets sent out during the outage attest (Figure 11.3).

We can go back to our trusty EDA example to see what can go wrong with communication. In fact, the early part of the report lays the blame for the fiasco largely on poor communication between the Department of Commerce and its unit, the EDA. From the report:

DOC CIRT sent two incident notifications to the EDA. In the first incident notification on December 7, 2011, DOC CIRT's incident handler requested network logging information. However, instead of providing EDA a list of potentially infected components, the incident handler mistakenly provided EDA a list of 146 components within its network boundary. Receiving this notification, the subsidiary unit, the EDA believed it faced a substantial malware infection, affecting all the listed 146 components.

DOC CIRT's mistake resulted in a second incident notification. Early on December 8, 2011, an HCHB network staff member informed DOC CIRT that the incident handler's request for network logging information did not identify the infected components. Rather, the response merely identified EDA components residing on a portion of the HCHB network. The HCHB network staff member then performed the appropriate analysis identifying only two components exhibiting the malicious behavior in US-CERT's alert. With this new information, DOC CIRT sent EDA a second e-mail incident notification.

DOC CIRT's second incident notification was vague. DOC CIRT's second incident notification did not clearly explain that the first incident notification was inaccurate. As a result, EDA continued to believe a widespread malware infection was affecting its systems. Specifically, the second incident notification began by stating the information previously provided about the incident was correct.

EDA interpreted the statement as confirmation of the first incident notification, when DOC CIRT's incident handler simply meant to confirm EDA was the agency identified in US-CERT's alert. Nowhere in the notification or attachment does the DOC CIRT incident handler identify that there was a mistake or change to the previously provided information.

Although the incident notification's attachment correctly identified only 2 components exhibiting suspicious behavior – not the 146 components that DOC CIRT initially identified – the name of the second incident notification's attachment exactly matched the first incident notification's attachment, obscuring the clarification.

DOC CIRT and EDA's misunderstanding continued over the next 5 weeks, though additional communications occurred between DOC CIRT and EDA. Each organization continued to have a different understanding of the extent of the malware infection. DOC CIRT believed the incident affected only two components, whereas EDA believed the incident affected more than half of its components. Several factors contributed to these different interpretations:

- DOC CIRT assumed EDA understood that its second incident notification superseded the first incident notification and that there were only 2 potentially infected components – not 146. However, DOC CIRT did not follow up to establish whether EDA understood the new information.

- EDA responded to the second incident notification by providing a sample of two components (on the list identified in the first incident notification and that were exhibiting malicious behavior) for forensic analysis. DOC CIRT believed the sample to be the same two components identified in the second incident notification.

- When DOC CIRT confirmed that the sample of 2 components was infected with malware, EDA believed that DOC CIRT had confirmed the malware infection for all 146 components listed in the first incident notification.

- DOC CIRT did not retain the first incident notification showing 146 components or document initial incident response activities. Therefore, when DOC CIRT management became involved in the incident response activities, they could not see that a misunderstanding had occurred.

Compliance

Compliance is the act of following applicable laws, regulations, rules, industry codes, and contractual obligations. Ideally, compliance requirements are best-practices developed to avoid well-known past mistakes. In practice though, compliance is often important because non-compliance leads to avoidable penalties. In any case, you need to be aware of any compliance requirements associated with incident response that are applicable to your context and act accordingly.

As an example of compliance requirements in incident response, the Federal Information Security Management Act[1] (FISMA) requires Federal agencies to establish incident response capabilities. Each Federal civilian agency is required to designate a primary and secondary point of contact (POC) with US-CERT, the United States Computer Emergency Readiness Team,[2] and report all incidents consistent with the agency's incident response policy.

---

[1] http://csrc.nist.gov/groups/SMA/fisma/index.html

[2] http://www.us-cert.gov/

As an example of FISMA compliance, when a known or suspected loss, theft, or compromise of PII (personally identifiable information) involving US Navy systems occurs, the Department of the Navy is required to:

I. use OPNAV Form 5211/13 to make initial and follow up reports,

II. send form US-CERT within 1 hour of discovering a breach has occurred,

III. report to the DON CIO Privacy Office within 1 hour,

IV. report to the Defense Privacy Office,

V. report to Navy, USMC, BUMED chain of command, as applicable.

Hardware and software

To be effective, the IRT needs the appropriate tools. A sampling of the hardware and software recommended by NIST 800-61 rev.2 for incident response includes:

- backup devices to create disk images or other incident data,

- laptops for gathering, analyzing data, and writing reports,

- spare computer hardware for "crash and burn" purposes, such as trying out malware and other payload found and considered "unknown,"

- packet analyzers to capture and analyze network traffic,

- digital forensics software to recover erased data, analyze modified, access, and creation (MAC) timelines, log analysis, etc.

- evidence gathering accessories such as digital cameras, audio recorders, chain of custody forms, etc.

One of your best friends during this part of the process is a search engine. A web search on a log snippet, an FTP banner, for instance, may reveal valuable information such as location of log files, configuration files, and other important clues to help the security team to build a more complete timeline for the event.

> Out of the 855 incidents analyzed in the Verizon Data Breach Report of 2013, 81% leveraged hacking, 69% included malware, and 61% featured a combination of both. Therefore, it is only natural to assume that most of the time the members of IRT will be involved in the investigation and analysis of a hacking or malware infection and use specialized tools extensively. We have therefore devoted an entire chapter to such analysis.

Training

IT is an ever-changing world. New technologies, new acronyms bring along new assets and new threats. It is the job of the security analyst such as you to maintain awareness of those new assets and threats, especially those that may introduce risks to the organization. Some of you may have the luxury of specializing in an area of security, such as encryption or forensics. The core members of the IRT, however, must be generalists. They must be able to step back from their day-to-day functions and have a 30,000 feet view of the enterprise, assets, controls, threat actions, and consequences.

A security certification is a good start, not necessarily because you will retain all the hundreds of pages of information that will be thrown at you, like being asked to drink from a fire hose, but because it offers a baseline set of information on all aspects of security, especially things you may not have thought of quite yet. Good certifications will build on the introductory information provided in this book.

One such certification, offered by the ISC² organization, is the Certified Information System Security Professional certification, or CISSP. The CISSP is based on what is known as the Common Body of Knowledge, information deemed important to security professionals around the world, including:

Access Control
Telecommunications and Network Security
Information Security Governance and Risk Management
Software Development Cryptography
Security Architecture and Design
Security Operations
Business Continuity and Disaster Recovery Planning
Legal, Regulations, Investigations, and Compliance
Physical (Environmental) Security

Other facets of training also merit consideration. Media Relations personnel, for instance, should be instructed on how to interact with the media, including the control of the message, the importance of not revealing sensitive information. Revealing technical details on how a malware infection was detected and controlled, for instance, could alert hackers and malware developers on how to sidestep the same controls in future releases of the malware. In certain situations, this control of the message goes directly against the principle that the public should always be communicated fully and effectively. Media Relations is a balancing act when it comes to incident response, much like implementing security controls: revealing too much may be a problem, revealing too little may also make matters worse.

Detection and analysis

The steps in the previous section ensure that the organization is prepared to an incident should it occur. In this section, we will look at the general incident detection and analysis process. Later in the book, we will take a more detailed look at some specific incident analysis techniques.

Initial documentation

According to NIST 800-61rev2, IRT members should ensure that the incident is properly documented, starting as soon as the event is detected. While this documentation will evolve as detection and analysis run their course, at the very least, information about the following items must be present in the documentation of an incident:

- The current status of the incident (new, in progress, forwarded for investigation, resolved, etc.)

- A summary of the incident

- Indicators related to the incident

- Other incidents related to this incident

- Actions taken by all incident handlers on this incident

- Chain of custody, if applicable

- Impact assessments related to the incident

- Contact information for other involved parties (e.g., system owners, system administrators)

- A list of evidence gathered during the incident investigation

- Comments from incident handlers

- Next steps to be taken (e.g., rebuild the host, upgrade an application).

Detecting an incident

Your organization has gone through the process of preparing for a security incident. You planned, trained, made a few purchases. Your analysis hardware is ready to go. Media Relations is prepped. Unfortunately, chances are your IRT will not have to wait for long to be put to the test. But how will the organization come to the realization that something is amiss? How will the incident be detected?

Visible changes to services One of the most common ways in which an organization discovers something is wrong with a system or data is through a visible change on the same data or system. Web defacement, for instance, is an example. Users of a website will quickly notice something is amiss when they visit the site and are greeted with the page shown in Figure 11.4.

FIGURE 11.4 Website defacement example

According to the VERIS Data Breach Report of 2012, an astonishing 92% of the breaches are reported by a third party. Let's put this into perspective, because it is pretty important. No matter what "silver bullet" a security vendor tries to sell you to protect your assets, to monitor the health of your security, chances are that when you have a breach, it will be reported to you by a third party.

Performance monitoring   Another typical scenario is the breach causing performance issue. At times, either as a direct or indirect result of malware installed by a hacker, a computer system may become sluggish to such an extent that it becomes noticeable either to users or to administrators.

One of the popular uses for hacked computers is the use of the machine's storage as a repository of data, either for illegally sharing music, movies, or pornographic material. The latter seems to gain lots of attention from other hackers and lurkers (folks who frequent hacking circles but do not share any data). Once a computer is exposed to a malware and pornographic material shared from it, a user on the computer will quickly notice a decrease in performance because most of the computer's CPU and network bandwidth will likely be used for downloading of that material. This generally results in a call to the help desk.

Understanding normal behavior

In order to detect anything that is "abnormal," administrators must first determine the baseline or normal behavior of the system. Some desktop computers in the university, for instance, are only used from 8 am to 5 pm, Monday through Friday. Therefore, the detection of a login attempt to these computers at 2 a.m. on Saturday should raise all sorts of warning flags.

PII monitoring   As a direct result of all the big breaches on large corporations and the resulting onslaught of coverage in the news, individuals have begun to be more careful with their personal information. As part of this process, users may head over to Google or other search engines and search for their own personal information, such as their Social Security Number (Figure 11.5).

Ten years ago it was common for professors to post students' grades in front of their office door. Instead of using names, in order to protect the students' identities, professors used Social Security Numbers (oh, the irony).

Now, ten years later, many professors still have the Word documents they used to post on their doors, with SSNs and grades. At times, these forgotten files end up in places where search engine crawlers pick them up and expose them to the world.

FIGURE 11.5   PII search

Google Alerts

Google Alerts is a tool offered by Google to help users keep track of topics of interest. A good use of the tool is to set it up to provide you with an alert every time your name is indexed by the Google crawler. You can enter the search query "John Doe" and instruct Google Alerts to send you an email as soon as it finds a new web page with the name John Doe in it.[3]

File integrity monitoring   File integrity tools are software applications that monitor the integrity of files in a computer system. If a monitored file on a computer is modified, the administrator of the system will be immediately notified. These tools are often part of larger suites called Host-based Intrusion Detection Systems (HIDS). They are host-based because they are applications that run on a computer host, versus Network-based Intrusion Detection Systems, normally referred to simply as IDS.

Take the web defacement situation, for instance. Had the index.html (or equivalent primary file) been monitored by a file integrity tool, as soon as the page's integrity was affected (by the change in content), the web administrator would have been notified. Many tools also have options to automatically restore a file when it detects a change. Popular examples of tools containing file integrity monitoring applications are OSSEC (Figure 11.6), Samhain, and Tripwire.

File integrity monitoring tools quickly bring to light the concept of an FP or False Positive. *A false positive is a find that appears to be a problem (a positive) but upon further investigation turns out not to be a problem (therefore, false).* You also learned about this concept in statistics

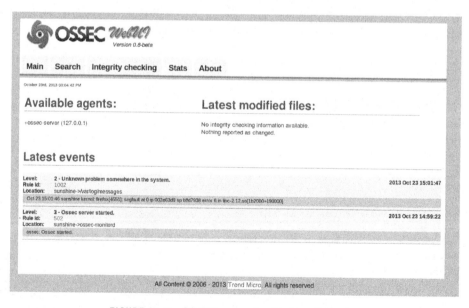

FIGURE 11.6   OSSEC, a popular file integrity tool

---

[3]You can setup Google Alerts here: http://www.google.com/alerts?hl = en

as a type-2 error. This concept is found in many "security detection" tools, from firewalls to vulnerability scanners.

Let's examine the specific issue of false positives in a file integrity tool. During installation of the tool, the administrator will be asked to specify what needs to be monitored. This is a decision that must be made carefully. What would happen, for instance, if you decide to monitor the integrity of the web server access log file? The access log file for a web server changes every time someone accesses your website. Therefore, warning bells would go off every time you had a visitor – a false positive.

While this may be "neat" for a slow website, on a busier site it would quickly cause you to neglect the warning. So, it is worth monitoring at all? In the case of a log file, the answer is no. But how about monitoring a configuration file? Or the index.html file on a website. Those may be worth monitoring.

Anonymous report   At times individuals may be hesitant to report adverse events in fear of reprisal. Most institutions have means for employers and other parties to report perceived or possible events anonymously. These events could be, for instance, potential fraud incidents, inappropriate use of the organization's computing infrastructure by managers or other administrative employees, allegations of sexual harassment over emails, etc.

In many cases, internal institutional policies **require** that any and all allegation received by these anonymous reporting mechanisms be investigated. While in a perfect world this may be a good policy to follow, institutions have to be aware of the fact that individuals in position of power within organizations are at times not liked. Blindly following allegations, repeatedly, without proper verifications, could itself be a threat action against a personnel asset (a manager, for instance) putting the institution at risk.

Log analysis   *Logs are records of the performance of a machine.* Logs are a security analyst's best friend. In terms of incident detection, logs are used by security administrators to determine the exact times when the system was under attack and what threat actions were used by a hacker (Figure 11.7).

In a Linux system, most logs are located under the */var/log* directory. The majority of the operating system logs are controlled by the syslog daemon. The */var/log/ messages* file will usually be the first one a security analyst will examine, looking for irregularities such as strange error messages, irregular reboots, etc. Log analysis is covered in more detail in a later chapter (Figure 11.8).

In terms of detection, your organization may have a Log Consolidation solution, or a full-blown Security Incident Event Manager (SIEM). In a Log Consolidation solution, logs from multiple systems and applications are consolidated into a separate server for monitoring, forensics, and performance analysis. SIEM systems integrate consolidation with analysis. These systems look for patterns of irregularities across multiple systems to determine the possibility of any threats or breaches.

For log analysis to be effective, it is key that the clocks between all the servers feeding their logs in to the log consolidation server be synchronized. This synchronization is important to ensure that timelines are interpreted correctly when hackers probe, attack, and breach multiple systems.

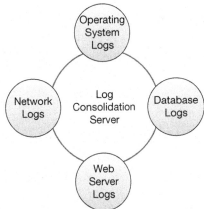

FIGURE 11.7   Typical logs consolidated

FIGURE 11.8 Log analysis

Log consolidation has another advantage. Besides being able to look at log events in one place, making it easier to slice and dice the data to look for specific events, it also copies the log data on to another server, maintaining the integrity of the log. This is particularly useful when examining data looking for evidence of fraud perpetuated by individuals with administrative privileges. A Database Administrator is generally able to cover his or her tracks on the database system server itself but a DBA should not have more than read-only permission on a log consolidation or SIEM server.

End point protection management consoles   End point protection or EPP is the evolution of our old friend the antivirus application. An EPP implies more than simply monitoring and protecting a computer system against a virus infection. EPP solutions usually include:

- Antivirus protection against malware "trying to install itself" on a computer, usually known as "On Access" protection or "Realtime" protection.

- AV protection with removal and/or quarantine of files that are found on your computer, already downloaded, either installed or not, through "On Demand" or "scheduled" scans.

- Firewall protection.

- HIDS, Host-based Intrusion Detection (optional).

- File Integrity (optional).

- Identity Theft (option).

- Children Access Monitoring (optional).

As you can see, EPP suites are quite a change from "just" a malware protection suite. Often times they also include "hooks" for management of other server applications, such as email, web servers, etc., getting closer and closer to a SIEM solution. While the cost or effort to install and configure a full-blown SIEM or log consolidation solution may be cost-prohibitive for an organization, EPP management consoles are often included with the price of the license for EPPs. Since even the smallest organizations invest in end point protection, they have the option of using EPP management suites to perform some log analysis functions (Figure 11.9).

Internal investigations   Finally, it is worth mentioning those events found by internal investigations. Notably, we are talking about investigations originated by Internal Audit, State Auditors (if you work at a State entity), Human Resources, University Police, or General Counsel. At times, these investigations may start with something totally out of the technical area but need IT help for further evidence. For instance, if an employee is fired and ends up suing your workplace

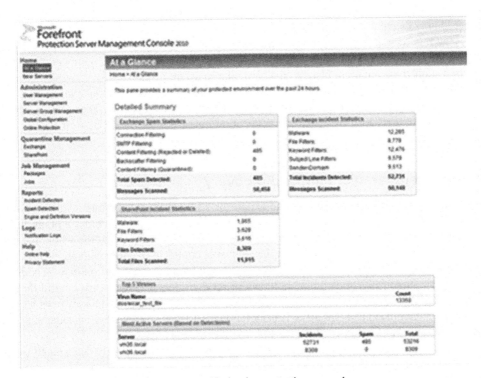

FIGURE 11.9   End point protection example

for unlawful termination, you may be asked by General Counsel to produce all emails between the executives of your workplace discussing the subject.

Another possible scenario would be internal auditors investigating a department's operations and find PII stored without approval from the security office and against policy. In this case, it is important to locate all irregularly stored information, classify it, and apply the appropriate controls before other audits (such as a credit card PCI audit, for instance) and other more severe problems threaten the data.

Analyzing the incident

Once there is an agreement that "yeah, there is an incident," the IRT will start the process of analyzing the incident. The goal of the analysis is to discover all adverse events that compose the incident in order to properly and effectively manage the next phase of the cycle – containment and eradication. If the incident is not analyzed thoroughly, your organization will get stuck in a loop of detection and containment, with each iteration bringing more and more potential damage to the confidentiality, integrity, or availability of the asset involved.

Analysis will obviously change depending on the situation. In practice, you always should try to gauge the return you could possibly get from the analysis. For instance, let's suppose there was a malware outbreak in the Chemistry Department. Ten computers in the open use lab were infected with apparently the same malware strain. All of them presented the same backdoor, the same botnet, and using the same port number. If you have the time and resources available it would be ok to take a close look at all the machines, look for log files for the backdoors, check to see if any traces of actual human connections were noted using the system. On the other hand, since these are all open use lab machines with no personal data stored in them, it may be easier to only examine a sample of the machines.

Internet Search Engines are an incredible source of knowledge that can be easily tapped to gain information during analysis. Everything from FTP banners to port numbers on botnets can be searched to gain more insight on a particular malware installation.

Finally, as part of the analysis, you should be able to determine the stakeholders and any possible restricted or essential asset that may be affected by the incident. These assets will be your primary targets for protection and eradication going into the next phase of the incident management.

Containment, eradication, and recovery

Containment is the act of preventing the expansion of harm. Typically, this involves disconnecting affected computers from the network. For many incidents, there comes a point during the analysis when an event merits containment even before the analysis of the whole incident has been completed. This happens when the analyst is confident that the ongoing events merit action, and/or determines that the risk to the asset is too high for events to continue as is. Since containment may involve temporary shutdown of services, this decision needs careful thought in balancing the expected losses from disrupted services with the expected losses from spreading harm to other machines. The same consideration has to be made when we consider **eradication**, the removal of the causes of the adverse event (Figure 11.10).

There is no secret recipe for finding this branching point. It is largely determined by the experience of those individuals who are part of the IRT, along with input from management if possible.

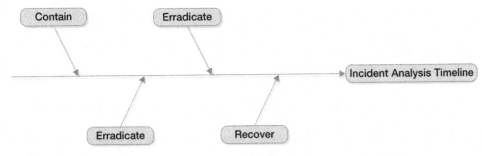

FIGURE 11.10   Containment, eradication, and recovery timeline

Going back to our open use lab example, once the first computer is thoroughly analyzed, the software on the machine can be wiped and reinstalled. This is the *recovery* point, when the computer is turned back to the owner for normal operations. If this situation included a professor's computer that should be investigated, the IRT group may consider obtaining a copy of the hard drive and then releasing the machine to be wiped, data backed up, and OS reinstalled. By obtaining a copy or disk image we can quickly release the machine to be recovered without impairing the end user's duties while the analysis period continues.

Considering a more urgent example, if during analysis the IRT members find out that a backdoor is being used to actively transfer PII from a hacked server to other off-campus hosts, the connection should be broken as soon as possible. Thereafter, the backdoor can be handled, either through network access control lists, firewalls, or actual removal of the backdoor from the server prior to analysis. In all situations, the confidentiality, integrity, and availability of the asset must come before the needs of the analyst.

IRT should be aware of the impact of acting upon an asset involved in an adverse event, both at the micro and macro levels. Here's a situation when decisions may change drastically as data is available for analysis.

1:00 pm: A machine in the College of Medicine is found to have a backdoor.

During analysis, a few things should come to mind right away. "College of Medicine" is one of those Colleges that "may" have HIPAA compliance requirements associated with the data. Find out immediately if the machine contains HIPAA data. If the machine contains HIPAA data it must be handled immediately.

1:10 pm: Computer <u>does not</u> contain HIPAA data. It belongs to a faculty in Radiology, outside the HIPAA zone.

After a quick phone call to the local administrator we find that the computer in question does NOT contain HIPAA data. IRT "could" move to act if needed. What is the threat action posed by the box?

1:30 pm: Computer determined to be part of a grant bringing 100 million dollars to the University.

There better be serious backing up from the College Dean and possibly from the Provost before anything is done to this machine that could even remotely jeopardize anything running on this box.

Certain actions performed by the IRT during containment may prove difficult to recover from. Actions performed to contain a specific situation may put the organization at risk in other areas. Restarting HR systems to finish removing malware may interrupt payroll processing if performed at the wrong time. For these reasons, to the extent possible, it is important to notify all stakeholders **before** changes are performed on assets for containment. Please note that IRT members must continue to observe need-to-know during these notifications. A payroll manager may have to be filled in as to why a server is being restarted, but not necessarily everyone in the payroll department.

Another decision that needs to be made during containment is whether to sit back and observe hacker behavior or immediately contain the problem. It all boils down to the potential amount of damage to assets. While the initial jerk reaction of system administrators is to immediately squash the bugs and remove all tracks, observation may be beneficial to the organization. It may reveal other attack vectors used by the hacker, other assets already under hacker control, and many other useful pieces of information.

IRT members and administrators have to be careful when pulling the plug on hackers. Efforts to do so should be orchestrated and coordinated as much as possible. Hackers have been known to turn destructive when found out, in an effort to further cover their tracks and remove all local logging information that may lead to their capture. Database administrators involved in fraudulent situations may set up traps that, when invoked, totally destroy the database and all data contained in it.

It is for this reason that FBI agents involved in sting operations against hackers forcibly and speedily remove individuals from keyboards and other input devices as soon as possible when they are caught. This minimizes the possibility that the hackers might initiate scripts to destroy assets and evidence.

Lessons learned

The final stage of the incident handling procedure is also what allows us to prepare for the next incident. In this final part, IRT members gather their notes and finalize their documentation. The documentation should contain all individual adverse events involved in this incident, together with time stamps and assets involved, as well as:

- Indicate which areas of the organization were involved in the accident and what was the resulting breach;

- How the threats were handled individually by each department and together under the coordination of the IRT;

- Extent to which existing procedures were appropriate to handle the issues and opportunities for improvement;

- The extent to which the assets were appropriately identified and classified, so that the IRT could make quick judgment calls as the situation evolved;

- Extent to which information sharing with stakeholders was done satisfactorily;

- Opportunities for preemptive detection to avoid similar issues from happening;

- Technical measures necessary to be taken to avoid similar issues in the future.

So, how was the EDA incident finally resolved?

In February 2013, over a year after the initial alert, the Office of the Inspector General at the Department of Commerce (DOC) assured the EDA and the DOC that the damage was limited to two systems. Assured that there was no significant incident, the DOC started recovery efforts in February 2013, and needed only a little longer than 5 weeks to restore EDA's former operational capabilities. By comparison, EDA's incomplete efforts spanned almost a year.

Specifically, the [DOC] provided EDA with enterprise e-mail, account management services, help desk support services, and a securely configured and uniform image for its laptops. Additionally, the Department restored EDA users' access to critical business applications.

The disaster

In the world of incidents there is that monster that has huge repercussion throughout the whole organization and can quickly bring a prosperous company down to its knees: the disaster. *A disaster is a calamitous event that causes great destruction.* A disaster may be considered a huge incident, or an incident so large that it involves multiple sub-incidents, or an incident that affects the entire organization. Whichever way you look at it, a disaster is an incident with major implications on multiple stakeholders.

Let's start with a few definitions. *Disaster Recovery (DR) is the process adopted by the IT organization in order to bring systems back up and running.* DR may involve moving operations to a redundant site, recovering services and data.

In 2002, a hardware failure in the student email servers caused all 30,000 student email accounts to be lost at the University of South Florida, including the data they contained. Immediately the DR plan kicked in gear, calling for the re-creation of all student email accounts. These accounts were to be initially empty but would allow students to start sending and receiving emails. Once that was done, all data mailboxes were extracted from tape and restored to the users' mailboxes. The entire DR process in this case took about 3 weeks.

DR is an extremely complex process and is something usually tackled by individuals with years of experience in the organization. In large organizations, there are often individuals solely dedicated to the subject. In all likelihood, you are not likely to be given DR responsibilities in the early part of your career, so the subject is not covered in detail in this book. The topic is introduced here to familiarize you with some basic concepts and to enable you to contribute to the process.

DR is a piece of the bigger picture, Business Continuity Planning or BCP. Business continuity planning is the process for maintaining operation under adverse conditions. During BCP, planners contemplate what would happen in case of a disaster, and what would be minimally necessary to help the organization continue to operate. In the case of the USF email system, questions included how students would turn in their assignments, which funds would be used to purchase new hardware, how to make any insurance claims, and what other effects did the outage have on the organization?

By its nature, BCP and DR involve and are often led by entities other than IT. For instance, it makes no sense for organizations to work isolated from each other when preparing for a hurricane or a tornado. Such events will affect the entire organization. HR may require that all individuals stay at home if there is a possibility of a hurricane level 4 or higher. Meanwhile, IT may need employees to physically be present to shut down servers and desktops. Co-ordination between these groups will ensure that appropriate actions are performed.

An important part of BCP is the Business Impact Analysis or BIA. *Business Impact Analysis is the identification of services and products that are critical to the organization.* This is when the classification of assets we've seen in previous chapters comes in play. Essential assets must be those that directly support the services and products that result from the BIA. The BIA then dictates the prioritization of the DR procedure.

The primary objective of any BCP/DR plan is to keep employees and their families safe. Nothing should be done that puts an employee in jeopardy, and preparations should be made to allow for methods of implementing recovery of assets that do not include hazardous situations. Here are some other things to consider:

- A call list, maybe something as simple as a card-sized list of phone numbers, is an incredibly useful tool for employees to have in case of a disaster.

- How you will inform fellow employees if local phone systems are down?

- If you back up your data to tape, locally, by a device attached to your server, how will you recover the data at a redundant site? Which data should be restored first?

- Does anyone besides you know how to restore the data? Are there instructions published somewhere? If the expectation is that someone will read a 100-page manual before initiating the restore, the procedure must be simplified.

- Are test restores done regularly? Tapes and other media go bad, get scratched, and become unreadable.

- Are there means to acquire new hardware to quickly replace the hardware damaged by the disaster? If cyber insurance is involved, does someone know the details on how to activate it?

Example case – on-campus piracy

These are the personal notes of a System Administrator on a case at the University of South Florida. This case happened prior to 2005 and all personal names and host names were changed to protect the individuals involved. Such detailed incident reports are difficult to find in the public domain because they are usually need-to-know and never published.

We will call the students Greg Apple and John Orange. Both students were undeclared majors. The SA's notes on the timeline of the incident are as follows.

Monday, Oct 17:

I received reports that the root partition on SERVER-A was full. It turns out two students (login names jorange and gapple) had been using /tmp to store about 10GB worth of zipped files. I removed most of the files.

In the evening, our Network Administrator sent me this mail:

"I wacked an account by the name of gapple on SERVER-A tonight . . . He had 2 logins from different sides of the country at the same time . . . On top of this he seems to have picked up a password file, which is in his account, from somewhere off the net . . . Also, do a last on this guy, it doesn't appear as if he ever sleeps . . . I'll talk to you in the morning. . . ."

The password file seemed to have originated from somedomain.com.

Together with the password file on gapple's account there was a file containing a long directory listing from a user "mikel". I did a finger on mikel@somedomain.com and 'bingo', there he was. I sent mail to root@somedomain.com but I did not get any reply.

Tuesday, Oct 18:

I noticed in the morning when I logged in to SERVER-A that jorange had a telnet session to somedomain.com. I decided to check his home directory and its layout looked very similar to gapple. I ftp'd some of the files he had stored on /tmp over to my PC and unzipped. They turned out to be pirated games. I started monitoring jorange's actions very closely.

Will (the network administrator) informed me that thepoint.com is a freenet site, with full fledged internet connections and shell access. He also told me he has an account there. Since I had not received anything from root@thepoint, I told Will to log in and see if he could snoop around "mikel's" directory, since it was 755. Will found 3 password files and more games.

****

From the log files, I have found connections from the following hosts to either gapple's or jorange's accounts:

- numsix@inca.anotherdomain.net – Jack Laughlin's account

- hopi.anotherdomain.net

- mikel@somedomain.com – Mike Lee's account

- server0.thriddomain.net – Randy Sharr's account

There might be more accounts compromised on these sites.

****

Evidence on gapple:

1. Password file from somedomain.com.

2. File containing listing of the directory thepoint.com:/˜mikel

3. Log files indicating logins from gapple@servera to jorange@servera.

Evidence on jorange:

1. Pirated software on /tmp. We have copies of the stuff locally on to another server but the actual files were removed last night before the account was closed.

2. Mail received by jorange from anonymous users, giving the location of a new site for pirated software. The existence of this new site was confirmed.

3. Log files of ftp transfers from somedomain.com, using a fake account mikel. The existence of the mikel@somedomain.com account and its contents – pirated software – were confirmed by root@somedomain.com.

As a result of these findings, both students were suspended from the University for breach of the Code of Ethics.

SUMMARY

In this chapter, we looked at the incident handling process. We saw that effective organizations do not wait for incidents to happen before figuring out how to deal with them. Rather, they proactively prepare to deal with information security incidents. Such preparation involved developing a policy to guide incident response, agreements on communication plans, procedures for establishing incident response teams, and acquiring appropriate tools to respond to incidents. Incidents are detected by noticing abnormal behavior. We saw that while responding to incidents, it may become necessary to disable services to contain the damage. Finally, we introduced concepts related to disasters or large-scale incidents.

CHAPTER REVIEW QUESTIONS

1. What is an information security incident?

2. Provide some examples of incidents, preferably some that you have experienced yourself.

3. What are the basic steps involved in handling an incident?

4. Which of the above in your opinion is the most important? Why?

5. What are the important activities involved in preparing for an incident?

6. What is an incident response policy? Why is it useful?

7. View the incident response policy for an organization (these are easily available online). What are the elements of the policy? What did you find most interesting about the policy?

8. What is the scope of an information security policy? Why is it useful to define the scope of a policy?

9. What is the incident response team? How is it constituted?

10. What are some common issues involved in communicating about incidents?

11. What is the need-to-know principle? Why can it be useful in incident handling?

12. What is compliance? What is its relevance for incident handling?

13. How can training help incident handling?

14. Pick an information security certification of your choice and read its curriculum? In about one sentence each, describe how three modules of the curriculum might improve your ability to handle incidents?

15. What are the common ways by which incidents are detected?

16. What is log analysis? What can it be used for?

17. If you used a file integrity tool such as OSSEC on your home computer, what folders would be most appropriate to monitor using the tool? Why? (you may want to try an open source tool such as OSSEC)

18. What are the goals of incident analysis?

19. What is containment? Why is it important? What are some measures you can take to contain the damage from a virus attack?

20. What is eradication? What are some measures you can take to eradicate a virus attack?

21. How can incident handling improve an organization's information security in the future?

22. Treat the last semester as an incident. Write a simple "lessons learned" paragraph following a template

analogous to the template used for information security incidents. Appropriately anonymize/generalize the lessons learned to maintain your privacy.

23. What is a disaster? What is disaster recovery?

24. What is business continuity planning? What are some things you can do as part of a business continuity planning exercise for your personal data?

25. What is business impact analysis? How is it useful?

EXAMPLE CASE QUESTIONS

1. Which of the incident detection mechanisms described in the chapter led to the detection of the incident?

2. Who would be the appropriate people at the university campus to be notified of the incident once it was detected?

3. What lessons did you learn from reading about the incident?

HANDS-ON ACTIVITY – INCIDENT TIMELINE USING OSSEC

In this exercise, you will use the copy of OSSEC that was installed during the hands-on exercise in Chapter 9 to monitor a simulated incident and construct an incident timeline.

To begin the incident simulation, switch to the super user account and execute the simulator script:

```
[alice@sunshine ~]$ su -
Password: thisisasecret

[root@sunshine   &tilde;]#    /opt/book/
incident-handling/scripts/begin_incident
```

```
###########################################
###########################

Simulated Incident has begun!
This script will run for 10-20 minutes.

###########################################
###########################
```

Once the script completes, start the OSSEC-WebUI interface by opening a web browser and visiting http://sunshine.edu/ossec

QUESTIONS

1. How did the attacker attempt to access the system? What account was his/her target?

2. Once the account was compromised, were any other accounts compromised?

3. Was any new software installed?

4. Were any new network ports opened or closed?

5. Were any accounts added to the system?

6. Generate a timeline of the major events that occurred in the incident. A Microsoft Word template for the timeline can be downloaded from http://office.microsoft.com/en-us/templates/timeline-TC001016265.aspx

CRITICAL THINKING EXERCISE – DESTRUCTION AT THE EDA

The EDA report is very useful reading for anyone interested in information security incident handling. For further thinking, here is another excerpt from the report:

Despite recovery recommendations from DHS and NSA advising EDA to focus on quickly and fully recovering its IT systems, EDA focused instead on

building a new, improved IT infrastructure and redesigning its business applications. In September 2012 (8 months after isolation), EDA leadership presented to the Commerce IT Review Board (CITRB) a request to reprogram funds to carry out its recovery efforts; the CITRB did not approve EDA's request. EDA estimated it would need over $26 million disbursed *in the next 3 years (an increase from $3.6 million to approximately $8.83 million, or about 2.5 times more, to the bureau's average annual IT budget) to fund its recovery efforts.*

1. Those suspicious of large government would use this information in the OIG report to suggest that the EDA merely used the incident as an excuse to destroy its existing IT infrastructure so it could secure funding for brand new IT equipment, an instance of gold-plating its infrastructure. How would you support or reject this suggestion based on the information in the report?

DESIGN CASE

You are asked by the Provost to prepare a one-page document describing what steps you would take in order to create an incident response team and prepare for hacking attacks. Prompted by a vendor of cyber insurance who convincingly presented a doom and gloom scenario, the Provost and President are concerned that Sunshine University would not be able to act quickly and decisively to resolve any issues that may occur and this will affect the image of the university. In your report, consider the following:

1. What points should be addressed in an incident response policy?

2. Which units should have representation on the IRT and why?

3. Argue for centralization of resources in terms of campus security.

4. Research the reporting requirements in your State in case of a breach.

5. Research the protection offered by cyber security insurance.

Incident Analysis

## CHAPTER 12

Introduction

In the last chapter, we saw an overview of the incident handling process. We looked at the different phases:

- Preparation: Laying down the infrastructure to resolve an incident when it occurs.
- Analysis: Figuring out and documenting as much of the incident as possible.
- Containment: Given the results of the analysis, determine what is the best way to process and remove any lingering effects of the incident.
- Lessons learned: Apply the newfound knowledge to remediate any issues found during the process, going back to the preparation phase.

The cycle of incident handling never ends. As new vulnerabilities come about, new technologies are deployed, new challenges appear. If something is missed during the preparation phase, when the organization tries to be proactive about its vulnerabilities, it will inevitably lead to adverse events.

In this chapter, we take a closer look at phases 2 and 3, analysis and containment. We will:

- Look at sources of information within the Linux and Windows operating systems.
- Learn how to extract information from those systems specific to the event we are reviewing.
- Learn how to create timelines indicating the pattern of the event.
- Look at examples of evidence of attack on multiple applications.

Log analysis

Most software applications and operating systems provide some sort of logging mechanism to record status information. The purpose of logging the tasks on an application varies.

- **Software developers** use logging to ensure the application is behaving as expected. For instance, the software developer may decide to dump the output of an internal command to the screen in certain situations. This is commonly known as running the application in debug mode.

- **System administrators** use logging information to do performance analysis on the production instance of the application. For example, SAs may monitor the logs to make sure the application has enough memory and disk space to run properly.

- **Security administrators** use logs during the analysis stage of an incident. In fact, access to system logs is likely the first item a security admin will request as part of an investigation.

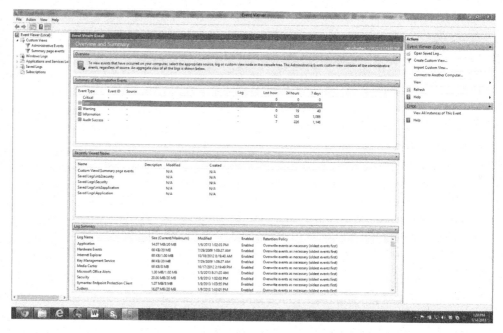

FIGURE 12.1 Event Viewer Screen on Windows 8

In this section, we will take a closer look at logs in general, both operating system logs and application logs.

Windows logs

Windows logs are also referred to as "event logs." Figure 12.1 depicts the interface Windows provides a user to peruse the logs. The program is known as ***Event Viewer***. There are other tools, open source and commercial, that can be used to dig into the event log files in Windows. A simple web search will come up with hundreds.

The left pane on the Event Viewer is the navigation pane. It provides the administrator the means to look at the different logs that exist in this system. On this pane, the administrator is able to create custom views, focusing on specific targets.

Event Viewer Home Screen

The Home screen of the Event Viewer, depicted in Figure 12.1, consists of three panes with different information on the log files.

Summary of Administrative Events pane   This pane contains a breakdown on the number of events per event type. If the administrator expands the event type by clicking on the "+" button next to the type, the number of events under that particular event type is further broken down by Event ID. Event IDs are classes of events under a specific type (Figure 12.2).

Recently viewed nodes pane   This pane contains the latest event log files viewed. It contains a description of the view (when available), the date the log file (node) was last modified (in

Summary of Administrative Events

Event Type	Event ID	Source	Log	Last hour	24 hours	7 days
Critical	-	-	-	0	0	0
⊞ Error	-	-	-	2	15	35
⊞ Warning	-	-	-	5	9	44
⊞ Information	-	-	-	24	627	1,595
⊞ Audit Success	-	-	-	68	223	1,192

FIGURE 12.2   Summary of Administrative Events pane

Recently Viewed Nodes

Name	Description	Modified	Created
Custom Views\Summary...		N/A	N/A
Windows Logs\System	N/A	1/14/2013 3:29:13 PM	7/29/2009 1:05:19 AM
Windows Logs\Applicati...	N/A	1/14/2013 3:29:14 PM	7/29/2009 1:05:19 AM
Windows Logs\Forwarde...	N/A		
Windows Logs\Setup	N/A	12/20/2012 8:09:35 AM	7/29/2009 1:08:23 AM
Windows Logs\Security	N/A	1/14/2013 3:29:13 PM	7/29/2009 1:05:19 AM
Custom Views\Administr...	Critical, Er...	N/A	N/A
Saved Logs\inb2security		N/A	N/A
Saved Logs\Security		N/A	N/A

FIGURE 12.3   Recently viewed nodes

Log Summary

Log Name	Size (Current/Maximum)	Modified	Enabled	Retention Policy
Application	14.07 MB/20 MB	1/14/2013 3:29:14 PM	Enabled	Overwrite events as nec...
Hardware Events	68 KB/20 MB	7/29/2009 1:08:27 AM	Enabled	Overwrite events as nec...
Internet Explorer	68 KB/1.00 MB	10/18/2012 8:19:40 AM	Enabled	Overwrite events as nec...
Key Management Service	68 KB/20 MB	7/29/2009 1:08:27 AM	Enabled	Overwrite events as nec...
Media Center	68 KB/8 MB	10/17/2012 2:19:49 PM	Enabled	Overwrite events as nec...
Microsoft Office Alerts	1.00 MB/1.00 MB	1/14/2013 3:26:01 PM	Enabled	Overwrite events as nec...
Security	20.00 MB/20 MB	1/14/2013 3:29:13 PM	Enabled	Overwrite events as nec...
Symantec Endpoint Prot...	1.07 MB/8 MB	1/14/2013 3:30:56 PM	Enabled	Overwrite events as nec...
System	18.07 MB/20 MB	1/14/2013 3:29:13 PM	Enabled	Overwrite events as nec...

FIGURE 12.4   Log Summary pane

other words, when something was actually written to the file), and when the file was originally created. Blank date lines indicate that the file was never created or log entries have never been appended to the file (Figure 12.3).

Log Summary   The last pane on the Home page is the Log Summary pane. It describes the attributes of each of the log files Windows is currently keeping. The Size/Maximum Column tells the administrator how much space is left for growth in the log file. If you see files that are nearing or at the maximum, it is likely that the records stored in those files are rotating and therefore being lost (Figure 12.4). This begs the question: how many days' worth of logs is the machine able to store before records are lost?

Usually you will notice that the Security Log will fill up the fastest, requiring rotation more often than the others. This is particularly true on Windows Servers. Depending on the user population of the server, extracting useful information from the Security Log files may be useless.

Also, note two more columns displayed on the Log Summary pane. At a glance, you can confirm whether a particular logging service is enabled, and you can also find out if the service is set to overwrite the existing information when the log file is full or discard new entries when full.

Types of event log files

By default, a few event log files are common to Windows OS since XP. You can see the Windows log files displayed on the left pane on Figure 12.2.

- The **application** log contains logging information from third-party applications and Microsoft applications not considered part of the operating system core distribution. For instance, video game log information, Microsoft Office logs, all these messages are logged within the application event log file.

- The **security** file is largely a repository of login and logout attempts by default. Its configuration can be adjusted so that it would log the creation and opening or closing of data files within the system.

- The **system** event log file holds operating system log messages. For example, network connection problems and video card driver errors are logged to the system event file.

  Windows 8 has two more standard log nodes:

1. The **Setup** node, which stores logging information regarding the installation of software applications.

2. The **Forwarded Events** log, which we will be discussed in a few moments.

Windows forensics example

Here is a quick, real-life example of using Event Viewer to gather data for analysis. At times even events classified as "informational" may carry important information for a security analyst. Take the screenshot from a compromised machine on Figure 12.5.

This computer had a McAfee antivirus installation running on it. Browsing through this log file, a few words should pop up immediately. In the general description, we see "Event ID 5000." This is not the original machine the log was exported. Therefore, Windows cannot tell which event generated the event. However, the included information points to "VirusScan

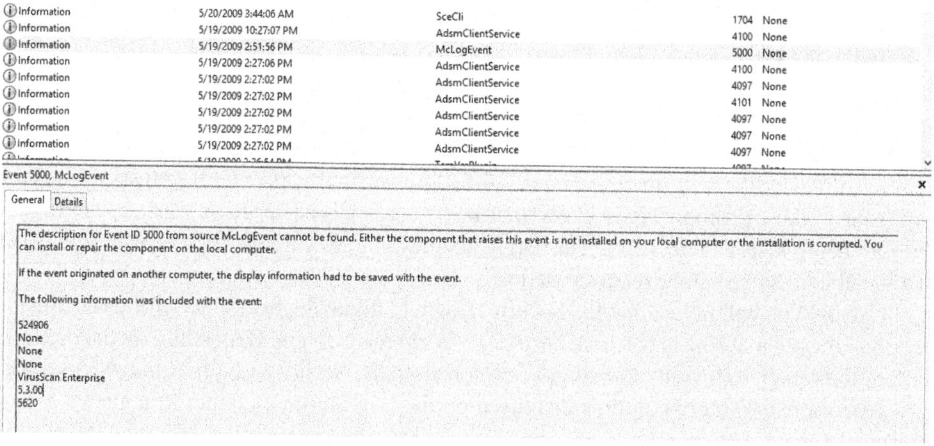

FIGURE 12.5 - Informational event screenshot

Enterprise" as the culprit. If you were familiar with the organization you would know that the AV engine version at the time of this incident was 5.4.1 (compared with the 5.3.0 text found) and the virus signature version was 5700, leading to the conclusion that the virus scanner was not up to date on this particular machine. An Internet search on "Event ID 5000" in connection with McAfee reveals that this could be an error raised if the On Access protection, the piece that keeps the machine from getting infected real time, did not start up successfully.

All of this information is from a single, simple informational event log message. At this point, the question on your mind should be: was the antivirus software application running on this machine at all?

Event criticality

Log messages are also tagged with labels indicating their level of urgency. When looking at the Event Viewer, you will notice that the Custom View folder contains the "Administrative Events" Custom View. This view comes installed by default with the Windows 8 installation and provides a view of all the "Critical," "Error," and "Warning" events from all administrative logs. These are the top level, most urgent log messages on a Windows system. Figure 12.6 shows a typical output of the Administrative Event view. According to Microsoft,[1] Windows has the following levels of criticality:

- **Information**: An event that describes the successful operation of a task, such as an application, driver, or service. For example, an information event is logged when a network driver loads successfully.

- **Warning**: An event that is not necessarily significant, however, may indicate the possible occurrence of a future problem. For example, a Warning message is logged when disk space starts to run low.

- **Error**: An event that describes a significant problem, such as the failure of a critical task. Error events may involve data loss or loss of functionality. For example, an Error event is logged if a service fails to load during start-up.

- **Success Audit** (Security Log): An event that describes the successful completion of an audited security event. For example, a Success Audit event is logged when a user logs on to the computer.

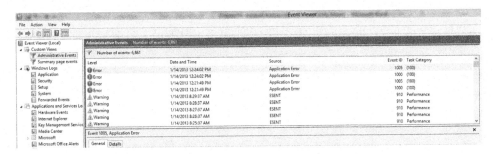

FIGURE 12.6   Windows Administrative Events view

[1]"How to view and manage Event Logs," http://support.microsoft.com/kb/308427

- **Failure Audit** (Security Log): An event that describes an audited security event that did not complete successfully. For example, a Failure Audit may be logged when a user cannot access a network drive.

UNIX have similar levels of criticality, but not quite the same. We will see those in the next sections.

When "Event Viewer (Local)" is selected on the left pane, the administrator is taken to the Overview and Summary page.

Unix logs

Now let's take a look at Unix logs. What we will see in the next few sections uses Linux but the idea, and very often the file locations and configuration files, also apply to other flavors of Unix, such as Solaris and AIX. For instance, one of the files we will look at is **/var/adm/messages** (Solaris) or **/var/log/messages** (Linux). The same file, with the same type of content, but in a slightly different location.

Syslog logging facility

Unix has a process especially designed to handle messages for programs that are "syslog-aware." As such, any programmer can use the facility to store log information on a location specified in the **syslog.conf** configuration file.

The syslog service is used by specifying what is known as **selectors**. Selectors are composed of two parts:

1. *Facility* specifies the service that produced the error message. Some of the available facilities are **auth, authpriv, cron, daemon, kern, lpr**, and **mail**. Log messages produced by the email subsystem, for instance, would be logged using the **mail** facility. Syslog also provides facilities for locally developed code to use. These are known as **local0** through **local7**.

2. *Priority* is one of the following: **debug, info, notice, warning, warn** (same as **warning**), **err, error** (same as **err**), **crit, alert, emerg, panic** (same as **emerg**). Priority classifies the message by criticality. Priorities are additive, meaning that when a priority selector messages with that priority and all higher priorities will be logged. For example, the selector **mail.warn** will match messages with the priority **warn**, **err**, **crit**, and **emerg**.

The configuration file is composed by combining a **selector** coupled with an **action**. The action could be:

- A filename, such as **/var/adm/messages**

- A forward to the syslog service on another host, such as @hostname

- Write the log information to the user's screen by specifying the username (or * for all users)

Here are some examples:

```
*.info;mail.none;authpriv.none;cron.none    /var/log/messages
authpriv.*                                  /var/log/secure
```

```
mail.*                          /var/log/maillog
cron.*                          /var/log/cron
*.emerg                         *
```

On line 1, all messages classified as **info** or higher priority regardless of facility (`*.info`) will be written to `/var/log/messages`. The only exceptions to this rule are messages with the facility `mail`, `authpriv` and `cron`. In lines 2–4, all messages with those facilities are written to their respective log files. Finally, all messages with the priority of **emerg** (typically only used if a system shutdown is eminent) are written to the screen of all users currently logged into the server.

Sidebar

There is a lot more to syslog configuration. There are also many syslog replacements, open source, and commercial, with improvements such as logging to databases. Unfortunately, these are beyond the scope of this book. The intent of approaching this subject, on Windows as well as Unix, is to give you enough background to be able to understand where to start looking for the logs. If you are involved in an investigation, you look at the **/var/log** directory and all files are empty does not mean someone removed them. It could be that the administrator simply put the logs in a different location.

Standard log files

When investigating an incident, the analyst should probably look at all files on the /var/log directory. Here are some of the most important.

messages or syslog   Most Unix implementations will include a messages file although some versions of Unix use **/var/log/syslog** instead. The information it stores, however, is essentially the same as the standard **/var/log/messages** file. Any and all informational messages using the syslog service goes to these files. As such, it is the first stop for an administrator looking for possible problems or a security analyst looking for traces of a break-in.

One of the nice things about Unix log files is that you can quickly dissect them using some of the tools we have learned so far. Take the snippet shown in Figure 12.7, for example. That chunk of log file was dumped to the screen with the following command:

zcat syslog.?.gz | grep -v snort | grep -v AptDaemon | grep -v dbus | less

```
Jan 13 07:30:01 inigo CRON[30617]: (root) CMD (start -q anacron || :)
Jan 13 07:30:01 inigo anacron[30620]: Anacron 2.3 started on 2013-01-13
Jan 13 07:30:01 inigo anacron[30620]: Will run job `cron.daily' in 5 min.
Jan 13 07:30:01 inigo anacron[30620]: Jobs will be executed sequentially
Jan 13 07:35:01 inigo anacron[30620]: Job `cron.daily' started
Jan 13 07:35:01 inigo anacron[30687]: Updated timestamp for job `cron.daily' to 2013-01-13
Jan 13 07:56:58 inigo cracklib: no dictionary update necessary.
Jan 13 07:57:09 inigo rsyslogd: [origin software="rsyslogd" swVersion="5.8.6" x-pid="722" x-info="http://www.rsyslog.com"] rsyslogd was HUPed
Jan 11 07:38:16 inigo kernel: [337129.385557] device eth0 left promiscuous mode
Jan 11 07:38:17 inigo rsyslogd-2177: imuxsock begins to drop messages from pid 5300 due to rate-limiting
Jan 11 07:38:17 inigo rsyslogd-2177: imuxsock begins to drop messages from pid 24379 due to rate-limiting
Jan 11 07:38:19 inigo kernel: [337131.708016] device eth0 entered promiscuous mode
Jan 11 07:38:25 inigo anacron[24018]: Job `cron.daily' terminated (exit status: 1) (mailing output)
Jan 11 07:38:25 inigo anacron[24018]: Can't find sendmail at /usr/sbin/sendmail, not mailing output
Jan 11 07:38:25 inigo anacron[24018]: Normal exit (1 job run)
Jan 11 08:17:01 inigo CRON[24910]: (root) CMD (   cd / && run-parts --report /etc/cron.hourly)
Jan 11 09:17:01 inigo CRON[25618]: (root) CMD (   cd / && run-parts --report /etc/cron.hourly)
Jan 11 09:17:49 inigo dhclient: DHCPREQUEST of 131.247.96.1 on eth0 to 131.247.174.245 port 67
```

FIGURE 12.7   syslog file evidence

which essentially directs the system to uncompress the contents of all files on the current directory from matching the pattern above, where "?" expands to any letter or number. Then remove any line containing the words "**snort**," "**AptDaemon**," or "**dbus**" and display the results through the pager command **less**. This was done to declutter the log file. In the Windows event log, this would be the equivalent of asking the program to hide any "Audit Success" messages for starters. This simple command line reduced the number of lines of interest from 3,600 to 1,000.

The reasoning behind the decluttering is simple. When you first start examining the log files, you want to look at abnormalities, odd events. Look at Figure 12.7 again. About half way through the picture, the following log line appears:

Jan 11 07:38:16 inigo kernel: [337129.385557] device eth0 left promiscuous mode

All log lines using the syslog service follow the same pattern: first a date, then the military time, the host name, the service logging the message, and finally the actual message. On this particular line, at 7:38 a.m. on January 11, the eth0 interface, the wired network interface that connects the host to the network, "left promiscuous mode." Ordinarily this would be a concern. An interface in promiscuous mode is essentially able to capture any and all data traffic it sees, including data packets that do not belong to it. In a switched environment, that may not be a problem. But in a shared environment, such as unprotected wireless access points, all traffic from all machines connected to this access point would be visible to this computer while in promiscuous mode.

Authentication log The next stopping point for the security analyst should be the authentication log, **/var/log/secure** or **/var/log/auth.log**, depending on the operating system. As the name implies, this file holds authentication and authorization information for the system. Figure 12.8 has a small sample.

This file was extracted from a desktop Linux box, containing no particular appealing data for a hacker. This box is what is known as a "crash and burn" station. It is set up, then destroyed,

```
Jan 14 00:17:01 inigo CRON[10982]: pam_unix(cron:session): session opened for user root by (uid=0)
Jan 14 00:17:01 inigo CRON[10982]: pam_unix(cron:session): session closed for user root
Jan 14 00:26:15 inigo sshd[11094]: Invalid user aadriano from 66.135.32.170
Jan 14 00:26:15 inigo sshd[11094]: input_userauth_request: invalid user aadriano [preauth]
Jan 14 00:26:15 inigo sshd[11094]: pam_unix(sshd:auth): check pass; user unknown
Jan 14 00:26:15 inigo sshd[11094]: pam_unix(sshd:auth): authentication failure; logname= uid=0 euid=0 tty=ssh ruser= rhost=host.insourceguy.com
Jan 14 00:26:17 inigo sshd[11094]: Failed password for invalid user aadriano from 66.135.32.170 port 47379 ssh2
Jan 14 00:26:17 inigo sshd[11094]: Received disconnect from 66.135.32.170: 11: Bye Bye [preauth]
Jan 14 01:17:01 inigo CRON[11694]: pam_unix(cron:session): session opened for user root by (uid=0)
Jan 14 01:17:01 inigo CRON[11694]: pam_unix(cron:session): session closed for user root
Jan 14 02:17:01 inigo CRON[12421]: pam_unix(cron:session): session opened for user root by (uid=0)
Jan 14 02:17:01 inigo CRON[12421]: pam_unix(cron:session): session closed for user root
Jan 14 03:17:01 inigo CRON[13133]: pam_unix(cron:session): session opened for user root by (uid=0)
Jan 14 03:17:01 inigo CRON[13133]: pam_unix(cron:session): session closed for user root
Jan 14 04:17:01 inigo CRON[13843]: pam_unix(cron:session): session opened for user root by (uid=0)
Jan 14 04:17:01 inigo CRON[13843]: pam_unix(cron:session): session closed for user root
Jan 14 05:17:01 inigo CRON[14551]: pam_unix(cron:session): session opened for user root by (uid=0)
Jan 14 05:17:01 inigo CRON[14551]: pam_unix(cron:session): session closed for user root
Jan 14 05:35:10 inigo sshd[14767]: pam_unix(sshd:auth): authentication failure; logname= uid=0 euid=0 tty=ssh ruser= rhost=5.79.16.183  user=root
Jan 14 05:35:12 inigo sshd[14767]: Failed password for root from 5.79.16.183 port 42917 ssh2
Jan 14 05:35:12 inigo sshd[14767]: Received disconnect from 5.79.16.183: 11: Bye Bye [preauth]
Jan 14 05:35:18 inigo sshd[14769]: pam_unix(sshd:auth): authentication failure; logname= uid=0 euid=0 tty=ssh ruser= rhost=5.79.16.183  user=root
Jan 14 05:35:19 inigo sshd[14769]: Failed password for root from 5.79.16.183 port 43352 ssh2
Jan 14 05:35:19 inigo sshd[14769]: Received disconnect from 5.79.16.183: 11: Bye Bye [preauth]
Jan 14 05:35:25 inigo sshd[14773]: pam_unix(sshd:auth): authentication failure; logname= uid=0 euid=0 tty=ssh ruser= rhost=5.79.16.183  user=root
Jan 14 05:35:27 inigo sshd[14773]: Failed password for root from 5.79.16.183 port 43658 ssh2
Jan 14 05:35:27 inigo sshd[14773]: Received disconnect from 5.79.16.183: 11: Bye Bye [preauth]
Jan 14 05:35:33 inigo sshd[14777]: pam_unix(sshd:auth): authentication failure; logname= uid=0 euid=0 tty=ssh ruser= rhost=5.79.16.183  user=root
Jan 14 05:35:35 inigo sshd[14777]: Failed password for root from 5.79.16.183 port 43746 ssh2
Jan 14 05:35:35 inigo sshd[14777]: Received disconnect from 5.79.16.183: 11: Bye Bye [preauth]
Jan 14 06:17:01 inigo CRON[15272]: pam_unix(cron:session): session opened for user root by (uid=0)
```

FIGURE 12.8 auth.log file

then set up again, and so on. Its purpose is to test new forensics tools. Look at the log file. Within a period of 6 hours, overnight:

- Someone using the login **aadriano** tried to login using ssh from **66.135.32.170**.

- Someone tried to login multiple times, probably with multiple passwords, to the **root** account from **5.76.16.183**.

Since there is no aadriano user on this box, we can only assume that this was an automated script, perhaps using a known password obtained somewhere for the user aadriano. A quick web search on the IP and the account brings up a web page from a *honeypot* site, a site which deliberately leaves itself open to attract and record intrusion attempts. The honeypot site has the actual passwords used on the attempts against it: **admin**, **aadriano123**, and **aadriano**. All attempts recorded on the honeypot site happened around the same date as our incident.

The next bullet is actually a bit more concerning. The IP belongs to a communications company in Russia. A search on the address reveals no records, no traces anywhere. While the first attack leaves clear tracks of being automated, the second may have been a targeted exploratory probe. The next step on the analysis process would be:

1. Check if the same IP hit any other computer on your organization

2. Check the full log, without the filtering, for the same IP

3. Check other log files on the same machine

Sidebar – Standard operating procedure for hackers

Once you get used to analyzing incidents, you will notice a pattern. Organized criminal hackers doing mass attacks usually split up their activities in three different phases, with three different teams working from three different locations:

First, comes the *discovery phase*. These are soft touches on your infrastructure in order to detect and analyze possible weaknesses. Port scans, limited login attempts like we've seen in this section, web server scans looking for specific vulnerable applications, all of this looking for the low hanging fruit.

After discovery, the *penetration phase* starts. The goal of the penetration phase is to use the information discovered on phase one to actually gain a beach head on the target organization. The discovery phase team turns in the information to the penetration team for the actual break in. Even if your systems were smart enough to block the connections from the first set of IPs involved in discovery, this new phase will use a brand-new set of address as the point of origin for the attack. The penetration phase activity would not be blocked.

Finally, we hit the *exploitation phase*. In this phase, some data may be extracted from the hacked machines. A few machines may be used to exploit other organizations. And a few may be left dormant in the hopes that it will not be discovered and contained.

wtmp   The wtmp file is not a text file, but a binary file which stores historical login and logout information. The Unix **who** command reads the **/var/log/wtmp** file and displays on the screen a list of the last logged in users. In addition, **last** will also report any reboots of the system

```
[2020][campoe.inigo: /var/log]$ last -a
campoe    pts/5        Tue Jan 22 09:13   still logged in    spinoza.acomp.usf.edu
campoe    pts/5        Thu Jan 17 21:55 - 00:31  (02:35)     pool-71-251-115-226.tampfl.fios.verizon.
net
campoe    pts/2        Mon Jan 14 10:25   still logged in    :0
campoe    tty7         Mon Jan  7 10:01   still logged in    :0
(unknown  tty7         Mon Jan  7 10:00 - 10:01  (00:01)     :0
reboot    system boot  Mon Jan  7 10:00 - 09:25 (14+23:24)   3.5.0-22-generic

wtmp begins Mon Jan  7 09:54:17 2013
[2021][campoe.inigo: /var/log]$ ■
```

FIGURE 12.9   Sample run of last

recorded on **/var/log/wtmp**. If you are looking for reboot times, the **last** command is always the easiest command to run and get a quick answer. The assumption is, of course, that the logs have not been altered. Figure 12.9 shows a sample output of the program **last** on a little-used desktop Linux box. It shows the user name, the pseudo terminal number associated with the login, the hostname, and the period of time the users was logged in. The "-a" switch at the end of the command tells the system to display the hostname at the end of the line. If that switch is not used, the hostname is shown on the third column and truncated as needed. That often makes it difficult to read the full hostname.

The wtmp file is rotated periodically. You may notice several wtmp files in /var/log, appended with a .1, .2, etc. These older files can be accessed by using the **last** command with a **–f** *<filename>* flag.

Sidebar – Admin's Best Friend

You can always find out more about Unix command and all the switches and options available by using the **man** command. For instance, **man last** will give you a complete description of the command, as well an indication of where in the system its log file resides. The man pages also cites related commands you may find useful.

utmp file   While the wtmp file stores historical information about logins, the **utmp** file indicates who is logged in to the system at the present moment. In some Unix systems, utmp is kept on the /var/adm directory. Most Linux distributions keep the file in /var/run.

Similarly to wtmp, the utmp is a binary file. Its contents are examined by using the "**who**" command. This command reads the utmp file and displays the username of those logged in, as well as some information about where they are logging in from.

Another, perhaps a bit more useful command is the "**w**" displayed on Figure 12.10. This command displays a bit more information about the system and it is usually one of the first things an analyst will run as soon as logged in. The **w** command shows:

- How long the computer has been up since the last reboot.

- Which real or pseudo terminals are being used.

- When the users logged in.

- Whether they are active or not.

```
[2033][campoe.inigo: /var/log]$ w
 09:53:28 up 14 days, 23:54,  3 users,  load average: 0.13, 0.08, 0.06
USER     TTY      FROM             LOGIN@   IDLE   JCPU   PCPU WHAT
campoe   tty7     :0               07Jan13 14days  4:22m  0.05s gdm-session-worker [pam/gdm-passwor
campoe   pts/2    :0               14Jan13 42:05   0.21s  0.21s bash
campoe   pts/5    spinoza.acomp.us 09:13    0.00s  0.12s  0.00s w
[2034][campoe.inigo: /var/log]$ ▉
```

FIGURE 12.10   Output of w command

- Load information.

- Command running by the user.

The output of **w** may not be very impressive on Figure 12.10, but it becomes quite useful on multiuser systems, where hundreds of users may be logging in and working at the same time. Let's assume that while executing the command. you see a user running the following command:

nmap 192.168.1.0/24 > ˜/.out/.output.pscan

Even if you do not know what the command nmap does, the fact that you have a user in your system who is storing data on a hidden file in a hidden directory should raise warning flags. A quick web search reveals that nmap is a powerful port scanner. The host specification indicates this user is scanning the entire 192.168.1 subnet. Even if this is not against policy, it warrants a check. If the FROM column displays a hostname that is not known to you, it may be time to enter incident response mode.

Web server logs

The majority of the incidents in the past few years involve some sort of web-based event, whether it is exploiting a Java vulnerability, downloading a tainted PDF file, or the ever so common SQL injection. In order to analyze this event, we need a sample of the web server log.

The following box shows a few lines on a log file of an application server running the PeopleSoft application. PeopleSoft uses a custom configured Apache web server as its front end.

```
xxx.2xx.89.16 - - [09/May/2012:11:41:37 -0400] "GET /login HTTP/1.1"
404 338
xxx.2xx.89.16 - - [09/May/2012:11:41:37 -0400] "GET /sws/data/sws_
data.js HTTP/1.1" 404 353
xxx.2xx.89.16 - - [09/May/2012:11:41:37 -0400] "GET /wcd/system.xml
HTTP/1.1" 404 347
xxx.2xx.89.16 - - [09/May/2012:11:41:37 -0400] "GET /js/Device.js
HTTP/1.1" 404 345
xxx.2xx.89.16 - - [09/May/2012:11:41:37 -0400] "GET /ptz.htm HTTP/1.1"
404 340
xxx.2xx.97.183 - - [09/May/2012:11:41:37 -0400] "GET / HTTP/1.1" 200
14257
xxx.2xx.97.183 - - [09/May/2012:11:41:37 -0400] "GET /authenticate/
login HTTP/1.1" 404 352
xxx.2xx.97.183 - - [09/May/2012:11:41:37 -0400] "GET /tmui/ HTTP/1.1"
404 339
```

```
xxx.2xx.97.183 - - [09/May/2012:11:41:37 -0400] "GET /admin/login.do
HTTP/1.1" 404 348
xxx.2xx.97.183 - - [09/May/2012:11:41:37 -0400] "GET /dms2/Login.jsp
HTTP/1.1" 404 348
xxx.2xx.97.183 - - [09/May/2012:11:41:37 -0400] "GET /login HTTP/1.1"
404 339
xxx.2xx.97.183 - - [09/May/2012:11:41:38 -0400] "GET /sws/data/sws_
data.js HTTP/1.1" 404 354
xxx.2xx.97.183 - - [09/May/2012:11:41:38 -0400] "GET /wcd/system.xml
HTTP/1.1" 404 348
xxx.2xx.97.183 - - [09/May/2012:11:41:38 -0400] "GET /js/Device.js
HTTP/1.1" 404 346
xxx.2xx.97.183  -  -  [09/May/2012:11:41:38  -0400]  "GET  /ptz.htm
HTTP/1.1" 404 341
xxx.2xx.89.16  -  -  [09/May/2012:11:41:38  -0400]  "GET  /robots.txt
HTTP/1.1" 404 343
xxx.2xx.89.16  -  -  [09/May/2012:11:41:38  -0400]  "GET  /CVS/Entries
HTTP/1.1" 404 344
xxx.2xx.89.16   -   -   [09/May/2012:11:41:38   -0400]   "GET   /
NonExistant1380414953/ HTTP/1.1" 404 355
```

On the sample above, the host 97.183 seems to be performing some sort of probe on the web server. Each line seems to be searching for a different application. Again using a web search, we find that "ptz.htm" is the front end for an AXIS security camera. The sws_data.js file belongs to the web statistics package Awstats. In addition to these findings, it seems like 97.183 is also attacking 89.16, which in turn is forwarding the attacks to this web server. Indeed, after further investigation, we determine that 89.16 is a proxy server for Peoplesoft.

Netflow logs

Netflow is a network protocol developed by Cisco to collect network IP traffic information. Through the years, it has also become supported by other network equipment vendors as the standard for this type of logging.

Here's a sample of information available from netflow. The lines were decomposed to facilitate the reading.

Date	Time	Source	Port	Destination	Port
Packets					
2011-12-01	00:11:19.285	66.2xx.71.155	34340	1xx.2xx.222.243	443
TCP 1 60					
2011-12-01	00:11:46.659	61.1xx.172.2	35590	1xx.2xx.222.243	80
TCP 1 48					
2011-12-01	00:18:58.992	71.xx.61.163	55194	1xx.2xx.222.243	80
TCP 3 152					
2011-12-01	00:18:59.594	66.2xx.71.155	36614	1xx.2xx.222.243	443
TCP 3 180					

Network logs such as this netflow log are key to being able to establish relationships between activities in multiple computers on the network. Besides the timestamp, the netflow logs indicate the source and destination of transactions. The port number is useful to determine the type of service running on the source and/or destination IPs. Finally, the number of packets is a good indication of the amount of information exchanged during that connection. From the snippet above, we can already determine a few things:

- 222.243 was probably running a web server on port 80. This is traditionally the port number for an unsecure (non-SSL) web server.

- The same IP was running a secure (SSL) web server on its standard port, 443.

- The amount of traffic on these ports is an indication of whether this was a popular web server or not. An out of the ordinary amount of connections could indicate that questionable content (such as porn, music, or movies) being distributed illegally.

- Since there was a web server running, it also means that there should be a log file somewhere on 222.243. If we want to find out what was transferred at a specific time we could find out, assuming the clocks on the netflow device and the web server were in sync.

As you can see, we can obtain quite a bit of information from four lines of netflow logs.

Other logs

Depending on the applications running on your system, you may have more logs to investigate which working on the analysis of the incident. The following are messages extracted from a server running WordPress, a Content Management System. It shows the WP application being attacked by a SQL injection attack.

```
[07-Dec-2012 02:40:49] WordPress database error You have an error in
your SQL syntax; check the manual that corresponds to your MySQL server
version for the right syntax to use near 'WHERE id = -1\'' at line 1 for
query SELECT text, author_id, date FROM WHERE id = -1\'
[07-Dec-2012 02:40:50] WordPress database error You have an error in your
SQL syntax; check the manual that corresponds to your MySQL server version
for the right syntax to use near 'WHERE id = 999999.9 UNION ALL SELECT
0x31303235343830303536--' at line 1 for query SELECT text, author_id,
date FROM WHERE id = 999999.9 UNION ALL SELECT 0x31303235343830303536--
```

General log configuration and maintenance

Operating systems and software applications come from the developer with default settings for log capture, but those default settings do not always fit the desired outcome. Like we mentioned in the beginning of this book, different IT personnel want to extract different things from logs, and what the user may want is not necessarily what the security analyst desires. For instance, the user may not care about records of login and logout to the desktop at all. Obviously, from the security analyst's perspective, that information is quite valuable. Therefore, the first task to accomplish when dealing with log configuration and maintenance is to determine the audience. Who will be interested in seeing the logs? Is there a compliance issue that requires the logs to be set up and record a specific activity? For instance, is my organization required by Federal Auditors to record any and all access to Social Security Numbers stored in my database? Is my organization required to maintain log information for a certain number of days? What information is the organization required to maintain?

These are all compliance questions, and compliance is not necessarily the same as security. Let's look at some baseline configuration changes and again ask the question "What should I be keeping?" with our eyes on the security aspect. Figure 12.11 is a screenshot of the entries on the security event log with default settings, from a Windows 8 Early Release installation.

We previously discussed the fact that the Security Log is usually the one that will fill up and rotate the fastest. And here is the reason: repeated, successful logins from users. In this case, we have a couple of options.

- **Increase the maximum log file size**. This would buy us some additional time and may be enough on personal computers to allow for a decent number of days retained. However, it is not a "one-size-fits-all" solution and may not be practical in an enterprise environment. The administrator may have to determine different log sizes for different computers depending on usage pattern.

- **Do not log "Audit Successful" messages**. This may sound like an acceptable answer, at least at first. However, it should not be option A for a security analyst. If you remove all successful logins from the logs you would also miss all the times when a hacker logged in to

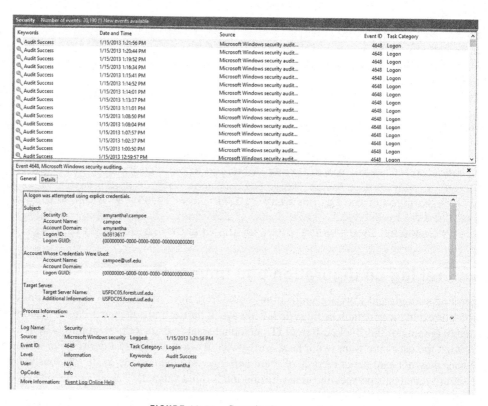

FIGURE 12.11 Security Log snapshot

the computer using a stolen password at 4 in the morning! See the sidebar on the next page for a practical example.

- **Rotate and archive the old file**. Another option would be to archive the file and start a brand new log. This is appealing because you can keep log files down to a short, more manageable size and keep a longer history. The drawback is the disk space usage. Let's say you'd like to keep the log files down to 20MB, keeping the last five copies. That would be 100MB for the security logs. What about the other log files? Usage may start creeping up.

The best option, if possible, is to transfer log files away to another machine dedicated to keep log information. Windows has added this option as of Windows 8. These exported events will show on the **Forwarded Events** log node.

The act of exporting logs from the original machine to a central box dedicated to log collection is known as **log consolidation**. From the security perspective, and compliance as well, exporting the logs is the best option for a variety of reasons. For starters, it allows for easier correlation of logs between different computers. With all applicable logs in one location, the security analyst does not have to go around gathering things. It is particularly difficult to collect logs if you do not know which hosts have been compromised. In a consolidated situation, the analyst could be looking on all access files for all connection attempts from one particular IP, for instance. The process is much quicker and simpler. And simple is good when you are in the middle of an incident. Minutes of downtime could translate into millions of dollars (Figure 12.12).

One of the very first things experienced hackers will do when they break into a computer, especially in an enterprise environment, is to clear and disable all the logs in an effort to cover their tracks. If the log entries are exported as they happen, in real time, to another machine, even if the local logs are corrupted, the security analyst will still have access to a pristine copy.

Exporting the logs also offers protection against the threat of abuse of privilege by administrators, since the server administrator can easily cover his or her tracks in a fraud situation by modifying logging information. Of course, here's the caveat: the logging machine, if set up, should **only** allow access on a need to know basis. Common practice is to only allow security personnel to access this computer, with read-only access handed out as needed to other administrators.

Live incident response

One of the first rules of forensics is to recover as much data as possible while the system is up and running if at all possible. At times, depending on the damage being caused, administrators have to shoot first and ask questions later, pull the plug on the machine, or disconnect it from the network.

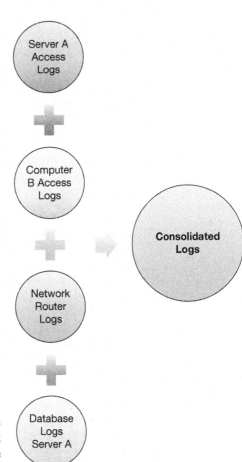

FIGURE 12.12   Log consolidation

However, if the situation allows, an analysis of the live, compromised system may provide investigators with more data. Live incident response involves the collection of both volatile and non-volatile data which the system is up. Volatile data is the data that would be lost on a reboot of the system: running processes, volatile memory content, current TCP and UDP connections, etc. Non-volatile data is the data stored in permanent storage devices, such as hard drives. Once collected, the data must be shipped off the machine through whatever means necessary. Popular applications used to send this data to another workstation (normally known as the *forensics workstations*) include **netcat** and **cryptcat**. Netcat creates a TCP tunnel between the computer under investigation and the forensics workstation, and it includes a MD5 hash checksum capability, which is desirable to ascertain the integrity of the data. Cryptcat is the encrypted version of netcat.

One such a program is the native *systeminfo* command. Figure 12.13 shows the output of systeminfo on a desktop Windows 8 computer. Interestingly, this is usually one of the first commands a hacker will run on a compromised computer in order to find out how powerful the machine is and how much storage is available. Systeminfo also specifies which patches have been applied to the system.

Sidebar – Hackers and patches

It is not uncommon for hackers to patch machines after they are compromised. This is not done out of the goodness of their hearts. They will patch the machine to ensure that no other hacker group gains access to the same machine.

In general, hackers prefer command line utilities so they can easily read the output and evaluate it from another system. It is common to find log files containing the output of these utilities all nicely wrapped up in one convenient package when investigating a compromised host.

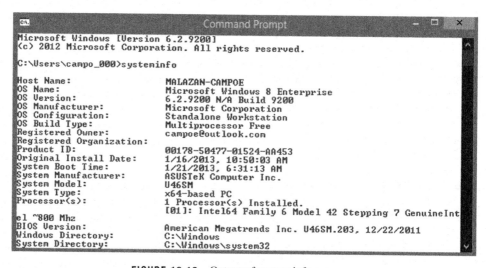

FIGURE 12.13 Output of system info program

Restoring files

Hackers generate logs. They also have payloads that are usually transferred to compromised systems, including the system profiling tools we have just discussed. These logs and tools are often removed from the system once the beachhead is established, but getting ahold of these files is usually a big plus for an investigation. Restoring files is also particularly beneficial on a personnel investigation, in a fraud situation, or irregular use of company resources.

There is a difference between **deleting** and **erasing** a file. Users normally think that by hitting the delete button on a Windows machine, they will effectively remove the file from the system. Other more sophisticated users realize that they must also "empty the trash." But few users know that even by taking both of these steps, the data associated with this file could still potentially be restored.

Here's a simplification of the process of file storage. When a file is stored on a computer, the data is sliced off into multiple pieces. The first piece will hold the information on **where** physically on the disk the other pieces are stored (also referred to as *metadata*). When a file is **deleted**, the operating system will delete the first piece, the address pointer, and leave the actual data pieces untouched but marked "usable."

In order to avoid data loss, the address pointer is replicated, sometimes in multiple locations on the system. If this first piece is rebuilt based on the backup pieces before the pieces marked available are reused, the entire file can be retrieved. Another method of file reconstruction is called *file carving*. With file carving, the carving application attempts to rebuild the file based on the contents of each data piece, and not based on the metadata.

Figure 12.14 shows the *System File Check* command being run on a Windows 8 machine. This command is usually run when the metadata for certain files are missing at boot time.

Sidebar

Based on the current conversation, how does one effectively "erase" a file? The simplest way is to overwrite the data pieces with random content. This removes all the actual information from each of the data pieces, making the file unable to be restored by carving or otherwise. Unfortunately, hackers have this information as well.

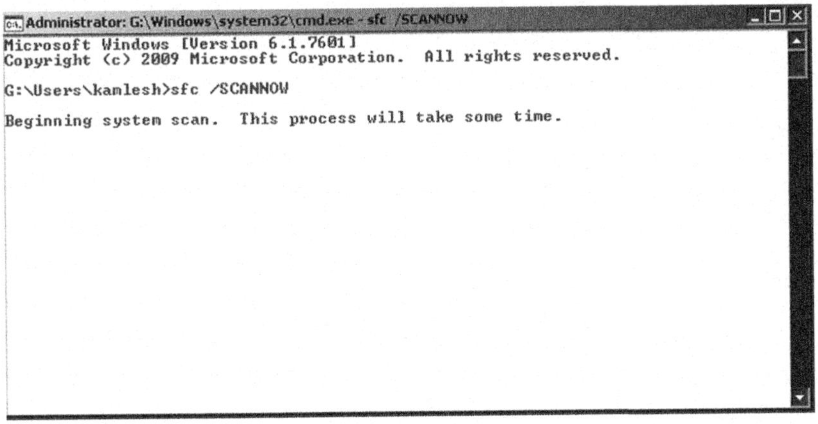

```
Administrator: G:\Windows\system32\cmd.exe - sfc /SCANNOW
Microsoft Windows [Version 6.1.7601]
Copyright (c) 2009 Microsoft Corporation.  All rights reserved.

G:\Users\kamlesh>sfc /SCANNOW

Beginning system scan.  This process will take some time.
```

FIGURE 12.14   The sfc command

MAC times

We already looked at timestamps for events found on log files of all varieties. Now we will talk briefly about timestamps associated with data files.

Every file, whether on Unix systems or Windows, have at least three timestamps associated with them. These timestamps are known as MAC times, and they are:

- **Modification Time** – indicates the time the file was last modified.

- **Access Time** – points to the time the file was last accessed or read.

- **Creation Time** – the time when the file was created.

Usually the Access Time is not very trustworthy, since it will change often. A virus scanner, for instance, may access all files on the system on a nightly basis when scanning for viruses. A disk defrag application may access the data snippets on hard drives in order to improve performance by removing "empty" spaces between data. Both of these activities could potentially affect the Access Time of files in the system. The tracking of Access Time may have even be disabled by the system administrator to improve file system performance.

The Creation and Modification Times, however, are a bit more reliable. While they can be changed programmatically, they are usually not touched by hackers.

So, let's assume that using the netflow logs, we find a suspicious SSH connection to a server we are investigating. Using the netflow log, we find the timestamp associated with the connection. Netflow also indicates a large number of packets being transferred into the server: some sort of payload was dropped into the system. However, the netflow logs would not tell us "what" was dropped. In order to find out what was the payload we have to examine the system in question. We could go blindly investigating directory after directory, trying to find out what looks out of the ordinary **or** we could build the server file timeline and determine which files were created around the time found on the netflow logs.

Figure 12.15 shows one way to look at MAC timestamps on a file in Windows. Simply select the file, right click, and then select **Properties**. You can also display the different dates on a whole directory by using File Explorer and displaying the appropriate column, such as in Figure 12.16. That would work for a quick look at a live system. However, if you need to examine an entire drive, it would be easier to use a tool that investigates directories in a recursive manner, such as **mac_robber** or another forensics tool.

Timelines

Once all the information has been gathered, it is time to build the incident timeline. Timelines are an essential part of the analysis process. Developing timelines on multiple machines and correlating them with each other and with network logs are a big part of forensics work.

Figure 12.17 shows a sample timeline for one of five different servers involved in an incident in 2006. The resulting report was 15 pages long and questionable activities on the Kenya server were often corroborated on the other servers. Scans initiated on Kenya were detected on Server A and vice versa. The entire timeline was built based on examination of a variety of log files found on the five servers.

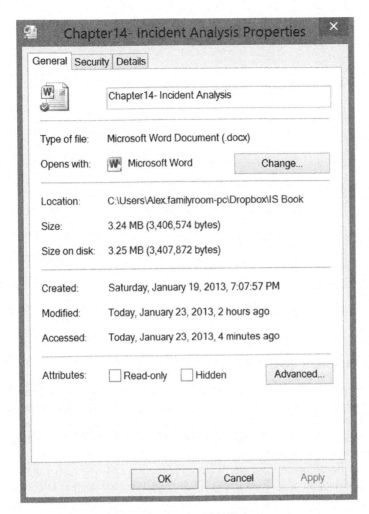

FIGURE 12.15 Windows MAC timestamps

Name	Date created	Date modified	Type	Size
Cache	1/19/2013 6:52 PM	1/19/2013 6:56 PM	File folder	
Cybersecurity Posters	1/19/2013 6:52 PM	1/19/2013 7:01 PM	File folder	
Final Drafts - Policies 2012 Revision	1/19/2013 6:52 PM	1/19/2013 6:56 PM	File folder	
Home Manuals	1/19/2013 6:52 PM	1/19/2013 7:17 PM	File folder	
IS Book	1/19/2013 6:52 PM	1/23/2013 5:44 PM	File folder	
ISW	1/19/2013 6:52 PM	1/19/2013 7:07 PM	File folder	
mSecure	1/19/2013 6:52 PM	1/19/2013 6:53 PM	File folder	
NotesPlus	1/19/2013 6:52 PM	1/19/2013 6:52 PM	File folder	
NUR3175 TO SHARE	1/19/2013 6:52 PM	1/19/2013 6:52 PM	File folder	
Perf Eval 2011	1/19/2013 6:52 PM	1/19/2013 6:57 PM	File folder	
Photos	1/19/2013 6:52 PM	1/19/2013 7:20 PM	File folder	
Public	1/19/2013 6:52 PM	1/19/2013 6:53 PM	File folder	

FIGURE 12.16 File Explorer with timestamps

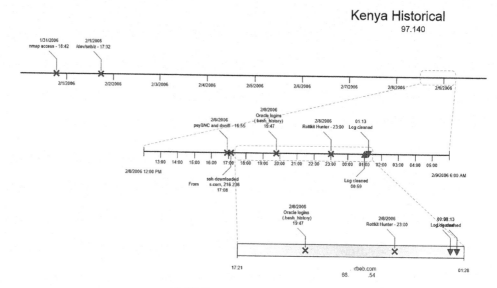

FIGURE 12.17 Sample timeline

Other forensics topics

IT forensics is an extremely broad topic that would require an entire semester to discuss. Proficiency only comes with experience in the area. Training is a constant, since computerized devices with network ability expand constantly, from smartphones to smart thermostats. More and more sophisticated electronic devices become "smart" and start taking a more integral part on the world we take for granted.

Some new developments are worth mentioning, as they bring major challenges to forensics. One such development is cloud storage. Take an application such as Dropbox, for instance. This is brand-new territory for security in general, as well as forensics. For instance, files stored with Dropbox are almost immediately shared with multiple computers in the accounts' Dropbox network. Also, files "deleted" on a computer Dropbox folder are not deleted on the Dropbox web portal and can easily be restored, as shown in Figure 12.18. How much access does an investigator have to Dropbox logs? Would it require a subpoena?

Smartphones and personal tablet devices also raise issues. We discussed the idea of BYOD before, employees using their personal devices for business, often times with access to proprietary, restricted company data. Forensic tools are now being developed that allow an investigator to analyze disk images and files from a smartphone. Most of these tools work on backup copies of the device, not on the device itself. This would imply either possession of the device in order to generate a backup or access to existing backup copies. Internal investigations are out, since gaining access to either one of these options would require the employee's cooperation (which is not always the case) or a subpoena.

Much like the rest of IT security, forensics has to keep up with the pace of technological evolution. Every time there is a new operating system revision, a new device with new filesystem types, forensics tools have to evolve and adapt to the new situation. There will always be a lag, and investigators need to be able to find alternative, creative answers when the situation requires.

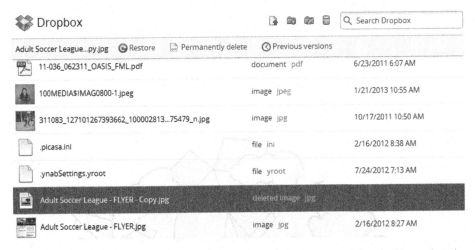

FIGURE 12.18   Information Security and IT Risk Management is not affiliated with or otherwise sponsored by Dropbox, Inc.

Example case – backup server compromise

Some time back, a computer housed in the information technologies department of a university was compromised. The machine was used as backup for credit card handling systems and was in the process of being rebuilt when hackers broke in. It is suspected that the intrusion exploited a known vulnerability in an outdated copy of the MySQL database server installed on the machine. The major cause for worry was that a critical file containing sensitive data was transferred from the machine prior to detection of the break-in. However, as a result of the organization's policies and their implementation, the file was heavily encrypted and therefore unreadable by the hackers without knowledge of the private key. This key was only possessed by two people within the organization.

The timeline of the incident is very instructive as it illustrates the blistering pace of these attacks and the need for prompt response by IT. All events listed happened on 1 day.

8:00 a.m.	Computer with IP address 1.2.3.4, registered to http://www.example.com, located in Tampa, FL, scans the entire university, gathering information on MySQL servers
10:21 a.m.	Computer with IP address 2.3.4.5, registered to Big ISP in Belgium successfully compromises the local computer
10:53 a.m.	Backdoor created on port 3000. This backdoor was used to run diagnostic programs on the machine and transfer data files
10:57 a.m.	Diagnostic tools uploaded to the server by hacker

11:01 a.m.	First diagnostic program (getallinfo.bat) finished. The program outlines the hardware profile of the machine, including • CPU speed • memory and disk space • listing of all patches installed • listing of the system events logged on the machine • complete list of all computers belonging to the same domain as the compromised machine
11:03 a.m.	Second diagnostics program (speed.bat) finished. It gathers some new information, including hardware information list of current processes running on the machine list of services information on user currently logged in
11:14 a.m.	File containing sensitive credit card information (datatodate.zip) was transferred from the machine. This file was heavily encrypted. The private key needed to decrypt the file is not housed on the hacked machine and is not believed to have been compromised
12:05 a.m.	Compromise detected and ticket created. Local administrators contacted
12:49 p.m.	File transfer backdoor restarted on the compromised server
1:00 p.m.	Machine removed from network by local administrators

The installation of the FTP server suggests that the hackers who compromised the server intended to make it part of a network of compromised computers used to distribute pirated software. What is surprising is that although this was not a targeted attack on machines containing financial information, the attackers nevertheless were able to instantly locate the file containing financially sensitive information. However, the information within the stolen file is safe due to encryption.

The following lessons have been learned and implemented following this analysis of the incident.

Access control list

The access control list is the first line of defense against attacks. The list is placed in the network and controls which machines are allowed to access services on the target machine.

Update MySQL server

This seemed to have been the source of the vulnerability that allowed the hackers to compromise the system. Therefore, simply patching the operating system does not solve all security issues. The local system administrator must be aware of all applications running on the computer and resolve critical security updates promptly.

Additional steps taken

- Full and complete review of operations and set up to assure secure environment.

- Program put in place to review IP access list and functional user system access to assure entries are necessary.

- Significant documentation on security measures and business recover plans have either been created or updated.

- Unnecessary open shares removed on production and backup servers.

- No longer storing these files on either server. If something is sent to our vendor, it is then deleted.

CHAPTER REVIEW QUESTIONS

1. What is incident analysis? What is the goal of incident analysis?

2. What is log analysis? What is the goal of log analysis?

3. Open up the Event Viewer on your computer. What is the most recent event in the Administrative Events pane?

4. What is the most recent entry in the recently viewed nodes pane?

5. What are the different levels of log criticality typically reported by Windows systems?

6. How can event criticality information in the Windows logs be useful?

7. What are the common locations of log files on Unix-based systems?

8. What is the syslog service?

9. What are syslog selectors?

10. What are the parts of a syslog selector?

11. What is the authentication log in Unix? How can it be useful?

12. What is the wtmp file? How can the information in the file be useful?

13. What is the utmp file? How can the information in the file be useful?

14. What information is commonly available from web server logs?

15. What are some of the benefits of log consolidation?

16. What is live incident response? Why is it important?

17. What are some basic principles of live incident response?

18. Why are timestamps important in incident analysis?

19. What are MAC times?

20. What is an incident timeline? Why is it useful?

21. What incident analysis issues are raised by popular cloud storage services such as DropBox?

    The following questions relate to your analysis of a faculty members hacked Windows laptop. You know this machine was hacked 3 days ago.

22. What tool can you use to view the event logs of the computer?

23. Which pane holds the Creation date of the log files?

24. What assumptions could you make if the Creation date of Application, System, and Security Logs are the same, 4 a.m. this morning?

25. Is there a way to have an educated opinion about the last time the hacker accessed the laptop?

EXAMPLE CASE QUESTIONS

1. How much time elapsed between the start of the scan and the theft of the file containing credit card information?

2. Had the attack gone unnoticed, what potential harm could have happened to the university?

3. What are some ways in which the detection of the incident could have been expedited?

HANDS-ON ACTIVITY – SERVER LOG ANALYSIS

In this exercise, you will analyze the server logs from a production web server.

To begin, let's look at the format of the log:

```
[alice@sunshine ~]$ cd /opt/book/chptr_12
[alice@sunshine ~]$ head -1 apache_
server.log
```

The file is the Apache "combined" log format and is made up of the following columns:

- IP address of the client (e.g., 127.0.0.1).

- The identity of the client according to inetd – this is a legacy field and is almost always set to "-"

- The username of the person requesting data if HTTP authentication is used, if authentication is not being used, this field will be set to "-".

- The time the request was processed (e.g., [16/Jan/2013:10:14:02 -0500]).

- The HTTP request sent from the client (e.g., "GET / images/gtalk.png HTTP/1.1")

- The HTTP status code (e.g., 200).

- The size of the transfer in bytes (e.g., 1506).

- The "referrer." The page that directed the client to request this resource ("http://www.sunshine.edu/").

- The "User Agent," which gives you information about the web browser and operating system used on the client ("Mozilla/4.0 (compatible; MSIE 7.0; Windows NT 6.0)").

Of these fields, there are only a few that we need to be concerned with. We will discuss why each of these pieces of data are important and demonstrate how to extract them using the cut command that you learned about in Chapter 10.

Client IP address

If there is a possible incident, you must know where the client is coming from. *Note: this data was taken from a production web server, so the IP addresses were modified to protect user's privacy.*

```
[alice@sunshine ~]$ head -4 apache_server.
log | cut -d"" -f1
YX.224.59.134
YX.224.59.134
YYP.63.193.132
YAY.247.53.103
```

Timestamp

Just as important is the client IP address, you need to know when a request was made to the web server.

```
[alice@sunshine ~]$ head -4 apache_server.
log | cut -d" " -f4,5
[16/Jan/2013:10:13:55 -0500]
[16/Jan/2013:10:13:55 -0500]
[16/Jan/2013:10:13:56 -0500]
[16/Jan/2013:10:13:58 -0500]
```

HTTP request

The HTTP request is broken up into three parts:

1. The method: GET is used for requesting data and POST is used for submitting data.

2. The resource (HTML page, image, PHP script, etc.) that is being requested.

3. The version of the HTTP protocol used. This is normally HTTP/1.1.

```
[alice@sunshine ~]$ head -4 apache_server.
log | cut -d" " -f6,7,8
"GET /favicon.ico HTTP/1.1"
"GET /favicon.ico HTTP/1.1"
"GET / HTTP/1.1"
"GET / HTTP/1.1"
```

HTTP status code

The HTTP status code the server sends back to the client. "This information is very valuable, because it reveals whether the request resulted in a successful response (codes beginning in 2), a redirection (codes beginning in 3), an error caused by the client (codes beginning in 4), or an error in the server (codes beginning in 5)."[2]

```
[alice@sunshine ~]$ head -4 apache_server.
log | cut -d" " -f9
404
404
200
200
```

User Agent

The User Agent string gives you important information about the client such as browser type and version and operating system version. *Note: this string is generated by the client's browser and can be modified, so don't assume this data is 100% correct.* This is often used in analyzing overall usage, such as determining the percentage of users accessing a web page with a mobile device.

```
[alice@sunshine ~]$ head -4 apache_server.
log | cut -d'"' -f6
Mozilla/5.0 (Windows    NT    6.1;    WOW64;
rv:21.0) Gecko/20130115
Firefox/21.0
Mozilla/5.0 (Windows    NT    6.1;    WOW64;
rv:21.0) Gecko/20130115
Firefox/21.0
```

```
Mozilla/4.0 (compatible; MSIE 7.0; Windows
NT 6.0)
Mozilla/5.0 (Macintosh; U; Intel Mac OS X
10_6_8; en-us)
AppleWebKit/533.21.1 (KHTML, like Gecko)
Version/5.0.5 Safari/533.21.1
```

Notice that we've used a quotation mark (' " ') instead of space (' ') as the delimiter for cut. This was because the User Agent contains variable number fields separated by spaces, but it always begins and ends with a quotation mark, making the quotation mark a more reliable delimiter.

Questions

Use the knowledge you've just learned on extracting the data from the file with grep, sort, and other string manipulation commands you learned throughout the hands-on activities in the text to answer the following questions:

1. How many unique IP addresses submitted requests?

2. What IP address sent the most requests? Were the requests successful? How do you know?

3. What is the most popular User Agent?

4. How many User Agents contain the words "iPad" or "iPhone" versus "Android"?

5. You've just been notified that there is suspicious activity on a machine in your network, YAY.247.114.164. Generate a list of all the resources (if anything) that were requested using this system.

6. Another web server on campus has been compromised through a vulnerability in the admin utility (wp-admin) of the Wordpress blogging application. It is not known what IP address the attackers used, but you expect that they are scanning other web servers to find vulnerable copies of Wordpress. Search the web server log for any scans and determine what IP address or addresses they are coming from

---

[2]http://httpd.apache.org/docs/1.3/logs.html

CRITICAL THINKING EXERCISE – DESTRUCTION AT THE EDA (CONTD.)

Much of the incident analysis at the EDA was performed by the external contractor. Here is what the OIG report has to say about the work:

> Within 2 weeks of beginning its incident response activities, EDA's cybersecurity contractor found the initial indications of extremely persistent malware were false positives – not actual malware infections. However, EDA's CIO sought guaranteed assurance that the components were infection-free and no malware could persist. External incident responders were unable to provide the assurance EDA's CIO sought, because doing so involved proving that an infection could not

> exist rather than that one did not exist. By April 16, 2012, despite months of searching, EDA's cybersecurity contractor was unable to find any extremely persistent malware or indications of a targeted attack on EDA's systems. Further, the NSA and US-CERT did not find nation-state activity or extremely persistent malware.

1. Do you agree with the standard of defense sought by EDA's CIO – an assurance that no malware could persist on the organization's systems?

2. Based on the report, what followed this finding from the contractor?

DESIGN CASE

The following is a summary of an incident you investigated for central IT.

APPSERVER1 was compromised in the evening of February 29, 2013. The hacker had access to the machine for about 1 hour. During his/her time accessing the machine, the hacker tried to access other machines within the Sunshine University network using a set of six different credentials.

The following investigative methods were used to determine the extent of the break-in:

- Extensive forensics investigation using Autopsy and Sleuthkit forensic toolkits to determine timeline of the events, locate and extract log files, backdoors, and possible keyloggers.

- Windows event logs were recovered and examined in detail.

- Inbound and outbound network connections to and from APPSERVER1 were examined as well.

- Special attention was paid to inbound and outbound traffic to the database server DB1, which holds restricted personal data for the university.

The hacker used a known password to Remote Desktop into the APPSERVER1 application front-end server. Further investigation revealed a list of credentials that seemed to have been compromised previously. The credential used

by the hacker to access APPSERVER1 was the only one still valid at the time. Password expiration at the university is set to 180 days.

Timeline table

2/29/2013 Sunday 7:31 pm	Initial signs of break-in, extracted from network flow logs. Off campus connection from 67.105.138.194 using Remote Desktop, registered to XO Communications and owned by Peaks and Plains Medical in Spokane, Washington.
2/29/2013 Sunday 7:37 pm	Machine is rebooted in an attempt to start a backdoor process listening on port 1034. These are usually FTP servers or bot control channels, allowing remote users to control the local machine without the need to use Remote Desktop. Sunshine University administrator is paged due to unscheduled reboot.
2/29/2013 Sunday 7:39 pm	Hacker attempts to connect to other machines within USF. Attempts were not successful.
2/29/2013 Sunday 8:42 pm	Hacker logs off the system. No additional logon attempts or hacker activity detected

QUESTIONS

1. When was the incident discovered and how?

2. What critical pieces of information are missing?

3. Based on what you know, what else would you consider looking into in order to make a better determination of the final consequences of the incident? Be as detailed as you can.

4. What would be your recommendations for improvement?

## CHAPTER 13

Policies, Standards, and Guidelines

Introduction

In earlier chapters, we took a broad look at the hazards and challenges organizations face when their businesses depend on data networks. Whether a government agency or private firm, all organizations face similar security challenges – how to best protect assets without impairing productivity and the bottom line. We also looked at various protective measures to protect assets, primarily performed by trained system administrators. We also looked at recommended procedures for reacting to adverse events, thereby controlling damage and minimizing the impact upon the organization.

In this chapter, we will step away from the technical world and discuss administrative mechanisms available to security analysts and system administrators. These mechanisms allow security administrators to guide the behaviors of IT users in the organization in a manner that reduces easily avoidable security hazards. Without these mechanisms, system administrators would spend enormous amounts of time fixing security problems that should not have occurred in the first place, at significant costs to the organization.

At the end of the chapter, you should be able to:

* Understand the difference between security and compliance requirements
* Distinguish between policies, standards, and procedures
* Understand the life cycle of a policy
* Identify a set of policies considered "a must" for any organization

Guiding principles

The administrative mechanisms used in the industry to guide end-user behaviors are policies, standards, and guidelines. These mechanisms allow security administrators to obtain executive level endorsement for information security objectives within the organization and translate these objectives to specific actionable items for all organizational members. When their experiences with handling incidents suggests to security administrators that the organization needs to change the way it deals with information security, they can bring suggested changes to the attention of top management for review. While top management is concerned about information security, it is also concerned that additional security usually impedes work, and can add substantial training costs to deal with the change. However, if the change is still warranted, top management will allow the change. The resulting information security practices are released as policies. Standards and guidelines emanate from these policies. Policies, standards, and guidelines need to be targeted and have clear objectives. In order to accomplish this, it is important to understand the basic principles of information security valued by the organization and use those principles as the underlying support of the policy. We will discuss some of these principles in the next few paragraphs.

First of all, the organization must comprehend the fact that security affects the organization and its employees and customers on a daily basis. Security is not something you do today, skip tomorrow, and then try it again next week. Sound principles of security must be embedded in any and all activities in the organization.

Next, understand the concept of "layers of security." There is no "one size fits all" solution for security problems. As a security analyst or a systems administrator you will find many companies out there trying to tell you that their product is absolutely indispensable and will resolve all your security problems. That will **never** be the case. If that was the case we would not see repeated in the news media, over and over again, cases of virus outbreaks, data leaks, and web defacements. The best way to fight back hackers, malware, and fraudsters is to implement multiple security systems in order to protect your asset. So, to protect the data in a file server you may have implemented a login system with complex passwords, biometric scans, a firewall, EPP, and encryption, hoping that one of these systems will catch a threat action.

Understanding other positions may also help with the writing of policies. Does the company prefer open source or commercial software? The different approaches may bring up different policy requirements. Does the company adopt one of the industry standards across the board, or is it more selective on what it adopts? Does it hire temporary consultants or does it strive to keep knowledge in-house?

Policy

According to the COBIT framework,[1] *"a policy is a document that records a high-level principle or course of action that has been decided on."* The emphasis here is on "high-level." Policies reflect principles endorsed at the highest levels of the organization. Executive time at these levels is very expensive, and these executives try very hard not to revisit an issue a second time. Therefore policies are written in a language that is general enough to deal with routine developments in business and technology. The other administrative mechanisms – standards, guidelines, and procedures – emanate from policies and provide specific actionable directions to all employees. Standards, guidelines, and procedures are written by experts such as system administrators and can change as the specific circumstances within the organization change. Thus, while a policy specifies a general direction for the organization to follow, without concerns for how to get there, standards, guidelines, and procedures focus on how to get where the policy desires to go.

For instance, the University of South Florida states the following on policy 0-516, SSN Appropriate Use Policy[2]:

> *Paper and electronic files containing Social Security Numbers will be disposed of in a secure fashion in accordance with state and federal retention and disposal policies.*

---

[1] COBIT 5 Glossary, http://www.isaca.org/Knowledge-Center/Documents/Glossary/glossary.pdf

[2] SSN Appropriate Use Policy, University of South Florida, http://generalcounsel.usf.edu/policies-and-procedures/pdfs/policy-0-516.pdf

There is no detail on how to dispose of paper containing SSN. The only requirement is that it is done "in a secure fashion" according to the law. The focus of the policy is that the records are disposed, and not how the disposal is to be implemented. That would depend on technology available, cost, etc. and will be described in standards, procedures, and guidelines.

Standard

A standard is a defined set of rules, accepted and adopted by several organizations. Some standards are referred to as "industry standards." These are activities, settings, and measurements that are accepted by all firms in an industry and should be considered the norm for operations.

NIST, the National Institute for Standards and Technology, is one of the foremost sources for standards in terms of IT security, at least for organizations within the United States. Even though their documents are usually carefully labeled as "recommendations" or "guidelines," they are seen as de facto standards for all organizations in the United States. Some examples have been seen throughout this textbook, and include the "Guidelines for Conducting Risk Assessments."

The International Organization for Standardization (ISO) is another organization accepted worldwide to produce standards with international scope. One of the most widely used ISO standards is 17799/27002, which deals with information security. According to their website, ISO 27002 *"establishes guidelines and general principles for initiating, implementing, maintaining, and improving information security management in an organization. The objectives outlined provide general guidance on the commonly accepted goals of information security management."* ISO/IEC 27002:2005 contains best practices of control objectives and controls in the following areas of information security management:

- security policy
- organization of information security
- asset management
- human resources security
- physical and environmental security
- communications and operations management
- access control
- information systems acquisition, development, and maintenance
- information security incident management
- business continuity management
- compliance

Once accepted by the organization, standards are mandatory. For instance, in order for an organization to declare itself ISO 27002-compliant, the organization **must** adhere to all regulations put forth by the standard. There is no such thing as "partial compliance."

Sidebar

In 2009, Symantec put together a nice poster referencing different standards and regulatory compliance requirements, in a clear fashion so the reader can quickly identify the similarities among each class of security requirement. You can find a copy here:

http://net.educause.edu/ir/library/pdf/CSD5876.pdf

Standards also are directly related and backed up by a policy. For instance, a policy could declare that all computers in the organization must have installed an end point protection solution put forth by the IT department and made available at the IT website. The standard would then specify which EPP should be installed. The advantage in this situation is simple. As we will see, usually a policy is harder to modify than a standard. By allowing IT to keep the EPP standard, the policy is allowing IT to make decisions in terms of EPP without necessarily having the burden of going through the entire policy life cycle and approval.

Finally, standards make a policy more meaningful. Take the example in the previous paragraph. Without a standard, EPP becomes a bit vague. EPP is a collection of applications that protect an end point. They **always** include an antivirus solution, but the following are optional:

- Host-based intrusion detection

- Firewall

- Scheduled virus scans or real-time scans

- Vulnerability assessment

- Website reputation

Without the standard, units would have a hodgepodge of solutions. The standard determines which of these options are important for the organization and forces all units to implement that solution.

Guideline

Guidelines are the procedures you tell units when "it would be nice if" things were operated or accomplished in a certain way, but it is not a requirement to do so. For instance, let's assume there is a new antivirus application that runs on iOS, and it works wonderfully. The IT department may be able to "suggest" that everyone should be installing and running this app on their devices, but without a policy stating IT has the ability to do so, this suggestion will remain a suggestion and will not be mandatory.

Some guidelines may evolve later to be standards. In a university without a centralized IT department it may be difficult for the security organization to must the support for a unified antivirus solution for all. That would involve convincing all units to give up their right to run any AV software they would like. Instead, IT security may be forced to put a guideline together, specifying the use of vendor "A" and the reasons why this should be done.

This scenario, when the reasons may be more political than technical, is when it is extremely useful to use the "carrot vs. stick" principle. If the IT security organization is able to

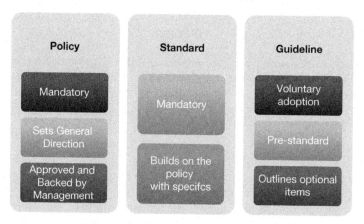

FIGURE 13.1 Policy, standard, and guideline

offer the software provided by vendor "A" for free to the other units on campus, many units will find the idea appealing and convert to using the software. This is the carrot approach.

But, to the point of this section, guidelines are adopted strictly on a volunteer basis. The document generated will continue to remain a guideline until there is enough authority granted by management to be able to make it a standard (Figure 13.1).

Why so much paperwork?

A typical complaint of technical folks is "why do we have to go through all this trouble? Why so much paperwork?" IT personnel are generally very hands on people, and documentation is not necessarily their forte. But the need to maintain policies goes beyond compliance. Done right, documenting these operations is not just added red tape and bureaucracy, it can actually improve the organization's functioning.

For example, security policies are a sign to customers, end users, and even employees, that the organization takes security seriously. For example, the City of Tampa, FL, posts the following on their security policy:

> *Providing you with a secure online experience is a high priority of the City of Tampa. We recognize that your information security is of the utmost importance, and we have devoted a great deal of effort to ensure that your personal information is safeguarded.*[3]

This policy indicates the importance the organization places on information security, which should be reassuring to concerned users. Policies also provide roadmaps for new employees and users. One common policy we will see in the next few sections is known as the "acceptable use policy" or AUP. The AUP describes to users the do's and don'ts of the system, things that are acceptable to do as well as things that would cause an end to services or employment. Here's a sample of AT&Ts IP services AUP:

> *Threatening Material or Content: IP Services shall not be used to host, post, transmit, or re-transmit any content or material (or to create a domain name or operate from a domain name), that*

---

[3]City of Tampa Internet Policies, http://www.tampagov.net/about_us/tampagov/internet_policies/security_policy.asp

harasses, or threatens the health or safety of others. In addition, for those IP Services that utilize AT&T provided web hosting, AT&T reserves the right to decline to provide such services if the content is determined by AT&T to be obscene, indecent, hateful, malicious, racist, defamatory, fraudulent, libelous, treasonous, excessively violent or promoting the use of violence or otherwise harmful to others.[4]

Policies force organizations to determine the value of information they generate in support of actual assets. Sometimes it may be advantageous to make this determination and document it in case of litigation. For instance, MIT has the following paragraph on their policy on retention of DHCP logs.

The DHCP server is configured to provide dynamic addresses automatically as needed. The logs of information are maintained on an IS&T-managed server. Each log is tagged with its creation date; once a day, the system deletes logs that are 30 days old.[5]

MIT is not the only organization to have their DHCP log policies in writing. Many universities do it for a very specific reason: to make organizations tracking violation of copyright laws aware that, if they are to pursue any infringement actions, they must notify the organization within 30 days (in the case of MIT) of the event detection.

Policies also ensure consistency across the organization. And consistency is a good thing. Academic organizations, for instance, are notoriously decentralized. Each college may have their own computing group, each administrative unit. While in terms of desktop support this model ensures that the individuals working on a workstation respond to the same person as the owner of the workstation, usually the College Dean, in terms of security it has the potential to create a panacea of solution. For instance, School of Architecture may decide that antivirus is a waste of funds and not to purchase any. College of Engineering may install a low-quality AV solution just because it is cheaper than others. College of Fine Arts may pay an exorbitant price for their license because they don't have the number of computers to be able to negotiate a better deal. A campus-wide policy affecting antivirus solutions would unify these units, forcing them to work with each other to achieve standardization, better pricing models, and many other benefits associated with consistent use across campus.

Note that this is not a statement that "centralized IT systems work better." Even if support is decentralized in an organization, certain aspects (such as security) must have a common baseline. Usually this can be accomplished by setting up minimum common denominators. For instance, the Windows Account Management Standard may be something to the effect that "passwords will not be shorter than 8 characters." This does not keep any department from making their own internal policy and having a password of a minimum of 12 characters.

Finally, the ultimate reason for IT personnel to support the development of a security policy is management backing. If the policy was developed the right way, inputs from all affected units and stakeholders would have been considered before its promulgation. This greatly improves acceptance of any constraints imposed by the policy. And much like the law, once the policy is in place, alleging ignorance will not exempt individuals from consequences. For instance, if the organization has a policy that computers not updating their virus definitions daily will be pulled off the network, and a user's computer is pulled off the network due to this reason, the user would have no recourse to complain.

---

[4] AT&T Acceptable Use Policy, http://www.corp.att.com/aup/

[5] MIT DHCP Usage Logs, http://ist.mit.edu/about/policies/dhcp-usage-logs

Policy cycle

Much like the incident response cycle, policies also work with cycles. Actually, incidents are often the driving force behind the creation of a new policy or the revision of an existing one. In the late 1990s, massive outbreaks of the "Melissa" and "ILOVEYOU" viruses drove the creation of centralized security policies for decentralized university organizations, and the naming of Information Security Officers for universities.

There are two separate and distinct audiences for a policy. An organization either writes policy for their employees and customers, or the policy is written to satisfy a state or federal regulation. Ideally the security administrator will be using the policy to address both audiences.

> At times there may be a specific need for formality in the writing of policies. We have all seen those policies before, when you need a translator next to you in order to figure out what the policy is saying. As a rule of thumb, don't use legal language unless you have to do it. Policies need to be written in such a way that employees and customers clearly and quickly understand what the writer is trying to say. If they are not written in clear language, the only audience the policy is addressing is the regulatory compliance, and it becomes "a policy for the sake of a policy": no one reads it, everyone has a vague idea of what it is about.

As often as possible, policies should be targeted at a specific issue. Some organizations write pages and pages of policies, expecting users to read and understand the entire document. By breaking up the policies into targeted segments regulatory compliance can be satisfied, and users will have an easier time finding what they are looking for. For instance, you may have one policy that addresses data protection, another that talks about user access, yet another that discusses data backup.

We previously mentioned that policies are often spurred by adverse events. When an event is large enough and grabs the attention of management it is common to see knee-jerk reactions in form of policy. We will discuss Impact Assessment in a few sections but it is a good idea to make sure policies that stifle productivity and usability are not put in place simply as a "knee jerk" reaction to an adverse event. Policies need to be well thought out and impact analyzed before adopted by an organization. This is especially true for security policies.

On one end of the spectrum, the security policies have to be strong enough to protect the confidentiality, integrity, and availability of the assets. Because of the need to protect, many organizations err on the protection side of the issue. However, you cannot strangle productivity and the mission of the organization in order to satisfy that goal. Your employees will have a tendency of keeping you honest as far as policies go. They are an extremely resourceful bunch, dedicated to doing their job or achieving their goal in the easiest possible manner. If they deem an activity or behavior to be the best way to accomplish their goal and you forbid them to do it, they **will** find a way around it. When your organization puts a policy together make sure users will actually be able to abide by them.

Now let's discuss the stages of the policy cycle are the following:

- Writing the policy

- Impact Assessment and Promulgation

- Review

Writing a policy

Now it is time to put pen to paper and actually start writing. Your organization may have a specific format for writing policies. In the absence of that, one of the best things to do is to search the web for similar policies from the same industry. So, if you work on a K-12, look at other schools and school districts. It is useful to look at your State first, since the State may have regulatory compliance issues that may have to be addressed on the topic you are tackling. Then, look at other policies, both nationally and internationally. This will ensure you cover as many sub-topics as possible.

Here we present a generic template which includes the sections you will find in almost any policy. The names may change a little, for instance some may choose to call the "Overview" the "Introduction", but the content of the sections will remain. For the sake of maintaining a similar thread throughout the section, the examples we will examine are all from higher education.

Overview

This is the first section in a policy. The overview tells users the reason why the organization decided that it would be appropriate to have such policy. Let's look at an example from the University of Arizona. This is from a general Security Policy[6]:

> *University resources, information and technology have become increasingly important to faculty, staff and students for academic and administrative purposes. At the same time, internal and external threats to the confidentiality, integrity, and availability of these resources have increased. Security breaches are commonplace and universities continue to be popular targets for attack. Critical university resources, such as research, patient care, business transaction, student, and employee nonpublic personal data, must be protected from intrusion and inappropriate use or disclosure. Devices must be set up and routinely maintained and updated so that they prevent intrusion and other malicious activities.*

In the first paragraph above, the university outlines that they value their institutional data. They also give a glimpse of some of the issues that will be covered on the policy. In the second paragraph, they elaborate on the purpose for writing the policy.

> *The purpose of this policy is to ensure that all individuals within its scope understand their responsibility in reducing the risk of compromise and take appropriate security measures to protect university resources. Access to university resources is a privilege, not a right, and implies user responsibilities. Such access is subject to Arizona Board of Regents and University policies, standards, guidelines and procedures, and federal and state laws.*

With this paragraph, they go back to some of the guiding principles we discussed earlier. Security is not the job of IT alone. Instead, securing their data is the responsibility of every individual in the university. They also set things up for the enforcement piece, stating that their access, including the access given to students, is not a right due to the paying of their tuition, but a privilege. And if the user abuses these privileges, there may be consequences.

---

[6] UA Security Policy, http://security.arizona.edu/is100

Scope

The scope section tells the user what or who is covered by the policy. Policies will always have a scope associated with it. Here's the scope for the Workstation Security Policy[7] at Emory College:

> *The workstation security policy is applicable to all workstations (Windows, Mac OS X, Linux) (including desktops, portables, and virtual machines) that fall under the administrative scope of ECCS.*

This is a very clear-cut scope. At one glance, the user can read it and determine whether their workstation is covered under this policy or not. However, organizations must be careful not to over-specify the target of the policy, unless there is a need for it. By noting *Windows, Mac, OS X, Linux*, ECCS is opening the door for loopholes. A simple ". . . and other Operating Systems" at the end of that list would cover the loophole. However, as is, a faculty member running an older Solaris Desktop Workstation would not be covered by the policy.

In another example of scope, the Kansas State University has the following scope attached to their Incident Management Policy:[8]

> *These procedures apply to all University personnel, units, and affiliates with responsibility to respond to security incidents involving University IT resources or data.*

KSU's policy is an excellent example of an Incident Management Policy itself, including data classification and very clear lines of responsibilities. If security is not the sole responsibility of the IT security group but instead it is shared by every user, this scope basically includes all employees and affiliates of the university every time institutional data is involved.

Definitions

Still in the "pre-policy" sections, where we set the stage for the actual policy, you may see a separate section for definitions. This is particularly useful when the subject matter of the policy may be unclear to the audience, or if the organization needs a bit more clarification on the scope.

As an example consider Georgetown's definition of ePHI, Electronic Protected Health Information:

> *Electronic Protected Health Information: ePHI includes any computer data relating to the past, present or future physical or mental health, health care treatment, or payment for health care. ePHI includes information that can identify an individual, such as name, social security number, address, date of birth, medical history or medical record number, and includes such information transmitted or maintained in electronic format, but excluding certain education and student treatment records. Not included within ePHI are student education records, including medical records (which are protected under FERPA), medical records of employees received by Georgetown University in its capacity as an employer, and workers' compensation records. Although these records are not covered under the HIPAA Privacy or Security Rules, other University Policies cover the confidentiality and security of these materials. There are special provisions in the law governing the release of psychotherapy records.*

---

[7]Workstation Security Policy, Emory College, https://wiki.as.emory.edu/display/ecitprocedures/Workstation+Security+Policy

[8]Incident Management, Kansas State, http://www.k-state.edu/its/security/procedures/incidentmgt.html

This definition is extremely important for Georgetown's HIPAA Policy,[9] since ePHI is at the heart of the HIPAA regulations. This definition not only specifies what **is** considered ePHI but also some clear examples of what is **not** considered ePHI, such as student records.

A popular term used in IT policies is "Information Resources." But what exactly is an information resource? Does it include an employee's smartphone? A student's laptop? A departmental fax machine? A faculty's telephone? Here's how the Marist College[10] defines Information Resources:

For the purpose of this policy, information resources refer to:

1. *All Marist College owned computer hardware, software, communications equipment, networking equipment, networking and telecommunications protocols, associated storage and peripherals;*

2. *All computer hardware, software, communications equipment, networking equipment, associated storage and peripherals that are connected to any Marist College information resource;*

3. *All computer hardware, software, communications equipment, networking equipment, associated storage and peripherals that store or transmit information that belongs to Marist College;*

4. *All data, information and intellectual property that may be transmitted over or stored on any Marist College information resource;*

5. *Any paper reports, microfilm, microfiche, books, films or any media containing information, data or intellectual property that is the property of Marist College.*

This is a very thorough definition of Information Resources. From now on in the policy, every time the words "Information Resources" are mentioned there should be no questions on what it refers to.

Statement of policy

We finally get to the section which will explain to the readers the actual policy we want to establish. The section will pick up all the concepts introduced in the first couple of sections – the purpose, the organization's guiding principles, the targets for the policy, and the definitions, and move it forward to the conclusion. The policy statement formulates how the organization will deal with a particular situation.

The next paragraph contains a piece from the University of Massachusetts Boston's Wireless Requirements and Procedures, discussing Wireless Access Points. WAPs are the point of connection between a mobile device and the rest of the network:

All WAPs connected to university infrastructure must be registered with IT and must comply with the technical standards and naming conventions specified by IT. The registration process requires information including the responsible university unit and designated liaison, as well as the location, purpose, and technical and operational information about the WAP. Registration can be accomplished using the online form located at the IT website. Such registration is intended for the identification of the WAP, to facilitate communications between all parties responsible for wireless

---

[9]HIPAA Policy, Georgetown University, http://policies.georgetown.edu/hipaa/sections/security/62953.html

[10]Information Security Policy, Marist College, http://security.marist.edu/policy.pdf

network support and operation, and to ensure compliance with all applicable UMass policies, standards, and guidelines, as well as federal, state, and local rules and regulations.

This is a common type of policy. Wireless Access Points or WAPs carelessly deployed on campus could easily cause problems. If settings are not done properly, individuals walking around campus could associate with the WAP accidently, opening themselves up to sniffing attacks. Also, tracking connections back to a particular user may not be possible.

Statements of policy will vary in length depending on the subject matter and the organization's choice of either grouping multiple security issues into one policy or splitting them up into multiple policies. As much as possible, the statement of policy will also outline the responsibilities for implementing the policy.

The Coordinator of Incident Response upon receiving a report is responsible for assessing its veracity, determining whether or not the event constitutes an IT Incident and classifying the IT Incident, and initiating handling procedures.

The above statement is part of Purdue's Data Security Incident Response Policy. It is just one of several statements specifying the responsibilities of the coordinator of incident response.

Enforcement

The enforcement section is usually the last section of the policy. It may refer to other policies for penalties. It is also rarely specific in the penalty. It will usually mention a range of possible measures, with phrases such as "up to and including" and "appropriate measures." These sections will also tend to use "may" instead of the more absolute "shall" or "must" used in the rest of the policy. Take Carnegie Mellon's enforcement section:[11]

Violations of this Policy may result in suspension or loss of the violator's use privileges, with respect to Institutional Data and University owned Information Systems. Additional administrative sanctions may apply up to and including termination of employment or contractor status with the University. Civil, criminal and equitable remedies may apply.

The enforcement section may also mention exceptions to the policy, or means by which a user would be able to apply for an exception of the policy. The same policy from CMU adds the following:

Exceptions to this Policy must be approved by the Information Security Office, under the guidance of the Executive Steering Committee on Computing ("ESCC"), and formally documented. Policy exceptions will be reviewed on a periodic basis for appropriateness.

The Information Security Office will not only approve or reject any requests for an exception but also review these requests from time to time to make sure they fit in with current tech threats, not putting the university at risk. Also note something common in policies in this paragraph: the exceptions will be reviewed "periodically." Not yearly, not every month, but periodically. This is done so that the ISO does not break its own policy by not reviewing them on a specific time table. If other pressing matters appear, the review can be delayed.

With all policies approved by the organization, compliance is mandatory. The following is another example, a snippet of the USDA security policy. It first specifies what was mentioned,

---

[11] Information Security Policy, CMU, http://www.cmu.edu/iso/governance/policies/information-security.html

that everyone involved with USDA data must comply with the security policy. Then, on the last paragraph, it speaks to the enforcement of the policy:

> *All users of information and AIS, including contractors working for USDA, are responsible for complying with this information systems security policy as well as procedures and practices developed in support of this policy. Any contractor handling sensitive USDA data is subject to the security requirements specified in this Departmental Regulation.*
>
> *Anyone suspecting misuse or attempted misuse of USDA information systems resources are responsible for reporting such activity to their management officials and to the ISSPM.*
>
> *Violations of standards, procedures, or practices in support of this policy will be brought to the attention of management officials for appropriate action which will result in disciplinary action, that could include termination of employment.[12]*

This paragraph does something very common to policies when it comes to enforcement. Instead of specifically stating that anyone does this will be fired immediately, it softens the blow by saying "up to" termination of employment. Making the statement in this manner allows management officials to apply their own penalties without necessarily having to fire the individual employee. In fact, this policy doesn't even set a low threshold for the enforcement. For all intents and purposes, a simple slap on the wrist may be enough.

Not to "pick" on this policy, but it is important to mention that this particular policy is also missing another important point required by COBIT guidelines. And that is the method for exemption. One alternative that would make this policy COBIT compliant would be to state that the perpetrator would be fired, then allowing an avenue for appeal due to special circumstances.

Impact assessment and vetting

Once the policy is written, it is strongly recommended that the policy be reviewed by all affected stakeholders. During this phase, the draft of the policy is circulated through stakeholders and feedback is requested. One of the questions posed to the stakeholders is whether the new policy or change in existing policy will have an impact on their department, beneficial or not. The organization has to be able to consider also the impact of a failure to pass new policy, as well as the impact of passing the same.

When we discuss policies and vetting the issue of Governance immediately comes up. Governance is the hierarchy of who makes decisions within the organization. In terms of policy, Governance reflects the committees or groups that have the ability to veto a policy before it becomes official. The University of Michigan[13] lists the following:

> *The following identifies the different levels of governance review and vetting of policies, standards and guidelines (initially drafted by IT policy development working groups):*
>
> *CISO/IIA Executive Director: Initial review of policies, guidelines, and standards*
>
> *IIA Council: First level of governance review for IT policies, standards, and guidelines*

---

[12] USDA Security Policy, http://www.ocio.usda.gov/sites/default/files/docs/2012/DR3140-001.htm

[13] Policy Development Framework, University of Michigan, http://cio.umich.edu/policy/framework.php

CIO: Second level of governance review for IT policies; final approval of guidelines and standards before adoption and dissemination to campus

IT Council: Third level of governance review for IT policies; new or substantially revised policies require IT Council approval

IT Executive Committee: Final level of governance review for IT policies; policies recommended for adoption as a new or revised Standard Practice Guide require approval of the IT Executive Committee.

There may be other levels of approval involved before the policy becomes official. Generally, in order for a policy to be applied to an entire organization, it also has to be vetted by other groups. Faculty members may have a say on the policy. Perhaps even student organizations. Some universities have specific "Policy Groups" setup with cross-campus representation, responsible for reviewing and approving or rejecting policies. Other universities handle policies within the Office of General Counsel. Here's an example from Cornell University:[14]

With the responsible executive's approval, the UPO will distribute the draft of the policy document to members of the Policy Advisory Group (PAG) in advance of a PAG review meeting. The responsible executive or the responsible office will present the draft policy to the meeting, where the document will be reviewed for practicality and clarity. After the PAG meeting, the UPO and responsible office will review and make accepted changes proposed by the PAG. Then, the PAG will recommend that the EPRG approve the reviewed document.

With the responsible executive's approval, the UPO will distribute the final draft of the policy to members of the EPRG in advance of the EPRG meeting. The responsible executive will present the final policy draft to this meeting, where the EPRG will deliberate on final approval of the policy, in particular its principles. The UPO and responsible office will make changes as directed by the EPRG.

Once the EPRG and the responsible executive have approved the document, the UPO will note on the document the date of final approval as the date the policy was "Originally Issued," and will promulgate the policy to the university community through a formal announcement.

The UPO (University Policy Office) handles the mechanics of the policy promulgation process. The PAG is the cross-functional group responsible for the approval. At Cornell the PAG actually meets from time to time to make policy decisions. In other universities, the vetting process may be done over email, with a deadline for comments to be brought forth.

As you can see, at times you may be talking several weeks before a policy goes through the promulgation process and is made enforceable. This is one of the reasons why technical details should be left out of policies as much as possible. By adding a reference to a standard on the policy and putting the IT organization in charge of the standard, things like minimum length of passwords, supported operating systems, and other dynamic IT items can be modified more easily with just an internal review.

While these extensive reviews appear to be unnecessary bureaucracy and red tape, they prevent the organization from developing policies that are difficult to implement, or which create inadvertent consequences among stakeholders. Rather than revise policies after encountering

---

[14]Formulation and Issuance of University Policies, Cornell University, http://www.dfa.cornell.edu/cms/treasurer/policyoffice/policies/volumes/governance/upload/vol4_1.pdf

resistance from these groups, and wasting your time as well as your credibility with top management, it is better to consider all possible problems with a policy before bringing it up to top management for approval.

Policy review

Once the policy or standard is created and promulgated, when should it be reviewed? There are a couple of triggers that should be considered, but one of the most common is the periodic review of policies. Universities are usually accredited by an outside academic organization. In Florida, that organization is SACS, the Southern Association of Colleges and Schools. Every 5 years, SACS sends a team of academic investigators to look at the university, its degree offerings, and overall policies and procedures. One of the things SACS specifically looks at is whether policies, including IT policies, are reviewed periodically. If a policy is 10 years old, has it been reviewed recently? Does it meet the current requirements of the institution? If not, does this reflect a systematic negligence on the part of IT? The rule of thumb is to have an internal review of all policies, standards, and guidelines at least once a year. Usually the folks in IT responsible for writing policies are also the same in charge of administration of the systems, to one extent or another. The yearly review period is the time when all triggers are considered to determine if a policy has to be reviewed.

One of the things that may expedite the review of a policy or standard is the advent of technology change. Ideally, the policy was written in such a way that new technologies may be addressed on the standard, instead of having to go through the entire promulgation process.

New projects deploying new or updated applications also may require a review. For instance, changing your employee portal to a new application could be a massive endeavor, which may very well require the change of policy, standard, and procedures at the same time.

Changes in regulatory compliance may require a reevaluation of governance. For example, the Higher Education Opportunity Act of 2008 forced universities to take a more concrete stance against the illegal sharing of copyrighted material, such as movies or songs. According to EDUCAUSE,[15] several sections of the HEOA deal with unauthorized file sharing on campus networks, imposing three general requirements on all US colleges and universities:

- An annual disclosure to students describing copyright law and campus policies related to violating copyright law.

- A plan to "effectively combat the unauthorized distribution of copyrighted materials" by users of its network, including "the use of one or more technology-based deterrents."

- A plan to "offer alternatives to illegal downloading."

Universities were required to make a good-faith effort for compliance by August 2008, even though the law was not going to be enforced until 2010. Failure to comply could result in massive financial losses for the university in terms of Financial Aid funds. Changes in compliances resulted in change in operations, which had to reflect on changes for existing policies.

---

[15]HEOA of 2008, EDUCAUSE, http://www.educause.edu/library/higher-education-opportunity-act-heoa

Compliance

Before we look at examples and some key policy issues, let's take a look at a topic that is commonly misunderstood: compliance. More importantly, let's understand the difference between a secure environment and a compliant environment.

Compliance, sometimes referred to as *regulatory compliance*, involves following **specifications** put forth by policies or legal requirements. Policies are often originated from (a) industry standards for the area, themselves driven by regulatory compliance, or (b) events with adverse effects on the organization. These legal specifications are often vague and confusing, especially in the case of compliance mandated by state and federal law. For instance, leak of Social Security Numbers in the past couple of years generated many State laws requiring protection of SSNs, without addressing the reason why organizations at times are required to collect SSNs.

But for security analysts it is important to understand the difference between security and compliance. Let's assume, for instance, that you maintain a highly secure server which stores restricted data for your company. In this hypothetical server, your company stores thousands of credit card information from their customers. You have set up 20 different controls to maintain the system secure, from a single account only known by you, multi-factor authentication, firewalls, etc. If the credit card data is not encrypted, no matter what else you have done to protect the data, the system may be out of compliance according to the Payment Card Industry (PCI) policy.

This is not to say that compliance is not important. Internal Audit and Compliance departments ensure that administrators and other employees adhere to the laws and policies governing the organization, so not to put the organization at undue risk. In the IT arena, the absence of an internal Audit and Compliance department that partners with IT on projects implies that the responsibility for abiding to all of the sources shown in Figure 13.2 are up to the IT department. If the compliance context is not available, security management and operations teams may well be doing what they believe to be the "right" things, but what could, in fact, be wasting effort and not achieving the needed results.

Compliance is a critical aspect of any project and, as such, should be considered at the planning stages of any endeavor. It is a lot easier to design with compliance in mind than to try to retrofit and accommodate those requirements later.

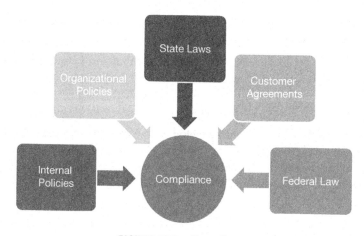

FIGURE 13.2 Compliance

Each state has its own set of regulatory compliance requirements. Some are directly aimed towards IT resources, such as California's Breach Notification Law. According to data-governance.com, *SB 1386 (the California Security Breach Information Act) is a California State law that requires companies that collect personal information to notify each person in their database should there be a security breach involving personal information such as their Social Security number, driver's license number, account number, credit or debit card number, or security code or password for accessing their financial account.*

Others indirectly affect IT operations, such as Florida's Record Retention laws. These are an extremely complex set of regulations with retention schedules that identify agency records and *establish minimum periods of time for which the records must be retained based on the records administrative, fiscal, legal, and historical values.*[16]

As if keeping up with State requirements was not enough, there are also Federal compliance requirements put forth by the many different laws and regulations, based on the type of industry or type of data your organization handles. Just like State regulations, some are directly aimed at IT resources. Others end up involving IT indirectly. Here are some of the best-known and most complex federal regulations. Any of these would take at least an entire week to study. We will just give you a brief summary.

HIPAA

The HIPAA Privacy Rule provides federal protections for personal health information held by covered entities and gives patients an array of rights with respect to that information. At the same time, the Privacy Rule is balanced so that it permits the disclosure of personal health information needed for patient care and other important purposes.

The Security Rule specifies a series of administrative, physical, and technical safeguards for covered entities to use to assure the confidentiality, integrity, and availability of electronic protected health information.[17]

GLB

The Gramm–Leach–Bliley Act (GLB or Financial Modernization Act) requires "financial institutions" to protect the privacy of their customers, including customers' non-public, personal information. Because universities also deal with a variety of financial records from students and their parents, universities also have a responsibility to secure the personal records of its students. Among the institutions that also fall under FTC jurisdiction for purposes of the GLB Act are non-bank mortgage lenders, loan brokers, some financial or investment advisers, tax preparers, providers of real estate settlement services, and debt collectors. At the same time, the FTC's regulation applies only to companies that are "significantly engaged" in such financial activities.

GLB is composed of two "rules": the Safeguards Rule and the Privacy Rule. According to the FTC website, the Safeguards Rule requires companies to develop a written information security plan that describes their program to protect customer information. The plan must be appropriate to the company's size and complexity, the nature and scope of its

---

[16]Record Retention Scheduling and Disposition, http://dlis.dos.state.fl.us/recordsmgmt/scheduling.cfm

[17]Understanding Health Information Privacy, http://www.hhs.gov/ocr/privacy/hipaa/understanding/index.html

activities, and the sensitivity of the customer information it handles. As part of its plan, each company must:

- designate one or more employees to coordinate its information security program;
- identify and assess the risks to customer information in each relevant area of the company's operation, and evaluate the effectiveness of the current safeguards for controlling these risks;
- design and implement a safeguards program, and regularly monitor and test it;
- select service providers that can maintain appropriate safeguards, make sure your contract requires them to maintain safeguards, and oversee their handling of customer information;
- evaluate and adjust the program in light of relevant circumstances, including changes in the firm's business or operations, or the results of security testing and monitoring.

FERPA

The Family Educational Rights and Privacy Act (FERPA) (20 U.S.C. § 1232g; 34 CFR Part 99) is a Federal law that protects the privacy of student education records. The law applies to all schools that receive funds under an applicable program of the US Department of Education.

Schools may disclose, without consent, "directory" information such as a student's name, address, telephone number, date and place of birth, honors and awards, and dates of attendance. However, schools must tell parents and eligible students about directory information and allow parents and eligible students a reasonable amount of time to request that the school not disclose directory information about them. Schools must notify parents and eligible students annually of their rights under FERPA. The actual means of notification (special letter, inclusion in a PTA bulletin, student handbook, or newspaper article) is left to the discretion of each school.[18]

SOX

The Sarbanes–Oxley Act of 2002 (SOX) introduced significant changes to financial practice and corporate management regulation. Passed in the wake of numerous corporate scandals, SOX is a complex piece of legislation that requires companies to make major changes to bring their organizations into compliance. The Act holds top executives personally responsible for the accuracy and timeliness of their company's financial data – under threat of criminal prosecution. Thus, SOX compliance has become a top priority for publicly traded companies.

In compliance with the Federal Act, the IT departments plays a major role in securing the accuracy and reliability of the corporate data. With the implementation of the Sarbanes–Oxley Act, information technology controls have become more popular. Here are some of the IT processes that would likely be investigated when checking for compliance:

- Security administration
- Data backup
- Change control
- Access control

---

[18] US Department of Education website, http://www2.ed.gov/policy/gen/guid/fpco/ferpa/index.html

Export Control Laws

Export Control Laws are a hot topic for research universities around the country. The laws prohibit the unlicensed export of certain materials or information for reasons of national security or protection of trade. Export controls usually arise for one or more of the following reasons:

- The nature of the export has actual or potential military applications or economic protection issues,
- Government concerns about the destination country, organization, or individual,
- Government concerns about the declared or suspected end use or the end user of the export.[19]

University research is subject to export control laws including the International Traffic in Arms Regulations (ITAR). These laws may also apply to research activities on campus, to the temporary export of controlled university-owned equipment including laptop computers containing controlled software or technical data, and to the shipment of research materials to foreign collaborators.

Key policy issues

Here is a quick rundown of some of the key issues any organization should be prepared to handle, either at the policy or standard level.

Acceptable use – The AUP is one of the main policies for an organization. It gives guidelines to users and customers on what is appropriate and what is not appropriate to do with information technology resources. Scope definition is important so that users understand what and who falls under the policy. The costumer AUP may be different than the employee's AUP. In a university environment they are usually the same. If there are any exceptions to the coverage they also should be mentioned. For instance, College of Medicine may need a stricter AUP due to the need for HIPAA compliance.

Information classification – This is the policy which outlines the definitions of criticality and sensitivity of the asset. Examples are important to clarify the intent of the classification. Definition of data ownership and custodianship are also part of this policy.

Network access – This policy spells out which types of users are allowed to connect to network resources. Students at the resident halls may not have access to datacenter subnets. Visiting professors may have to go through a special process to get network privileges. Visitors may only be able to access the guest wireless network if they use their cell number for registration.

Remote access – Specifies the acceptable means by which an employee is allowed to access resources from outside the organization network. This may also include requirements on accessing data through smartphones and other personal devices. Is remote desktop an acceptable option, or should the employee use a VPN connection?

---

[19] UC Berkeley, Export Controls, http://www.spo.berkeley.edu/policy/exportcontrol.html

Encryption – What type of data requires encryption? When is a web server required to use SSL? Do test and development environments also require encryption? Can certificates be self-signed? Is it acceptable to send restricted information unencrypted over email?

Contingency planning – Specifies the disaster recovery plans. The policy should establish a clear line of command in case of a localized or generalized disaster, with reporting lines and alternatives in case someone cannot be reached. It designates an executive as the appropriate person to be responsible for the declaration of a disaster. It refers to other standards and procedures for the specifics on what to do with each system in case of disaster.

Incident response – The incident response policy describes the general procedure in case of an incident with adverse effects in the organization. It specifies who is supposed to lead the incident response team, who will be in charge of communications, both internal and external. It will determine when an incident has to be escalated, and how to handle the escalation. It provides the chair of the IRT the latitude to make one-sided quick decisions in order to protect the organization's assets.

Authentication and authorization – What are the accepted methods of authentication? What roles can an individual user take? How soon after termination of employment will the user's account be revoked? Are departments allowed to request an extension to this time period? Who has the right to receive an account on a system?

Example case – HB Gary

HB Gary is an information security company with a subsidiary called HB Gary Federal. As the name suggests, this subsidiary aimed to attract information security business from various US federal agencies such as the CIA, FBI, etc. Unfortunately, due to weaknesses in its software and poor implementation of password policies, most of the company's emails were stolen by hacktivists affiliated with Anonymous and Lulzsec in or about February 2011. The publicity associated with the incident made a laughing stock out of the security company seeking security business from some of the highest security organizations in the world. On May 2, 2012, federal prosecutors charged five individuals with this and other associated crimes.

An article in Ars Technica describes the attack in detail. HB Gary had developed a custom content-management-system (CMS) with the help of third parties. Weaknesses in the CMS made the software vulnerable to SQL injection attacks. Exploiting this vulnerability, the attackers downloaded the entire user information from the site. Though the passwords had been encrypted, two key executives at the security firm – CEO Aaron Barr and COO Ted Vera – violated common password recommendations in two important ways: (1) they used simple passwords and (2) they used the same password not only for the CMS, but also for email, Twitter, and LinkedIn. This information about two of the company's most privileged executives followed by some clever social engineering allowed the attackers to download all the company's email and deface the company's website.

The indictment and the Ars Technica article are interesting reading. As is the Wikipedia article on Lulzsec.[20]

---

[20] Stephen Colbert had his take on the incident, "Corporate hacker tries to take down Wikileaks," http://www.colbertnation.com/the-colbert-report-videos/375428/february-24-2011/corporate-hacker-tries-to-take-down-wikileaks (accessed 07/23/2013). Warning: NSFW (not safe for work)

REFERENCES

http://arstechnica.com/tech-policy/2011/02/anonymous-speaks-the
-inside-story-of-the-hbgary-hack/

http://www.wired.com/images_blogs/threatlevel/2012/03/Ackroyd-
et-al.-Indictment.pdf

http://en.wikipedia.org/wiki/LulzSec

SUMMARY

In this chapter, we distinguished between compliance and security. Whereas compliance refers to following specified procedures, security refers to minimizing harm. We distinguished between policies, standards and procedures, which are the three primary forms of formal documents that guide information security in organizations. Given the relative permanence of policies, we walked through the generic process to establish policies that are best likely to accomplish their objectives. We also listed a minimal set of information security policies that we believe every organization should draft.

REFERENCE

SANS Policy Templates, http://www.sans.org/security-resources/
policies/

CHAPTER REVIEW QUESTIONS

1. What is an information security policy?

2. What is the goal of an information security policy?

3. What is a standard?

4. How are standards different from policies? How are the two similar?

5. What is a guideline?

6. How are guidelines different from standards and policies? How are the three similar?

7. What is the policy cycle? Why does policy development proceed through a cycle?

8. What are the components of a typical information security policy?

9. What is typically included in the overview section of an information security policy?

10. What is typically included in the scope section of an information security policy?

11. What is typically included in the definitions section of an information security policy?

12. What is typically included in the statement of policy section of an information security policy?

13. What is typically included in the enforcement section of an information security policy?

14. What is impact assessment and vetting of a policy? Why is this activity important before a policy is adopted?

15. What is policy review? When is it usually performed? Why is a policy review useful?

16. What is compliance? Why is it necessary? What are some of the laws with which your employer has to comply? (if you are not currently employed, consider your educational institution as your employer for the purposes of this question)

17. What is the difference between compliance and security?

18. What are the main compliance implications of HIPAA for information security professionals?

19. What are the main compliance implications of GLB for information security professionals?

20. What are the main compliance implications of FERPA for information security professionals?

21. What are the main compliance implications of SOX to top management of firms?

22. What are the main compliance implications of HIPAA for information security professionals?

23. What is an acceptable use policy?

24. What is an encryption policy?

25. Determine if the following should be considered as a **guideline** or worked through the process as a **standard**. Justify your answers.

   a. "All systems storing SSN must be registered with IT Security"

EXAMPLE CASE QUESTIONS

1. What are the provisions of US Code sections 982(a) (2) (B) and 982 (b) (1)?

2. What specific offenses were committed by the attackers, as listed in the indictment?

3. Based on the incident, what specific policy recommendations would you recommend for the company to prevent damage from similar attacks in the future?

HANDS-ON ACTIVITY – CREATE AN AUP

(Recommended: Form a group in your class to complete this activity.)

With your group, create an acceptable use policy for the use of Sunshine State computing accounts. When constructing the policy, consider the following information:

1. The policy will apply to all computer accounts belonging to students, staff, and faculty of Sunshine State University.

2. The policy should include a list of actions/behaviors that are prohibited with Sunshine State computer accounts.

3. The policy should include laws and/or regulations that affect the acceptable usage of system accounts.

4. The policy should include consequences for violation.

Once your group has created the policy, save it on your Linux Virtual Machine as `/home/shared/business_finance/information_technology/website/it/policy.html` which can be viewed at http://it.sunshine.edu/policy.html.

Create a three- to four-line summary of the policy suitable for warning users of the terms of the policy at system login and save it as `/etc/motd`. Be sure to include the URL of the policy so that users can read the full text.

`/etc/motd` is the "Message of the Day" file. It is a text file which is printed out to users when they login to relay important messages such as acceptable use guidelines.

Open a new terminal window and use SSH to view the message of the day:

```
[root@sunshine ~]# ssh alice@sunshine.edu
```

Deliverables

1. Submit a copy of the policy.html file.

2. Submit a copy of the /etc/motd file.

CRITICAL THINKING EXERCISE – AARON SWARTZ

Aaron Swartz was a highly respected and extremely skilled computer programmer. At the age of 14, he was one of the creators of the popular RSS service, which allows users to follow content from websites. Aaron also had an intense desire of getting information from behind pay walls so users could access the information for free. Unfortunately, the intensity of this desire led him to surreptitiously download almost all the contents of the JSTOR digital library of academic articles using MIT's network. Almost 4.8 million articles were downloaded in spite of repeated attempts to stop him.

This incident led to a criminal prosecution under the Computer Fraud and Abuse Act (CFAA), and apparently a demand from prosecutors that he go to prison as part of any plea deal. Aaron, long suffering from depression, was unable to deal with the stress and was found dead in his apartment on January 12, 2013. The death was considered a suicide.

Aaron's death generated intense pressure to revise the Computer Fraud and Abuse Act. Aaron's supporters were aghast that a genius such as Aaron would be pushed to his death merely for violating acceptable use policies and other contractual agreements. Rep. Zoe Lofgren of San Jose drafted a law called Aaron's law that would prohibit prosecution under the CFAA for violating acceptable use policies or other contractual obligations if such violation was the sole basis for determining that unauthorized access had occurred.

Other experts argue that Aaron's crime was not merely a violation of acceptable use policies. Aaron stealthily overcame the attempts by JSTOR and MIT to stop the contentious downloads, thereby guilty of false representation.

REFERENCES

(There are many articles about Aaron Swartz on the Internet. The following are the primary sources for this case.)

Schwartz, J. "Internet activist, a creator of RSS, is dead at 26, apparently a suicide," New York Times, 01/12/2013

Sellars, A. "The impact of 'Aaron's Law on Aaron Swartz's case," 01/18/2013, http://www.dmlp.org/blog/2013/impact-aarons-law-aaron-swartzs-case (accessed 07/16/2013)

Healey, J. "One bit of Aaron Swartz's legacy: Fixing a bad law?" Los Angeles Times, 01/16/2013

Computer Fraud and Abuse Act, http://www.law.cornell.edu/uscode/text/18/1030 (accessed 07/16/2013)

CRITICAL THINKING QUESTIONS

1. Do you think Aaron's death is the result of "prosecutorial overreach"?

2. You are the prosecutor in this case. Would you do anything differently, for example, settle for a minor penalty, given Aaron's immense contributions to technology?

DESIGN CASE

During a meeting involving state auditors and university officials you notice that many Sunshine University Deans and Directors make extensive use of tablets and smartphones. Not only that, but they also use applications such as Google Drive and Dropbox to move documents from one device to another seamlessly. You bring this concern to the Dean of the College of Business, who is sitting next to you in this meeting.

Write a policy on the use of cloud-based personal storage space to store university institutional data. The policy must have an overview, scope, definitions, statement of policy, and enforcement. At a minimum, consider and address the following:

• The policy will only apply to the College of Business.

• Is the general guidance that users should or should not store data on the cloud? Please justify.

• Is there any class of data that must never be stored on personal cloud accounts?

• Will the enforcement measures be different for faculty and students?

In addition to the policy, research and outline the Terms of Service for two personal cloud-storage services, indicating any possible problems these terms of services may bring to the university and to the user, including limited liability, uptime restrictions, etc.

## CHAPTER 14

IT Risk Analysis and Risk Management

Overview

This chapter integrates most of the concepts discussed in previous chapters into an overall framework to deal with information security. The previous chapters have taken a bottom-up approach to security, discussing individual concepts in detail. This chapter takes a top-down approach, beginning with the concerns of society and top management as they relate to information security. These constituencies are less concerned with the technology and more interested in minimizing the economic impacts of information security. The phrase "IT risk management" organizes all issues associated with information security, utilizing inputs from both management and technology experts.

Issues important to top management typically receive lot of attention from many quarters. Since top management cares about risk management,[1] a number of popular IT risk-management frameworks have emerged. We provide a quick tour of these frameworks. We then distill ideas from these frameworks to create a risk-management framework that is consistent with the standard frameworks we have used for other related concepts in earlier chapters. At the end of this chapter, you should know:

- The relevance of risk management to top management
- IT risk-management frameworks
- Risk analysis – identification and assessment
- Risk management – mitigation, preparation, and response

Introduction

Risk is a quantitative measure of the potential damage caused by a specified threat. In prior chapters, we have built up the knowledge base required to analyze and manage risks. In Chapter 6, we have discussed threats in detail. We can build on that idea in this chapter to discuss an issue that draws the attention of top management – risk management.

Since risk management is driven by top management concerns, in this introductory section, we set the topic of risk management within the overall context of managing an organization.

---

[1] In spite of this concern, only about 5% – 25% of Fortune 500 companies are prepared to deal with crises. These crisis-prepared companies have to tackle about 33% fewer crises, live about 25% longer, have double the ROA and have higher reputations than companies that just react to crises (Mitroff, I. I. and M. C. Alpaslan (2003). "Preparing for evil." Harvard Business Review 2003(April): 109–115.).

We then discuss the standard risk-management framework developed by NIST to guide IT risk-management activities.

Risk management as a component of organizational management

The performance of an organization is assessed using some measure of profitability.[2] More profitable organizations are more valuable than less profitable organizations. Accordingly, the primary focus of managers is to maximize their organization's profits. We may write this managerial concern as:

$$\text{Manager's decision problem} = \max(\text{profit}) = \max(\text{Revenues} - \text{cost})$$

Managers can accomplish this goal by using some combination of increasing revenues (generally by raising prices or selling more units) or by reducing costs. Much of the management literature and most of the typical MBA curriculum are devoted to guiding managers to reach these goals. However, when running organizations on a day-to-day basis, managers find unusual things happening all the time, many of which can significantly affect the organization's profit-maximizing equation. For example, we have seen earlier how TJ Maxx made provisions for $118 million to deal with the fallout from its credit card incident. Since these incidents can affect the organization's profits, they need to be managed. At a very high level, *managing the financial impacts of unusual events is called risk management*. To represent this, we can modify the manager's decision problem as:

$$\max(\text{Revenues} - \text{cost} - \Delta), \text{ where } \Delta \text{ is the impact of unusual events on the organization.}[3]$$

There are broadly two approaches to risk management: (1) making risks (Δ) predictable and (2) minimizing and preparing for these risks.

The standard approaches for making risks predictable are insurance and hedging. These are some of the most important activities of the financial sector of the economy. For example, buying flood insurance for your datacenter makes the financial impact of flood events predictable, equal to the annual premium paid to buy the insurance. While the idea sounds unusual, you should know that this is an important component of IT risk management. We (the authors) are not experts in designing and pricing financial instruments, so we leave the details of this approach to the experts in finance. However, we would like to emphasize that top management understands this approach well and always considers it seriously. So, do not be surprised if you hear the term "insurance" in the context of IT risk management.

That leaves us with minimizing and preparing for risks. This is the approach we discuss in the rest of this chapter.

---

[2] Not all organizations aim for profitability. Non-profitable organizations such as universities are a huge sector of the economy, accounting for over 10% of all US jobs (http://www.urban.org/nonprofits/index.cfm). While these organizations measure their outputs using criteria such as number of students graduated and number of patents obtained, even these organizations are concerned with putting their resources to optimal use, and their managers share most of the same risk-managers concerns as managers in for-profit organizations

[3] Δ stands for delta, an industry-standard term for deviations from normal behavior

Another classification that we find interesting is between offense and defense. All sports teams have a mix of offense and defense. In our domain, organizations invest in IT as an offensive measure in the profit equation – to attack costs and complexity or to battle for customers in more markets. Information security is the defensive arm of the equation. It focuses on ensuring that the organization's existing competitive advantage is not lost due to improper IT implementations.[4,5]

With this background, we will now look at the standard IT risk-management framework developed by NIST.

Statutory reporting of risk factors by top management

As an example of the importance of risk management to top executives, publicly traded companies are required by law to report the risk factors facing their company to investors.

Item 1A. Risk Factors.[6]

Set forth, under the caption "Risk Factors," where appropriate, the risk factors described in Item 503(c) of Regulation S-K (§229.503(c) of this chapter) applicable to the registrant. Provide any discussion of risk factors in plain English in accordance with Rule 421(d) of the Securities Act of 1933 (§230.421(d) of this chapter). Smaller reporting companies are not required to provide the information required by this item.

From §229.503(c),[7] risk factors for newly issued securities include, among other things, the following: (1) lack of an operating history; (2) lack of profitable operations in recent periods; (3) financial position; (4) business or proposed business; or (5) lack of a market for your common equity securities or securities convertible into or exercisable for common equity securities.

Example: AAPL 10-K (Oct 31, 2012)[8]

In its 10-K filed on 10/31/2012, among other risk factors, Apple reported the following two risk factors, which directly to IT:

The Company's business and reputation may be impacted by information technology system failures or network disruptions.

The Company may be subject to breaches of its information technology systems, which could damage business partner and customer relationships, curtail or otherwise adversely impact access to online stores and services, and could subject the Company to significant reputational, financial, legal, and operational consequences.

Risk-management framework

A framework is a structure for supporting something else. In the management literature, frameworks are used when a large number of ideas are to be organized in a manner that can be

---

[4] One of our students summarized this idea by reminding us of the quote: "*Offense sells tickets, defense wins championships*"

[5] Another related area is ensuring that new risks created in the organization due to IT investments are well managed. For example, some spectacular financial losses have occurred because of rapid financial trading enabled by IT systems. This is also not discussed in this chapter. But an excellent discussion can be found in *Westerman, G. and Hunter, R. (2007). IT Risk: Turning Business Threats into Competitive Advantage (Hardcover). Boston, MA, Harvard Business School Press*

[6] http://www.sec.gov/about/forms/form10-k.pdf

[7] http://www.law.cornell.edu/cfr/text/17/229.503

[8] http://investor.apple.com/

understood and memorized by many people, i.e., management frameworks support the organization of related concepts to accomplish a goal of interest.

Many frameworks are popular for risk management, including CERT's OCTAVE, ISO 27002 from the International Standards Organization, and the NIST 800-39 guidelines on managing information security risk. In addition, leading vendors such as Microsoft[9] and Google[10] publish their own recommendations for information security risk management. All of these guidelines present similar ideas and represent the results of the collective efforts of the best minds in the industry to manage IT risks. Any of these guidelines would be an excellent basis to develop an information risk-management plan for your organization.

> It is strongly recommended that you adopt and follow one of the standard risk-management frameworks to develop your risk-management plan, making any adjustments for your specific context. It is generally a bad idea to develop your own risk-management plan from scratch. You are very likely to miss many important concerns, which you will only discover at great cost when a threat exposes the omission in your risk-management framework. It would be wise to remember Benjamin Franklin on this matter, "*experience keeps a dear school, yet fools learn in no other.*"

Our preference in this book is to present ideas in a consistent manner across chapters. We believe it facilitates comprehension and memorability. We find the NIST 800-39 guidelines to be the most suitable for our purpose since it is very compatible with the way we have presented information in earlier chapters. Accordingly, we base the rest of this chapter on these guidelines. We integrate many of the ideas covered in earlier chapters (such as the threat model and the disaster life cycle) within the NIST risk-management framework. For completeness, toward the end of this chapter, we also provide a quick overview of the other popular frameworks.

The NIST 800-39 framework

The NIST recommendations for managing information security risk are published as special publication 800-39.[11] The current version is dated on March 2011. The 800-39 guidelines were developed with inputs from the Civil, Defense, and Intelligence Communities to provide an information security framework for the federal government. The 800-39 guidelines (and the discussion in this chapter) are very general and do not attend to the specific concerns of high-security environments such as military bases or special laws such as HIPAA. Those environments will use more stringent procedures than those suggested by NIST 800-39. However, the 800-39 framework is very useful for the majority of commercial and non-profit organizations and hence are suitable for our purposes. If you work in a high-security environment such as a military base or bank, the institution will provide you with additional risk-management guidelines specific to that environment.

IT risk is defined as the risk associated with the use of information systems in an organization. This is one of the many risks facing organizations. NIST recognizes that risk management is not an exact science. It is the best collective judgment of people at all ranks and functions

---

[9] http://technet.microsoft.com/en-us/library/cc163143.aspx

[10] https://cloud.google.com/files/Google-CommonSecurity-WhitePaper-v1.4.pdf

[11] http://csrc.nist.gov/publications/nistpubs/800-39/SP800-39-final.pdf (accessed 12/20/2012)

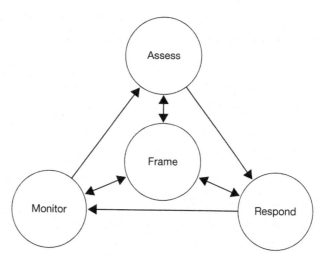

FIGURE 14.1   NIST 800-39 risk-management framework

within an organization about suitable measures to protect the organization. The 800-39 framework recommends that senior leadership be involved in IT risk management, and that IT risk management be integrated in the design of business processes.[12]

IT risk-management components

The 800-39 framework identifies four components of IT risk management – (1) the risk frame, (2) the risk assessment, (3) the risk response once the risks are assessed, and (4) ongoing risk monitoring based on the experiences gained from risk response activities. These are organized as shown in Figure 14.1.

The risk frame establishes the context for risk management by describing the environment in which risk-based decisions are made. This clarifies to all members in the organization the various risk criteria used in the organization. These criteria include (i) assumptions about the risks that are important; (ii) responses that are considered practical; (iii) levels of risk considered acceptable; and (iv) priorities and trade-offs when responding to risks. Risk framing also identifies any risks that are to be managed by senior leaders/executives.

> In a classic example of risk framing that was highlighted during the 2012 Presidential debates, there was only one reference to terror in the President's 2001 State of the Union address. The very next year, after the 9/11 attacks, there were 36 references to terror in the 2002 State of the Union address.
>
> Doesn't that make clear a change in the risk-frame of the executive branch of the US Government in just one year?

---

[12] A very interesting link on IT risks for school administrators: http://dangerouslyirrelevant.org/2012/08/26-internet-safety-talking-points.html (accessed 07/22/2013). Appeared in Bruce Schneier's blog, 9/15/2012

Within the context of the risk frame, *the risk assessment component identifies and aggregates the risks facing the organization*. Recall our definition of risk as a quantitative measure of the potential damage from a threat. Risk assessment develops these quantitative estimates by identifying the threats, vulnerabilities in the organization and the harm to the organization if the threats exploit vulnerabilities. We discuss risk assessment in greater detail in the next section.

Risk response addresses how organizations respond to risks once they are determined from risk assessments. Risk response helps in the development of a consistent, organization-wide, response to risk that is consistent with the risk frame. Following standard business procedures, risk response consists of (i) developing alternative courses of action for responding to risk; (ii) evaluating these alternatives; (iii) selecting appropriate courses of action; and (iv) implementing risk responses based on selected courses of action.

Risk monitoring evaluates the effectiveness of the organization's risk-management plan over time. Risk monitoring involves (i) verification that planned risk response measures are implemented; (ii) verification that planned risk responses satisfy the requirements derived from the organization's missions, business functions, regulations, and standards; (iii) determination of the effectiveness of risk response measures; and (iv) identification of required changes to the risk-management plan as a result of changes in technology and the business environment.

The arrows in Figure 14.1 illustrate the risk-management processes and the information and communication flows among the risk-management components. The activities in the outer circles are performed sequentially, moving from risk assessment to risk response to risk monitoring. The risk frame informs all the sequential step-by-step activities. For example, the threats identified from the risk frame serve as inputs to the risk assessment activity. Similarly, the outputs from the risk assessment component (risks) serve as the input to the risk response component.[13]

Risk assessment

Once the risk frame is established, we can build on the threat model developed earlier to create a risk assessment model.

Disambiguating risk assessment and risk analysis

The risk assessment component in the NIST 800-39 framework includes two activities – identifying risks and quantifying these risks. What NIST calls risk assessment is often also called risk analysis, with the term risk assessment referring to the quantification aspect of NIST's risk assessment component.

The specific context should help you disambiguate the meaning of the term risk assessment.

Risk assessment model

The threat model introduced earlier is reproduced in Figure 14.2. Threats involve motivated agents attacking assets. When conducting threat analysis, we typically do not conduct a formal analysis of the potential outcomes of the threats. Our concern during threat analysis is limited to identifying potential problems.

---

[13] The 800-39 document uses bi-directional arrows everywhere in the figure. We have used directed arrows to connect the outer circles. We believe this better represents the sequential nature of activities and information flows from risk assessment to response to monitoring

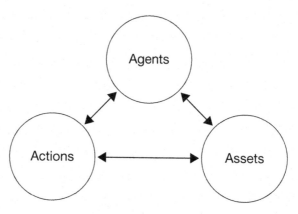

FIGURE 14.2   Threat model

For example, one of the threats identified was a remote hacker (agents) compromising the user credentials database (asset), by stealing these credentials (action). During threat analysis, we did not consider the potential impact of such a threat. Specifically, we did not worry about what the hacker might do with such information.

Risk assessment can be seen as adding an analysis of outcomes to the identified threats. Our definition of a risk as a quantitative measure of the potential damage caused by a specified threat can be written as:

Risk = damage as a result of a specified threat, or

Risk = damage(threat), i.e., risk is the damage output as a function of the threat input

Since the threat itself is composed of an agent, an action, and an asset, we can write the equation for risk as:

$$\text{Risk} = \text{damage(agent, action, asset)}$$

This is shown in Figure 14.3. We can use this figure to identify risks and write them down as risk statements, which provide all the information necessary to communicate information about risks to concerned parties. Building on our example threat of a hacker stealing user credentials, we can write the associated risks as:

Risk 1: A remote hacker (agent) may steal (action) user credentials (asset) and try these credentials to access banking websites (action). This may lead to lawsuits, which will drain profits as well as management time (damage).

Risk 2: A remote hacker (agent) may steal (action) user credentials (asset) and try these credentials to access banking websites (action). This may lead to adverse publicity, which may hurt our business in the short term (damage).

In other words, the same threat may be associated with multiple risks, if the threat can cause multiple forms of damage.

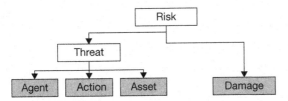

FIGURE 14.3   Risk assessment model

The risk assessment model of Figure 14.3 shows that even a small set of assets and agents can lead to a large number of threats and risks. For example, the combination of two agents (remote attacker and disgruntled employee) and two assets (information assets and hardware assets) can result in four potential threats. If we add two forms of damage to the mix (financial loss, information loss), we have eight potential risks to consider. In the real-world, even the smallest businesses deal with tens of assets, agents (who can be driven by multiple motives), and damages, which can result in tens of thousands of potential risks (if we just multiply the number of agents, assets, actions, and damages). But most organizations can only deal with perhaps 5–10 risks at any given time. This is why risk frames are important – to prune out unlikely risks.

Once the risks are identified, quantitative measures for the risks are developed by estimating the likelihood and potential damage upon occurrence of the risk. We then calculate the risk as the product of the likelihood and the magnitude. Continuing with our example of the hacker, say we estimate the probability of such an attack in the coming year at 1%. Also, say that for risk 2, we estimate the monetary damage from lost sales at $10,000 in profits. We can quantify the risk in this case as:

$$\text{Risk} = \text{likelihood} \times \text{magnitude} = 0.01 \times \$10,000 = \$100.$$

By developing similar estimates for all the identified risks, we can prioritize the risks within our risk frame.

Other risk-management frameworks

The NIST 800-39 framework is a very general IT risk-management framework. There are some other information security risk-management framework, with the ISO 27000 series and the CERT OCTAVE being among the most popular. There are many consulting firms which help organizations to implement the recommendations of these standards. We provide a brief overview of these two standards here for completeness.

ISO 27000 series

The International Standards Organization (ISO) has reserved the ISO 27000 series of standards (i.e., standards starting with the digits 27) for information security matters. As of December 2012, this series includes six standards ranging from ISO 27001 to ISO 27006. These standards cover the following topics:

ISO 27001: The standard that specifies the requirements for an information security management system (ISMS)

ISO 27002: The standard that specifies a set of controls to meet the requirements specified in ISO 27001

ISO 27003: Guidance for the implementation of an ISMS

ISO 27004: Measurement and metrics for an ISMS

ISO 27005: The standard for information security risk management

ISO 27006: The standard that provides guidelines for the accreditation of organizations that offer ISMS certification

The ISO 27001 standard states that the ISO adopts a process approach for implementing information security. All processes follow Deming's Plan-Do-Check-Act (PDCA) model. During the planning phase, organizations establish policies and procedures to manage information risks. These procedures are operated in the do phase. During checking, process performance is measured against the plan specifications and presented to management for review. In the act phase, review results are used to improve policies and procedures in the next iteration of the plan phase.

You may note the parallels between the NIST 800-39 and ISO 27001 standards. The NIST assess phase maps to the ISO plan phase, the respond phase to the do phase, and the monitor phase to the ISO check and act phases.

ISO 27002 documents a set of security techniques, which map to the controls we have discussed throughout this book. The controls in the standard are divided into the following sections: (i) asset management; (ii) human resources security; (iii) physical and environmental security; (iv) communications and operations management; (v) access control; (vi) information systems acquisition, development, and maintenance; (vii) information security incident management; (viii) business continuity management; and (ix) compliance.[14]

ISO 27005 specifies that the information security risk-management process consists of seven sequential steps: (i) context establishment; (ii) risk assessment; (iii) risk treatment; (iv) risk acceptance; (v) risk treatment plan implementation; (vi) risk monitoring and review; and (vii) risk-management process improvement. Following the PDCA recommendation of ISO 27001, ISO 27005 aligns these activities with the four phases as shown in Table 14.1.

As you can see, there is considerable overlap between the ISO and NIST recommendations as they relate to information security.

OCTAVE

Carnegie Mellon University (CMU) hosts the well-known Software Engineering Institute (SEI). SEI is a federally funded organization that has over the years taken the stewardship for coordinating various activities important to the software industry. It started off by developing recommended guidelines for improving the software development process. In recent years, it has taken leadership in information security and maintains the central repository of bug reports released by major software vendors. Another popular initiative of the SEI is the OCTAVE methodology for information security management.

---

[14]We have only touched briefly upon business continuity management in this book. This is because most fresh college graduates will only have limited responsibility for business continuity. We have chosen to maintain our focus on the information security topics that are most relevant to college graduates within the first 4–5 years after graduation

Table 14.1 Alignment between ISO 27001 information security (IS) management system components and ISO 27005 IS risk-management process components

Information security (IS) management system process stage	IS risk-management process stage
Plan	Context establishment
	Risk assessment
	Developing risk treatment plan
	Risk acceptance
Do	Implementation of risk treatment plan
Check	Continual monitoring and reviewing of risks
Act	Maintain and improve IS risk-management process

OCTAVE stands for Operationally Critical Threat, Asset, Vulnerability Evaluation. The methodology corresponds to the risk assessment phase of the NIST 800-39 framework. The description of the OCTAVE methodology provided below is adapted from the overview provided at the SEI website:[15]

The OCTAVE Method was developed with large organizations in mind (300 employees or more). These organizations generally maintain their own IT infrastructure and have the capability to manage their own information security operation. OCTAVE uses a three-phased approach to examine organizational and technology issues, assembling a comprehensive picture of the organization's information security needs. The three phases are:

Phase 1: identifying critical assets and the threats to those assets

Phase 2: identifying the vulnerabilities, both organizational and technological, that expose those threats, creating risk to the organization

Phase 3: developing a practice-based protection strategy and risk mitigation plans to support the organization's mission and priorities

OCTAVE is comprised of a series of workshops, either facilitated by outside experts or conducted by an interdisciplinary analysis team of three to five of the organization's own personnel. The method takes advantage of knowledge from multiple levels of the organization. These activities are supported by a catalog of good or known practices, as well as surveys and worksheets that can be used to elicit and capture information during focused discussions and problem-solving sessions.

As you may have observed, there are many parallels between the OCTAVE and other information security risk-management frameworks discussed earlier (NIST 800-39 and ISO 27000).

IT general controls for Sarbanes–Oxley compliance

Thus far in this chapter, we have discussed general information security risk-management frameworks that are usable in a wide range of industries. While these frameworks should be

---

[15]http://www.cert.org/octave/octavemethod.html (accessed 12/28/2012)

helpful in most contexts, in contexts where the stakes are very high, specific legal requirements for IT risk-management methodologies have emerged. One such context is financial reporting in publicly traded companies. This context has been a big driver of recruitment of freshly graduated information security professionals in the last decade. It has introduced terms such as SOX, section 302, section 404, internal control, and IT general controls into the information security lexicon. Given this importance, we provide an overview of this context in this section.

The Sarbanes–Oxley Act of 2002

In the final years of the 20th century, America witnessed one of the most euphoric rises in stock prices in its financial history. The business potential of the Internet led to investors bidding up the prices of any company associated with the Internet. The phenomenon is now known as the "dot-com boom." Analysts developed metrics such as "dollars per eyeball" to justify these prices. Whereas companies whose stock prices are over 20 times annual income are generally considered expensive, during this time companies sported billion dollar valuations with no profits and many companies sported valuations in excess of 100 times annual profits. In the late stages of this frenzy, when people began to question these lofty valuations and companies came under pressure to justify their stock prices, executives at some well-known firms forged their account-books either to show sales that did not actually occur (MCI-Worldcom) or to hide costs (Enron). Many of these executives profited personally from these forgeries.

When the cases came to trial, leaders at these companies denied culpability and took the plea that they had signed off on the financial statements based primarily on their trust in their accounting staff and auditors. They argued that the firms' operations were so complicated that it was impossible for them to know all aspects of the financial statements. However, management experts, the public, and lawmakers were convinced that the managers knew exactly what they were doing and the pleas of ignorance were merely attempts to exploit legal loopholes and avoid penalties.

These trials brought to light two important details of stock markets. One, that the retirements of most Americans were tightly linked to stock markets because most retirement funds have no choice but to invest the majority of their assets in the US stock markets to achieve the growth required to help people retire gracefully. When large companies such as Enron and MCI-Worldcom manipulated their statements and eventually collapsed, it hurt the retirement assets of almost every American worker. Two, that firm leaders could push a lot of wrongdoing in their firms through verbal and implicit directions that left no paper trail that could be used during court trials.

Under heavy pressure to do something, Congress passed the Sarbanes–Oxley act in 2002. The act is named after its two primary sponsors, Senator Paul Sarbanes (D-MD) and Representative Michael G. Oxley (R-OH). The voting pattern indicates the overwhelming legislative support at the time for the law. It received 423 of a possible 434 votes in the house and 99 of the 100 possible votes in the senate.

Sarbanes–Oxley – important provisions

From the legal perspective, the law had one major impact. Sections 302 and 906 created a new criminal provision, making CEOs and CFOs of publicly traded firms criminally liable for untrue statements in public filings. CEOs and CFOs are now personally liable for the veracity of financial information presented in public filings. Prior to Sarbanes–Oxley, prosecutors had to establish malicious intent for untrue statements to be considered a criminal offense. For reference, the relevant provisions of the act are reproduced below.

EXHIBIT 14.1 | EXCERPT FROM SEC. 302 OF THE
SARBANES–OXLEY ACT

SEC. 302. CORPORATE RESPONSIBILITY FOR FINANCIAL REPORTS.

(a) REGULATIONS REQUIRED.—The Commission shall, by rule, require, for each company filing periodic reports under section 13(a) or 15(d) of the Securities Exchange Act of 1934 (15 U.S.C. 78m, 78o(d)), that the principal executive officer or officers and the principal financial officer or officers, or persons performing similar functions, certify in each annual or quarterly report filed or submitted under either such section of such Act that—

(1) the signing officer has reviewed the report;

(2) based on the officer's knowledge, the report does not contain any untrue statement of a material fact or omit to state a material fact necessary in order to make the statements made, in light of the circumstances under which such statements were made, not misleading;

(3) based on such officer's knowledge, the financial statements, and other financial information included in the report, fairly present in all material respects the financial condition and results of operations of the issuer as of, and for, the periods presented in the report;

(4) the signing officers—

   (A) are responsible for establishing and maintaining internal controls;

   (B) have designed such internal controls to ensure that material information relating to the issuer and its consolidated subsidiaries is made known to such officers by others within those entities, particularly during the period in which the periodic reports are being prepared;

   (C) have evaluated the effectiveness of the issuer's internal controls as of a date within 90 days prior to the report; and

   (D) have presented in the report their conclusions about the effectiveness of their internal controls based on their evaluation as of that date;

. . .

EXHIBIT 14.2 | EXCERPT FROM SEC. 906 OF THE SARBANES–OXLEY ACT

SEC. 906. CORPORATE RESPONSIBILITY FOR FINANCIAL REPORTS.

...

''(c) CRIMINAL PENALTIES.—Whoever—

''(1) certifies any statement as set forth in subsections (a) and (b) of this section knowing that the periodic report accompanying the statement does not comport with all the requirements set forth in this section shall be **fined not more than $1,000,000 or imprisoned not more than 10 years, or both**; or

''(2) **willfully certifies** any statement as set forth in subsections (a) and (b) of this section knowing that the periodic report accompanying the statement does not comport with all the requirements set forth in this section shall be **fined not more than $5,000,000, or imprisoned not more than 20 years, or both**.''.

EXHIBIT 14.3 | SECTION 404 OF THE SARBANES–OXLEY ACT

SEC. 404. MANAGEMENT ASSESSMENT OF INTERNAL CONTROLS.

(a) RULES REQUIRED.—The Commission shall prescribe rules requiring each annual report required by section 13(a) or 15(d) of the Securities Exchange Act of 1934 (15 U.S.C. 78m or 78o(d)) to contain an internal control report, which shall—

  (1) state the responsibility of management for establishing and maintaining an adequate internal control structure and procedures for financial reporting; and

  (2) contain an assessment, as of the end of the most recent fiscal year of the issuer, of the effectiveness of the internal control structure and procedures of the issuer for financial reporting.

(b) INTERNAL CONTROL EVALUATION AND REPORTING.—With respect to the internal control assessment required by subsection (a), each registered public accounting firm that prepares or issues the audit report for the issuer shall attest to, and report on, the assessment made by the management of the issuer. **An attestation made under this subsection shall be made in accordance with standards for attestation engagements issued or adopted by the Board.** Any such attestation shall not be the subject of a separate engagement.

From a business perspective, section 404 of the Sarbanes–Oxley act introduced the concept of standards-based verification of internal control. Prior to the passage of the Sarbanes–Oxley act, auditing firms used their own battle-tested procedures to verify that firms had robust processes to prevent fraud. However, the events of the dot-com boom revealed that auditing firms could be persuaded through fees and promises of future engagements to compromise on their assessments and certify suspect financial reports. Accordingly, the Sarbanes–Oxley act required that the verification of internal procedures be based on rules that were established by government, not the industry. Section 404 of the Sarbanes–Oxley act is shown below. The directive in the section that is relevant to our purposes is highlighted in bold.

The net result is that, since 2003, firms are required to verify that their internal controls comply with the standards established by the Sarbanes–Oxley act. We provide a high-level overview of standards and associated procedures in the rest of this section.

PCAOB and auditing standards

Sarbanes–Oxley (popularly called SOX) created a body called the Public Company Accounting Oversight Board (PCAOB) to develop the standards to be used for SOX attestations. Adapting from the organization's website,[16]

The PCAOB is a nonprofit corporation established by Congress to oversee [the audits of public companies and broker-dealers, with the goal of investor protection]. The Sarbanes-Oxley Act of 2002, which created the PCAOB, required that auditors of U.S. public companies be subject to external and independent oversight for the first time in history. Previously, the profession was self-regulated. The five members of the PCAOB Board, including the Chairman, are appointed to staggered five-year terms by the Securities and Exchange Commission (SEC), after consultation with the Chairman of the Board of Governors of the Federal Reserve System and the Secretary of the Treasury. The SEC has oversight authority over the PCAOB, including the approval of the Board's rules, standards, and budget. The Act established funding for PCAOB activities, primarily through annual fees assessed on public companies in proportion to their market capitalization and on brokers and dealers based on their net capital.

The PCAOB has published standards for all aspects of auditing.[17] The standards of greatest interest to us are AS5 - "An Audit of Internal Control Over Financial Reporting That Is Integrated with An Audit of Financial Statements" and AS12 – "Identifying and Assessing Risks of Material Misstatement." AS 5 guides the overall SOX engagement, something you are quite likely to participate in if you join one of the professional auditing firms. Within the SOX audit, AS 12 provides guidance for IT.

Section 21 of the AS 5 standard specified the overall direction of a SOX audit as:

21. The auditor should use a top-down approach to the audit of internal control over financial reporting to select the controls to test. A top-down approach begins at the financial statement level and with the auditor's understanding of the overall risks to internal control over financial reporting. The auditor then focuses on entity-level controls and works down to significant accounts and disclosures and their relevant assertions.

---

[16] http://pcaobus.org

[17] http://pcaobus.org/Standards/Auditing/Pages/default.aspx

Section 36 of AS 5 directs auditors to paragraph 29 and appendix B of AS 12 to deal with the impacts of IT upon the audit process:

36. The auditor also should understand how IT affects the company's flow of transactions. The auditor should apply paragraph 29 and Appendix B of Auditing Standard No. 12, Identifying and Assessing Risks of Material Misstatement, which discuss the effect of information technology on internal control over financial reporting and the risks to assess.

Section 29 of As 12 essentially directs auditors to appendix B of the standard:

29. The auditor also should obtain an understanding of how IT affects the company's flow of transactions. (See Appendix B.)

Finally, appendix B of AS 12 includes the following:

APPENDIX B – CONSIDERATION OF MANUAL AND AUTOMATED SYSTEMS AND CONTROLS

. . .

B4. The auditor should obtain an understanding of specific risks to a company's internal control over financial reporting resulting from IT. Examples of such risks include:

- *Reliance on systems or programs that are inaccurately processing data, processing inaccurate data, or both;*

- *Unauthorized access to data that might result in destruction of data or improper changes to data, including the recording of unauthorized or non-existent transactions or inaccurate recording of transactions (particular risks might arise when multiple users access a common database);*

- *The possibility of IT personnel gaining access privileges beyond those necessary to perform their assigned duties, thereby breaking down segregation of duties;*

- *Unauthorized changes to data in master files;*

- *Unauthorized changes to systems or programs;*

- *Failure to make necessary changes to systems or programs;*

- *Inappropriate manual intervention; and*

- *Potential loss of data or inability to access data as required.*

For convenience, Figure 14.4 shows how the above guidelines for IT audits flow from section to section in the auditing standards.

Internal controls

What is the ultimate goal of all the activity associated with Sarbanes–Oxley? The term used is "internal control over financial reporting." This is defined by the PCAOB in appendix A of AS 5 as:

A5. Internal control over financial reporting is a process designed by, or under the supervision of, the company's principal executive and principal financial officers, or persons performing similar

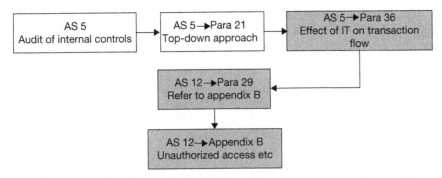

FIGURE 14.4   Sarbanes–Oxley auditing guidelines workflow for impact on IT

functions, and effected by the company's board of directors, management, and other personnel, to provide reasonable assurance regarding the reliability of financial reporting and the preparation of financial statements for external purposes in accordance with GAAP and includes those policies and procedures that –

(1) Pertain to the maintenance of records that, in reasonable detail, accurately and fairly reflect the transactions and dispositions of the assets of the company;

(2) Provide reasonable assurance that transactions are recorded as necessary to permit preparation of financial statements in accordance with generally accepted accounting principles, and that receipts and expenditures of the company are being made only in accordance with authorizations of management and directors of the company; and

(3) Provide reasonable assurance regarding prevention or timely detection of unauthorized acquisition, use, or disposition of the company's assets that could have a material effect on the financial statements.

Internal control over financial reporting is a subset of the overall control activities at the firm. In the Sarbanes–Oxley domain, *control activities are defined as procedures, methods, and policies that responsible persons use to reduce the likelihood of occurrence of risky events to acceptable levels.* This definition is consistent with the definition of IT security controls we have used in this book – safeguards used to minimize the impact of threats.

IT general controls

The bulk of the internal control audit activities are performed by auditors and accountants. However, these professionals rely on IT experts to assist in the evaluation of the controls exemplified in Appendix B of AS 12. These activities have traditionally been called IT general controls.

The current versions of the auditing standards do not seem to have a definition for the term "IT general controls." However, AS 2, which has been superseded by AS 5, included in para 50.[18]

50. Some controls (such as company-level controls, described in paragraph 53) might have a pervasive effect on the achievement of many overall objectives of the control criteria. **For example, information technology general controls over program development, program changes, computer operations, and access to programs and data help ensure that specific controls over the processing**

---

[18] http://pcaobus.org/standards/auditing/pages/auditing_standard_2.aspx

of transactions are operating effectively. *In contrast, other controls are designed to achieve specific objectives of the control criteria. For example, management generally establishes specific controls, such as accounting for all shipping documents, to ensure that all valid sales are recorded.*

While even AS 2 only provided example and did not formally define IT general controls, para 50 suggests a definition. Based on para 50 of AS2, general controls may be contrasted with specific controls in that general controls provide the underlying platform for the accomplishment of many specific controls. For example, if an IT system allows users without passwords to record transactions, the likelihood of fraudulent transactions increases significantly, weakening the effectiveness of specific controls designed to verify different business activities. Therefore, maintaining a secure IT infrastructure through IT general controls is important to reliably verify business activity. Based on this, we define IT general controls as *control activities performed by IT that ensure the correct processing of business transactions by the organization.*

In a Sarbanes–Oxley engagement, IT experts are involved in the auditing of IT general controls.

Procedure for verification of IT general controls as part of a SOX audit

Following the top-down guiding principle of AS 5, the industry has developed the following procedure for an audit of IT general controls over financial reporting.[19]

1. Look at the firm's financial statements

2. Identify material line items

   a. What an average prudent investor reasonably ought to know

3. Identify business processes feeding into these items

4. Identify IT platforms that support these processes – OS, database, applications, web-server, network

5. Verify that IT general control objectives are satisfied for these platforms

6. Report material weaknesses

   a. Deficiency that can result in material mis-statements to occur or remain undetected

This process is repeated annually, to comply with the provisions of the SOX act. For # 5 in the list above, 12 control objectives have been identified based on industry best practices, including items such as managing changes and managing data.[20]

Compliance versus risk management

The example of Sarbanes–Oxley in the domain of IT general controls over financial reporting that was introduced in the previous section shows that a lot of risk-management activities are mandated by law and regulations. Earlier, we have defined compliance as the act of following

---

[19]For more details, please see the ISACA document at http://www.isaca.org/Knowledge-Center/Research/ResearchDeliverables/Pages/IT-Control-Objectives-for-Sarbanes-Oxley (accessed 1/1/2013)

[20]See figure 1 on page 11 of the ISACA document referred above

applicable laws, regulations, rules, industry codes, and contractual obligations. If the bulk of risk-management work is defined by laws and regulations, you might wonder why any organization should take the effort of developing its own risk-management plan based on NIST 800-39 or ISO 27000. Why not outsource risk management to legislators and industry experts, and simply comply with the laws, regulations, industry codes, etc. that these experts develop?

If you give this some thought, you will realize that compliance is only a subset of risk management, requiring a minimal set of risk-management activities to prevent catastrophe that can affect others. Compliance does not regulate risks that affect only you or your organization. For example, you are entitled to risk your money on lotteries, squander your income on unwise purchases, and consume alcohol within the privacy of your home, etc. Since any adverse outcomes of these actions are limited to you alone, there are no regulations or codes preventing you from performing these activities. However, when you drive on the road, your dangerous conduct can put other drivers at risk. Therefore, we require drivers to comply with safe driving laws and there are stiff penalties for driving under the influence of alcohol.

Similarly, in IT risk management, compliance activities ensure that your organization's conduct does not put investors and other organizations at risk. But you alone are responsible for ensuring that your actions do not put your own organization at risk. Risk management covers everything that you do to prevent harm to yourself.

Selling security

IT security is not an easy sell. Upper management usually thinks in terms of Return on Investments and oftentimes it is difficult to quantify the return on something that "may" happen, like a power failure or a hacker incident. Even though it is easier to justify the expenses based on existing, known incidents, certain organizations are still hesitant to commit resources to security.

One of the best strategies is to try to include a certain percentage to be spent in security in every project started within IT. For instance, a project involving Identity and Access Management may also include the cost of software needed to encrypt personal data such as Social Security Numbers. And if the software agreement is negotiated correctly, the same software may be licensed to include the permission to encrypt other restricted data on other servers as well.

Unfortunately, one of the easiest ways to obtain funds is to capitalize on incidents that happened with other, similar organizations. A leak of Social Security Numbers on nearby Universities will without a doubt raise questions about the internal security of your own University. The students will be asking how protected their SSNs are, and maybe so will the local media. During these times, IT may receive windfalls of funds to improve the security stance of the infrastructure. It is important to have a strategy always ready to be able to use these situations and not just waste funds purchasing resources that are not needed.

Example case – online marketplace purchases

On December 5, 2012, the US Attorney for the Eastern District of New York announced the arrests of six Romanian and one Albanian national for defrauding US customers on popular Internet marketplaces such as eBay, AutoTrader.com, and Cars.com. The arrests involved co-operation among law enforcement agencies in Romania, Czech Republic, United Kingdom, Canada, and the United States.

The fraudsters posted detailed ads for expensive items such as cars and boats on the popular online markets though none of the posted items actually existed. They used co-conspirators called "arrows" in the United States to open bank accounts using high-quality fake passports. These arrows responded to enquiries from potential buyers and collected payments.

Payments from unsuspecting victims were transferred out of the United States by the arrows as cash or wire transfers. In one case, $18,000 in cash was mailed out of the US inside speakers. In another case, money was used to buy an expensive watch, which was then mailed to the fraudsters. The total estimated earnings of the gang was $3 million.

REFERENCE

http://www.justice.gov/usao/nye/pr/2012/2012dec05.html

SUMMARY

In this chapter, we looked at risk analysis and the different frameworks available for risk analysis. We used risk analysis to relate the contents of this book to the overall managerial objectives of a firm. The NIST 800-39 risk analysis framework allowed us to present all the information in earlier sections of the book in a format consistent with recommended standards for risk analysis. We saw that risk analysis associates each threat with all possible outcomes and provides a mechanism to quantify risks for comparison and evaluation. We also saw a specific risk-management framework mandated by the Sarbanes–Oxley act, which is used by publicly traded firms to assure investors of the reliability of financial reporting.

CHAPTER REVIEW QUESTIONS

1. What is risk? What in your opinion are the three greatest IT risks you face in your personal life?

2. What is risk management? List one or two activities you can perform to make the risks identified in q1 more predictable.

3. List one or two activities you can perform to minimize and prepare for the IT risks you identified in q1.

4. What are frameworks? Why are they used in management? Very briefly (in 1–2 sentences), name a framework you have studied in another class. How did the use of a framework help your understanding of the topic organized by the framework?

5. What is the objective of the NIST 800-39 framework?

6. What are the types of organizational risks listed in NIST 800-39 (page 1, para 2 of the standard)?

7. Look at the latest 10-K filed by Apple Computer (or if you prefer, another leading publicly traded technology vendor, say Microsoft, Oracle, Dell, IBM, HP). List all the risks identified by the company as risk factors (summarize them as short phrases each). Classify each of these risks as one of the organizational risks listed in NIST 800-39.

8. Provide a brief overview of the NIST 800-39 risk-management framework. Draw a figure showing the components of the framework and the relationships of these components to each other.

9. What is IT risk management? How is IT risk management related to an organization's overall risk management?

10. What is the IT risk frame, as defined by NIST 800-39? What is the role of the risk frame in IT risk management?

11. What is IT risk assessment, as defined by NIST 800-39? What is the role of risk assessment in IT risk management?

12. What is IT risk response, as defined by NIST 800-39? What is the role of the risk response in IT risk management?

13. What is IT risk monitoring, as defined by NIST 800-39? What is the role of risk monitoring in IT risk management?

14. How are risks related to threats?

15. During the risk identification phase of risk assessment, what are the items that need to be determined to identify a risk?

16. Write the risks you identified q1 as risk statements, following the examples in the chapter as the template. Clearly identify all the components of the risk in each risk statement.

17. For each risk in q16, use your best judgment to estimate the likelihood and impact of each risk. Using these estimates, quantify each risk and rank the risks based on these estimates.

18. Provide a brief overview of the ISO 27000 series of risk management standards developed by the International Standards Organization (ISO). How are they related to the NIST 800-39 standards. If you had to choose one of these, which one would you choose as your reference standard for IT risk management? Why?

19. Provide a brief overview of the OCTAVE methodology developed by the SEI. How is it related to the NIST 800-39 and ISO 27000 standards?

20. What are some of the important provisions defined by the Sarbanes–Oxley act?

21. What are some of the important differences between the provisions of sections 302 and 404 of the Sarbanes–Oxley act.

22. What is internal control as defined by the Sarbanes–Oxley act?

23. What are auditing standards?

24. Briefly describe the top-down auditing procedure for the verification of IT general controls as part of a Sarbanes–Oxley audit.

25. How is risk management different from compliance?

EXAMPLE CASE QUESTIONS

1. Read the announcement by the US Attorney's office at the link provided in the case. List as many mechanisms used by the fraudsters to convince potential buyers of the legitimacy of the advertisement?

2. Based on this incident, what precautions would you recommend to a friend contemplating the purchase of an expensive item online?

HANDS-ON ACTIVITY – RISK ASSESSMENT USING LSOF

In this activity, you will learn the use of the lsof command to audit which commands are using network connections and produce a risk assessment of your Linux Virtual Machine.

To begin, switch to the super user account and run 'lsof -i' to view all open network connections:

```
[alice@sunshine ~]$ su -
Password: thisisasecret

[root@sunshine ~]# lsof -i
COMMAND    PID    USER   FD   TYPE   DEVICE  SIZE/OFF  NODE NAME
sshd       1862   root    3u  IPv4   11083      0t0    TCP *:ssh (LISTEN)
sshd       1862   root    4u  IPv6   11085      0t0    TCP *:ssh (LISTEN)
ntpd       1870    ntp   16u  IPv4   11113      0t0    UDP *:ntp
ntpd       1870    ntp   17u  IPv6   11114      0t0    UDP *:ntp
ntpd       1870    ntp   18u  IPv6   11118      0t0    UDP v6.sunshine.edu:ntp
ntpd       1870    ntp   19u  IPv6   11119      0t0    UDP [fe80::a00:27ff:fef6:cadf]:ntp
ntpd       1870    ntp   20u  IPv4   11120      0t0    UDP sunshine.edu:ntp
```

```
ntpd      1870     ntp 21u  IPv4  1878265     0t0  UDP 10.0.2.15:ntp
mysqld    2148   mysql 10u  IPv4    11438     0t0  TCP *:mysql (LISTEN)
master    2276    root 12u  IPv4    11742     0t0  TCP sunshine.edu:smtp (LISTEN)
master    2276    root 13u  IPv6    11744     0t0  TCP v6.sunshine.edu:smtp (LISTEN)
httpd     2316    root  4u  IPv6    11985     0t0  TCP *:http (LISTEN)
qpidd     2335   qpidd 10u  IPv4    12079     0t0  TCP *:amqp (LISTEN)
qpidd     2335   qpidd 11u  IPv6    12080     0t0  TCP *:amqp (LISTEN)
dnsmasq  13558  nobody  4u  IPv4  1877904     0t0  UDP *:domain
dnsmasq  13558  nobody  5u  IPv4  1877905     0t0  TCP *:domain (LISTEN)
dnsmasq  13558  nobody  6u  IPv6  1877906     0t0  UDP *:domain
dnsmasq  13558  nobody  7u  IPv6  1877907     0t0  TCP *:domain (LISTEN)
dhclient 13624    root  6u  IPv4  1878166     0t0  UDP *:bootpc
httpd    31152  apache  4u  IPv6    11985     0t0  TCP *:http (LISTEN)
httpd    31153  apache  4u  IPv6    11985     0t0  TCP *:http (LISTEN)
httpd    31154  apache  4u  IPv6    11985     0t0  TCP *:http (LISTEN)
httpd    31156  apache  4u  IPv6    11985     0t0  TCP *:http (LISTEN)
httpd    31157  apache  4u  IPv6    11985     0t0  TCP *:http (LISTEN)
httpd    31158  apache  4u  IPv6    11985     0t0  TCP *:http (LISTEN)
httpd    31159  apache  4u  IPv6    11985     0t0  TCP *:http (LISTEN)
httpd    31160  apache  4u  IPv6    11985     0t0  TCP *:http (LISTEN)
```

The output from this command gives you several valuable pieces of information about the programs running on your system such as:

- The name of the program that is running (COMMAND)

- The user the program is running as (USER)

- The process id of the program (PID)

- The port the program is connecting to and/or awaiting connects on (NAME)

The final column (NAME) is the most interesting. The entries are in the format server:port (STATE) where server is the computer (name or IP address) the process is connecting to and port is the name of the service the process is using. The port number the process is connected to is resolved to a service name by looking it up in /etc/services. Port numbers can be used for multiple services, so this lookup isn't always reliable, but it is usually a good guess.

Connection listings starting with an asterisk (*) are not connecting to an external server; they are listening for a connection to be made to them, hence the LISTEN state appended to many of these entries.

Search the web for more information on each of the processes listed in the lsof output and compile the information into a table.

Example:

Process	Description	Port number	Listening for connections	Connecting to another host
ntpd	Network Time Protocol – This service synchronizes the system time with network time servers	123	Yes	Yes

QUESTIONS

1. In your opinion, what services (if any) could be a security risk and may need to be disabled?

2. Instead of disabling a service, what other controls could be put in place to mitigate the risk?

CRITICAL THINKING EXERCISE – RISK ESTIMATION BIASES

In recent years, there has been a lot of research on how people are biased in estimating risks. Cass Sunstein, one of the most eminent legal scholars of our time stated that "diverse cultures focus on very different risks, with social influences and peer pressures accentuating some fears and reduce others. Cascades, the availability heuristic, loss aversion, and group polarization are highly relevant here." In an article in the New York Times, Prof. Jared Diamond described how people ignore hazards with a low likelihood of occurrence at each opportunity, but with a very high frequency of opportunities, for e.g., driving. In a related stream of research called cultural cognition, Prof. Dan Kahan of Yale University states that "culture precedes facts," in that people selectively accept and dismiss facts in a manner that supports their views.

REFERENCES

Sunstein, C.R. "Laws of Fear: Beyond the Precautionary Principle," Cambridge University Press, March 2005. Available at SSRN: http://ssrn.com/abstract = 721562

Diamond, J. "That daily shower can be a killer," New York Times, 01/28/2013

Schneier, B. Cryptogram, February 1, 2013

Kahan, D.M., Slovic, P., Braman, D., and Gastil, J. "Fear of democracy: A cultural evaluation of Sunstein on risk," Harvard Law Review, 2006, 119, Yale Law School, Public Law Working Paper No. 100, Yale Law & Economics Research Paper No. 317. Available at SSRN: http://ssrn.com/abstract = 801964

CRITICAL THINKING QUESTIONS

1. During IT risk assessment, what are some ways that estimation biases can lead to overestimation of insignificant risks and underestimation of important risks?

2. It is suggested that overestimation of a risk necessarily leads to an under-recognition of some other important risk. Do you agree with this assessment? Why, or why not?

DESIGN CASE

Now that you have finished the class, it is time to wrap up. You have been working at Sunshine University for a year now and the President and Provost ask you to put together a Risk Assessment for the organization. Create a simplified RA for the year based on all the Design Cases you have worked on so far. Here are some guidelines:

- Review and re-evaluate all Design Cases for all chapters in the book in order to prepare the Risk Assessment document.

- Make the RA easy to read.

- Use graphs to demonstrate your points.

- Compare the current status of Sunshine University with other Universities when possible.

- Research possible challenges brought up by new technologies.

- Close with a few items proposed to improve the security stance of the University.

Password List for the Linux Virtual Machine

There are a number of pre-configured accounts included with the Linux virtual machine used in the hands-on exercises of this text. The following table includes several accounts that are used in the exercises. For a full list of accounts and passwords, you can open `/root/passwords.list` in a text editor on the virtual machine.

Username	Password
root	thisisasecret
alice	aisforapple
bob	bisforbanana
charlie	cisforcookie
dave	disfordog
eric	eisforelephant
fred	fisforfrog

Glossary

Access audit: the process to determine what access each individual should have based on the data provided by the Person Registry and the current security policies.

Access control: the act of limiting access to information system resources only to authorized users, programs, processes, or other systems.

Access control models: a description of the availability of resources in a system.

Access control list: a list of permissions attached to specified objects. Often abbreviated as ACL.

Access management system: the policies, procedures and applications which take the data from the Person Registry and the Systems of Record to make decisions on granting access to resources.

Access registry: a utility that provides security administrators with a single view of an individual's accounts and permissions across the entire organization.

Action: the activity performed by the agent in order to affect the confidentiality, integrity, or availability of the asset.

Active Directory: the collection of technologies that provide centralized user management and access control across all computers that are "members" of the domain.

Active Directory Federation Services: a service that extends the Active Directory system to support federated access to local and external resources using SAML and related protocols. Commonly abbreviated as ADFS.

Advanced persistent threat: a sustained, human-intensive attack that leverages the full range of computer intrusion techniques.

Anomaly-based detection: the process of detecting deviations between observed events and defined activity patterns.

Asset: a resource or information that is to be protected.

Asset criticality: a measure of the importance of an asset to the immediate survival of an organization.

Asset owner: the individual or unit with operational responsibility for all unanticipated functions involved in securing an asset.

Asset sensitivity: extent of damage caused to the organization by a breach of confidentiality or integrity of the asset.

Authentication: the process that a user goes through to prove that he or she is the owner of the identity that is being used.

Authentication token: a unique identifier or cryptographic hash that proves the identity of the user in possession of the token.

Availability: ensuring timely and reliable access to and use of information.

Biometric devices: devices that analyze the minute differences in certain physical traits or behaviors, such as fingerprints or voice patterns, to identify an individual.

Biometric markers: observable physical differences among people.

Block encryption: the process of converting a plaintext block into an encrypted block.

Brute-force attack: amethod by which a hacker tries to gain access to an account on the target system by trying to "guess" the correct password.

Buffer overflow vulnerability: the situation where a program is able to put more data into a storage location than it can hold.

Business impact analysis: the identification of services and products that are critical to the organization.

Central Authentication Service protocol: one of the leading open source single sign-on technologies, especially in higher education.

Certificate: a bundle of information containing the encrypted public key of the server, and the identification of the key provider.

cd: the command (change directory) that allows us to switch to another directory. The target folder name is specified as the argument to the command.

Checksum: a value computed on data to detect error or manipulation during transmission.

Ciphertext: the encrypted text that is unintelligible to the reader.

Cloud computing: the delivery of software and other computer resources as a service over the Internet, rather than as a stand-alone product.

Compliance: the act of following applicable laws, regulations, rules, industry codes, and contractual obligations.

Computer security incident: a violation or imminent threat of violation of computer security policies, acceptable use policies, or standard security practices.

Compromised passwords: passwords on the system that are known to unauthorized users.

Confidentiality: preserving authorized restrictions on access and disclosure, including means for protecting personal privacy and proprietary information.

Configuration: the act of selecting one among many possible combinations of features of a system.

Controls: safeguards used to minimize the impact of threats.

Control activities: procedures, methods, and policies that responsible persons use to reduce the likelihood of occurrence of risky events to acceptable levels.

Credentials: the piece (or pieces) of information used to verify the user's identity.

Cross-site scripting: a vulnerability that occurs when user-supplied input is used without verification as part of the output served to other users.

Cryptanalysis: the art of breaking ciphertext.

Cryptographic algorithm: a well-defined sequence of steps used to describe cryptographic processes.

Cryptography: the art or science of rendering plain information unintelligible, and for restoring encrypted information to intelligible form.

Deep packet inspection firewalls: devices that examine the data carried by a packet, in addition to the protocol headers, to decide how to handle the packet.

Default allow stance: a firewall configuration that allows all packets into the network, except those that are explicitly prohibited.

Default deny stance: a firewall configuration that blocks all packets, except those explicitly allowed.

Deferrable asset: an asset that is needed for optimal operation of the organization but whose loss of availability would not cause major issues to the organization in the near term.

Demilitarized zone: see perimeter network.

Denial of service: the unauthorized prevention of access to resources or the delaying of time-critical operations.

Digital signatures: cryptographic transformations of data that allow a recipient of the data to prove the source (non-repudiation) and integrity of the data.

Disaster: a calamitous event that causes great destruction.

Disaster recovery: the process adopted by the IT organization in order to bring systems back up and running. Commonly abbreviated as DR.

Discovery service: a service that provides the user with a list of the trusted organizations that they can choose from to authenticate.

Distributed denial-of-service attack: the use of many compromised systems to cause denial of service for users of the targeted system. Commonly abbreviated as DDoS.

Domain controller: the server that implements the active directory rules within a domain.

Encryption: the cryptographic transformation of data to produce ciphertext.

End point protection: the security implemented at the end-user device.

Essential asset: an asset whose loss of availability would cause immediate severe repercussions for the organization.

Evasion: the act of conducting malicious activity so that it looks safe.

False positive: a find that appears to be a problem (a positive) but upon further investigation turns out not to be a problem (therefore, false).

Federation: bridging the gap between authentication systems in separate organizations.

Federation metadata: a document containing a comprehensive list of all federation members and important data, such as organization and contact information, for each identity providers.

Federation provider: the entity responsible for all administrative tasks related to running the identity federation, such as membership management, creating and enforcing federation policies, and managing the Public Key Infrastructure (PKI) needed for cryptographic operations.

Firewall: a form of protection that allows one network to connect to another network while maintaining some amount of protection.

Framework: a structure for supporting something else.

General assets: assets that are found in most organizations.

Group policy: an infrastructure that allows you to implement specific configurations for users and computers.

Hash functions: encryption methods that use no keys.

Hidden files: files whose existence is hidden from users by default.

Home directory: a user's personal space on a computer, analogous to the Documents folder in Windows. The term is popular in UNIX systems.

Host-based IDSs: software applications installed on individual hosts that monitor local activity such as file access and system calls for suspicious behavior. Sometimes abbreviated as HIDSs.

Hot spares: redundant components that are housed inside a server and that can replace the failed component with no downtime.

Identification: the presentation of a user identity for the system.

Identifier: a string of digits which uniquely identifies an identity in an SoR.

Identity: a distinct record stored in a System of Record.

Identity enrichment: collecting data about each individual's relationship to the organization.

Identity management: the processes of identifying individuals and collating all necessary data to grant or revoke privileges for these users to resources.

Identity matching: the process of searching the existing Person Registry for one or more records that match a given set of identity data.

Identity merge: combining the new or updated record with data associated with the existing person record.

Identity reconciliation: the process of comparing each discovered identity to a master record of all individuals in the organization.

Idiosyncratic assets: assets that are distinct to an organization.

Incident response policy: standard methods used by the organization for handling information security incidents.

Information asset: digitally stored content owned by an individual or organization.

Information security: protecting information and information systems from unauthorized access, use, disclosure, disruption, modification, or destruction in order to provide integrity, confidentiality, and availability.

Information security controls: safeguards used to minimize the impacts of information security threats.

Information security model: a representation of the core components of information security, showing the relationship of these components to each other, and excludes everything else.

IT general controls: control activities performed by IT that ensure the correct processing of business transactions by the organization.

IT risk: risk associated with the use of information systems in an organization.

IT system: an assembly of computer hardware, software, and firmware configured for the purpose of processing, storing, or forwarding information.

Infrastructure as a Service: a business model in which an organization uses hardware equipment such as processors, storage, and routers from a service provider. Commonly abbreviated as IaaS.

Input validation vulnerability: a situation where user input is used in the software without confirming its validity.

Installation: the act of writing the necessary data in the appropriate locations on a computer's hard drive for running a software program.

Integrity: guarding against improper information modification or destruction, and includes ensuring information non-repudiation and authenticity.

Intellectual property: creations of the mind (inventions, literary and artistic works, and symbols, names, images, and designs) that can be used for profit. Commonly abbreviated as IP.

Interior firewall: a device that limits access to the organization's internal network.

Internal agents: people linked to the organization, often as employees.

Internal network: the location of all the organization's information assets. Also called the militarized zone.

Intrusion detection systems: hardware devices or software applications that monitor IT systems for malicious activity or violations of usage policies established by the system administrator. Commonly abbreviated as IDS.

Intrusion prevention systems: technologies that build on IDS and attempt to stop potential intrusions.

Kerberos: an authentication protocol that allows nodes in an insecure network to securely identify themselves to each other using tokens.

Kernel: the software which provides controls for hardware devices, manages memory, executes code on the computer's CPU, and hides the details of the underlying physical hardware from user applications.

Key loggers: software that tracks (logs) the keys struck on a keyboard, typically trying to gather usernames and passwords.

IT-related legal assets: contractual arrangements that guide the use of hardware and software assets within the organization.

Logs: records of the performance of a machine.

Malware: software or code specifically designed to exploit a computer, or the data it contains, without the user's consent.

Missing authorization vulnerability: a vulnerability that happens when a software program allows users access to privileged parts of the program without verifying the credentials of the user.

Mission statement: short (preferably one or two sentences long) expression of an organization's services, its target market, and its competitive advantages.

Model: a representation of the real world.

Monitoring: the act of listening and/or recording the activities of a system to maintain performance and security.

Mono-alphabetic substitution: encryption scheme of replacing individual letters with other letters for the purpose of encryption.

Need-to-know: an information management principle where a person is only provided the information that is necessary to perform their job.

Network firewalls: hardware or software that prevent the dangers originating on one network from spreading to another network.

Network IDS: device that monitors network traffic and application protocol activity to identify suspicious connections.

OAuth: a mechanism that allows a user to grant access to private resources on one site (the service provider) to another site (the consumer).

Open source software: software in which anyone is able to modify the source code and distribute his or her changes to the world.

Operational responsibilities: the responsibility of an individual or entity for a specific function related to the use of an asset.

Operating systems: software that manages computer hardware and provides common services to user applications.

Operating system updates: software updates that fix issues with the low-level components of the system software.

Packet filtering firewalls: firewalls that examine the protocol header fields of packets flowing through the firewall to determine whether to allow the packets to enter the network.

Packet sniffing: the act of intercepting and monitoring data passing through a computer network.

Parent directory: the directory (folder) directly about the current one in the file-system hierarchy.

Partners: any third party sharing a business relationship with the organization.

Passphrase: a sequence of words that serves as a password.

Password: a secret series of characters that only the owner of the identity knows and uses it to authenticate identity.

Password capturing: the ability of an attacker to acquire a password from storage, transmission, or user knowledge and behavior.

Password cracking: the process of generating a character string that matches any existing password string on the targeted system.

Password expiration: the duration for which the password may be used before it is required to be changed.

Password guessing: the act of repeatedly trying different passwords associated with a user account, such as default passwords and dictionary words, until the correct password is found.

Password management: the process of defining, implementing, and maintaining password policies throughout an enterprise.

Password policy: a set of rules for using passwords.

Password replacing: the substitution of the user's existing password with a password known to the attacker.

Password synchronization: ensuring that the user has the same username and password in all systems.

Patch: software that corrects security and functionality problems in software and firmware.

Patch management: the process of identifying, acquiring, installing, and verifying patches.

Perimeter firewall: the firewall that lies between the external network and the organization.

Perimeter network: the network that lies between the external network and the organization's internal network. The perimeter network hosts external services such as http, smtp, and DNS. The perimeter network is commonly called the demilitarized zone.

Permutation: a specification of the output position of each of the k input bits.

Person Registry: the central hub that connects identifiers from all Systems of Records into a single "master" identity and makes the correlation and translation of identity data (such as Student ID to Employee ID) possible.

Identity creation: the function that creates a new person record and identifier in the Person Registry.

Personal identification number: a short (4–6 digits), numerical password. Commonly abbreviated as PIN.

Phishing: attempting to compromise a user by masquerading as a trustworthy entity in electronic communication.

Physical controls: traditional non-technical methods of preventing harm.

Policy: a document that records a high-level principle or course of action that has been decided on.

Proactive testing: the act of testing a system for specific issues before such issues occur.

Procedural controls: prescribed plans of action that govern the use of computer resources.

Procedural vulnerability: a weakness in an organization's operational methods, which can be exploited to violate the security policy.

Protocol-state-based IDS: an IDS that compares observed events against defined protocol activity for each protocol state to identify deviations.

Public-key cryptography: encryption methods that use two keys, one for encryption and another for decryption.

Reactive monitoring: the act of detecting and analyzing failures after they have occurred.

Recursion: the act of defining a function in terms of itself.

Redundancy: surplus capability, which is maintained to improve the reliability of a system.

Reputation-based end point protection: predicting the safety of a file based on a reputation score calculated using the file's observable attributes.

Required asset: an asset that is important to the organization, but the organization would be able to continue to operate for a period of time even if the asset is not available.

Restricted asset: an asset in which disclosure or alteration would have adverse consequences for the organization.

Risk: a quantitative measure of the potential damage caused by a specified threat.

Risk assessment: identifying and aggregating the risks facing the organization.

Risk frame: describing the environment in which risk-based decisions are made. This helps in establishingthe context for risk management.

Risk management: managing the financial impacts of unusual events.

Risk monitoring: evaluating the effectiveness of the organization's risk management plan over time.

Risk response: defining an organization's response to risks once they are determined from risk assessments.

Role: an individual's relationship to the organization. Also called affiliation.

Role-based access control: granting individuals in specified job roles the access privileges associated with the corresponding system role. Commonly abbreviated as RBAC, it assigns permissions to user roles rather than to individual users.

Rootkit: collections of software programs designed to hide the existence of certain specific computer processes or programs from normal methods of detection.

Controls: safeguards used to minimize the impact of threats.

Scope: the part of the incident response policy that specifies the targets of the policy.

Secret key cryptography: encryption methods that use one key for both encryption and decryption.

Separation of duties: a constraint where more than one person is required to complete a task.

Service level agreement: the specification of what and how IT will deliver and manage the expectations of the customer or system owner. Commonly abbreviated as SLA.

Shell: a text-based program that allows the user to interact directly with the kernel.

Shibboleth: an open-source identity management and federated access-control infrastructure based on Security Assertion Markup Language (SAML).

Signature: a sequence of bytes that is known to be a part of malicious software.

Single point of failure: a part of a system whose failure will stop the entire system from working.

Single sign-on: technology that allows a user to authenticate once and then access all the resources the user is authorized to use. Commonly abbreviated as SSO.

Social engineering: the art of manipulating people into performing desired actions.

Software as a Service: a delivery mechanism in which an application and all of the associated resources are provided to organizations by a vendor, typically through a web browser. Commonly abbreviated as SaaS.

Software assets: software tools needed to manipulate the organization's information to accomplish the organization's mission.

Software update: the act of replacing defective software components with components in which the identified defects have been removed.

Software vulnerability: an error in the specification, development, or configuration of software such that its execution can violate the security policy.

SQL injection vulnerability: the use of unvalidated SQL input in applications.

Standard: a defined set of rules, accepted and adopted by several organizations.

Steganography: hiding information in a way such that no one suspects the existence of the message.

Substitution: specification of the k-bit output for each k-bit input.

System administration: a set of functions that provides support services, ensures reliable operations, promotes efficient use of the system, and ensures that prescribed service-quality objectives are met.

System administrator: the person responsible for the day-to-day operation of a technology system.

System of Record: records from which information is retrieved by the name, identifying number, symbol, or other identifying particular assigned to the individual. Sometimes abbreviated as SOR.

System profiling: the act of putting together all the assets inventoried, grouping them by function, and understanding the dependencies between these assets.

System security officer: the person responsible for writing, enforcing, and reviewing security operating procedures in an organization.

Technical controls: the information security measures built into the information system itself.

Threat: the capabilities, intentions, and attack methods of adversaries to exploit or cause harm to assets.

Threat agent: the individual, organization, or group that originates a particular threat action.

Threat model: interactions between relevant agents, actions, and assets facing an organization.

Tokens: physical objects (or in the case of software tokens, stored on a physical object) that must be presented to prove the user's identity.

Unencrypted data vulnerability: the situation where sensitive data is stored locally or transmitted over a network without proper encryption.

Unrestricted assets: assets not classified as restricted. It is the data that, if leaked or viewed by someone, would not cause problems for the organization.

Unrestricted uploads vulnerability: the vulnerability created when files are accepted by software without verifying that the file follows strict specifications.

User management: defining the rights of organizational members to information in the organization.

Viruses and worms: computer programs that adversely affect computers and propagate through the network without the user's consent.

Vision statement: a statement that articulates the organization's aspirations.

Vulnerability: a weakness in an information system that gives a threat the opportunity to compromise an asset.

Web mashup: a web page or application that combines data from one or more web-based APIs into a new service.

Zero-day exploit: an attack that compromises a previously unknown vulnerability in computer software.

Zombie: a computer connected to the Internet that has been compromised in such a way that it performs malicious tasks at the direction of a remote controller. Typically caused by the installation of a zombie client.

Zombie client: the software that takes directions from a remote computer and uses the infected computer to perform malicious tasks as directed.

Index

CPSIA information can be obtained
at www.ICGtesting.com
Printed in the USA
BVOW04s2007020117

472085BV00018B/9/P